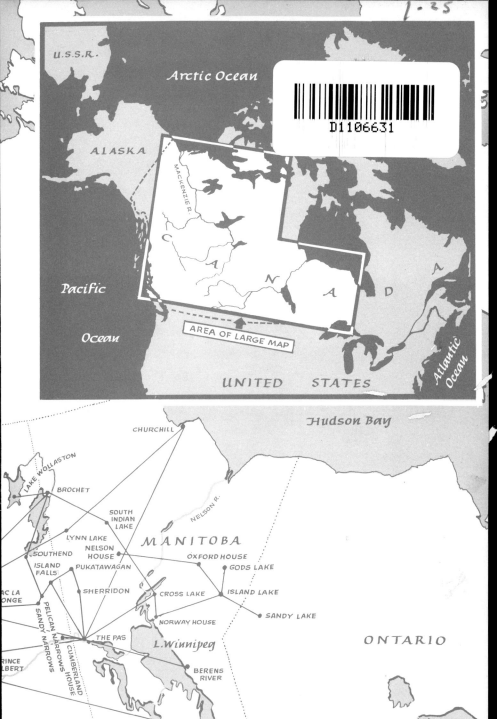

ARCTIC WINGS

ALBERTA CATHOLIC SCHOOL
TRUSTEES ASSOCIATION
11328 - 100th AVENUE
EDMONTON, ALTA.

ARCTIC WINGS

WILLIAM A. LEISING, O.M.I.

DOUBLEDAY & COMPANY, INC.

GARDEN CITY, NEW YORK

Imprimi Potest: Rev. Joseph Turcotte, O.M.I.
Acting Provincial

Nihil Obstat: Rev. Charles Gilles, O.M.I.
Censor Librorum

Imprimatur: Paul Piché, O.M.I.
Titular Bishop of Orcisto
Vicar Apostolic of Mackenzie

Nihil Obstat: Gall Higgins, O.F.M. Cap.
Censor Librorum

Imprimatur: ✠Francis Cardinal Spellman
Archbishop of New York
August 12, 1959

The nihil obstat and imprimatur are official declarations that a book or pamphlet is free of doctrinal or moral error. No implication is contained therein that those who have granted the nihil obstat and imprimatur agree with the contents, opinions or statements expressed.

To Our Lady of the Snows

Chapter One

UP ON the bend of the world where the polar fox and the wolf prowl the shelf ice of the glaciers, I found the vast land of the snow people, the Eskimos. Their untamed country scarred my hide and their rugged way of life is forever engraved on my soul. I went there to teach and I was taught. I return now with nineteen years of gleanings from this far horizon where I found a land veiled in fog and mystery and where I found a people who can laugh even when they are starving!

What strange force pulls a man in the direction of adventure and the unknown? What internal longing sends a woman to Africa to teach and nurse the people of those strange lands? What really sent me into the high Arctic? For a complete answer I must run back to my college days. Like most young fellows, I did not focus too much attention in any special direction; that is, not until I became a friend of William Stanton, a missionary priest from up home in Buffalo, New York. I paid little attention to cultivating the friendship of priests, although I always respected them. They visited our home often when I was small, but most of them always spoke of serious things that held little interest for me. William Stanton was interested in football and liked those fellows who gave their all for the school. He was a practical man with a keen eye for special plays and for the fellow who had to struggle to keep abreast of the team. We had several good visits when I thumbed a ride home with him and finally on one of these rides he plucked the sensitive chord. "It's none of my business," he began one day, "but have you decided on a special field for the future?"

A few other people had verbally taken me by the shoulders and pointed me in a definite direction. I wondered if he was going to be just another person telling a little boy what to do!

"What did you decide to do for a life's work?" he asked, and he was dead serious. I liked this man. He spoke to me as an equal.

"I am seriously thinking of becoming a doctor," I said with growing pride.

"Fine," he mused. "We need good doctors." Then he screwed up his eyes in a mass of wrinkles and sat silent for a few miles. "A doctor has a wonderful purpose in life, to heal the ills of humanity, but remember, the body ultimately dies. I work with patients that live forever, human souls!"

For over a year the echo of those words bounced around in my mind, but my main interest centered on hitting a pass receiver with a football at forty yards and getting a passing mark in ethics. Then one spring day during my second year at St. Bonaventure's College the dean called me to the visitors' room.

"How is the medic doing these fine golf days?" Father Stanton met me at the door. He was the last person I wanted to see. Spring was in the air and in my blood. I could not get out of class soon enough and onto the tennis court or the golf course. And here was a man with the one question I was trying to avoid.

"What are your weekend plans?" he asked, probably sensing my very thoughts.

"Oh, just the usual study periods and perhaps the old round on our little golf course."

"Good," he said, steering me into the room and closing the door. This must be it, I thought to myself. He's going to try to talk me into something. "I just arranged with the dean to take you to the baseball opener at Yankee Stadium," he almost whispered. "How about it?"

"Wonderful." I beamed, startled at this change in events.

"You have to return for class Monday morning at nine o'clock and we can drive it easily." And off we went to see the Yanks trim Boston.

On the return trip, after spurts of conversation and silence, Father Stanton was off and running on his pet subjects, "souls that live forever" and the life of a missionary.

"Tell you what I'll do," he said after a couple of hours of discussion. "Because I believe that a person must have knowledge of anything before he makes a judgment on it, I am willing to make a bargain with you. Spend six months at our novitiate and study the life of a priest. If at the end of that time you decide not to study theology, I will guarantee your way through medical school."

"That's quite a tempting proposition, Father, but I can't understand why you want to take such a chance on a farmer."

8

"Then you will accept?" he said eagerly, ignoring my question.

"I want to think this over for a few months. Your offer makes quite a definite change in my life."

Five months and several discussions later I found myself in the tranquillity of the Oblate Fathers Novitiate in Tewksbury, Massachusetts.

Here was a different life. We started with what seemed to me to be a real endurance test in kneeling, during a spiritual retreat of a full seven days. From early morning until late evening we had enough religious exercise to give a fellow spiritual indigestion. In fact, during those days, the thought often occurred to me that this must be one of the acid tests. For the first time in my life I caught myself thinking seriously about what the future held for me. The other novices, who had spent some years in the preparatory seminary, were not only familiar with all the terms of religious living but even voiced opinions on the mission field they had chosen! I had not even served a Mass before those days!

Was this the life for me? Was I spiritual enough in my thoughts and actions to become a representative of Christ? When would I know for sure? How would I know? These thoughts kept pushing me for over two months before I had the courage to go to our novice master, Father Charles Barry.

"I've been having some doubts about being in the right place, Father," I began. "When does a fellow know for sure what he is supposed to do in this life?"

"I have been wondering when you would come to see me about that," he began. "Most of the other novices have been in several times. I was beginning to think your mind was pretty well settled on that score."

"Far from it, Father. I feel very uncertain about many things, especially this business of being a priest." I told him of Father Stanton's offer and explained that many people, including my good parents, would like to see me become a priest. He combed strands of white hair off his freckled forehead with long, limber fingers, and so much understanding was scribbled in the crow's-feet around his smiling eyes.

"I know about that six-month deal with Father Stanton, but believe me it will be a first-class miracle if you know a certain answer to your problem by that time." He looked at a picture on the book stand. "My mother was sure I would be a priest when I was ten—God bless her. I did not know for sure until the Bishop called me officially for my subdeaconate and I stepped forward."

"There is so much said and discussed by the Brothers about the 'call' and a 'vocation,'" I began.

"Yes, yes, that all sounds so sure." He nodded assuringly. "There are many stories about the Holy Spirit coming down in the quiet of some candlelit chapel and whispering the secret words into the ear of some young man or woman. Most of this is just hopeful wanderings of a pious imagination."

"But how does a fellow know, Father? There must be some sign or some way in which God does single out a person for His work."

"Yes, Brother, there are some signs, but each case is different. Many factors direct a man or a woman into special walks of life. A good home is usually the foundation. For a call into God's service, a person must first of all pray and ask for divine help and the advice of his fellow man."

Father Barry was not a big man, but he spoke with authority and assurance that made him a giant as far as I was concerned.

"You just continue your daily life, and when the time comes to decide, God will give you that extra push of grace necessary to make the right decision."

With this good man as my adviser the months passed and so did my worries. The six months of my bargain went by and I decided to remain and make certain of my calling one way or the other.

Then in May 1935, while I was studying philosophy at Newburgh, New York, six of us Brothers were building a handball court when we heard the double-barreled voice of Father John Tully, our Superior, summoning us to meet some visitors.

He introduced us to Bishop Fallaize and Father Mansoz of the Arctic missions of the Mackenzie. We shook hands and kissed the Bishop's ring, but he would not let us kneel on our left knee as is the custom. "The Bishop just dropped by on his way North to see our house of studies and to meet you Brothers." Then, addressing the Bishop, he said, "This is their period of manual labor, Your Excellency. I am sure you will excuse them for not being in their soutanes."

The Bishop's face lit up with a smile and his eyes took in all of us behind thick glasses. "I will excuse them, Father," he said, stroking his well-trimmed white beard and throwing a look full of meaning at Father Mansoz. "Down in the missions of the Arctic, we often exchange our cassocks for coveralls. I believe I can say with pride that this fellow wore out more coveralls than soutanes, eh, Père?"

"*Mais oui,*" replied Father Mansoz, looking up at the six-foot Bishop. "You had your period of manual labor too, Bishop, in that coal mine on the Arctic coast."

I liked these men immediately. They were interested in our work and looked like "the working missionary" we heard about in our conferences. The Bishop was the taller of the two and in his early fifties. What I could see of his face showed signs of wind and frost burn. He had broad, square hands and crooked fingers from working in the cold. Father Mansoz was a few years younger and heavier-set, with a square face behind a graying beard.

"You must find this country warm, Bishop, after all those years on the cold Arctic coast." Father Tully mopped his face.

"We have our share of heat too, Father. In fact I have seen eighty degrees at Coppermine on the Arctic coast in July!" This was a surprise to me.

"What sort of people are those Eskimos? Are they friendly?" I found myself asking the Bishop.

"In the fifteen years I spent among them, I do not recall one of them getting into a fight or openly losing his temper," he answered proudly. Then he immediately looked at his hands and tried to straighten a crooked finger. "They are friendly, but their life is such a constant struggle for survival that they have no ear for such inedible things like faith and hope and love. It will take many years and many men's lives to lead these Eskimos to know God." He told us how the missionaries had to travel constantly to reach the people, since the Eskimos and Arctic Indians had to spread themselves over the broad land to find enough game to keep alive.

"Our Fathers and Brothers do most of our building too," Father Mansoz said just behind me, joining our interested circle.

That visit of the northern missionaries shed new light on this life of a priest. For the first time I saw real adventure in it and a challenge that appealed to me. These missionaries were devoted men, yet they possessed a special brand of lightheartedness I liked. They were practical too, and their openhearted frankness of the existing problems rang with a sincerity that aroused my interest. I would like to work with men of their caliber.

My meditations of the following months started from the meditation book in chapel but usually ended with me on the tail end of

11

a dog sled, fighting the cold and the wolves to reach the souls of the Eskimos in God's polar attic. My doubts about whether I had a call to be a priest began to disappear. All I could think about was preparation. I had lost so much time in the fog of indecision. Now not only did I want to be a priest, but most of all I wanted to qualify for a missionary. Over the five years of studies that remained I read every book available on the Arctic. My purpose in life began to focus on a clear picture. I envisioned myself as an Arctic missionary. Now I had something special in mind to prepare for. How many years and hours of daydreaming I had spent just wondering aimlessly, without a definite thought of what I wanted to be and what I wanted to do. Now I had my teeth into something solid and something real. I would bend every effort of my life to bring the God I knew to the Eskimos and to all those who did not know Him.

During our last year of theology I wrote that special letter to Father General in Rome stating my preference as to where I would like to be sent after my ordination. I volunteered for the Arctic missions of the Mackenzie and I prayed that my request would be honored. This hope was known only by my Superior. My parents would know about it later. I did not want to cause them any anxiety, especially on one of the big days in their lives, May 27, 1940. On that memorable morning, in the Oblate chapel of the Miraculous Medal in Washington, D.C., His Eminence, Francis Cardinal Spellman, ordained sixteen Irishmen and myself to the holy priesthood.

After the ceremony he greeted us with individual good wishes and on taking leave of us said, "As your ordaining bishop, I ask you to recall always this day with the thought that you are ambassadors of Christ, priests of God, not for eight hours a day, but for twenty-four hours a day, seven days a week, and three hundred and sixty-five days a year so long as you live, and you will be the happiest men on earth and in heaven."

I have often recalled these words, but most of all I remember my father consoling my mother when my letter of obedience came from Rome that thirteenth day of August 1940. "He is a priest of God now and he must go where he is sent. Our work is done. We brought him up to love and serve God."

On September 2, after a short summer home, I was on a train rumbling to the West. My heart and mind were still held close to Mom and Dad and my little sisters and brothers back at the station where we cried our good-bys. I think a son or a daughter never forgets that good-by look on the faces of loved ones when they leave home for war or for a mission from which they may never return. It's a picture that returns and returns regardless of the years and the home-comings.

Those first two days, as the cornfields of Illinois and Iowa slid by and our train thundered across the Dakota prairies, I was mentally back home on our little farm dreaming of chicken-feeding time and of our black dog, Tiger. Would I ever return to belt his shaggy head when he leaped on my clean suit and slobbered all over me? No doubt Mom was wondering where I was tonight while she stood at her favorite place, the kitchen sink, and looked out of the window at the rows of sweet apple trees. Dad always had a last evening look at his chickens about this time, checking their water troughs and mash hoppers. And my brothers and sisters would be gathered around the kitchen table doing their homework. I never realized the tap roots of family love were planted so deep in a man's heart. I knew now I had really left home, for I felt very much alone out here on this wide prairie of the great Northwest.

Chapter Two

ARLY on the fourth day, when the train slowed down, our conductor called out: "Edmonton, Alberta, next stop. All out for points North." I collected my baggage quickly and sat by the window. The scene had not changed from that of the last two days. Black angus and whiteface cattle stood knee-deep in wheat stubble, chewing and looking at the train. Far out on the prairie I saw a tractor creeping along towing two grain wagons. Then abruptly the stubble fields were no more. Houses, gravel streets, big yards of yellow tractors and red combines slid by, gleaming new, in the morning sun.

"Welcome to Edmonton, Gateway to the North," a large sign guided us into the station. From all appearances this was a typical western city with modern trimmings. I followed the stream of passengers, and in a few minutes my taxi was zigzagging through busy streets lined with stores and early shoppers. My idea of Edmonton included red-coated Mounties, bearded prospectors, and perhaps even some Indians on the streets. I saw none of these on my way to St. Joachim's, the Oblate house.

"Here we are, Father," the taxi driver called out. "The Fathers must be having some kind of a celebration. This makes my fourth trip today," he mumbled half to himself, digging out my bags. I paid the man and bent to gather up my bundles.

"Welcome to Edmonton, *mon Père*," I heard from the door of the porch. *Mon Père*—my Father! I must get used to the French language now. This fellow must mean me, I thought, looking around. Before I could take a step, a big hand clamped on my shoulder and I looked into the kind, dark eyes of a Brother. "I am Brother Borghese," this burly six-footer said, descending on me with a handshake and a welcome I could feel was real. "I look after the door here and I saw your name on a telegram you sent to Father Superior saying you would be coming this morning. Excuse my English, Father, I do not have much practice here in this French

14

parish." After a few words he picked up my bags. "Come, I'll show you the room I saved for you. One of the Oblate missionaries from the Mackenzie is being consecrated tomorrow at St. Albert, and we have a houseful of visitors."

Brother led me to the room, served my Mass, and pointed me in the direction of the dining room. I had just poured a cup of coffee when a heavy-set gray-haired priest shuffled in and introduced himself. "I am Père Le Treste from the Mackenzie."

My ears pricked up at that last word! Here was a man I must know. He was from the North! When he learned of my new assignment, his close-set little eyes were alerted.

"Welcome, Father, we need you," he said, coming closer and putting a heavy hand on my shoulders. "I am a Frenchman, as you can tell by my miserable English, but I have always had a soft spot in my heart for you Americans. I met some of them in 1898 when they passed my little mission on the Athabaska River on their way to the Klondike gold rush. Naturally I gave them lodging and helped them, along with many others in those days, with a little of my grub. Of course they all promised to return and repay me. To my great surprise, three years later two of them came to see me all the way from California. They came to reimburse me. They struck it rich, they said, but their good luck was due to the little kindness I had offered them on their way. Father," he went on with hoarseness in his voice, his fingers biting into the muscle of my arm, "those wonderful Americans paid me a new little chapel for my Cree Indians."

Emotion had come over him, revealing the kind and great heart of this man. We not only had coffee together but spent half that day on a walking tour of Edmonton.

Three blocks south of the Oblate house we came to the high bank of the North Saskatchewan River, which divides the city. "That was my road for over forty years." Father Le Treste said. "I used to camp there with the Indians." He looked down on the smooth rolling greens of the golf course. "This was my jumping-off place for the five-hundred-mile trip to Lake Athabaska and the Chipewyan Indian country. I was young in those days, not fat and clumsy like this." He patted his 250 pounds. Looking to the south, across the river, he pointed out the new buildings of the University of Alberta and told me how the city had grown on a diet of fur, cattle, and wheat trade from a few thousand to a quarter of a million people. We climbed the stairs to the Parliament buildings and went up to the high dome to get a good view of the city. From the tallest building, the Hotel MacDonald, smaller buildings and homes fanned out for some fifteen square miles.

"Seems to be a religious city, Father. I count fifteen church spires with ease."

"There are over forty different denominations here even though this is not a big city," Father Le Treste explained. "People from all over the world have settled here, and in some cases half a dozen families of a special denomination erect their own church."

I picked out the airport where aircraft landed and departed. Father pointed out the five hospitals and our silver spired Oblate Parish Church.

"Notice that tall building in the direction of the grain elevators to the northwest?" he asked with a serious note in his voice. "Can you read the sign on top if it?"

"Looks like a big six to me," I squinted.

"You've passed the eye test for a good traveling missionary." He smiled broadly, starting down the stairs. "That building is Six Brewery and, after the church, it is the last stopping-off place to replenish a man's supplies of snakebite medicine before a long trip." He chuckled.

Next morning we rode together to St. Albert, seven miles north of the city, where the new Bishop was to be consecrated. He gave me a bump-by-bump account of the road he had traveled so many times by horseback and dog sled on his way north to visit his beloved Cree Indians.

"Mark my words," he said. "One day this will be the trail to the Mackenzie and the crossroads from your great country to Alaska."

After twenty minutes we reached the village of St. Albert, which I had read about so often in missionary annals. It was a small settlement of some two hundred souls living in frame houses on the flat of a ravine. We crossed a small river and climbed the opposite embankment to the mission grounds and the church on the hilltop. Automobiles, light delivery trucks splattered with mud, and even some horses and prairie wagons were lined up along the fence beside the church. Little groups of people stood about, visiting. Father Le Treste pointed to the small, original mission church that had been built in 1862 by the first Oblate missionary priest in those parts, Father Lacombe, known as the black-robed voyager.

The church, the Oblate mission house, and the massive old folks' home conducted by the Grey Nuns were built on the highest point of land in the area and presented a beautiful and colorful view from the church steps, looking south across the valley of the Sturgeon River. During this time, and ever since I heard the news that a new Bishop would be consecrated for the Mackenzie Vicariate, I was most anxious to get a look at him. However, I knew this was impossible until after his retreat just prior to the ceremony of consecration. This is the usual procedure in preparation for such a high office in the church, even as it is the custom before ordination to the priesthood.

Father Le Treste chose a very advantageous place for us to view the ceremony. Over two hundred priests and dignitaries and close to a thousand people jammed the little church as Archbishop Gabriel Breynat of the Mackenzie and Bishop Jean Louis Coudert of the Yukon Vicariate consecrated Most Reverend Joseph Trocellier as Bishop of Adramytte and co-adjutor Bishop of the Mackenzie. It was the Feast of Our Lady's Nativity, September 8—the day on which I had pronounced my first vows and a special day for all Oblates of Mary Immaculate. I learned later that the new Bishop chose this day because of his great devotion to Our Lady.

After the two-and-a-half-hour ceremony, the new Bishop came down the center aisle of the church, imparting his blessing. We were fortunate enough to leave the church a little ahead of the crowds, so that I could get a picture as the new Bishop stood on the church steps blessing his Oblate Brothers. He was a big man, almost six feet tall, and in all those robes he looked like a 250-pounder. Immediately I judged him to be a jolly fellow, since most hefty people are of a happy nature. After blessing the Oblates, he came directly to where I was kneeling at the edge of the group and blessed me, putting both hands on my head. "Welcome to our northern family," he said in a low voice. I kissed his ring and when we shook hands he pulled me to my feet. "Archbishop Breynat showed me your letter and I am so glad you have come to our northern missions." He smiled, and went on to give his blessing and greeting to the Nuns, who were kneeling beside me.

I looked over the new faces of the missionaries, hunting for those two familiar bearded gentlemen I had met at Newburgh some five years ago. After the Bishop's greeting, I thought of them. He had the same warm friendly hello in his kind brown eyes. It was real. When I felt the grip of his handshake, I knew at once that I was a member of his Arctic family. On this, one of the greatest days of his life, he expressed concern and the warm welcome I needed then in this new country among so many new faces. Suddenly I awakened to the fact that he had addressed me in English—with a heavy French accent—but he spoke easily. This was a real blessing. After hearing everyone speak French the previous evening, I had visions of dull French grammars instead of dog sleds and jackpine country!

For all my traveling, I might have been back in the French quarter of Lowell, Massachusetts, or Quebec City. I really felt lost in the crowd that bubbled with the excitement of the hour and buzzed in French. I realized then and there that if I was to live in this new world I would have to learn the language and all the customs of these people. I was made aware of this again two days later, after the excitement of the consecration, when the Bishop asked me, "*Avez-vous du tabac?*" (Have you any tobacco?)

I threw up my hands, saying: "I guess the first thing I will have to do is learn how to speak French."

"Excuse me, Father, I forgot myself." The Bishop smiled, finding his tobacco in a back pocket, and filled his pipe. His voice had a baritone pitch and it came from the depths of his barrel chest.

"What kind of supplies did you bring for this cold country of ours?" he managed between puffs.

We went out to my trunk on the porch, and I opened it, reeling off the number of shirts, trousers, socks, and other clothing.

He bent down and carefully picked up a pair of bathing trunks. "This looks like a typical American packer. I remember them from the First War army days, when they liberated me from a prison in Germany. The Americans' boxes would come from home and they had everything in them from soup to nuts." He let go of the bathing trunks and started fingering the pile of socks. "How many pairs of these have you?"

"About two dozen, I believe. Do you think that's enough?"

"Yes," he said, smiling. "I would think that is a plenitude of socks, *n'est-ce pas?* You could allow me to carry six pairs," he said with a chuckle.

I was to learn that the Bishop, who could think of all the needs of his men, could not remember to supply himself with enough clothing. For after the socks came shirts, collars, and "anything that would burn in his pipe."

These little things spoke a language I could understand and they told me he was a very human and understanding man. To borrow things in this manner seems to be characteristic of men in community life who take the vows of poverty. Very often a man in South Africa might find in his laundry a shirt or a handkerchief that belongs to a fellow missionary in Japan or the Arctic. I found out that about the only thing an Oblate priest can call his own is his Oblate cross. His clothing, his shoes, and even the cord that holds the cross must be replaced. His breviaries become soiled and torn; his very body becomes scarred and bent with the years.

While this man whom I had met only forty-eight hours ago should have been a stranger—and more so, considering his position as Bishop—in this simple act of borrowing my socks I sensed very forcibly the bond that made us brothers with a common need.

"They are very nice socks, Father," the Bishop said, pocketing them. "Now you will have to move your trunks and those bags." He looked straight ahead and marched purposefully beside me on the porch like the master sergeant he had been. I sensed he was leading up to something serious—my first assignment. "You have heard of Le Scolasticat at Lebret, Father?"

"Yes, Bishop."

"There is a wonderful school there to learn French. They have excellent professors and the regulation is—how you say?—profoundly academic."

My vistas of the Far North began to shrink to classroom dimensions and the smell of chalk instead of pine needles. Lebret, four hundred miles southeast, was pretty far in the wrong direction.

"You would like that, Father?"

"Ye-e-ss, Bishop." I hesitated.

A big smile creased his face. "You are not only a big boy, but you are a big liar, I think."

I squirmed.

"You would not like to study French and you do not like to go back to school, n'est-ce pas?" He did not wait for my answer. "So I will take you myself into the North. We will go to Fort Smith, and there you will meet the professor pratique, Père Mansoz. You will not only learn French but some of the Chipewyan Indian language as well."

Two days later, having narrowly and happily escaped the clutches of formal language tutoring, I boarded the famous "Muskeg Special" bound for Fort McMurray, three hundred miles to the northwest. The train was aptly named because the tracks were laid over soft, wet, spongy ground commonly known as muskeg.

It had taken engineers some six years of backbreaking toil hauling logs to complete the railway in the 1920s. They followed the height of land as best they could, worming or twisting around the base of the higher hills, and followed the river beds of the famous Christina and Clearwater rivers to McMurray.

I had plenty of time to get a good look at this country as we sped along at twenty-five miles an hour. One hundred miles north of Edmonton we left the wheat fields and the tilled land, and the trees grew within twenty feet of the train. This was the first solid bush country I had ever seen. Down North we call it bush country since there are just spots of heavy timber and more than half the land is either water or just willows, tagler, and alder bushes. When the Bishop pointed out the first Indians during our long stop at Lac la Biche, I was a little disappointed. I expected feathers and fancy colorful clothes.

"Northern Indian tribes dress mostly in caribou or mooseskin clothing like this fellow coming toward us."

A middle-aged man came up to the Bishop, knelt, and kissed his ring. The Bishop smiled, but I could see he was surprised at this sudden recognition. Then the Indian hesitated a little and offered me his hand. I liked his solid grip and the true smile playing around his eyes. He did not speak, but the expression on his ruddy, tanned face said he was happy to meet us. He sat facing us, and when he crossed his legs I noticed he was wearing moccasins with rubbers over them. In less than ten minutes an odor of smoked meat tickled my nose.

At home when I was a boy we butchered pigs in the fall and I always liked the tangy smell of the smokehouse where the hams and homemade pork sausage were hung. The Bishop told me later that the Indians smoked the moose and caribou hide for a day or two, depending on its use, to toughen it and change its color from white to dark orange and brown. At the succeeding stops along the way more Indians came aboard, and it seemed that their moccasin telegraph was in good working order, for in about an hour after boarding the train they would work their way in our direction to meet their new Bishop.

"Our missionaries for almost a century have brought ninety-eight per cent of these people into the Church and, as you see, they taught them well."

For two days and two nights we rolled over the muskegs and finally ground to a stop where the tracks came to an end at Waterways, Alberta, at six in the morning. Fog hung in the valleys and the only moving thing we saw was the station agent.

"Is the boat still here?" the Bishop asked him when our baggage was collected in a pile on the gravel pathway.

"You are in luck, sir," the agent told us. "Some spare parts for a boat engine came on this train and Captain Lou Martin waited for it."

Just then the two local missionaries came on the run. Greetings were short. "We just put two Grey Nuns on the boat. It is waiting for you," Father Pat Mercredi puffed, talking to all of us. He was excited in all this confusion of the new Bishop's coming, the boat leaving, and getting the Sisters aboard on time. He was taking no chances on having his passengers stranded for three weeks and another boat.

"You have at least an hour," the agent cut in. "We have to load all this freight on that boat."

This gave us time for our Masses and a short visit over coffee. Father Mercredi gave the Bishop a report on his three Cree missions along the railroad, and Father Chouinard had the good news that his new school registered seventy pupils.

A truck came for us at eight-thirty, and fifteen minutes later the whistle of the *Pelly Lake* sent a shrill blast down the valley and we began to move north. Our boat was really a tug that pushed three two-hundred-ton barges loaded with everything from food to mining machinery. Our route was three hundred miles long over the Athabaska River and Lake and then one hundred miles over Slave River to the rapids at Fitzgerald, Alberta. Eight passengers were aboard, including Sister St. Omer, a fifteen-year veteran, and a new recruit, Sister Des Lauriers.

As the last houses of McMurray disappeared around the bend of the river, I regretted not having a better look at this famous settlement.

Almost two hundred years ago, Peter Pond, the great explorer and trader, stopped here on his western tour. Indians, too, always made this a camping place on their way to Chipewyan. Fishing was good at this junction of the Clearwater and Athabaska rivers, and the Hudson's Bay Company started trading about 1850 when the place was known as the Fort at the Forks. A few years later Inspector J. D. McMurray set up his office here and the settlement was named after him.

But surely I would be here again someday. Now I must live this wonderful hour, this beautiful day of September 12. I had hoped for it and dreamed about it over my books in Washington, and now I was really on the river, going north. Even though a frost had tinted the leaves, it was a warm day. The sun was out and I sat on the forward deck in a light windbreaker. Every bend of the river was a possible bears' playground or a pasture for moose or jumping deer. Three-hundred-foot steep banks walled the river. I learned later these are hills of tar sands that cover the entire area. Over the years prospectors and oil companies have come with a gleam of ambition in their eyes when they saw these hills of potential wealth. Here was oil actually oozing out of the ground! Presently there is one extracting plant some sixty miles down-river where about fifty men are employed.

Captain Lou took me around his boat, from the wheelhouse to engine room, where two Gardner diesels strained every muscle to push the laden barges. Dog sleds packed in bundles of six were stacked with canoes and small jolly boats on the roof decks of the three barges, and barrels of oil were everywhere.

"We keep these doors locked because of valuable foodstuffs like coffee and liquor." Lou slid one barge door open. "Some of our deck hands may get the notion to do a little trading on our stop-overs if we tempt them with all this food." He pointed to stacks of sugar and flour. "People have to shop once for a whole year down North, Father. Almost half of this bargeload is for your missions down in the Arctic—for next year. These supplies will remain at Smith in your warehouse this winter, and next summer will continue on their way north."

On the evening of the second day, during our fourth meal of stew, the Bishop looked at Sister Des Lauriers with a serious eye and asked if she was enjoying her first boat ride in the great North.

"*Oui, Monseigneur,*" she said, a little embarrassed at being singled out by the Bishop.

"No doubt you learned many things in the convent?"

"*Oui, Monseigneur.*"

"You know how to pray, I am sure. Now, *ma chère Soeur*, do you know how to cook?"

Sister Des Lauriers stole a look at her companion. "A little, Bishop," she answered.

"Good," His Excellency exploded. "Perhaps you could stay here in the galley and persuade this engineer-chef that God provided something besides stew for the table."

22

Sister bowed her neatly bonneted head as she promised to try.

The next morning she stopped me on deck and asked, "Do you think the Bishop would like a spaghetti dinner?"

"Well, Sister, I've known His Excellency only a few days, but since he made his studies at St. Giorgio in Italy, I feel sure he would enjoy a good dish of spaghetti."

As we were speaking our flotilla neared the shore and the pilot called out to the deck hand to secure the head line of the barge to a stout tree. In a matter of minutes the tug was free of her barges and we were going down-river, headed for an island. The commotion brought most of the passengers on deck, though not Captain Martin who was still asleep in his cabin after a long night at the wheel. The tug slowed and scraped to a stop against the cut-bank of the willow-covered sand island.

"Don't be wary. I go for a goose I see on far end of the sand bar," the Cree Indian pilot called to us from the open window of the pilothouse. The words were no sooner uttered than he leaped over the rail with his .22 and disappeared into the willows. We could see nothing from behind the screen of trees, and no one went ashore after the Bishop's warning.

"I suggest we all remain here on the boat," he had said quietly. "That young fellow has a certain hunting glint in his eye, and anything that moves may be fair game."

We sat quietly, waiting for the report of the rifle. The engineer came up on deck and told us that an Indian was always hunting, no matter what kind of work he might be doing. Zing, went the rifle shell over our heads! Minutes later our pilot broke from the willows and stomped aboard, mumbling to himself.

"He missed the goose," the Bishop whispered in my ear.

Doors banged in the pilot's cabin and bells rang to get the engine started. Our boat jerked in reverse, then forward at full speed back to the barges.

Some twenty feet from the barge, bells rang and the tug shuddered as our engines reversed, but it was too late. Our tug hit the barge with a thud and a splintering of timber!

"What in tarnation are you trying to do?" yelled the captain, storming out of his cabin in his long underwear. "You've wrecked my tug! Look at that bow post."

"I can fix that, Mr. Martin," the pilot said, coming meekly from his cabin.

This was developing into a rhubarb and I decided to bow out

and see how the new cook was doing. As soon as I slid the galley door open a strange sight met my eyes. Sister, dazed, was just picking herself off the floor, spaghetti stringing from her bonnet and all over her habit. At the time of the crash she had been thrown from a stool near the stove. The pot of cooking spaghetti had spilled over her, burning her face. I went to her quickly and helped her to the wall bench.

After I explained quickly what happened, she took a few relaxing breaths and stole a glance into the mirror nailed to the wall near the stove. "My, I look awful," she said, managing a little smile and picking a long string of spaghetti from the folds of her bonnet.

Just then I heard the Bishop's heavy steps and knew he was coming into the galley. In a glance he took in the situation, and before Sister spotted him he turned on his heel and went back up on deck. I thanked God for Sister's sake and helped her clean up the galley.

"The spaghetti was good, eh, Father, what was left of it?" the Bishop said as we sat on deck that evening. "She wore that spaghetti and ketchup like a sergeant wears his medals. I was a supply sergeant in the French Army, Father, I know." Then he slapped his knee and laughed at the memory of Sister.

"The Grey Nuns down North will welcome her with open arms. They like their companions to laugh and be able to keep the family spirits high," he continued in a meditative mood. "You'll like the Grey Nuns, Father. They have been working with Oblate Fathers for over seventy years, teaching in our schools and nursing in our hospitals. Frankly, I believe they do more with their great works of charity for the people and especially the children, than we missionaries who follow the people to their hunting grounds."

This trip and the companionship of the Bishop and the little incidents of daily life aboard began to give me the tempo of northern life. It was so open and friendly, and with plenty of time even to hunt! Through it all I began to note a very fine thread of the survival philosophy of life in the fabric of every person I met, from the Bishop to the youngest lad of an Indian trapper.

On our third morning I was awakened by the gabble of ducks and the honking of geese. We were on the great delta of the Athabaska. Everywhere I looked, water fowl filled the air and some flocks were swimming along the riverbanks. Again that gleam came into the eye of our pilot, but Captain Lou was now at his side! They were both busy scanning the water ahead for new sand bars and rocks that usually appear in autumn when the river is low.

As I listened to the Bishop and watched Captain Lou with an eye on the ever-changing view as we moved north, I began to suspect that this would be a land of surprises, of bumps and lumps and even spills! I would indeed have need for a professor who was *pratique,* and I wondered what he would be like.

Chapter Three

BEFORE I met the Père Professor I met the mosquitoes. They came up out of the willows on the river flat in swarming black waves when our boat docked at Fort Fitzgerald. We were all flailing ourselves, waving hats in the air and trying to put up some kind of defense against these pests. Like most people, I thought mosquitoes went no farther north than the Jersey swamps, but these northern monsters made the Jersey variety look anemic.

While the two Sisters and I were beating ourselves blue to keep the insects away, the Bishop puffed great clouds of smoke on his pipe and grinned. "Don't you mind these mosquitoes?" I asked.

"After nineteen years in this tough weather of the North, I am tough meat," he answered, smiling. "Those little beggars know enough to choose the filet mignon," he continued, turning to glance in the direction of the Sisters.

"Bonjour, bonjour, Monseigneur," came from behind us.

"It's Brother Brodeur from Fort Smith," Sister St. Omer whispered to her young companion as the Brother knelt in the dust to receive the Bishop's blessing.

When the Bishop introduced us, I noticed he had an iron grip and looked at me with a pair of dusty gray eyes.

"Welcome to our country, Father," Brother Joe said in heavy French-accented English that put me at ease. I had visions of meeting people who spoke only French. "I am stationed at Fort Smith. We travel a very dusty sixteen-mile road along the high bank above the Slave River rapids," he said, brushing dust from his jacket. Dirt streaked his lean face where sweat had run from a graying hairline. I walked with him to a waiting red truck and noted he was about five feet ten, with well-knit muscles that bulged to the tune of at least 190 pounds. "Before I entered the Oblate Brothers I used to work as a lumberjack in the shanties near the Quebec boundary, and I met many of your countrymen.

That's where I learned to speak English," he continued, loading our bags on the truck. "Do you speak any French, Father?"

"No, Brother, we have very few French-speaking people in western New York. In school I studied German so I could speak and write to my father."

"Well, you will hear a lot of French up here, especially around the missions. We all speak it. I will teach you," he added, laughing, and helped the Sisters aboard. I climbed on top of the trunks and baggage, and from that seat had my first good look at the town.

Evening had come, and the dust of a busy day was settling, mixed with smoky fog down on the willow flat. Lights began to flicker from cabin windows high on the rocks north of this little settlement of perhaps three hundred souls. From the gatherings on the waterfront and the chatter, it was apparent that the docking of a boat was an event in this town. A big searchlight hung a curtain of dust from the pilothouse of the tug to the open doors of the barge, where heavy iron-wheeled trucks rattled down the gangplank. The unloading had begun and no doubt would continue through the night.

All the while the mosquitoes were buzzing and biting, and I was relieved when we began to move. But in a few minutes we were holding handkerchiefs to our faces and choking with dust. It swirled up like heavy smoke, and the poor Sisters huddled under their capes, coughing. From the time the lights of Fitzgerald disappeared until the truck stopped at Fort Smith, we were enveloped in a cloud of dust—the very last thing I expected to find in the country of eternal snows!

When the truck stopped and the dust began to settle, a barrage of "bonjours" greeted the new Bishop. Missionaries, nuns, Indians, and dogs gathered as the circle grew around him. I was looking for a familiar face—and I think the Bishop was also, as he moved slowly toward the black hulk which I supposed was the mission. A rattling of chains at the rear of the truck reminded me that Brother Joe had not forgotten us.

"Are you people still alive up there?" He grinned up at me.

I coughed my answer and brushed my dark suit, now light gray! The little Sisters were in truth Grey Nuns—and very disturbed at being seen in such dishevelment by their new Superior. I guided them down the small ladder and was passing their baggage to Brother when I saw the face I was looking for approaching the truck. He had not changed. I climbed down and worked my way into the group to shake hands with my professor, Père Mansoz.

"Welcome to the North," he greeted me, shaking and squeezing my hand and brushing my face with his bristling beard in the usual French manner. This was the same wonderful missionary I had the pleasure of meeting in Newburgh over four years ago. Now I was in the North, and with a man of God I had so admired as a model missionary!

That evening I met some of the other Fathers and Sisters, but my mind was on one man and what steps he would take to make a missionary out of me. After my five-day look at this vast country and its strange people I realized how much there was to learn before I could even think of myself as a missionary like these men.

That night a quiet room and a bed were so welcome after days of grinding trains and river-barge bunks that I was aware of nothing until a loud clatter of bells wakened me at 5 A.M.! I looked outside. It was still night! Bright stars twinkled in a dark sky. Then I heard a strange new sound, a heavy roar like Niagara Falls. I could see nothing from my window but was convinced it must be the famous Slave River rapids I had read about. Another bell rang and I hove to and followed the routine of the house.

After Mass and breakfast, Father Mansoz led me on a tour of the entire mission—the grounds, the school, and finally the hospital. I met the Brothers on their way to work. There was Brother Le Gall in his mid-sixties, almost six feet tall, quiet, white-bearded, heavy-set, with large work-hardened hands.

"This is the Brother who carved a farm out of the wilderness fourteen miles west of here," Father said as we left him near a woodpile twice the size of a house. "When the muskegs freeze we will go to the farm."

We inspected the warehouse, the garage where Brother Joe was working on his truck, and the little church of St. Isidore.

"We are so lucky to have a man like him around," Father said quietly as we left Brother Joe. "He is a master at engines and such a handy man to fix things and keep everything operating around a mission. Most of us from France are not too mechanically inclined, but I found out that even a Frenchman will bury his pride, get greasy hands, and swing an ax if he gets hungry and cold enough." Father laughed.

At the hospital, a three-story frame building with room for thirty-five patients, I met most of the Sisters.

"When I get confused or when I'm in doubt about correct grammar in my sermons, this is my professor," Father said as he introduced me to Sister Paulette Fortier, a petite nun with a doll's face and the smallest hands I had ever seen.

"Welcome to the North, Father," she said in English that had the dainty lace trim of a French accent.

"Perhaps you could give this helpless American a few lessons in French when he comes to visit the patients." Father Mansoz nodded in my direction.

"*Avec plaisir, mon Père.*" Her French was clear and distinct. Unlike the other nuns, she was in a most impressive white habit, which I learned later all the nursing Sisters wore.

We went in the rooms and wards to greet the patients. This was my first look at tuberculosis in its most horrible form, squeezing the life out of these Indians in a slow but sure death.

"We try to cure them, Father, but it's all but hopeless in most cases," Sister explained. "We have such a limited supply of drugs here in the North."

In the months and years that followed, I learned all the answers to the questions that coursed through my mind that day. And since then great medical strides have eased the pain and minimized the death rate.

"You can come a few times a week to visit the patients," Père Mansoz confided as we left the hospital. "They will like to hear your English, and you can practice your Chipewyan on them."

"When do I start my lessons in that language, Father?"

"Oh, you have just started," he said, looking over his glasses, which had a habit of sliding down his broad nose. "You recall this phrase I used in almost every room we visited: *Nazon dzine usson?*"

I had heard those words, but they were just guttural sounds to me.

"*Nazon* means 'good,'" Père Mansoz explained. "*Dzine* means 'day.' *Usson* is the interrogation. In other words, 'Is this a good day for you?' And the patient would say *ech* for 'yes' and *ille* for 'no.' Tomorrow morning at nine we will have a lesson from the book."

And the next day I started my formal studies in Chipewyan. I was more fortunate than earlier missionaries, who had to work out their own grammar. There were now two good grammars and Father Le Goff's dictionary, the Fathers having devoted much time preparing these books so that young missionaries could learn the language quickly. Weeks went by while I listened and tried to twist my tongue around the new words. Evenings my throat was sore trying to simulate the sounds uttered by my teacher. I had become more than a little discouraged. Finding myself again at a desk in a small room smelling of books and pencils instead of the fresh pine-scented forests and the crackle of a campfire was not the active dog-trail life I had imagined as a student.

About three weeks after my arrival—about the time my discouragement began to show—Father Mansoz came up with a sure-fire remedy. It was on one of those real Indian-summer days, when the sun had dissolved the fall mists and put a warm golden glow in the air. My studies had become a grind, and both my teacher and I began to lose patience. Father Mansoz looked over his book and out of the window to the jackpine country with a faraway look in his eye. A discussion had begun over the pronunciation of the *r* among the Chipewyan people, and one of the Fathers who had spent most of his missionary life among the Indians around the Athabaska country was of the opinion that the *r* should be pronounced like the Greek *rho*. Father Mansoz gave me a half-hour argument why it should be pronounced like an ordinary *r*. All of a sudden, as though an alarm went off inside him, he jumped up from the table.

"Enough of these books for today. Come with me," he said, making a beeline for the back door. I followed to the small warehouse, and by the time I caught up to him he was taking off his cassock and working his way into a pair of coveralls. He pointed to a shelf of clothing and told me to hang my cassock on a nail and try on a pair of coveralls. "I want to show you something more interesting than the Greek *rho*."

I suspected he was going to take me to visit some Indian family, and I had visions of showing my ignorance of their language. Just then he surprised me by reaching into the upper-floor joists and slowly drawing a .22 rifle from its sheath! A new look came over his face—a young, vibrant look.

"This is the right time of the year to give you a few other lessons in something just as necessary in the North as learning the Indian language. Hand me that box of cartridges."

We left the warehouse and set off on the narrow trail, Indian-fashion, headed for the heavy timber. I half ran and stumbled to keep him in sight. Suddenly as I rounded a bend, Father Mansoz was down on one knee with a finger to his lips, pointing to a tree with his gun. I looked but saw nothing. He crept forward slowly. I followed, searching the lower pine branches for something, when I tripped over a piece of dead wood and went flat on my face.

Père Mansoz kept muttering in French and cautioned, "Don't scare the birds. Look where you put your feet." I could see his white beard bobbing as it jutted from his blue jacket, but he never looked back. I was glad.

He caught my attention again, pointing to a tree. I looked and looked, but still did not see anything. Then he raised his gun, still working his way forward. He stopped, went down on one knee, and shot. "*Voilà*, the first partridge of the day," he called to me, running into the alder bushes to the fluttering bird.

"Now do you think you could spot one?" He smiled broadly, swinging the bird around by the neck. (This is the usual method we use to kill grouse, partridge, pheasants, ducks, and geese after they are shot.)

I had to confess that I had not seen the spruce hen until the shot bird came tumbling out of the tree. With a twinkle of pride he explained in low tones as we walked slowly, keeping close to each other.

"First of all you must remember they have the camouflage. So you must use your ears." Then Père Mansoz twisted his mouth and produced some woodland noises that can best be described as "clurk-clurk-clurk." He also pointed out to me that the tail of this bird, the sharp-tail grouse, is the thing that ultimately gives him away. "You see, Father, when you hear that clurk-clurk-clurk, you look over there and *voilà*, pretty soon you see the flicker of the tail and you have him in the pot."

Father Mansoz turned the rifle over to me and pointed me down the narrow trail. He cautioned against quick movements, for from the time they are young these birds are wary of foxes. In spite of all my watching and listening, it was this sixty-year-old Frenchman who again spotted a grouse—in fact, four of them sitting on heavy branches near the trunk of the tree.

I followed his coaching, shooting the lower one first, and was pleasantly surprised to see the grouse fall. The remaining three seemed to wait their turn, and they too fell.

"This time of the year," Father Mansoz explained, "and with no wind in the trees, they will sit like stones, but watch them fly when the blast of zero winds comes in from the Barren Lands."

This was the beginning of my northern life, of happy, wonderful days and years with one of the kindest and warmest men I have ever known.

Father Alphonse Mansoz, the quiet teacher and alert hunter, was really a Brother Oblate of Mary Immaculate. To the natives he was "the man with a golden heart." He taught me not only the Chipewyan language, but most of all the northern way of life. With forty years of schooling in this area, he usually punctuated his advice with personal experience.

"When I came north I measured almost six feet," he said one day, eying me up and down. "This dry country does things to a man. Right now I'm over an inch shorter, but a little fatter here." He chuckled, slapping his waist, which to me looked quite normal. Despite the loss of an inch in height he was still a powerful man and could pick up a hundred-pound sack of beans from the warehouse floor and ease it up on his shoulder without a grunt. And he could also deliver a blistering sermon to his Chipewyan Indians and keep them in line.

"Never guess at anything when you travel up in this country," I can still hear him say as he paced the floor at the mission. And I can still see that crooked finger warning and coaching me when I packed for a trip to the Indian camps. He would always check my sled to make sure I had an ax, extra clothing, and footgear. "Up here you can't afford to guess. You don't guess about anything. You don't guess about how many packs of matches you have in your camp sack. Look and make certain. And always make sure you have your .22 and at least four boxes of ammunition and a knife. It is your best payload, you know," he would add, puffing away on his pipe.

Even now I remember those pipes he smoked. They were a curious, evil-smelling collection. "I'll admit I smoke too much," he would confess. "Look, this pipe of a week is beginning to bowl-crack already. Still," he would add, rubbing the hot bowl along his nose, "a pipe is sometimes a man's best friend."

Along with the irregular verbs in the Chipewyan language, my professor introduced me to the cosmopolitan populace of Fort Smith. On our daily walks through the settlement we met new faces and strange names. There was big John Beaver, the ex-chief, with his black hat, and Mrs. Beaver with their half dozen little Indians. And Jim Squirrel and his family in the back yard of our hospital with howling sled dogs tied to the bushes around their log cabins. Farther down the road lived the Maurice Beaulieus in their one-room fourteen-by-fourteen log house with an attic where the children and visitors slept. Other Indian families lived south of the mission in one-story log cabins, usually the single-room style. In the center of town, one lot east of the mission, was a squat log building with a huge chimney. The doctor, mayor, and Indian agent lived here in the person of Dr. J. A. Urqhuart. Our paths crossed at the hospital. He was a big, friendly man, always a gentleman, showing respect and receiving it from everyone. Anyone with trouble—physical or otherwise, great or small—found that the range of his generous attention included them.

Across the street and to the east of the doctor's residence was the Royal Canadian Mounted Police barracks, the grounds of which included a nine-hole golf course and the local jail. Four Mounties and the inspector lived here, the central police office for the Mackenzie District. South of the barracks stood the Anglican mission house and church, but there was now no minister. Father Mansoz said the last minister was a kind man who took daily walks to the hospital to visit the sick before he became ill and left for his home in the east. North of the Royal Canadian Mounted Police lived my very dear friend, Leo Mercredi, and his family. Mr. Mercredi was my first guide when I visited the people east of Smith. I have often thought how much faith this man must have had to trust me with his great dog team. Perhaps he was confident that the dogs knew more about the country than I did and that they would bring me back or come for help in case of accident.

The Hudson's Bay Company store and hotel stood next in line, high on the sandy bank, a good one hundred and fifty feet above the roaring rapids of the Slave River. On the waterfront the Bay had a long single-story warehouse from which their boats were loaded with supplies that were trucked over the sixteen-mile portage from the Fitzgerald warehouse or direct from the barges during the summer. It was here on the river that I saw the first float-equipped plane land with our weekly mail. Even two hours before it was due the natives always gathered to witness this feat of daring in those boiling waters below the rapids. I was often there, too, dreaming of seemingly impossible things—like flying a plane for the missions instead of driving a slow dog team or sitting for days on a river boat.

That fall when the cold weather blew in from the northwest in late October and early November, the little settlement grew smaller, like a turtle retreating into its shell. All the transport people left for the south on the last boat from Fitzgerald. The trappers, which included Indians, Metis, and whites, gathered their supplies, hitched their dog teams, and "marched them" out across the frozen river to their trap lines. The roar of the rapids changed from a deep-toned summer bass to a kind of baritone in the crisp drying zero air. Each morning a low cloud dusted the little settlement with snow crystals, the frozen breath of the rapids.

By All Saints' Day, November first, the winter population of some two hundred souls had settled down behind heavily frosted windows and smoking chimneys. They ventured outside only when necessary. There was no plumbing or electricity in those early days; we gathered wood for fuel and melted ice for water. On mild days, rabbit snares were set by the children after school hours. They gave me lessons in that sport and I taught them catechism a half hour each day. With the great exodus to the trapping grounds in November, there was a sharp decline in school attendance. At first I thought it was illness or just a case of playing hooky.

When I brought up this question one morning Père Mansoz sighed ruefully. For over thirty-five years, he explained, he had begged the people on the trap lines to send their children to the mission's boarding school at Fort Resolution, two hundred miles north, on the south shore of Great Slave Lake. He had stressed the importance of an education and especially the training and formation of their character, but only twenty-five per cent had sent their children.

"What about the boys and girls who are still in the settlement and do not attend school? They can't accomplish much if they come only a few days a month, Father."

"I am aware of this situation, and believe me, I have written letters and begged the authorities to enforce the laws of compulsory education," he answered, forcefully slapping the table. Then in a more subdued manner he added: "But the reply is always the same: 'In time these conditions will be remedied.' Meanwhile the children grow up to be ignorant and continue to follow the same pattern as their parents—'live for today, tomorrow will take care of itself.'"

This was just one of many discussions we had on that school question, because it seemed to me to be the most important work in the settlement. These children would be the citizens of tomorrow, and all they knew or thought important was snaring rabbits or catching squirrels. After a few meditations on this subject I followed the advice of Father Mansoz and continued his practice of visiting the families and asking their assistance. By mid-November four families decided to use the most convincing of all arguments, a willow switch, when their youngsters skipped classes. I saw a new light of interest in the eyes of our day-school teacher, Sister Rose Ann Gregoire, when the attendance increased and remained constant. She was a veteran of twenty-five years in Indian schools and, like all teachers, became discouraged when her pupils skipped classes and made her repeat lessons, thus retarding the entire school. This Grey Nun had the patience of a seal-hunting Eskimo, and rather than use her persuasive ruler on the knuckles of some of the more accurate spitball artists, as I knew she would have liked, she just put them on the dunce seat or gave them a writing punishment. Our little school could accommodate fifty pupils, but we were fortunate to have thirty-five steady students ranging from the five-year-olds in kindergarten to the fifteen-year-olds in eighth grade. The girls outnumbered the boys—and outranked them in high marks on their report cards. Yet the boys tried and kept at their books even though the twelve who attended school would have preferred snaring rabbits or shooting at ptarmigan with their slingshots.

Because I was really a boy at heart, too, in this new untamed land, and Father Mansoz knew it, he called me to his room one evening in early December with news that was music to my ears. "How would you like to take a week off from class to visit some Indian families east of the river?" he asked, reaching for a map.

"That would be just fine, Père. But how would I travel? We have no dog team here."

He had already arranged that end of it. I was to travel with a man who knows the country, Leo Mercredi. He had a number-one dog team and was the brother-in-law of Father Laferte, our native priest at Fitzgerald. I was to leave after dinner the next day, which would allow time enough to get to the first settlement at Salt River, some nineteen miles north.

That same evening we packed my Mass kit with new linens, hosts, and fresh candles. "I usually pack the Mass wine in two or three bottles and bury it deep in my sleeping bag to keep it from freezing and from being broken on the rough trail," Father Mansoz advised, handing me three newly filled half-pint medicine bottles of red wine. "This is my squeezings from three years ago. You will like it and I don't believe it will freeze unless you get into thirty-five and forty-below weather."

Later that year he taught me how to make altar wine from white raisins by just adding water and allowing the mash to ferment for some seventeen days at room temperature. No sugar was added when the mixture stopped "working"; we bottled it and in a few months it was ready for use.

Father Mansoz gave me his rabbit-skin sleeping bag, and before that night was over I packed and repacked time and again, always forgetting something. This was a moment I had been dreaming about for almost six years—hitting the trail as a real northern missionary. Before sleeping, I had thought of home and made a mental note to write first thing in the morning. Leaving the mission with its home atmosphere was not easy either. I began to like the spiritual climate around the house, where men had stopped saying "I" and began saying "we." There is such a wholesome sense of belonging to the family when all are recognized as equals and respected for their opinions. St. Isidore's mission was my new home now and I liked it.

While packing the remainder of my trail gear the next morning Father Mansoz came in, followed by a medium-sized man with very dark eyebrows and a smile that set like a built-in fixture on his tanned face.

"This is your trail guide, Mr. Leo Mercredi."

"Hello, Father," Leo said in clear unaccented English as he sized me up. "I hope you fit in my sled." He grinned, turning to Father with a wink. Then a flurry of French went past my ears like the swish of rockets. Again shifting gears into English without even clearing his throat, Leo turned to me and asked if I had a rifle. I went to the clothes closet and dug out my Marlin .30-.30 in the new canvas case the Sisters had made for it. This rifle, a memento of home, had been given to me by a great hunter and sportsman, the Right Reverend Monsignor Anthony Veit of Hamburg, New York, who had baptized me. The gun gleamed as I slipped it from its new case and handed it to Leo, whose eyes lighted up. "*Très bien,*" he said, levering it open. "Excuse me, Father. I always check on a gun to make sure it is not loaded before I handle it." He sighted the Marlin and hefted it. "This is a real gun. I was asking Father Mansoz about one, since mine is at the bottom of the river. Last spring on the return trip from my trap line the ice suddenly gave way while I was crossing the river

36

and my sled slipped into the water. We finally saved the sled, but my rifle slid into the river. All I have now is a .22-caliber. We need a larger gun in case we run into moose, caribou, or even wolves."

When he mentioned wolves I thought it was time to tell him that my experience with a rifle was limited to a little target practice. He promised to give me a checkout on it and assured me there would be ample opportunities to practice on moving targets!

Leo came back with his dog team at eleven o'clock. We packed the sled with a small tent, bedrolls, my Mass kit, food for ourselves and the dogs (fish) for six days (packed in a small tin camp stove), a trail ax, and our two guns lashed well forward on top of the load. A deep seat was left for me near the backboard of the sled, on which the handles are attached for the driver. Behind the backboard was a kind of pouch for shells, tea pail, and seven dog chains to tie our team to trees at night. By the time our sled was packed it was so near lunch hour we joined the Community for a last good meal cooked by the Sisters.

The dogs were yelping and straining at their tie chains when we came from lunch. They were anxious to move to keep warm in that twenty-below-zero weather. The sky was a dull gray with just a smudge of red to the south.

"We will follow the old wagon trail to Salt River," Leo told Father Mansoz while he untied his lead dog, Timber. "I don't want to discourage this young missionary and give him a bad impression of our dog-team express by taking that rough bush trail."

"Leo will teach you how to handle a team," Father Mansoz assured me. "He will help you, too, if you get your tongue tangled in that Indian language. And don't be afraid to speak even though you make mistakes—that's the way I learned to speak Chipewyan. Now, have a safe trip," he added with a warm handshake. "Don't forget to give my special regards to all my people at Salt River. Visit every tent and cabin," he called as our team lunged ahead.

We were off in a flurry of snow, and I was hanging on with every muscle. "Cha, cha," Leo called, and Timber lurched off to the right, pulling Blackie, a younger dog following him, right off his feet! The wheel dog next to the sled was a red, squat, mean-looking creature that snapped at old Shaggy ahead of him every chance he got. "Redzie, march," Leo barked at him, and that red face turned and gave me an ornery look. "Yurh, yurh." Leo tilted the sled to the left and Timber did a cross step like a Derby winner and pulled the whole to the left after him.

"March, march!" Leo cracked his long blacksnake whip, and the team began to move at a fast clip. Timber was a long-legged pacer, and the other six dogs had to gallop to follow him. His stub tail of four inches was always at full mast, like those of the five dogs following him. Redzie's tail was always held down, ever protecting himself from the whip.

In a few minutes we were past the edge of town, riding in a two-foot-deep trail through the tall jackpine. Very quickly I learned that a dog sled has a lot in common with a speedboat on choppy water. Both ride their passengers close to the surface and give an exaggerated sense of speed as they hit the bumps. There was just a half inch of hickory board between me and the trail, and on that loaded sled I could feel every wrinkle in the road. Our speed of about seven miles an hour really put fangs into that below-zero wind. A halo of frost formed around my face on my parka fur, and my nose felt like a piece of cold metal. After an hour we came to a clearing where the trees were cut and corded.

"Turn your back to the wind," Leo called down to me. "It could freeze your face out here." I worked my way around and faced the rear. My driver not only had his face circled with frost, but even his eyebrows and eyelashes were white.

"That breeze is cold out here in the open," he said, holding onto the sled with one hand and rubbing his face and chin with the other. His beaver-skin mitts hung on a cord around his neck, and his right shoulder was white with frost from his breath. I was thankful then for the heavy black bearskin mitts Father Mansoz had lent me. They kept my hands warm as toast.

From this new position I had a good view of Leo tooling that sled. When the trail sloped to the left, his left foot flicked out for leverage as he heaved and righted the sled. Climbing steep hills, he would leave the sled and run behind to lighten the load. On the hill crest he hopped back on and trailed his foot in the snow, breaking the speed of the sled as we careened downhill. When we reached the tops of two of the higher hills, we stopped for a rest. I welcomed the chance to stretch and get some circulation back in my legs.

"I'm happy about your rifle, Father," Leo said. "Back about a mile I noticed some buffalo tracks. Sometimes they can be mean and refuse to move out of the road. One shot high over their heads usually sends them on their way." He told me they would not charge us because of the dog team. Dogs and wolves are their enemies. All the rest of the way, I watched for signs of buffalo but saw none. I was not unhappy about this, for I must admit that a prickly fear of expectation kept me coiled for action since I had heard wild animals were around us.

It was evening when we saw the lights of the Salt River settlement—all two of them! Our dogs stopped near the fish rack of Joe Nodaway.

"He must still be out on the trap line." Leo pointed to the stakes where dogs had been kept. Someone opened the cabin door nearby, and the hissing gasoline light that shone out at us was blinding. My guide led the way into the cabin and shook hands with an Indian woman with long straight black hair.

"This is Mrs. Joe Nodaway, Father."

"Welcome, Yaltri," she said, using the Chipewyan word for "Father." As she offered me her hand she was almost knocked over by a little boy, about four years old, who ran at her, yelling in fright. She patted his head and told him I was a young brother to Father Mansoz and that I was going to stay and say the Big Prayer (the Mass) in the morning. The young lad peered from behind his mother's buckskin skirt and stopped crying, fascinated when I took off my steamed glasses and cleaned them. I must have looked more than a little frightening in those white-frosted glasses.

Leo insisted I make myself at home while he went out to get our supplies and stake out the dogs. I wanted to help, but he assured me there would be plenty of time for that when we camped alone on the trail. "Tonight we have a roof over our heads and all the comforts of home, thanks to Joe and his wife," he said, smiling at Mrs. Joe. She returned a shy little smile and went to fire up her stove.

The cabin was about ten by fourteen feet, with a six-and-a-half-foot ceiling. One four-pane window looked out toward the fish rack to the northeast. The other window faced the southwest, and a five-foot door opened to the southeast. Roughhewn logs dressed the four walls. A metal picture of the Sacred Heart was nailed over the door, and a well-fingered calendar hung on the wall above the table. Near the door, four wooden pegs supported parkas, mitts, a couple of pairs of old moccasins, and a red-fox pelt. The stove was a round barrel affair that nested lengthwise in a box of sand in the center of the cabin floor. A flat piece of metal bolted to the top of the stove was covered with a few fire-blackened pots and a large cast-iron kettle with a heavy cover. I wondered what they were cooking in that big pot for just three people.

This was my picture of the cabin at a glance while I slipped off my parka and mitts. Something was missing, and when Leo shouldered his way in with our sleeping bags I knew what it was. They had no bed! Immediately I became a little concerned. Not only did that floor look hard, but I wondered where we would all find a spot to unroll our blankets! When I heard the bedlam of barking dogs and the little boy ran to the door, calling his father, I began to realize that this was home to these people regardless of how poor and simple it was. They were happy here. And, too, this is how missionaries made the rounds in one of the largest mission fields in the world. All across the Canadian Northland people lived like this. No doubt this very night other missionaries were visiting other cabins somewhere in this vast frontier country. Father Mansoz had spent many evenings here and probably said Mass for the people of this little settlement at the little table Mrs. Nodaway was setting. Nine families made their home here where the Salt River empties into the Slave River because the fishing was good and because these people ran trap lines in the vicinity.

Leo entered with more baggage, followed by a stocky man, who flung three frozen rabbits on the floor near the stove.

"This is Joe Nodaway," Leo said, pulling his parka off over his head. A smile tried to work its way out of Joe's cold, red face. His hand was like ice, but I could feel power there and friendship too. He said nothing, just nodded and looked me over. Leo spoke very rapidly to him in Chipewyan, but all I could get was the word "Yaltri." Joe nodded approval, sat on a box, and began unlacing his moccasins. All the while the little boy clung to his father's pants leg and gave me the eye—and all the distance he could muster. I thought of the bag of candy Father Mansoz had given me, saying I might need it to "melt the ice." Now I knew what he meant.

"You will wash hands, Yaltri?" The low, feminine voice of Mrs. Nodaway startled me. There she stood at my elbow with a white enamel basin of water, soap, and a clean towel. I never noticed her getting it. I thanked her, set the basin on the box where I was sitting, and washed up. When I took the towel from my face, the basin was gone and I just caught a glimpse of her leaving the cabin. I was going to clean the basin myself, but she was two jumps ahead of me. While the two men washed, chatting away in Chipewyan, I unlaced my moccasins and tried to follow the workings of an Indian housewife. She had just about everything at arm's length and she made every move count. While keeping an eye on the cooking pots on the stove, she opened various boxes for tableware and food. Her quick yet measured movements, her face and dark lively eyes told me she was in her early thirties. Her dark hair was now rolled neatly at the nape of her neck. An apron covered her blue blouse and buckskin skirt of caribou skin. A little silver cross dangled on a leather thong about her neck, and I noted that she wore a gold wedding band. When I questioned Leo about her later, he told me how these women can transform themselves and dress, even while they seem to be doing nothing else but cooking.

The table was set with a square of checkered gingham for a tablecloth, enameled cups, saucers, and plates, and knives, forks, and spoons. Pepper and salt were on the table in their original boxes and sugar and jam in tins—all for packing and traveling. Three empty boxes served as chairs.

We gathered at the table and all stood while I said a prayer. Father Mansoz had instructed these people well, and their faith in God was solid and real. They reverently bowed their heads and folded their hands. The little boy, Gabriel, watched as I made the final Sign of the Cross and tried to follow me—but with his left hand. His mother took the chubby little right hand in hers and signed him with the cross. The prayer over, we sat down to a supper of roast moose—a "first" for me, but a delightful one. The meat was succulent and tender, and I didn't miss potatoes or other vegetables.

"They were all contained in the gravy anyway," Leo said later that evening. "You won't miss those green vegetables at all after a while. Just so long as you have good meat and fish, your hunger will be satisfied."

I had proof of that when I looked at Joe. He was a picture of health—a man who spent himself physically yet seldom, if ever, had any green vegetables. While his wife did the dishes, Joe began to find his tongue and told us how glad he was to have the visit of a missionary, but he was sorry the other people were away at their traps except one other family. I told him I would try to return for Christmas, and his face lighted up.

"They will all be here, and we will have singing at Mass?" he questioned. I assured him we would, and that made him happy. He hugged little Gabriel, who sat on his knee, listening. The other family, with two little girls about eight and eleven, came in at nine o'clock. Their cabin was the largest of the settlement and it was decided we would have the Christmas Mass there.

About nine-thirty I noticed Mrs. Nodaway was fingering a rosary, and I knew it was time to say the evening prayer. This was a custom Father Mansoz told me he had started the second year he visited the Indian families. I saw they were faithful to the practice, for as soon as I took out my rosary the men knelt at their chairs and crossed themselves. This was the one prayer I could say in Chipewyan, and they responded in good rich voices, proud to hear I could pray in their language. After the first decade Gabe fell asleep in his mother's arms and she laid him on a wolf skin and covered him with a blanket.

While we had tea, Joe opened our sleeping bags on one side of the stove while his wife arranged their bed on the other side, where little Gabe was sleeping soundly. When the beds were stretched out Joe set a lighted candle on a box between our beds.

"Good sleep, Yaltri," he said, touching my shoulder. No doubt he knew I would find more hard spots on his cabin floor than in my soft bed at the mission. And Joe was right. Even with Father Mansoz' rabbit-skin sleeping bag under me I kept squirming and turning to get comfortable. Leo was dead to the world in ten minutes and all was quiet except for the crackle of the fire and Joe's heavy breathing. This was my first try at sleeping on the floor and, from the looks of this country, I knew it would not be the last. For the first time I realized a spring bed was a luxury. But I managed to doze off anyway, and the next thing I knew Leo was nudging me—it was time to get up. The others would be here for Mass in half an hour.

I shook myself awake and dressed quickly. Joe had the fire going, and I noticed even little Gabe was up and dressed. When the other family arrived, I began the Mass at the altar set up on the dinner table. Leo served and the people said prayers aloud in Chipewyan. I thought it was about as close to Bethlehem as the real thing, and the simple faith of these good people made me feel very humble and unworthy to carry God to them.

While Joe and Leo packed the sled and hitched the team, I said a few prayers and dressed into my trail gear. It was a new day, but a cold one. A west wind was blowing snow off the tree tops—a sign that stormy weather lay ahead. Joe's thermometer read thirty-one below zero. Bright stars still winked at us from a dark sky, even though it was after nine o'clock. I could just pick out the dull gray-white land of Salt River to the north of our cabin, but drifting snow made the dull light of early morning more black than gray. I was thankful that Leo was along, otherwise I am sure I would have spent the day with Joe or returned to the mission. My guide did not seem to worry about the darkness or the impending storm. He hitched the yelping dogs, put the rifle aboard, and with hasty good-bys we were off in a swirl of flying snow.

"Hang on tight, Father," Leo yelled. "The trail gets rough through here, and soon we will be going down the steep river-bank." He was not telling a lie. I thought the end of my spine was being pounded by sledge hammers. The sled yawed, pitched, went up over small rises into the air and down with a bang that made my bones crack! I was thanking God that Leo stopped the team after our race down the riverbank.

"We will have to help the dogs with the sled over these hummocks of ice," he said. "They sure run with open throttles in the morning, those dogs. It's a wonder they don't freeze their lungs." He was breathing deeply, a heavy mitten shielding his mouth and nose from the cold air. Out here on the river the wind began to have fangs that bit right through my pants legs and even through my parka and into my back and shoulders. Now I knew it was thirty-one below zero!

We were soon on our way again, grunting with the dogs to push and heft our sled across the rough ice. Some ridges were five and six feet high. These we by-passed when possible because it took at least ten minutes to chop our way through them. Some of those ice cakes were four feet thick! The wild wind pushed at us and sometimes enveloped us in gusts of blowing snow, so that I could not see Timber. Through it all Leo kept urging the team on until we struck the soft snow in the willows across the river.

"You guide the sled now," he directed. "I will cut a trail for the dogs." He slipped into his snowshoes, tying them snugly over his moccasins. "You will notice a rope trailing some twenty-five feet behind the sled." He pointed. "That is attached to Timber's collar. If you should fall off, or if you want to stop the team, just grab that rope. It's a kind of emergency cord that stops the team. When we are about to start, take the sled by the horns and rock it to break it free of the snow. This helps the team get rolling." Off he tramped then, Timber at his heels.

We moved slowly in the soft snow. I had to help the dogs, pushing the sled at times or just walking behind it to lighten their load. It was daybreak now, but a very dull gray day with no shadows. Swishing willows cut me in the face and smarted like iodine in an open wound. We climbed steadily, plodding on for over an hour before reaching the black spruce ridge. About a mile deep in timber we hit a good trail, and I became a passenger again. The trees shielded us now from the stinging wind, and the dogs became frisky again, with Timber setting a fast pace. Powdered snow filtered down through the trees as the wind dug its strong fingers into their hair, bending and twisting their stiff trunks. The trail followed an easterly direction over small open muskegs, frozen creeks, rivers, and through some poplar country.

At about one o'clock we stopped at the eastern edge of heavy timber in the lee of the storm and made a fire. I toasted four doughnuts the nuns had packed for us, while Leo made tea. The dogs dropped in their tracks, gulped a few mouthfuls of snow, and lay quietly, content for the chance to rest. We ate standing with our backs to the fire, warming our hands on the hot cups of tea, and feeling the warmth of the fire on the backs of our legs.

Our pace was fast after lunch, for Leo thought it wise to make tracks while the light lasted, and the trail was hard and firm over small lakes. By three o'clock we climbed into rocky country, where the trees were dwarfed and twisted by the ripping winds. The landscape changed as we went east over these hills of solid granite. Out here a kind of speedway for the racing wind left many bald surfaces where our sled rumbled over bare rock. The gray sky was turning dark in the north when we careened down a steep slope into a flat of soft snow. It was like riding on foam rubber after those rocks. Again Leo went on ahead with snowshoes and I guided the sled until a few stars began to twinkle in the dark sky. When we came to a growth of spruce and tamarack near what looked like either a ravine or a river, my guide decided this was the place to camp.

"We can't reach Star Lake tonight in this blizzard," he said, kicking off his snowshoes. "This will make a good campsite because it is a good vantage point for spotting moose or caribou down in that ravine. Besides, it's sheltered from the wind." We unhitched the team quickly and tied them to trees behind some

44

outcroppings of rock. This made a wall between the dogs and the ravine, with our tent in the center, facing south.

"Keep your rifle handy," Leo advised when we had the dogs in their places. "Leave it in its case, but unbuckle the top flap so we can slip it out quickly. Moose begin to travel about this time of evening. As you work, keep an eye on the eastern end of that ravine, and I will watch the west," he said, getting our tent out of the sled.

We cut two small trees to make floor space, shoveled away the snow down to the moss, using our snowshoes for shovels, and set up our tent. This was my first outdoor camp, and no doubt Leo realized he had a number-one greenhorn on his hands. I'm glad he had God's gift of patience, because I kept up a constant barrage of questions.

"You can melt snow now for our tea," he directed me when our camp stove was set up. "Dig a hole in the snow and get the icy snow crystals just above the moss. It not only makes the water taste better, but it makes twice as much as a pail of fresh surface snow." He warned me against tapping the pail of snow as it melted. "Otherwise the snow will be toasted by red-hot sides of the pail. This gives the tea that coal-oil taste." He wrinkled his nose.

While I cut some dry wood and lit the stove, Leo cut four or five small pine trees and stripped off their branches to make a soft warm flooring in our tent. During these camp chores we kept an eye on the ravine. I wanted to spot a moose just to prove to myself this was not a dream. Everything I had read about the North and the life of a missionary was now a reality. Here we were, camping out on the edge of a forest, the lobo of wolves and the range of caribou, moose, and wild buffalo. Here we would find the Indians who made this untamed land their home. I was coming to teach them about the God Who created all of us and how they should respect His laws and prepare for their future life of eternity which He promised all those who love Him and keep His commandments.

My thoughts were interrupted by a sudden barking of the dogs which made me blow out the candle and sent me scurrying out of the tent to see what was up.

"I just fed the dogs for the day," Leo said, coming toward me with an empty fish sack. "You may as well bring the rifle into the tent and lay it on the floor to keep it cold. I don't believe we will

45

spot game any more with this sudden darkness." He pointed toward the ravine, which was just a black void now, a half-mile-wide corridor for the blowing snow.

Inside our tent the fire was crackling on its meal of dry spruce. We lit two candles, shed our parkas, and dusted the frost off the fur hoods so it would not melt and freeze. The two caribou skins Leo had packed in the bottom of our sled made a warm floor over the small pine boughs, and we felt warm and cozy after our day in wild, cold wind. Now we had time to cook and eat a good meal of white fish. I brewed a big pail of tea under Leo's direction and kept an eye on him as he opened the fish, cleaned and roasted it. We lingered over our tea and doughnuts for more than hour, talking. Our tent gave a gentle ruffle once in a while to remind us that the wind was still master of the snowy world outside. At an early hour we said our rosary together, added a special prayer for good weather, slipped into our warm sleeping bags, and blew out the candles.

I recall that night very often when I have problems that keep me awake, and the very thought of that wonderful sleep often puts me to sleep now. We continued our rounds the next day, visiting the Indians, spending the night with them, and then traveling on. It was exciting, wonderful, and educational in a thousand and one ways. I not only learned how to travel, drive dogs, make camp and cook, but most of all I learned how to deal with these wonderful people of the forest, who lived their simple lives outside the perimeter and rush of our southern world. In complex situations Leo Mercredi was my live dictionary. His big regret was that we did not see a moose or a caribou during the entire trip!

"Maybe their sixth animal sense prompted them to keep away while you had such a keen hunter along." Father Mansoz patted me on the back and winked at Leo. "Sometimes I have traveled a month out there, visiting the Indians, and was just lucky to shoot a rabbit."

I gave a full account of my trip, the baptisms and other sacraments I administered, and especially the present state of well-being of the families. Father Mansoz had known these Indians as children, and his keen interest fired my zeal to learn about them and help bring happiness into their lives. I needed teaching and training, and my professor *pratique* was a persistent but very patient man.

During that first winter he either sent me out on short trips or took me along with him. We rode roughshod over bush trails, ricocheted off icy rocks, got slapped in the face with willow whips at forty below zero, brought smiles of real joy to God's children of the woods, and returned content with the thought that we were fulfilling our role as messengers of God. I was learning how to walk those first faltering steps of a northern missionary, and I found happiness in this land that was now my new home.

Chapter Four

ONE killing cold day in February during that first winter at Fort Smith, I had just settled at my desk for an afternoon of study when the front door of the mission flew open and an excited voice called, "Yaltri, Yaltri, come."

I knew Father Mansoz was away for the weekend, acting as chaplain for the Brothers at the wood camp, and the elderly Father Laffont was at the hospital, visiting a Cree patient, so I went to see what this was all about.

A young lad of about fourteen came toward me, pleading, "Father, you come. My little sister, she die, I think." His parka was covered with hoarfrost and his face was burned red from the cold.

"Where do you come from?" I asked in English, shaking the cold thin hand he held out to me. His small slanted eyes opened wide when I spoke. He understood. From his doll-featured face, I took him for a Cree and I was relieved when he understood me. My knowledge of Cree was limited to about two words!

"Fitzgerald. I started early this morning, but I have only four poor dogs. There was new snow on the trail. You will come, Father?" he pleaded again.

I asked him to wait while I discussed this with Father Laffont at the hospital. The doctor happened to be out of the settlement at the time on a sick call, so Father decided I should go immediately, taking a few simple medications along from the Sisters' supply. Father Laffont spoke to the boy in Cree in an attempt to learn more details on the illness of the little girl, but the answers were always the same: "She is very sick." I learned that his name was James Drygeese and that his little sister's name was Theresa. Father said he knew the family and that they were fine people.

It was late in the day to start on a twenty-mile trip, especially at this time of the year when the days had only three hours of good daylight. While we made preparations the light was already fading from gray to twilight and it was only three o'clock in the afternoon! Then, like an answer to a prayer, young Theodore Mercredi came to the mission to request a Mass for his uncle, Father Laferte, who was off on a long trip upriver. Father Laferte's absence from Fitzgerald explained why the Cree boy had sought help from us. I sent him home on the run to ask his father if he would be my chauffeur with that fine dog team of his to Fitzgerald.

Before I had all my bags packed, Leo was there, smiling and ready to go with his frisky team. We loaded the trail gear with my baggage, and by four o'clock Timber was setting a fast pace over the new trail. There was a fifty-below-zero nip in the air, and little puffs of steam arose from the dogs as they raced along. Jimmy followed, urging his team to keep us in sight. We changed places four times on that trip. I drove the team and ran behind the sled awhile to keep the circulation in my legs, and Leo was glad to snuggle into the warm eiderdown we had stretched in the sled. Eerie wolf howls and the high-pitched whine of lynxes kept our team alert, and whoever rode the sled had his hand on my rifle—just in case.

What if we arrived too late? I thought over and over again. While the sled whistled over the snow in the night, I thought of another story and another place where men were racing against time with oxcarts in the jungles of Africa to reach a sick man. In 1937, Father Paul Schulte, O.M.I., the famed flying priest, had visited us in Washington, D.C., and recounted graphically some of his flying exploits in South Africa. "I would like you to know a Brother missionary," he lectured. "He was a young man with many years of usefulness before him, but he died a horrible death, alone in a remote jungle of South Africa. Fever killed him before the news of his illness reached the outside world. And the pity of it all is that he might be here today if I had been there to fly him out with my plane. He was just like one of you fellows. What a waste of manpower."

A plane up here in the North! That would be a Godsend. Why, I could fly these twenty miles, pick up the sick person, and have her in the hospital all within an hour! Perhaps, someday, but now was now. Even at dog-team pace, Father Mansoz managed to reach out and teach his people God's message of love. Until the good Lord sees fit to help change this transportation, I must be satisfied and do my best with the tools at hand.

Well after midnight we ran into a bedlam of howling, barking dogs, the first sign that we were arriving in Fitzgerald. Leo pointed

Timber at the only cabin where light blazed from a window out on the sparkling crystal snow. Dogs from half a dozen teams of visitors cut loose with deep-throated growls as we neared the small cabin. The door opened, letting out light, steam, and three men. I recognized one oversized fellow by his dark curly hair and cherry-red face—it was Joe Bourke, a Cree who worked for the Hudson's Bay Company during the summer and spoke English quite well. His Cree brothers were proud of him.

"I just came into town an hour ago, Father," he said, shaking hands. "It's a bad case, and I was glad Jimmy went for help."

I explained that the doctor was away and Father Mansoz was at the wood camp. We went inside, but I had to come out of that cabin immediately, choking for air!

It was small wonder that the little girl was dying. She must have been suffocating. There were fourteen people in the single room, which was no larger than ten by fourteen. I had Joe ask them to leave, and like chickens from a coop they left the cabin. The women ran curious eyes over me as they drew their black shawls about them, some with children on their backs. Inside again, I met Jimmy's mother kneeling by the sick girl, who was wrapped in blankets on the floor. Her little face was drawn and her lips were white from pain.

"She will die, Father?" Jimmy asked.

"Only God knows that, Jim. You must pray with your ma. God will do what is best for little Theresa. She suffers very much." I pointed to her dark eyes, wide open but seeing nothing.

Her pulse was very weak and her breathing labored. While I administered the sacrament of Extreme Unction for the dying the family said the Rosary in Cree. I could hear the people from outside the cabin answering the prayers. This manifestation of faith and family love was something none of my reading about these people had prepared me for. It was rooted so deep that perhaps many eyes had missed it. This cabin with its roughhewn log walls, moose-skin moccasins drying on a line above the stove, no bed except caribou skins on the floor—this was the place they knew and loved as home.

Mrs. Drygeese just knelt there praying, tears of real love for her little girl spilling over her tanned face. She seemed to be in her fifties, but now I know she was only in her middle thirties. Her husband was off on his trap line to the east and would not be returning until Easter. This frontier life had added the extra years.

To the best of my knowledge, the little girl was suffering from spinal meningitis, and out there in the hinterlands I knew only a miracle could save her—a thought I kept to myself. We made Theresa as comfortable as possible, turning her on her side, with hot towels on her back. It relaxed her a little and eased her breathing. I asked the people who waited outside to return to their homes and thanked them for their kindness to this stricken family. Joe Bourke translated my message to them in Cree and some came to me and kissed my hands tearfully. I knew now why Father Laferte loved Fitzgerald.

Theresa lay very quiet for two hours, and I said my Divine Office for the new day by candlelight. Mrs. Drygeese went to sleep sitting on the floor, her head against the cabin wall. Jimmy fell asleep too—near the stove, tired and most probably very hungry after over fourteen hours on the trail. Joe had the key to the mission house on the hill and started a fire there to thaw out the place. Every half hour he came to the cabin to poke up the fire, quiet the dogs, and meet any visitors with news of the situation. He was just entering the cabin with an armful of wood when Theresa suddenly awoke and let out a piercing scream! Everyone jumped up. I went to her, but it was all over. No pulse, no respiration; her eyes were finally closed in death. I blessed her with holy water and handed the sprinkler to her mother, who also blessed her, murmuring in Cree. I learned from Joe later that she kept repeating, "My baby, I love you, I love you."

It was half-past four in the morning when Theresa passed away. Her mother washed her and put on her white First Communion dress, which was decorated with mosquito netting for lace. Joe told me he would make the coffin first thing in the morning in Father Laferte's workshop, where the mission kept wood for that purpose.

I left Mrs. Drygeese and went up to the mission for a few hours of rest. After my Mass that morning I called on the local Mounted Police to register the death officially, and he accompanied me to the cabin. Rigor mortis made it difficult for me to get a rosary around Theresa's little hands, which her mother had folded on her breast. Since we had to be the undertakers and there was no embalming, it was decided to bury her the following morning. All that day and until late at night people came to pay their last respects with a prayer for Theresa. Old ladies with their walking sticks tucked their pipes in their pockets and murmured a prayer as they looked on the little girl. Most of them said the same thing: "She is now a little angel," and they would smile at me, shake my hand with their two hands, sign themselves with the cross, and go out into the cold, dark night to their homes.

Indeed these people had feelings for their little ones. Their love was silent and profound, yet very warm and human. They gave me a lesson in faith that made a far greater impression on my soul than anything I had ever experienced before. These people of the woods, who had learned only a few years before about life beyond the grave, had the grace from God to believe in heaven with all their heart and mind and soul. Their life in this world of snow and ice and mosquitoes was one of constant struggle to survive. Even in their simple minds they reasoned that a good and merciful God certainly must have a better place picked out for His everlasting heaven than this miserable land of earth. Regardless of the race or riches of men, they must leave everything one day and die like little Theresa.

At the funeral Mass next day I consoled these wonderful people with a few words on the eternity of happiness God has in store for all those who love Him and keep His commandments. After Mass the little pine coffin was pulled by Jim and Joe Bourke to the cemetery, where Joe had picked out a grave in the frozen earth. I said the ritual burial prayers, and Theresa was lowered to her rest in the graveyard at the edge of the forest. Jim and Joe closed the grave and marked it with a white cross bearing the name and the dates of her birth and death. The custom here was to build little wood fences three feet high around the graves—a custom surviving from the early days, to protect the dead from foxes and wolves.

"My husband will make a small white fence for her grave in the spring, Father," Mrs. Drygeese told me on the way home. She did not cry any more. Her tears were all spent. "We will miss our little girl very much, Father," she added when I said good-by. "Please say a Mass that God in His goodness will send Jimmy another baby sister." She pressed a worn dollar bill in my hand. I knew how much that dollar meant to her, so I gave it back and promised I would say my Mass for her at the end of the month.

This was the first of many sick calls I made in the years that followed, and on each of them I was reminded of the deep-seated love and devotion of these people for each other. Greed and envy have not yet entered their hearts to kill the real germ of family love implanted by the Creator.

At Easter time the people came one hundred and fifty miles over the snows to celebrate the Feast of the Resurrection and receive Communion. On Easter Sunday afternoon, when many trappers came to the mission with news of their life out on the line, Theresa's father was among them, a frail-looking man with pinched features and a sallow complexion that hinted the possibility of tuberculosis.

"Thank you, Father," was all he could manage between coughing and the emotion that seized him when he saw me. "The snow came early in the barren country where I was trapping, and many of the fox pelts were rubbed, but here is a little something I thought you might like for your mother." He handed me a small flour sack. "Those are two of the best silver foxes I had in my catch." I opened the bag and held them up, thanking him. "See the fur on the neck and over the haunches? That is where the fox rubs it off when he runs over trails out in deep snow." He rubbed the fur with his thin hand. I told him I did not expect any material reward and begged him to keep the fur.

"Please, Father," he pleaded. "My wife and I talked it over and we decided you should have them. One favor we ask; could you say a Mass for our little girl?" I promised Charlie Drygeese I would, and also that I would add another for his family. He was happy.

"You must come out and visit us trappers one of these years, Father. We had real good caribou hunting this fall," he said, looking at two other visitors for affirmation. They nodded agreement with shy smiles and left the mission with him.

"That would be a fine trip for you after Christmas next year," Father Mansoz said later. "Charlie is a poor fellow but he is a good honest man. His trap line is not in the best location, and I'm working with the game warden to extend it a little for next year." While he spoke he held up the fox pelts by their noses and shook out the fur. "They will make a fine souvenir. Just make sure that you are as honest as Charlie. Don't even hint to your mother that you caught them, or she will think you came North to be a trapper rather than a missionary." There was a twinkle in his eyes as he looked at me over his glasses.

And this was my baptism into missionary life at Fort Smith,

53

Northwest Territories. Learning two new languages, listening to Père Mansoz' clurk-clurk of the grouse, sleeping out under the stars at thirty below zero, sitting at a campfire and listening to the wild cries of life in the North woods, and comforting these people in their hour of sorrow. This was the life that had often elbowed its way into my meditations during student days. Now it was a reality! After seven and a half years of preparation I was trying to stretch my legs and follow in the footsteps of those trail-blazing missionaries of yesterday. Father Lacombe was the referee between the railroad builders and battling Indians, fighting for a place to live and hunt. He taught both sides that there was room enough for all to live and became famous as a peacemaker. Father Grollier was the frontiersman, unsatisfied until he reached "the end of the land" at the Arctic Ocean where the last man lived who could learn of God. His body lies buried on a pine ridge at Good Hope, just under the Arctic Circle, testimony to his zeal to reach all men with the message of his Master.

And here still in sight was the successor to the missionary giants of yesterday, Father Mansoz. Whenever I saw him coming down the path with long strides that stretched his cassock to its limit, I always wondered what his next move might be to test the mettle of this tenderfoot.

Chapter Five

EACH day during March and April the sun climbed higher and higher in the southern sky, and by early May it remained above us long enough to melt the winter snows.

On the long prairie west of the mission, the last ski plane in late April had to wait until the early-morning freeze to take off. This was one of my haunts whenever I could find an hour to spare and I knew an aircraft was due. Actually there was no airfield as such at Fort Smith in those days. The prairie had been cleared by the Brothers for farming, and in the fall, after the first good freeze and snowfall, it was used for a landing field. Now only a few of the higher snowdrifts along the willows and the timber to the west remained. Rivulets of water trickled from the southern slopes of hills and rocks. Black spots began to appear on the ice along the shoreline where creeks spilled their thaw waters into the river.

"Hear that?" Father Mansoz cocked his good ear to the sky one evening as we returned from supper. "Those are long-necked sand cranes coming north." Then he found them with his eyes and pointed. "Over there, just above the trees. They fly low in the spring." I saw them flapping enormous wings that seemed to hit the tree tops, their legs stretched out like flat tails.

"They are the vanguard birds. Soon now we will hear the music of the spring migrations," he said, rubbing his hands. "The longer you live in the North, the sweeter the sound becomes."

In the days that followed, the crows came in pairs to pick the carcasses of foxes and dogs from the thawing river ice. Flocks of geese, ducks, and sea gulls flew north over the settlement, some landing on the prairie airport, now covered with water. By the last week of May I saw the first robins and blue jays. Spring had come with new life and warmth. Spots of bright green grass began to appear and the willows sprouted new buds.

On these warm days more of the old folks began to appear. At first they just stood against the warm logs on the sunny side of their cabins, smoking their pipes. Then when the slush of spring was gone and the sand paths dried, they came to the hospital to visit sick relatives and friends. The new sun of spring brought life back into their old bones for another year.

Every day trappers returned from their lines with bloody wrappers on their sleds from caribou and moose kills. Their dogs stood strong and heavy-furred from a long hard winter on the trail. With wide grins of pride on their snow-tanned faces, these hardy men of the woods toted sacks of fur to the Hudson's Bay store. This would be their credit deposit for a summer's food supply, plus a grubstake for next fall. While the husband bargained with the trader, his wife looked over new prints for a dress and chose something for each of the children. After a price was agreed upon the fur was sold and the man of the house bought food for his family, and perhaps a new outboard motor to push his canoe over the river to the fish nets during the summer. With arms full of the good things they dreamed about during the long winter, they trudged off to their log cabin.

One morning in the last week of May the whole settlement came alive with the news that the river ice was moving north! A Royal Canadian Signal lad won the ice-pool jackpot of sixty dollars for guessing the day and the hour.

"Let's go and see what the ice will carry away this year," Father Mansoz said, closing the Chipewyan grammar. "Two years ago the entire Hudson's Bay dock and a section of their warehouse were swept down-river. One thing for sure," he added as we hurried down the sandy road, "Fort Smith is built a good hundred and thirty-five feet above all that ice, and there's no chance of a flood in case of an ice jam."

When I saw that wild river rip up huge cakes of ice seven feet thick and heave them high on the riverbank with such force that tall, heavy spruce trees were shaved off like willows, I realized what Father was talking about. A man who had seen forty breakup seasons was allowed to conjecture and draw conclusions. Alphonse Mansoz had come to Fort Smith at the turn of the century.

On our way to the river that morning we passed an old log building which had been Father's first residence. It was now used as a warehouse by the Northern Transportation Company, its windows boarded shut and its door locked. Father Joussard had built it in 1888 with an ax and whipsaw, I learned. He preached the first missions to the Indians of Fort Smith, making annual trips south from Fort Resolution. As we watched the river, Father Mansoz glanced back from time to time at the old log house that must have held many precious memories of his young missionary days. Father Joussard had been his professor *pratique*.

The deep-throated growl of the rapids now wheezed and whined like some prehistoric monster gasping for breath. Great chunks of ice were ground against the granite rocks. Spring thaw had poured into the river from hundreds of creeks, and now it had gigantic power and washed great pieces of ice ashore thirty feet above the normal water line. A huge piece of ice barely nudged a fifty-ton tugboat and toppled it off its log cradle as though it were an empty fish box!

"Looks a little like the spring of '18,' eh, Father?" came a voice behind us.

"Mickey Ryan!" Father Mansoz seemed pleasantly surprised. "When did you get back?"

"With the last ski plane of the season," Mickey said.

Father introduced me to this dark curly-haired Irishman with the warning that although he was only five feet eight he used to be one of the best boxers in the middleweight class—a compliment Mickey waved off shyly.

"So you remember the flood of '18?' That always makes me a little sad," Father began, rubbing his bearded chin. "When I think of those supplies for a whole year for all our missions washed down-river off the McMurray docks, I always recall the winter that followed. I was at our boarding school at Resolution in those days, and we ate fish, moose, and caribou for five months! No flour, no sugar. Luckily we had salt from the farm here at Smith."

"I lost three horses and two wagons in that flood, Father. It all but broke me," Mickey added, looking at the river. And I imagined many of those people standing there on the riverbank could recall one or more dark days in their lives caused by the spring floods. Most of the watchers just stood silent, watching, waiting to see what the savage beast of a river would do this year. Then Mickey pointed and said, "There goes a section of our dock." We looked and caught sight of the last timbers of the Hudson's Bay dock going under water. I watched but never saw so much as a plank again. By noon most of the heavy ice floated down-river, and those who knew the river agreed we would have no flood this spring.

I learned more about Mickey Ryan from Father Mansoz as we

returned to the mission. "He and his brother Patrick will go down in the history of this country as the Transportation Brothers," Father said. "They began first with dog teams, then horses, and carried the mail as regular as the sun three hundred and fifty miles north from McMurray to Smith. Every four weeks they made a round trip, whether it was fifty below zero or even colder."

For years there was only a trail between Fitzgerald and Fort Smith around the rapids, and when everyone else lacked courage the Ryans tackled the problem with their characteristic determination and built a twenty-mile road over muskeg and sand. For the first eight miles they slashed down trees and brush and built a corduroy foundation over the spongy muskeg. Oxen and horses sank to their knees in the soft mushy tangle of roots, mud, and water, and they could carry only two hundred pounds apiece. The Ryan brothers had spent over two years building the road, which, when completed in the early twenties, became the portage that opened this North country.

"And do you know what?" Father Mansoz stopped to make his point. "Mickey came to me and told us we could use the road without a toll charge! It was a Godsend to us in the development of our missions."

That evening Father told me how Mickey Ryan started a fast passenger service between Edmonton and McMurray in 1925 with an old Hudson super-six car, known as "the speeder," equipped with flange rail wheels to ride the new railroad tracks.

"Remember the *Pelly Lake* you took to come North?" Father Mansoz asked. "It's a big tug of over fifty tons, quite a package to cart around. Well, Mr. Mickey Ryan pulled that boat out of the river here at Fort Smith and decided he could haul it up that eight per cent grade. Most people told him he was crazy, that it might get away from him and smash in a heap of firewood. Mickey had a good engineer with him, a man by the name of Joe Lacombe, who drove one of Ryans' two new Lynn tractors."

On the morning of the big pull over a hundred people had gathered on the high bank to watch. Lacombe rode the first tractor, and another young fellow drove the second. Mickey gave a shout and waved his arms. The exhausts spouted blue smoke, and slowly the cables tightened. Twenty men on each side of the boat broke the skids loose from the packed snow with sledge hammers, and very slowly the huge boat began to inch forward. Joe Lacombe sat tense on his machine, his eyes on Mickey, who was walking backward ahead of the tractor. Past the halfway mark, just when everyone thought the boat was as good as up, the second tractor coughed and stalled! Mickey waved and called to Joe to keep it coming. The tractor threw out black smoke, dug its claws deeper into the frozen hill, and the whole load came up right to the top of the hill.

"That is your Mickey Ryan. Quite a man, eh?" Father said proudly.

Spring breakup in the North means exactly that. When the snows melt and the ice runs out of the rivers, the tranquillity of the winter is broken. The soft tinkle of sleigh bells and the snow-muffled barking of the dogs gives way to the rumble of trucks and tractors moving tons of supplies north. Warm weather in the sixties and sunshine for eighteen hours a day hatched out millions of flies and mosquitoes to torment us as we loaded and unloaded supplies. Very quickly I learned that the summer months mean more physical than mental work down North. Father Mansoz and I were in coveralls most of the day, unloading the truck for the Brother who hauled foodstuffs and supplies for the missions from the boats at Fitzgerald, Alberta.

The big news that summer was that the Bishop had purchased a new diesel-powered tug to pull the barge of supplies for the down-river and Arctic coast missions. Over the last ten years personnel in our schools and hospitals had increased to such an extent that the small red barge of forty tons capacity and the little tug, *Guy*, could not handle the volume of supplies required during the long winter.

On a particularly warm day in June as Father Mansoz and I were working at the warehouse we learned that the new boat was on the portage and would be passing through the settlement at any minute. We cleaned a little of the dust off our faces and arrived in time to see the new white tug ride gently down to the river. Most of the settlement gathered to watch, including the Bishop, who was most anxious to see the boat safely afloat below those dangerous rapids.

The Ryan brothers had long since turned over their transportation equipment to the Hudson's Bay Company, and the Bishop had contracted with Northern Transportation, Ltd., for this work. This company was operated by Eldorado Radium Mines on Great

Bear Lake to carry supplies to their mine and haul out the ore to a refinery.

We approached the boat, perched on its cradle parallel to the river and held by stout cables, which prevented it from sliding into the water over the greased ways on which the cradle rested. The underside was a dark red, and the five-hundred-pound bronze propeller almost buried in the built-in tunnel under the stern. The builder, Mr. Denholm of McMurray, was explaining the engine to Brother Jurczyk, and I heard him say it had a 120-horse-power medium-duty Atlas diesel. The boat measured sixty-five feet in length and fifteen feet in width, and the amazing feature was its water line—only thirteen inches from the bottom! It hardly seemed possible that fifteen inches of water would float this big boat, but the Bishop assured me it was. The ship had been built for shallow rivers and delta work.

Just before launching the Bishop blessed the new boat and christened it *Sant' Anna,* after her benefactress. Then the cables were slackened on the capstans and she slid down the ways into the Slave River. Some of the Sisters came aboard to examine the staterooms, which would accommodate four nuns very comfortably. They would enjoy a rest now on their river voyages from one mission post to another. Their rooms were in the bow, under the pilothouse, directly ahead of the engine room. We explored the entire boat—the galley with its table for ten and built-in food lockers, the cabins for engineers and pilots just aft the pilothouse, and the pilothouse itself with its big brass-trimmed helm and the huge ship's compass set in alcohol. There was a fresh-paint aroma in all the rooms, and the brass hardware sparkled. The Sisters and Brothers were like children with a new toy. In all the excitement no one noticed the quiet arrival of another boat until it was almost alongside.

"The *Guy* is here from Resolution," I heard Father Mansoz call from somewhere on deck. There was a rush for the stairs and ladders. A red barge pushed by a little white tug inched its way toward us. Two nuns waved from the forward deck of the barge and a tall, stern-looking fellow stood in front of them with a rope coiled in his hands, ready to heave a line ashore. High on the top of the pilothouse of the tug, the pilot waved and the man on the barge sent the coil of rope in an arc that landed at Father Mansoz' feet.

"Welcome to Fort Smith, Frère Kerautret," Father shouted as

he picked up the rope and made it fast to the stern post of the *Sant' Anna*.

Brother stood looking in open-mouthed admiration at the new boat. When the barge drew alongside and he stepped aboard, I felt the hard grip of his rough-skinned hands.

"I bring special greetings from your friend, Father Charles Gilles," he said, smiling. Forty years in this cold land had burned scars into his face, but his eyes were young—and spoke friendship without an accent.

"Brother? Or Admiral, I should address you." The Bishop came up behind us. "How do you like this boat?"

"Now you have a real *bateau*, Bishop. But I am too old to be your captain. A new boat needs a new man." He looked off to the pilothouse of the *Guy*. "And I believe you have a very capable fellow in that young pilot, Brother Sareault." The Bishop affectionately patted his old captain on the back with the assurance that he would be aboard the new boat to direct the young Brother.

"You must be the new Father from the States," Brother Sareault said climbing aboard the *Sant' Anna*. "My home used to be in Nashua, New Hampshire, before I came North twenty years ago."

It felt good meeting a fellow countryman up here, especially a man like Brother Henry Sareault, one of the best river pilots on the Mackenzie, I learned later. He was at ease with himself and the world, and it was relaxing just to talk with him. One of the first qualities I noted in this broad-shouldered well-built Brother was that he held a very healthy respect for St. Christopher and that he had both feet planted in solid faith and trust in God.

We looked at the new boat together and he regarded everything, especially the pilothouse and the helm, with a kind of reverence that sparkles in the eyes of every man of the sea. The Bishop knew his men and very soon Brother Sareault moved his duffel bag into new quarters.

Summertime was precious time in the North, and the old red barge was loaded and shuttled to Resolution for a trial run of the *Sant' Anna*. She returned to Smith with a new barge of one hundred ton capacity, built at the mission shipyard at Resolution early that spring by Brothers Bruyère, Szczepaniak, Jurczyk, and L'Ecuyer. Built of British Columbia fir with keelsons three feet deep, the entire structure was braced with one-and-a-half-inch steel tie rods. The deck was dropped three feet below the gunwales to carry the weight on and below the water line for stability on the lake. The cabin rose seven feet above the deck with a well-trussed roof on which more light supplies like canoes and dog sleds could be stacked. Wide loading doors were at midships, as well as entrances and two staterooms at the bow and two at the stern for extra passenger accommodations. Every available hand worked late for three consecutive days until the hull had her capacity load.

A sudden blast from the ship's horn set off a flurry of hasty good-bys and orders to loose the shore cables. The *Sant' Anna* was off to the North on her maiden voyage. Father Mansoz raised his work-hardened hand, blessing the voyagers, and strains of the *Ave Maris Stella* reached us above the deep roar of the rapids. Brother Sareault captained his new ship with just pride and waved his cap to us from the bridge. Now he had a real boat with power to guide that precious barge of cargo fifteen hundred miles down-river into the Arctic.

St. Christopher must have kept an eye on his champion, because in just six weeks the *Sant' Anna* was back for another hundred tons that we had ready for her. The new boat completed a perfect season, setting a stiff precedent for future years.

The warm summer passed swiftly with all the activity of transportation, and autumn frosts changed the green world of the forest to gold and brown. I hung my coveralls in the closet and was contemplating a quiet winter of studies when my professor reminded me that our meat supply was dangerously low for the long winter.

"Usually I receive enough moose meat from my people to tide us into the caribou season in December, but this must have been a very lean summer," Father Mansoz said one morning after class. "Fortunately I mentioned this to the ranger of the Wood Buffalo Park a few weeks ago and he gave me some hope. He said he would write to the authorities in Ottawa for permission to shoot some buffalo for our meat supply."

He looked worried, for I knew he felt the responsibility of keeping bread on our table. Some four or five days after this conversation, when I had completely put aside the idea of meat for a diet of Chipewyan verbs, Mike Dempsey, the ranger, arrived with the good news that he had permission to shoot sixty buffalo bulls for the mission hospital and school meat supply.

"There's just one hitch," he said hesitantly. "The government doesn't have anyone available to help me hunt the buffalo and I'm getting too old. My eyes are not as good as they used to be."

"Oh, we can supply some help and even some grub, Mike," Father said encouragingly. "Brother Joseph is a good hunter and a woodsman, and you can take Mr. Beaulieu along to help with the skinning."

Thoughts of the possibility of a buffalo hunt were just about bursting right out of my mouth, when Father looked in my direction. "How would you like to go along on this hunt, Father? It would be good to have a priest out there for Mass on Sundays especially."

"Did you ever handle a rifle, Father?" Mike asked before I could speak.

"Not very much. I shot a few squirrels."

"He looks strong enough to help us pack the meat." Mike winked at Father Mansoz. "I'll give him a few lessons with a rifle." Then he turned his brown eyes on me and grabbed my knee. "You would like to come, wouldn't you, Father?"

"Very much, Mr. Dempsey, if Father Superior thinks I can be of any help to you."

"Good, and from now on the name is Mike." Then in a business-like manner he turned to Father Mansoz. "In our surveys of the park we found a good concentration of buffalo around the old mission farm. Could we make our headquarters there?"

"Certainly, Mike, and when will you be ready to start the hunt?"

"In about three days."

"Fine. I will have the supplies ready and the men also." Father Mansoz smiled my way.

When Brother Joe Brodeur heard the news that evening he was jubilant. "I will clean the old chapel at the farm, Father, and we will have Mass every day," he said with a little question in his voice. I nodded and he was smiling from ear to ear.

All the preparations made the hours and the days fly by, and before I had time to worry about the danger of the hunt, Mike had me packed aboard his sled and we were off for the mission farm. The snow was new and fresh, covering the fallen trees like a heavy sheepskin and creating grotesque shapes along the trail. A snap of twenty below zero made the old trail underfoot hard, and Mike's team found it easily and galloped along in high gear.

After an hour we exchanged places, and Mike had just settled himself behind a new pipeful of Old Virginia when we rounded a bend and ran head on into another team.

Immediately there was a fight and just one big heap of snarling dogs, growling and snapping at each other. Showers of snow fell on us and the dogs from the low pine branches. I heard the loud snap of a bullwhip. As soon as I heard the voice I knew it was Vincent Beaulieu, one of our Indian workmen from the mission. Mike was out of the sled and in the middle of the fight, working down into the pile to sort out his prize leader, Cockles.

"Take this line to a tree." Mike flung a coil of rope toward me. It was the head line tied to Cockles' collar. I gave it a turn around a spruce and began to heave away, while Mike pulled the dogs apart.

Meanwhile Vince grabbed a tie chain from his sled and beat his fighting team into subjection until they lay cowering in the snow. Their harnesses were tangled and twisted, and some tugs were chewed off entirely. Mike's wheel dog, Muscles, snapped at his tugs, cut himself loose from the sled, and in one powerful lunge snapped the tail off Rusty, Vince's lead dog. The old ranger dug both hands into the fur on his wheel dog's neck and yanked him loose.

"Chain this devil to a tree," he puffed, his brown-moccasined foot on the dog's neck.

In a few minutes we had our dogs under control, and Vince came back to our sled when his team was secured to trees fifty yards or so up the trail. He had worked for the mission over twenty years and was as tough as a pine knot and always willing to work until he dropped in his tracks.

"Too bad I didn't hear you coming. I could have pulled my team off into the bush and let you pass. Why don't you have bells on your dogs, Mike?"

"Bells on a buffalo hunt? Now, Vince, we want to shoot some of those wise old buffalo. I'm afraid if we rang a bell on them they might kick up quite a snowstorm and hide in the thick timber." Mike winked at me. "I like to surprise not only the buffalo, Vince, but those sneaky old wolves too. Maybe we can bag a few and have some of their thick pelts for our camp."

"How did you find the old mission farmhouse, Vince?"

"It had a busted window or two, Father, but I fixed them with boards and left the load of hunting gear in the kitchen."

"How is the wood situation?"

"Fine, Mike. I cut enough for a few days and filled the wood box. The place will be still warm from my morning fire," Vince said.

When the teams were lined up, Vince was off for Fort Smith and we continued on to the mission farm. The new snow had cotton-balled the trees and bush country, and low, snow-laden jackpine limbs salted us as we zigzagged and bounced over the trail.

Back at Fort Smith, Brother Joe was packing supplies for six weeks of hunting. He would come to the farm on the big bobsled with the horses in a few days and Vince would follow with his dog team.

While riding along cozy and warm in the sled I began to daydream about those last days when we packed for the hunt. Father Mansoz told me how Mike finally became a buffalo ranger. To my surprise, I learned that this Irishman had been born in Quebec at Fort Coulonge and was a veteran dog-musher. He was more at ease with a bullwhip out on the trail than cooped up like a rat in a push-up shoving a pen in his office at Fort Smith. In the middle twenties, after World War I, he elbowed his way to the northern fringe of civilization at Fort Chipewyan on Lake Athabaska. Handy with tools and people, he worked on river and lake boats in summer and signed a contract to cut firewood for the mission until Christmas. From January to April he joined the Ryan brothers' dog-team postal service from McMurray to Smith, some two hundred and seventy miles. Here he learned to live off the land, to camp, and especially how to mush dogs.

Regardless of his wanderings, he always kept a duffel bag at Chipewyan, and soon the whole town knew why. Mike had met a girl to his liking at the mission school, Miss Rosalie Mercredi, whom he courted whenever he came to Chipewyan, and in the fall of 1927 they were married.

That year the last of the buffalo from the National Park in Wainwright, Alberta, were being shipped north and the Irishman found a door open to the life he loved on the open range. He joined the flotilla of buffalo-laden barges and left his new bride of a few weeks in a small log cabin near her people. From bull cook to dog driver over a very difficult trail, Mike finally became a full-fledged ranger. Naturally he manufactured reasons to get home every few months, and with the years ten little Dempseys brought happiness into Mike's busy life.

For more than ten years Mike spent himself devising ways and means to protect and better the park conditions with telephone and radio communications, cabins and new trails. In 1940 he and his family moved to Fort Smith and Mike was appointed chief ranger of the Smith Wood Buffalo Park. He examined the park area, made a study of the animals, and learned their winter and summer feeding grounds. No one was better qualified to hunt buffalo than this man who had worked so diligently to preserve them.

While we stopped for a rest and tea on our way to the farm that November day in 1941, Mike made me realize that even though we were allowed now to kill a few buffalo he was still held responsible for the preservation of this last big herd.

"The taxpayers of Canada spent over four million dollars to keep these animals from becoming extinct," he said. "We will have to select our animals with care and be sure only the older bulls are in our sights when we shoot."

While we finished our tea and the dogs rested, he told me the story that made this hunt possible. "From 1925 to 1928, 6673 prairie buffalo were transported from Wainwright, Alberta, to this new 17,300-square-mile range west of Fort Smith. They came 400 miles by rail and 257 down the Slave River to Buffalo Landing, 17 miles south of Fitzgerald, where we turned them loose."

Mike talked, but his eyes roved along a young growth of spruce. "Keep your .22 rifle handy. We may see a few rabbits."

He told me that when Columbus discovered America scientists estimated that 60,000,000 buffalo existed in North America, the greatest number of sizable four-footed creatures on earth! Then so ruthlessly were they slaughtered that by 1889 not a single wild buffalo existed in the United States. There were only 256 alive, all privately owned. After a careful survey of the animals was made in North America a special subspecies was found to exist in Canada's sub-Arctic Slave River country. Known as the wood buffalo, this animal was larger, tougher, and darker in color and had a heavier coat of fur and different horns, which curved in toward the forehead. When the question of a buffalo park came up, the Canadian Government paid special attention to the Slave River country, the only place in the world that still possessed some two thousand wild buffalo.

"We made a fence of rails from the river, some four hundred yards into a clear prairie, so the buffalo would not cross the river to the east but would go west to the vast grazing lands," Mike related.

"Since we moved the animals here in '25, they have been on the increase," the old ranger concluded, putting the grub box on the sled. "Our last count was well over fifteen thousand head, and weeding out a few will be good for the herd."

Soon after lunch we left the high pine country and followed a serpentine trail over low poplar and willow flats. The sky was gray, and a very light shower of snow salted the willows and made Muscles' dark fur turn gray. Mike spoke little to his team, but he did crack the snake once in a while, and Cockles would give a leap and put life into the rest of the dogs.

Mike Dempsey had a 306 Springfield rifle for distance shooting and I had my Marlin .30-.30 carbine with a long octagonal barrel for close work. The old buffalo hunter often remarked on the trip that I would have to help him with the actual shooting.

"My eyes are a little foggy from those long snowshoe treks on the Ryan mail route in March and April. When the new sun hits that snow, it's blinding. After all these years it has weakened my eyes. Now they want to close after an hour or so out in the snow," he added, rubbing his poached eyes with the back of a gnarled hand.

I was buoyant with expectancy that November afternoon, and I believe Mike noticed it. All he talked about was hunting. As the sled creaked over the trail my thoughts went back to Father Mansoz. He had often talked about the mission farm and described it as a haven for game. "That's the place for ducks and moose in the fall. That's the real spot for rabbits, prairie chicken, and sharp-tail grouse," he used to say, looking over his glasses toward the woods. He told me I would have the time of my life on this trip, not only enjoying the excitement of the hunt, but also doing some real missionary work. "Some of the Salt River Settlement Indians will come to Mass when they hear a priest is at the mission farm. They are good people even though they may not be able to come to Mass daily. Be sure you see my Indians on Sundays. I baptized most of them," he had said with a nostalgic glint in his eye. Father Mansoz loved hunting, and I know he must have been thinking of other years when the little mission depended on his gun and his strong young back to carry the meat home. My own liking for hunting went back to the time I was nine, when I caught a raccoon on my way home from school. My father sold the pelt and bought me my first gun, a .22 rifle.

"Well, here is the river," Mike said matter-of-factly, and pulled the .22 from its sheath. I looked around and saw only poplar bush.

"The river is just a few hundred yards ahead," he explained. "I stopped here so you could walk ahead a little and surprise any rabbits or grouse that usually hang out along this riverbank. In a mile or so you'll come to the old mission farmhouse. Just follow the trail along the river. You can't miss it. I'll rest the dogs a little and have a pipe."

Those were welcome orders for my cramped legs, and it felt good to walk. I thought of Mike as I took off down the trail. He was almost sixty years old and still full of fire, with enough get-up-and-go to head a buffalo hunt. Then I recalled that he had run behind the sled for over an hour! Could I follow this fellow hunting? Mike weighed about one hundred sixty pounds, and I knew now Father Mansoz was right when he said, "That Irishman can lick his weight in wildcats."

A flutter of wings scared me out of my wits. It was a grouse. I followed as it flew and lit on the low branches of a short jack-pine. *Slowly, very slowly, shoot the bottom one first,* I could hear Father Mansoz' voice over the miles, and remembered his coaching. I aimed carefully and shot! The lower one came down in a flurry of snow and flashing wings. Down on one knee, I took aim and bagged number two! Mike would smile when he saw these. He was so anxious for fresh meat.

Some fifteen minutes of walking brought me to a clearing, and there was the farmhouse. Wind and prairie sand had blasted and bleached the pitted logs, and the rains of thirty Aprils and Septembers had washed out the clay chinking between the logs. But it was a large two-story house. I judged it to be at least thirty feet wide and twenty-five feet long. A door and four windows faced me on the first floor and two windows looked out from the second. Two square sheet-metal Yukon chimney stacks poked their rusty tops from the steep-pitched tin roof. Half a dozen freshly cut dry spindly spruce trees lay against the house, and an old dog collar with half a trace still attached hung on a spike by the door. Vince had shoveled the snow away from the door but apparently had not walked very far to throw out his rabbit bones and coffee grounds!

I stood my .22 against the house and went inside. It had that musty, mouse-dropping odor of abandoned houses. The bare board walls were smoke-blackened, and large four-by-eight hand-hewn joists overhead anchored a network of dusty cobwebs. In the middle of the room stood a cast-iron box stove, one leg of which had been replaced by a huge stone. Heat cracks furrowed the wrinkled cheeks of its fire box, and one stove lid was now a rusty pie tin! I examined the rusty stovepipe up to the ceiling, and it looked safe. A stairway in the right corner of the room led upstairs, and there I discovered a room the length of the house. The floor was bare and still had a new-lumber look, with a pile of straw in one corner someone had used for a bed. I examined the rest of the smokestack, stuffed some straw in an old mouse-nesty grain sack, and plugged a broken window.

This was the house built by Brother Yves Le Gall in 1911, and from what remained I could see he had built it to last. Most of the logs were full length, pegged and dovetailed at the corners.

While I lit the fire and prepared our supper I recalled Father Mansoz' account of the beginnings of the farm and of the great work of Father Ed Gouy, who in 1911 had built a cabin and a barn on the high bank of Salt River, some twenty miles from Fort Smith. The summer was dry, so a good trail was cut through from Smith, a stack of hay cut for the six head of cattle and four horses, and the famous farm of St. Bruno came into being.

Brother Le Gall, now in his seventies and doing odd jobs around the mission hospital, broke ground on the big prairies with the hired help of several Indians. Fathers Gourdon and Gouy took turns driving the team and encouraged Brother and his men as they slashed down the huge spruce trees along the riverbank to build the barns and sheds. To kill off the tormenting mosquitoes, Brother tapped the soggy muskegs with drainage ditches into the Salt River and built log corrals for his cattle and winter feed stacks.

By the early thirties Brother Le Gall became the most northern rancher in Alberta, his grazing lands stretching into Northwest Territory. Even though the farm produced wheat, potatoes, and good hay after several years of strenuous tillage, transportation to the farm over the muskegs from Smith was always a problem. Brother had to wait for the blistering below-zero days of winter to freeze the muskegs before he could travel. Then in the middle and late thirties the growing buffalo herds hunted green pastures in the northern section of their range. They rode roughshod over the farm, crashed through corrals, devouring the precious winter feed for the stock, and even killed some of the cattle in their stampede for greener pastures.

This last invasion discouraged farming, and Father Mansoz decided with the Brothers and the Bishop to abandon the idea of ranching as a meat supply for the northern missions. With the Indian boys they rounded up the cattle, drove the one hundred head to Fort Smith a dozen at a time, and slaughtered them for the table. All that remained now of Brother's sweat and prayers was this old house. During the summer of 1940 a forest fire broomed the country and made ashes of the log barns, corrals, tools, and sheds. Fortunately the old house stood apart from the rest on the open prairie, and the long hot arms of the fire could not reach it.

The noise of barking dogs and a loud "Cha, cha!" heralded Mike's arrival. Standing just outside the door, I could see him hunched over and fighting the rolling of the sled as it careened and bounced toward me in the early darkness.

"Any luck?" he called, pulling the team to a stop near several posts that looked like relics of a garden fence.

I held up the two grouse that lay in the snow near the butt of the gun, and helped him unhitch his team. We staked out the dogs, each to a post, a good distance apart to keep them from fighting. It is not uncommon to see three-year-old dogs with ears or a tail missing. They are born scrappers.

"I usually keep my lead dog near the front door," Mike called to me, pulling Cockles toward the house by the scruff of his neck. "He makes a very good watchdog and warns me by pawing on the door if any game or wolves are near."

Inside the house I lighted our kerosene lantern and fired up the old stove. With a short-haired broom I found upstairs I began to uncover dried rabbit skins, ptarmigan bones and feathers, dead mice, dried duck wings, and moose hair. No doubt a few hunters had camped here in September. Mike cut up some firewood, and while the dog feed cooked on an outside fire he carried in our supplies and filled all our pots with clean snow for our water supply. When I carried out my box of sweepings, Mike was skinning the spruce hens and Muscles was having his hors d'oeuvres of the entrails and heads.

By six-thirty that evening, our outside chores attended to and the pot of spruce hens and rice cooking on our rosy-cheeked stove, we began an exploration of the house—as Mike put it, "just to make certain there are no ground squirrels or a black bear in one of those spare rooms."

Next to the stairway, a door opened into a large kitchen, about thirty by twenty feet, with handmade cupboards and a short sturdy table—a kind of meat chopping block—all knit together with wooden pegs. At the far end was a heavy box-ovened ranch stove, and at the opposite end another door led under the stairway to a good-sized dining room with a long oilcloth-covered table. Three other doors led to bedrooms to the left of the main room, and the fourth door opened into the old chapel. After sweeping out the place, I set up my portable altar at one end of the room and stretched out my sleeping bag on the floor. Mike took the room facing the front of the house to keep an eye on the dogs.

Our cooking pot steamed and sent an appetizing aroma throughout the house, giving it that warm feeling of home. Mike brewed the tea and I washed off the small square table near the window. It looked more like a butcher's block, with dried blood, rabbit hair, wax from candles, and even an odd bean lodged in its wide cracks! Now I knew why Mike had insisted on a good supply of newspapers when I was packing the supplies. It would make an excellent tablecloth to cover what I missed in those cracks.

With the diligence of a bachelor cook the old ranger gently ladled the spruce-hen stew on our enamel plates and, along with the bread and jam we had brought along from Smith, we sat to a tasty supper. The house was getting comfortably warm now, so we shed our parkas and used a lot of conversation to digest our meal. With the heat and smell of food in the old house, some mice began to scurry around the floor and along the beams overhead. I think Mike noticed that they disturbed me.

"On one of my first buffalo hunts with Brother Sareault we had a lot of mice," he said. "Our camp was on a high bank of the Peace River, and those little mice got into everything. One morning Brother noticed something in the syrup can and on closer inspection saw a very dead mouse." As he recounted the incident, Mike picked his grouse bone clean and chewed away. "In those days we had very meager supplies and Brother was careful not to waste anything. He scooped up the mouse, threw it out in the snow, and set the can back on the table. After breakfast that morning I guess the poor Brother thought he had done me an injustice and recounted what had happened. I told him that since he had eaten some of the syrup with the rest of us I would forgive him." Mike chuckled.

After dishwashing, I added more jackpine to the fire and said my Divine Office and prayers for the day while Mike lit his pipe and inspected the hunting gear.

It was November, the poor souls' month. Sitting there in the lantern light with the warm stove crackling behind me, I was disturbed by thoughts that perhaps the souls of Fathers Gourdon and Gouy were in purgatory. They must have sat at this very table years ago saying these very same prayers! I said my Office for them that evening. "Brother Le Gall used to spend at least an hour in chapel with God when his long day was over," Father Mansoz had told me.

When I closed my breviary, Mike was anxious to break the silence. "Better give me a hand lifting those grub boxes on that old kitchen table," he began. "Brother Joe doesn't like the taste of mice droppings in his rice." He winked. "I hope Brother and Vince arrive early tomorrow afternoon so we can get this camp ready for real hunting on Wednesday. There's a pile of wood to cut and ice to haul from that pond over in the bush for our water supply."

While I took off my moccasins and hung them on the drying bar above the stove, Mike gave me a few tips on buffalo hunting and especially on the importance of tying the dogs when an animal is spotted—a lesson he learned on a hunting trip with Brother Sareault near La Bute, north of Chipewyan. They had spotted two bulls on a prairie, and even though it was late in the day they decided to shoot them. In the excitement, Mike related, he forgot to tie his team, and after the first shot they took off after the buffalo. His sled turned over and scattered grub box, knives, spoons, ammunition, and everything else all over the prairie.

"We shot the buffalo, then began hunting for our knives and supplies in every buffalo track. With darkness coming on in thirty below, it taught me quite a lesson," Mike said, scratching the tar and ash of a day's smoking from his pipe.

That busy day in the cold had made my head heavy, and we sacked in about nine o'clock. Whether or not the mice ran over me that night, I do not remember. Sleep came too quickly.

After Mass next morning, which Mike served, we enjoyed an oatmeal breakfast in lantern light and put on our footgear for the outdoors. Mike planned on a five-hour walk "just to give me a look-around."

"Buffalo may be grazing in some of the small prairies nearby," he began, eying his plug of chewing tobacco for the first chew of the day. "We need camp meat, and a fellow could run into a jumping deer, a caribou, or even a moose!" The snow was over three feet deep and loose around there, so we left the house on snowshoes at eight-thirty that morning, taking Cockles with us "just for luck." "He has a nose for game and he heels well," Mike said.

With his old wood insulated 306 Springfield riding the crook of his arm, Mike stomped off, blowing steam in the crackling morning air. It was just fifteen below zero. His clothes smelled of butchering and pine-fire cooking, and gravy drippings added a glitter to his Davy Crockett fringed parka that hung some eight inches above his knees. Cockles followed, sending out little puffs of white, like a dinky engine pushing a big freight car.

We followed an old wagon road that cut through patches of poplar and spruce and over small prairies. Mike stopped to point out different landmarks, and the short stops gave me a breather my first day on snowshoes. About one-thirty that afternoon Cockles became alive and began sniffing the ground toward the woods on our right. When I reached Mike, he spat a stream of golden juice on the white snow.

"Some old buffalo tracks here, probably a week old," he said. I saw the tracks almost drifted full of snow. Drifts trailed off the small chunks of snow shoveled up by the huge hoofs marking the trail into the nearby bush.

"Those animals could be ten or more miles away or they could be bedded down in that timber. Here, Cockles," Mike called. "We'll circle back to the camp toward Salt River and pick a good smooth place for crossing with the meat. Sometimes strong winds during freeze-up cause rough ice," Mike added, cutting off a new chew of tobacco. I learned that he never lit his pipe on a hunt because buffalo can smell smoke from a great distance.

My legs began to feel numb from pumping those snowshoes, and I kept looking to see if the moose-leather thongs were cutting through my caribou mukluks. It felt as if they were and I could visualize blisters. But I could not whimper with a veteran like Dempsey breaking trail. Mike was only five feet eight and no more than one hundred and sixty-five pounds, but he was limber and cat-muscled. His hands were huge, grizzled, and work-scarred. His nose was big and pudgy from freezing and being rubbed. His face always needed a shave—except on Sunday morning when he attended Mass in town. Then it was usually decorated with a few small corners of paper to plug razor cuts. But these accidental wrappings covered a wonderful personality that expressed itself in his sparkling eyes, his ready smile, and always a good word. In the ten years I knew him I never saw him try to climb the ladder of society over the backs of his fellow men, regardless of some of the snubs and saddle-burred remarks he received because his wife was a native of Fort Chipewyan. And he never visited in the fort without Rosalie at his side.

About four o'clock we came to Salt River, and the old buffalo tracks disappeared on the smooth ice. "These tracks are over a week old." Mike nudged the frozen snow with his toe. "See how drifts have formed with the directions of the wind?"

A light snow was falling, and it was getting colder and dark when the old house came into focus. I was glad—my legs were very tired. Cockles began to whine and trotted ahead of us, anxious for his supper. We could see smoke coming from the chimney, and there were dogs around the house, evidence that Vince and Brother had arrived.

Brother Joe called out to us, and as I opened the door I smelled the delicious odors of rabbit stew with fresh onions. Mike fed the dogs with mash Vince had cooked, and we shed our trail gear and hung it up to dry. By six o'clock we sat down to a tasty supper and talked of what we might expect within the next few days. Later we knelt and said the Rosary, thanking God for His blessings and asking for His protection on the hunt.

Brother Joe shared my chapel bedroom, and we retired to pray our Office for the day, after which we joined Mike and Vince around the stove. The stories of the hunt ran along in high gear that evening and, just as a cook seasons a roast before putting it into the oven, Mike tucked us all into our sleeping bags well spiced for hunting dreams.

Several times during the night I was awakened by mice scampering over my face, but they did not seem to bother Brother Joe. He breathed deeply in his corner under Father Mansoz' rabbit-skin blanket, sleeping the sleep of the just. I thought of this man and the events that had led him to the Oblate Brothers. Twenty-five years ago his wife had died giving birth to their first child.

74

"Whatever made you decide to become a religious Brother?" I recalled asking him one evening while we were skinning beaver at Little Buffalo Falls.

"Well, Father Bill," he began, "I loved my wife so much and I wanted to preserve that love in my heart. If I married again I was afraid of making comparisons and perhaps making myself and someone else very unhappy. I consulted my pastor and spent many hours alone with God before a decision was definite to devote my life helping others as a Brother."

He was a man of high caliber, with such a sincere deep faith and a realistic love of God that they always influenced the people around him. Through his parish priest he learned that the Oblate Brothers are religious men bound by the same vows of poverty, chastity, and obedience as the missionary priests. He learned that they are the men who dig the potatoes and know the ring of an ax in the north woods, men who can pilot a river boat and diagnose the belly-ache of a diesel engine. He learned that they are the power behind the preaching missionaries. He learned of the Brother carpenters, electricians, plumbers, but most of all he liked the idea that these men were united in one big family. He reasoned these must be happy men, and he was not disappointed.

A sure sign that Brother Joe measured up to all the high standards of an Oblate Brother was the great respect the Indians had for him. They know that when he reprimands them they deserve it, and they regard his word as law. Mike was always trying to change Brother's serious outlook on life with his Irish humor—and Vince agreed with everything Brother Joe said and took sides with him good-naturedly against the Irishman. With men such as these I spent six weeks I can never forget. This was a real hunt, I realized, not so much for sport, but the daily-bread kind, for meat. With visions and dreams of howling wolves and charging buffalo, I drifted off to sleep.

A racket at the stove awakened me, and I noticed Brother was already up, kneeling beside his sleeping bag, saying his morning prayers. In about a half hour I was ready to say Mass, and Mike asked if I would say this Mass for his family. Rosalie had sent a note with Brother that his daughter Margaret was sick.

After Mass we had breakfast. Porridge, a good helping of beans, and a slice of bread, washed down with coffee, refueled us for the twenty-five-below-zero weather. We packed a small knapsack with tea, frozen rolls, salt, and our skinning knives, plus a box of

75

ammunition. Mike and I were to leave early, a good hour and a half before daylight, and strike out for the Big Prairie near the foot of the Buffalo Mountains, where the salt flats lay.

"Very likely we will see buffalo around that area," Mike pointed out to Brother Joe on a small map. "You and Vince leave camp one hour after daylight with both dog teams and follow our tracks. When you reach the edge of the woods, tie the teams there. That should be around eleven o'clock, just about the time to listen for some shooting. Make a fire and have your lunch. If you don't hear us shoot by twelve-thirty, keep coming with the dogs, but when you get to open country have a good look around before you break out of the bush into a clearing. Buffalo may be out there, and we don't want to scare them. If you should see buffalo or moose," he went on, pulling on his mukluks, "don't kill more than two! We should hear your shots and we will back-track."

This was sound advice, because we could not skin and dress more than two buffalo and return to base camp by seven in the evening. With our outdoor gear on, including field glasses, we made a final check for matches and were off in the starlit, breath-crackling, cold morning. The dogs came alive when we passed, and Cockles pawed the snow, eager to come along. Mike had not intended taking him, but Cockles had other ideas.

"He may be a great help to us and save a lot of walking," Mike said, walking over to free his leader.

This was the big day, and I was more excited than I cared to show. Years before coming North I had read about buffalo hunts, and now I was part of one. Our snowshoes squeaked on the drift-packed snow, and my nose was prickly with cold from about a five-mile-an-hour southwest wind. After yesterday's short hike, my leg muscles felt about as flexible as the limbs of the frozen trees, but with Mike and Cockles and the unexpected around every clump of swamp willows only a broken leg would have grounded me in camp.

Across Salt River and over three small prairies we trudged before gray dawn crept up the eastern wall of the sky and began to snuff out the stars. Delicate snow crystals bouncing off my face felt like hot sparks from an emery wheel. We were cutting through a patch of alder when Cockles became excited. His tail wagged and he sniffed the air, looking out over the prairie ahead of Mike.

"Something alive out there," Mike said, rubbing and blowing

his hands to get circulation back into his shooting finger. "Have a look around with your field glasses, Father. Buffalo could be along the edge of the timber or out there on the prairie and almost camouflaged with matted snow on their hide. See those hills?" He pointed directly across the flat country toward the Buffalo Mountains. "There's an island of thick bush and yards of muskeg separating it from the main timber line of the mountain. Our buffalo could be behind that island, munching muskeg grass. Do you see any sign of tracks in the snow?" I looked but could not make out any signs of tracks or life.

It was almost two miles across that open prairie, and the wind had saber teeth. A few hundred yards from the bush Cockles really began to yelp. Mike had to stop several times and quiet him. My hands were stiff with cold when we reached the woods, and we stopped just in the timber, out of the wind, to rub the blood back into our numbed fingers.

"Better load your rifle now," Mike mumbled, looking over a pocket-weary piece of chewing tobacco. "I have a feeling we will see something over this ridge. Buffalo usually take a rest in the draw between this island and the hill beyond. You walk down about five hundred yards, then we will enter the timber together." He pointed to the west. "From the top of this hill we will be able to see the prairie muskeg and have a good shot at anything in the draw." I walked the five hundred yards, looked back, and Mike waved me into the woods.

It was a good twenty-minute climb to the top of the ridge. Then all at once there was muskeg in front of me. To the right I saw nothing. *Bang!* A shot echoed against the hills. I levered a shell in my rifle, turning toward Mike. One black hulk lay on the prairie —and three buffalo were coming toward me. Mike shot again, but all three kept coming. They were just between me and heavy timber when I squeezed a shot at the last one. I heard it hit. Snow dust rose from his packed hide. He faltered just a little but kept going. I aimed, pulled ahead of him ten inches, and shot again. Down he plunged, plowing into the snow headfirst as though someone had cut off his front feet. Cockles was racing down the prairie after the others. I reloaded my rifle and approached carefully.

"Look at his eyes," Mike had cautioned me. "If they are closed, get away fast and be ready for a charge from a mad bull! If they are open, your animal is dead." My buffalo was giving a few kicks with his powerful hind legs, and his nostrils spouted red blood on the snow. Coming close, I saw his eyes open, and he kicked his last. He was dead. I looked toward Mike and saw him working over his animal, no doubt cutting the jugular vein to bleed the buffalo, so I did likewise.

"If Brother and Vince heard our shots they should be along in a couple of hours and give us a hand," Mike commented, coming up behind me and eying my buffalo. "You bagged a good-size bull there, about like mine." Each animal was about sixteen hundred pounds, and they certainly were the dark hybrids, results of the interbreeding of the wood buffalo and the plains buffalo.

Skinning and dressing animals of this size out there on the prairie presented difficulties. I slashed a few dead trees with my trail ax and packed the wood out to the kill with Mike, and we soon had a fire going some ten feet from the dead buffalo. It was nearly two o'clock, and a cup of hot tea and some toasted bannock gave us new stamina for the job ahead of us. Mike put a final edge on our old hickory skinning knives and we started on the buffalo I shot, opening the skin from under the chin down to the tail. We skinned out the legs and began to peel back the heavy hide. There were at least two inches of ice and snow matted into the kinky fur on the back of the buffalo. Every ten minutes we had to melt the fat off our knives back at the fire and put a new edge on them.

"Try not to touch the hair with your knife," Mike cautioned. "In this cold weather it's like cutting into wire. Don't worry about leaving a little meat on the skin. The tannery will trim that off before making coats for the Mounted Police out of these robes."

After the top side was exposed, we took off the front shoulder and hindquarter, then Mike directed me to stand clear and he poked the point of his knife into the distended belly. A foul odor and steam came out. Carefully we rolled out the fat-lined intestines from a stomach that must have weighed at least 175 pounds. We had to cut hand holds into it to roll it out. While it was still warm, Mike cut the lining from the stomach. "It's fat and makes real good dog feed," he said.

Carefully Mike lifted out a second stomach about the size of a good water pail. "This is what we call the Eaton's catalogue. Hold your nose," he cautioned, and a slash of his knife laid the stomach open. When its odorous contents spilled out, I saw the sectional booklike structure. The center had a heavy skin wall, and each side had about twenty compartments of about an inch and a quarter in width, separated by a thin membrane.

"This makes a good snack for the dogs, but watch," he said, tossing a chunk to Cockles. The dog caught it in his mouth, then let it go quickly and started eating snow to wash out his mouth. The dog then sniffed the soggy mess, bit into a corner of the meat, and gave it a vigorous shake. "That's one piece of meat they clean before eating," Mike said, washing his knife.

After washing his hands in the snow near the fire, the old ranger tackled the head.

"That is one of the largest bulls I have run into." Mike chewed away and made an effort to lift the trophy by a horn. It weighed at least two hundred pounds. We cut through the one-and-a-half-foot-thick neck, severed the head from the rest of the carcass, and then I watched the Irishman cut out the big steaming tongue, which he said weighed at least six pounds.

"Now we will do the roll-over, Father. You take the front leg and I'll try this one," he directed, bending and digging out the snow for a hand hold on the big shank. A few grunts, and over it flopped, sending a good five gallons of jello blood over the white snow. It was then I noticed that Cockles had returned from his "lunch hour." He sat on his haunches by the fire with front feet erect, looking, smelling, and dripping saliva. Mike had trained him well. We had put a new edge on our knives and more wood on our fire when we heard the dog teams approaching. It was Brother Joe and Vince.

Brother Joe was cold and we all decided on a tea break. It felt good to stand with our backs to the fire, warming our hands and telling Brother and Vince how we shot the buffalo. Blood had splashed on us, and my mukluks were stiff. The heat felt good on the back of my legs. Vince, hungry for fresh meat, rolled back the bloody skin, looped out the rack of the hump ribs with his trail ax, brushed at them with his mitten, cleaning off some black buffalo hair, and pushed them in the snow before the fire.

The hump meat is considered to be the very best part of buffalo, like the tongue of caribou or the tail of the beaver. Brother Joe gathered a pail of fresh snow while I fished some doughnuts from our supply in the sled.

The aroma of roasting buffalo ribs and watching Vince munch on one as though it were an ear of corn gave us all an appetite. I ate the meat from three flat hump ribs, and it was succulent and tender. Hot tea and toasted doughnuts made a grand repast and gave us new strength and warmth.

"Guess I'll get going on the other buffalo, eh, Mike?" Vince jumped up, rubbing his hands and tramping on the pine boughs before the fire.

"Yes. Take Father's knife and be careful not to puncture the intestines. You know what a mess it makes of the meat. Better start a fire going near the other kill to give you some light," Mike directed. Vince was already hopping over the snow like a jack-rabbit. He had some special equipment, this Chipewyan Indian—six well-formed fingers on each hand and six toes on each foot.

We dressed and cached the meat of the first buffalo and folded the three-hundred-pound hide. Mike cautioned against piling the pieces of meat on top of each other, otherwise they would freeze in one chunk. With a little snow and some spruce boughs or willows over our cache, it would be safe from marauding wolves for at least three nights. The human scent and fresh blood would act like a shield until the meat could be dog-sledded to the base camp and lifted up onto a seven-foot stage behind the house.

Vince was just about the fastest man I have ever seen with a skinning knife. With the fire flashing on his knife as he worked on the second buffalo, it was like watching the whirring blades on the cylinder of a threshing machine. He really did a kind of elf's dance there in the shadows, slicing, pulling, and skinning away. In less than an hour, we had the second buffalo cached and I was bouncing over the trail toward camp behind Vince's team. Our first day was a success and the pattern of the hunt was set. We came home with buffalo liver, hump ribs, and bloody mukluks—the signs of good hunting.

Next day we were lucky again, as we were throughout the week. Each day we were fortunate enough to locate two buffalo early enough in the day to skin and dress them before dark. So the hunt went on week after week, until we reached our quota of sixty buffalo. The meat was sledded back to Fort Smith by our good friend, Alois Gaillard, a layman from Switzerland, who has been giving his services to us at Smith and presently at Fort Chipewyan these past thirty years or more.

"Welcome back to civilization," Father Mansoz called as our dog team pulled in at Fort Smith after six and a half weeks of hunting. "From that thirty-ton pile of frozen meat in the ware-house, I know you had a good hunt."

Before I realized we were an attraction, a dozen people had gathered around to hear about the hunt. Several little Dempseys came a running and clung to Mike's parka. He patted their parka-hooded heads with affection and continued to unload my gear from his sled.

"This is a little sack of meat I took for the family," he said, hefting a fifteen-pound flour bag. "The family is always eager for a little fresh meat when I come home." Father Mansoz nodded, smiling approval of Mike's thoughtfulness for his loved ones.

That evening before sleep came I thought of Mike's little bag of meat and also of the mountain of buffalo carcasses in the warehouses. In the mission schools and hospitals down the Mackenzie River, many people were waiting anxiously for their little bag of meat. If we had an aircraft, how simple it would be to fly the frozen meat to their tables. Now it was a question of packing the meat in ice until river transport carried it by refrigerator barge to its destination. There would be the rush of canvas-covered trucks very early in the morning, while it was still a little cool, to get the frozen meat safely aboard. But if one of the hundred-and-fifty-pound chunks of meat thawed out before the cook needed it, a mold would form and many pounds would be lost. More than ever, I began to realize the importance of transportation in the missions and how an aircraft could revolutionize life in this country.

The outside world buzzed with the news that Hitler was turning a blitzkrieg on Europe with undreamed-of airpower. Whole countries were being bombed and destroyed. Perhaps from this boiling pot of war great changes would come to our world of the North. Buffalo meat would be a much better air cargo than bombs!

Chapter Six

O

N the morning of June 20, 1942, Fort Smith awoke in its usual drowsy manner, rubbed its eyes, blinked, and looked startled at an invasion. Two thousand men had moved into town overnight!

Chipewyan Indians stood along the dusty streets as huge D-8 caterpillar tractors thundered past, towing boats, barges, and heavy oil rigs on mammoth trailers. The patients and even the Sisters craned their necks from hospital windows to see the convoys of dark green trucks pass in a flurry of smoke and sand, hauling thousands of tons of pipe and oil and men. Children ran to the school windows—the teacher's head above their little ones—straining to see "all those tanned men" marching in squads to the river to unload pipe. One thousand two hundred and eighteen colored troops from the 388th Regiment had set up their tents that night on the bend of the street known as "Ax-handle Alley," deep in the poplar wood south of town. The 45th Station Hospital Unit under Major Lowell Privette, M.D., established themselves in Ryan's wheat patch some two hundred strong. And by noon news had filtered through the dust that the 89th Engineer Battalion was cutting the bush and building an airport three miles north of town. At one o'clock the Hudson's Bay Company closed its doors with a sign announcing, "All Sold Out." So did the other two private traders in town.

What was happening to the town? "Those Americans have come into the North and that is the end of our peaceful days," was the comment of our Archbishop. And by the looks of things today, he was right.

When the Japanese set off the burglar alarm at Dutch Harbor and we learned that someone was at the back door, the tranquil North was really jolted awake!

"I give to you assurance that the people of the United States will not stand idly by if domination of Canadian soil is threatened," President Roosevelt had said in Kingston, Ontario, in 1938. And as a result of the friendly co-operation of nations to preserve peace, the Permanent Joint Board of Defense, of equivalent United States and Canadian sections, was created in 1940. This Board recommended several projects for the North that sprang into being in 1942 and made the sub-Arctic a place of strategic importance.

Four great projects had been proposed by the Joint Defense Board in 1942, and these were executed by the civilian and armed forces of both countries. The Alaska Highway was built over the mountains from Dawson Creek to Fairbanks. A telegraph line, the Caltel, was constructed along the highway, providing not only an overland road but telecommunications. Third, airfields were built throughout the entire northwest of Canada, establishing what was known as the Northwest Staging Route for delivering planes to Alaska and Russia. And, last of all, there was the Canol pipeline and road from the oil at Norman Wells on the Mackenzie River to Whitehorse in the Yukon. The first three defense projects are still in use and have aided in the modern development of the Northwest. The pipeline has since been dismantled, but its secondary effect—the very fact that it broke into the isolation of the North with the modern air, river, and highway transportation—has changed not only the people but the face and pace of the entire country.

Because the tide of war turned toward Alaska in 1942, oil and its products had to be quickly supplied in vast quantities. Ten years before the Pearl Harbor disaster the Standard Oil Company of New Jersey, through Imperial Oil, Ltd., of Canada, acquired holdings of oil deposits along the Mackenzie River, forty miles north of Fort Norman, where oil was first located in 1920. This was a matter of a few hundred miles and some mountains. Government officials and petroleum experts turned their attention to the Mackenzie at a special meeting in Washington, D.C., on April 29, 1942, and in less than six weeks Task Force 2600 was born. Recommendations were submitted on that twenty-ninth day of April to enlarge the Norman Wells oil field and lay a pipeline to Whitehorse, where an oil refinery would be constructed with a capacity of three thousand barrels a day.

Task Force 2600 began to move North. Airports were cut out of the forests at McMurray, Alberta, three hundred miles north of the modern city of Edmonton, and along the river route at Embarras Portage, Fort Smith, Fort Resolution, Hay River, Fort Providence, Mills Lake, Fort Simpson, Fort Wrigley, and two airports at Norman Wells, one on either side of the Mackenzie River. Men and materials, medicine and the dying were flown from place to place. The work was expedited between these settlements by air support before the slow river traffic was organized.

Meanwhile north of the settlement of Peace River as a crow flies to Fairbanks, Alaska, another corps of engineers and Army personnel began the project of a highway over the Rocky Mountains to Alaska. This was a long and serious project that took its toll of lives and equipment. Earth-moving machines of great size were developed and used for the first time, and literally mountains of dirt and gravel were moved to effect a passable road over the mountains. This established the back road of defense—the famous Alcan Highway across northwest Canada into Alaska.

Many new stretches of road were built in and about the settlements along the Mackenzie to facilitate local transportation, but only winter trails made connections with the Alcan Highway. At Fort Smith the portage roads were rebuilt and an extension was pushed a hundred miles north. This road was cut toward Hay River into the Wood Buffalo Park.

The first fourteen-unit convoy of B Company of the 89th Engineers left Fort Smith on February 10, 1943, with pontoon-bridge equipment. I was sent along on this trip as chaplain by Father Mansoz, and the trucks proved to be rougher than dog-sled traveling. The leader of the convoy was a cigar-smoking sergeant who kept an especially heavy foot on the gas pedal. He bounced those Mack tractor trailers over frozen ruts and rocks and even made them play leapfrog over fallen trees. There was not time for scenery. I braced myself, wishing all the while the designers of these trucks had supplied safety belts. After sixty hours the convoy arrived at Providence on the Mackenzie River, 290 miles north of Smith.

We were welcomed by Father Michael when we stopped at the Sacred Heart School. The children flattened their noses against the windows to see the trucks, and one of the Sisters came out of the school with her children to get a closer look at her countrymen. She was Sister Mary Mack, a Grey Nun from Boston, who was delighted to see that an American missionary had made the first automobile trip from Smith to Providence.

"Did you happen to bring any candy along for the children,

Father?" she asked confidentially. When I told her I had over a hundred pounds of hard candy from the G.I.'s she was jubilant.

"Bring all those soldiers in our refectory for a warm lunch." She motioned me toward the school. "They must be hungry and cold after that long ride."

No second invitation was needed for the boys of the 89th. Some of the more fortunate ones had tasted the hospitality and home cooking of the Grey Nuns at Fort Smith and at Resolution. They left their engines running to keep the motors from freezing and came on the double.

"I hope you won't mind this invasion, Father." Lieutenant Barker ran up to me, puffing, leaving his Jeep in the middle of the road. "They all just insisted on coming along. I know it's just to get a look at the children and give them a little candy. Some are very lonesome for their own little ones."

Lieutenant Barker was in charge of A Company, which had arrived in Providence in September. With fifty-four men, his task was to build a fifty-seven-hundred-foot airstrip and a four-mile road north to the settlement. The airport clearing had been begun by civilians, but they left when A Company moved in. Log cabins had been built in a hurry before winter set in, leaving them in rather primitive quarters.

I left the G.I.'s in the care of the Grey Nuns and visited with Father Michael and Brothers Gosselin and Marchessault at the old log-cabin mission. Our trip to Providence by truck over a road was a great event to these men, isolated as they were at the headwaters of the Mackenzie, some forty miles north of Great Slave Lake. When I explained that we had traveled along the western shore of the lake all the way to the rapids five miles south of town, they were surprised.

"You did not cross on Big Island?" Father Michael asked. "That is fine high land with few muskegs. Father Grollier started this mission there in 1858."

The mouth of the Mackenzie is shallow and rocky, with Big Island in mid-river. Father thought this would be easier to cross than the steep-banked Kakisa River, which cuts into the Mackenzie along the bank we followed. He did not figure on bulldozers and the fact that we carried bridge equipment.

That evening after the boys returned to camp I had a wonderful visit at the mission and a tour of the school. I learned that Bishop Grandin founded the mission at Providence in 1862 and that the first convent and orphanage were erected in the next two years. The Grey Nuns arrived in August of 1867, and the present boarding school to accommodate a hundred children was completed in the mid-thirties. The mission house of logs was built in the 1890s, and that night I could feel drafts of cold north winds. Over the years mice had found a haven there too, but I was so tired from being belted around on the new road that I slept soundly under a heavy feather bed.

The following morning I had just finished my Mass when the trucks rumbled up, ready to return to Fort Smith. I invited the drivers in for a mission breakfast, after which the children gave us a cheery send-off. The day was clear and cold, thirty-five below zero, and we had trouble with frozen windshields. Once across the river in the bush country, the trucks began to warm up and speed up. I thought the loaded trucks had given me a rough ride, but now the driver and I bounced around in the cab like dice in a dealer's cup. By five that afternoon we were all grateful when the convoy reached Hay River.

"I feel like a tin can that fell into a cement mixer." Corporal Jim Powers stretched and rubbed his bruises. He was on the short side, but his arm muscles were always popping buttons on his shirt sleeves. When he laughed—and this seemed to be a built-in fixture with Jim—his eyes closed automatically.

Lieutenant Gilligan lent me a Jeep to go over to the old Indian settlement on the east bank of Hay River to spend a few hours with Father Dessy, and Jim came along as my driver.

"Since September 3, 1942, when Gilligan of A Company and fifteen men arrived to complete the airstrip, the town of Hay River has been turned upside down," Father told us. "When that first big-wheel plane landed here on November 15, every Indian in the vicinity of forty miles came to see it. Now they all want to work for the Army and quit trapping."

I consoled this slim, tall Belgian missionary with the news that other settlements along the river had also felt the impact of visitors and that he should work along with the officers in charge to keep his people in line.

Finally, without a major accident, we returned to Fort Smith, recorded our successful trip, and regular traffic convoys began to move over the new road.

Like Hay River, our whole North country received the shock of "southern invasion," but it had been softened by a hundred years of work by men and women of sacrifice and long-range vision—the missionaries. These devoted men and women braved a frontier unparalleled in history. Besides the common barriers of language and strange customs, they had to battle cold and famine and flies. Distance was a millstone around their necks, almost an iron curtain. More than half of their lives was spent in traveling.

They had to delve into a new language and master it in order to learn the thought processes of the people. With patience and determination, these men and women of God set up facilities for education and learning, appealed and received aid from a government that realized what a tremendous undertaking they had attempted. One, two generations passed before their efforts began to bear fruit. Those brave, generous souls gave the best they had—their very lives—to prepare the Indians and Eskimos for today.

When the Army and civil engineers took the last of their men from the North in 1944, a white cross remained at the head of the runway of the Fort Simpson airport. Pfc. J. H. Nylund of Headquarters and Service Company, under Major Laurion, lost his life when a frozen tree snapped and punctured his lung as he rode a bulldozer to cut the new airstrip. At Fort Smith, Privates Clarence Tucker and William E. Logan were burned to death in an explosion, and on August 15 Corporal Ira Brasington, Jr., was drowned in Waterways, Alberta. These were some of the men I knew who gave their lives to establish a chain of airports and set up an inland defense backing up our west coast against attack. New confidence fired the hearts of defense workers. They were assured that their homes were safe from intruders.

The North was now linked with the outside world. Mail service was established with regularity, and the people of Fort Smith began to blink their eyes and awaken to new sights and sounds. Fresh fruits and vegetables were now on sale at the local stores, and new faces appeared in town almost daily. We could see the great changes effected in our people by the war. History records that entire civilizations have had their faces not only scarred but so radically changed in a matter of a few months that it can almost be said that a new class of people has been born. The mixing of blood in social life and the intermingling of new ideas with people from foreign lands have an awakening effect, especially upon those souls who have been living a kind of monastic life of isolation like our northern peoples. When Alaska was purchased from Russia it aroused only critical remarks of "Uncle Sam buying an icebox." And when the United Kingdom turned over to Canada all her rights in the Canadian Arctic in 1880, even less concern was voiced. But during World War II, when the search for base metals and uranium hit its stride, our North country was literally invaded with prospectors as well as airport builders and petroleum probers. The Indians left their traps hanging on trees, packed their duffel bags and tents, and became the trail blazers and guides. Then came April of 1944.

"I'll have to make a few personnel changes this fall to keep those new gold hunters in line at Yellowknife," the Bishop said casually that morning at the breakfast table. However, I caught just a flash of that episcopal eye in my direction.

After breakfast, on the return to our house, the Bishop cleared up the whole situation. "I will need a companion this summer for my trip down the Mackenzie River. Do you think you could help pilot the boat?"

"It would be a pleasure, if you don't mind portaging over a few sand bars!"

"I thought of that," he began, hunting for a paper on his desk. "I plan to take a Brother along who knows the river and who will teach you how to read a map—and read the water too."

"This morning you mentioned Yellowknife, and I caught just a glance in my direction——"

"Oh, that will not be urgent until late August," the Bishop cut in. "You could pack just a light bag and we will take the plane to Edmonton tomorrow. I have some other work for you more urgent than Yellowknife."

On the flight to Edmonton I had my first good look at the country. How wonderful and how fast an aircraft could move over these lakes and rivers and hills. A boat on the river looked as though it was anchored, except for its wake. Yet with these thoughts I wondered what the Bishop had up his sleeve for me in Edmonton.

Brother Borghese met us at the door of the Oblate house. "You are leaving the North after only four years?" he began teasing me, winking at the Bishop. "Too cold for you up there, I suppose?"

"No, Brother," the Bishop said. "This fellow developed a few muscles riding the dog sled, and now I want him to learn how to use them in a special way. I know you used to work with a dentist years ago while you studied theology." His Excellency turned to me. "This will be a little surprise to you, but I wonder if you could take a kind of quick refresher course in dentistry and then come along with me this summer down the Mackenzie and repair the teeth of our missionaries. We have had no dentists down in our country since the war started."

"I was just a dentist's helper and did very little of the actual work. I'll need a very good teacher."

"Dr. Alfred Clermont will help you. We will go and see him this evening."

That evening—and every day for a month—I not only saw Dr. Clermont and tested his patience with a million questions but I even absorbed his free hours on weekends learning how to make dentures and drill out cavities. It was fully understood, of course, that I would attend to just the simple dental needs of the missionaries during this absence of dentists and that I would send all complicated cases outside. As a sendoff Dr. Clermont gave me his portable dental case with instruments I would require for extractions and fillings.

At McMurray we purchased a motor-driven scow from a Mr. Greenwood. Bishop Trocellier decorated the interior with a coat of white paint while I inspected the power plant. With a transfusion of gas, oil, and a full grub box, we chugged away down the Athabaska over the Smith Portage and down the Slave River to Fort Resolution. This was a highlight of the trip I had been waiting for, a meeting with my classmate, Father Charles Gilles. Since 1938 he had been stationed here at St. Joseph's Mission, and this was our first visit in six years. However, because the weather was fair and the lake calm, the Bishop decided to make his official visit on our return trip. So before we had time to trade mission experiences, our pilot, Brother Kerautret, blew the departure whistle and we were away down the fifteen hundred miles of the wide Mackenzie River to the Arctic Ocean.

There were moans of pain from my amateurish dentistry and ohs and ahs when new Obediences were handed out by the Bishop. After fifteen years as an isolated missionary in the Liard mountains among the Slave Indians, Father Le Cote raised his dark eyebrows and smiled with relief when the Bishop transferred him to the big mission at Simpson. At Wrigley, I had to extract all the teeth of Father Feuvrier. Archbishop Breynat, who had joined our crew at Resolution, offered Father a sip of cognac to kill the pain.

It was a summer of adventure and some consolation too. At Aklavik I ran into my first Eskimos when I attended the school children. They were always smiling and never flinched in pain. There on the rim of the Arctic Ocean I met Brother Herman Beauchemin, whose friendly face and spontaneous joviality melted the stoicism of the Eskimos. They loved this short, plump man of God and always invited him to visit their boats. They knew he was the master marine mechanic of Aklavik and liked his ideas and friendly advice. Later, I too leaned on Brother Herman for his many skills.

I had just a glance at the real Arctic, but enough to pull my attention to that land of the midnight sun when we finally turned south. The Bishop navigated and we washed our boat over a few sand-bar portages while I nursed the old Kermath engine. At Wrigley in late August we found Father Feuvrier in high spirits, his mouth healed—and enough brandy in his medicine bottle to salute the Bishop!

"This box must contain my new choppers," he said, smiling and handing me a package from Edmonton. He was right. Like most of the plates Dr. Clermont made for me, they fit with a little grinding of the bite.

"Now I can eat caribou and moose meat again." Father smiled, moving his lip and tongue over his new teeth. "You know, Bishop, I was getting a little tired of fish—after five months of it!"

It was mid-September when we arrived at Resolution. I spent many hours attending the dental needs of the new Indian children at St. Joseph's boarding school. Father Gilles arranged a potato-harvest bee, with the boys on one side of the patch and the girls on the other. In three days we not only picked up over five hundred bags of potatoes but he and I had another great reminiscence of college days.

Fall would slip rapidly by, so I began making plans for my new Obedience to Yellowknife. The Bishop told me there was plenty of repair work to be done on the old rectory and that a new St. Patrick's Church should be built.

"You're going to need lumber," I suggested.

"Naturally." He smiled. "How are you with a hammer and saw?"

I admitted I had done a bit of carpentry around home. In this brief moment I realized that this new appointment to Yellowknife was not so much a call upon my rather limited linguistic abilities as an English-speaking assistant but rather a summons to bend my back and flex my muscles.

"There is a spot on the Slave delta," the Bishop continued, "where there are some sawmills. A Mr. Allen McDonald runs one of those mills. You can see him and make some kind of a deal."

So at last I was a missionary on my way to Yellowknife, via a sawmill!

"You need lumber, eh, Father?" Mr. McDonald began after we met and I told him why I had come. "Well, you find me a good cat-skinner for about five weeks and I'll give you the forty thousand square feet of lumber you need and barge it for you to Yellowknife."

"You mean if I can dig up someone to handle your caterpillar you'll make us a present of this lumber?"

"That's right."

"Good. I'll guarantee to get you a man," I said.

"Where?"

"Don't worry. Just have faith, Allen. I'll get you a cat-skinner," I promised.

The mosquitoes and bulldog flies were very hungry that September of 1944. There were evenings when my neck was so bloody it looked as if someone had been trying to hack off my head with a dull Swede-saw!

Each morning at the lumber camp I said Mass in McDonald's cabin, and usually some of the Indians employed at the sawmill joined us as Allen served the Mass.

The first job was selecting the timber and blazing all the spruce of fifty or more feet with twelve-inch butts or over. Some of the white spruce on the delta run as tall as seventy feet. Often we found patches of rough-barked poplar, or balm of Gilead, growing straight to sixty feet with three-foot butts. This is used for flooring or decking. I did keep my eye open for a few twenty-inch butts which would give us some sixteen- to eighteen-inch-wide planks to make church pews. Four Indians followed us with Swede-saws, felling and branching the trees.

"When is that cat-skinner of yours coming, Father?" Allen asked me several times. "We could use him now," he said after the third day of cutting.

Next morning I had to tell him the truth. "I will drive the cat."

He just stood and shook his head. "Do you know how to handle one of those things? They can be dangerous in the bush."

When I assured him I had had a few hundred hours on a caterpillar he checked me out on several peculiarities of this particular machine.

It had been a few years since I jockeyed a caterpillar tractor, but in a half hour I was turned loose and began to swamp the cut logs through the muskegs and tangled brush to the mill. The country was mostly muskeg and required a lot of timber cribbing and adjusting to keep the mill operating efficiently. In two and a half weeks we cut our quota, and it was time to shove off across the Great Slave Lake for Yellowknife. October was upon us and the weather was changing rapidly, with heavy frost every night. A light fall of snow powdered the land on the last morning of our sawing.

We interlaced the lumber on the broad flat deck of the barge to prevent the rolling seas from sliding it off or shifting the cargo, and we strapped it with logging chains.

As Allen tied a bowline knot on the end of a rope to secure the tug alongside the barge, he said over and over again: "We had better let these waters quiet down a little, Father. I would not like to lose that barge of lumber. It represents too much sweat and hard work."

I said Mass aboard the boat at ten-thirty that evening, and an hour later the lake was calm and we began the trip under a rising yellow moon. I even had a stretch at the helm, for we were heading straight for Outpost Island. That island, across the wildest hundred miles of water on Great Slave Lake, had been used for a tungsten mining venture in the mid-thirties. Some buildings and docking facilities still remained, making a good port in case we ran into a storm. Besides, it lay just off starboard on our way to Yellowknife.

About two o'clock the next morning Allen took over the helm, telling me to go below and have a rest. I checked over the engine, pumped a few barrels of oil into the tanks, and went to my cabin. As I knelt to say a Rosary to the Queen of the Sea, the boat slowly began a peculiar pitch and roll. I finished my prayers and went on deck. Off to the west, great billowing cumulus clouds were boiling up and blacking out the stars. The air was heavy, yet a light breeze made a little chop on the water. I could smell rain.

"There's a storm brewing," Allen warned, looking to the west and then back at the barge of lumber. "Batten down the hatches and secure all the deck gear. Make sure all the porthole windows are locked."

A new life boat was lashed to the guard railing with half-inch manila rope, and our heavy three-inch hawser was well secured to the stern tow post. Inspecting below decks, I advised Mrs. McDonald that we were due for a blow. "You had better close those windows and if necessary tie the children in their bunks. We might roll and toss like a cork and they may be thrown around here and injure themselves."

The wind increased steadily and within a half hour twenty-five-foot waves were crashing against our little tug. We pitched and rolled, the alternating taut and slack of the hawser jerking us back and forth as the barge behind us was buffeted in the angry seas.

Allen hung onto the helm and I kept below decks, checking the power plant, a forty-horsepower medium-duty engine. All at once there was a tremendous boom as a heavy wave pounded the boat. I felt the swish of water on my back and turned to see water pouring in through two windows that had been smashed by the impact. As each wave rolled against us more water poured into the engine room. Now I began to move and to worry. We were in trouble. Grabbing the handle of a small wobbly bilge pump, I began pumping for all I was worth. It was a race against the rising tide on the floor of the engine room. The water rose halfway to my knees. I laugh now to think of my small efforts. I was like St. Augustine's little child at the seashore trying to empty the ocean into a small hole in the sand. This would not do. The water was gaining on me. I took a half-empty five-gallon oil pail, quickly cut the head with a pair of tin snips, tossed the oil overboard through a broken window, and began to bail out the oily bilge.

Fortunately we did not have to worry about the ignition system or wet spark plugs. We had a diesel engine that ignited its fuel with compression. The batteries for the diesel starting system were high on a wall shelf, and the engine-driven generator was still two feet above the water line. I bailed steadily for one hour until my hands were raw with blisters, but I gained on the storm.

To plug the windows I ripped my old hunting jacket in two pieces, stuffed it part way in the windows, and nailed a board over them.

When I thought it safe to leave the bailing I checked on Mrs.

McDonald and the children. They were all sick from the pitching and yawing of the boat, and the water was up to the mattress on their bunks. I told Mrs. McDonald there was no real danger now since I had boarded up the broken windows.

There was a small opening in the engine room on the lee side of the boat. I hooked this square panel open and poured out more bilge water with my bailing can, using a gallon syrup can to fill the big bucket. It was slippery work. Oily bilge made the floor as slick as ice and I barked my knees and elbows falling against the engine and on the floor. Deep within me I had the fear that at any moment this little boat could break in two. It was not a new boat. For a dozen years it had plied the Mackenzie River, serving our missions, before Allen had purchased it and replaced a few of the timbers and planks.

I climbed on deck and noticed the little time-yellowed framed picture of Bishop Guy nailed to the inside wall of the cabin. In the depth and silence of my soul I asked him to help us from his place up there—near the Big Fisherman, St. Peter, who knew all about these angry waters.

Once on deck, I hugged the cabin railing and saw Allen clutching the helm, sea water streaming from his face. What a night that man had spent in his lonely vigil at the wheel! I climbed over the wheel deck and shouted to him that all was safe below. He nodded and pointed to the distant islands. Suddenly the boat lurched so sharply that we were nearly pitched into the boiling sea. We hung on for our lives.

"Look at the barge!" Allen shouted above the wailing wind.

Our barge was tilted almost on end! Then we saw it happen— the steel binding chains burst and the wind caught some of the top boards and whipped them into the water. Stunned, we watched helplessly as our precious cargo slid into the lake. The barge righted herself and yawed back and forth a few times. Then as she dipped toward us down the crest of a wave we saw that all was not lost. There was still a four-foot pile of lumber on the barge. It was about then that I noticed our lifeboat was gone. Allen saw me pointing to a white speck bobbing up and down in the breakers. He just shook his head and looked ahead at the approaching islands.

It was impossible to change course to avoid the lashing of the waves. Taking them on our bow would send us westward into the open lake to Providence. If we went along with the wind on our stern there was the chance of being swept into the rocks and reefs of that archipelago dotting the eastern end of the lake. Our only chance was to remain on course, and I returned below decks and continued to bail water.

My hands were crusted with dry blood and open blisters, and every pail gained in weight. Slowly the boat stopped pitching and the motor slowed down. I looked out the window and was relieved to see that we were nearing an island. It was about five-thirty in the morning when the boat eased up to the weather-beaten docks at Outpost Island.

We tied three lines to the piling, and Allen helped his wife and children from the boat. Soon a fire was roaring on the rocks and the coffeepot put on to boil. I bound my hands with some bandages from the cabin, and Allen changed into dry clothing. What a relief to have our feet on solid, still ground again.

I wanted very much to say a Mass of thanksgiving that morning, but my hands were too swollen and sore. We said a thanksgiving Rosary sitting there by the fire and the children answered loud and clear above the wind. After thanking God, Mrs. McDonald went to work in the galley and Allen and I did a big clean-up of the boat. About ten o'clock we had a good meal and the children ate heartily, seasickness forgotten.

By noon the storm had quieted and we set out once again toward Yellowknife. Passing the islands, we scanned the water for lumber but failed to see even a two-by-four. Most of it was carried to the west shore of Rae Arm, Allen figured.

About three in the afternoon we sighted the black mine shaft of the Negus Mill and also the white shaft and buildings of the Consolidated Mining and Smelting. They lay to port along the hillside as we chugged down the quiet blue waters of the bay. Directly ahead of us the town proper nestled around a huge rock with a water tank on top.

"That's Yellowknife, Father," Allen said. "It always reminds me of a fat mother goose with her goslings clustered about her."

We rounded an island, and then I saw what Allen meant. New tents, new lumber shacks, and some new white houses were all packed around the base of the rock.

"That's your place with the small white cross on top." Mrs. McDonald pointed. She had the children on deck to see the view as soon as we entered the bay.

We headed straight for the shore in front of our house, and

before the boat was tied a tall, bearded priest was coming toward us at a fast clip.

"Hello, hello," he called, and leaped aboard. "I'm Father Gathy."

Immediately I noticed his huge, capable hands. He greeted Allen and Mrs. McDonald and began playing tricks with his long beard that made the children laugh.

"What happened to your hands?" he asked, taking my bags.

"I picked up a few blisters along the trail, Père. They will be ready for work in a few weeks," I assured him.

I was grateful to Allen, who gave Father a short rundown on our trip, because my thoughts at the moment were still scrambled. Battling that storm on the lake and trying to adjust to these new surroundings had given me a little mental indigestion.

"We have a big city here," he puffed, lighting his pipe nervously for the fifth time. "There are hotels, stores, a bank, a cinema, even a liquor store down the street! Come, I'll show you our mission house," he said, leading the way with long strides. Everyone we met was friendly and greeted us with a big "Hello, Father."

Opening the door of the mission, Father Gathy said, "This is a very small house, as you see. Like everyone else here, we too are just pioneers. I bought this place from a family that tried to strike it rich but, like so many others, left with empty pockets." It was just a one-story three-room frame building sitting on the rocks. "Every spring I crawl under it, jack it up, and add a few more logs of shoring to keep it out of the mud," Father explained, pointing to a door that would not close. "The winter frost heaves these houses so far out of shape that even some of the window glass gets broken."

We cleaned out one of the rooms that had been used as a storeroom, and I unpacked my bags and began to get acquainted with this new mining town. Even though it is two hundred miles north of Fort Smith, Yellowknife had more of the *outside* activity in its character.

The lure of the gold strike in 1935 started the boom that is still echoing down Yellowknife Bay. We were seven hundred air miles north of Edmonton, yet there was daily mail service (weather permitting) and a constant influx of fortune hunters. Mineralogists and prospectors who picked rocks in many parts of the world were drawn to this gold-in-blue-quartz mecca in the Rae Arm of Great Slave Lake. Their eyes sparkling like diamonds in aged settings, they came with hope for that "big strike." Everything they had went into a grubstake. Daily Father Gathy was approached for "fare money home" from those who "went for broke." He was able to help many of them because "those who sold their claims too soon" always left "eating money for the poor."

During the day, power saws whined and a dozen trucks and autos rumbled over the graveled roads. At night outboard motors droned on, and from the mining mills we could hear the heavy thump of the big diesel engines that ran the compressors so the men could breath fifteen hundred feet under the lake.

Many evenings at the mission I listened to old mossbacks, prospectors, and trappers unfold the scroll of their experiences. Darcy Arden was one of those colorful, entertaining visitors I'll never forget. He tied his dog team at our fence late one afternoon when Father Gathy was away preaching a retreat at Fort Resolution. Darcy was a trapper, buffalo ranger, prospector, and now a mink rancher. He worked with Mike Dempsey in the Wood Buffalo Park and prospected on Great Bear Lake, where he met Father Gathy. I persuaded him to share a bachelor supper that particular evening just to hear him recount stories of the early "raw-fish days."

"Father Gathy and I were traveling down-river on one of the boats some years ago," he began, "and we picked up three tenderfoot prospectors along the way. Those fellows were hankering to play poker. Of course they did not know Father Gathy was a priest, as he was in coveralls." Darcy laughed, slapping his knee. "They insisted on his joining in the game, and before he sat down he said, 'I may win all your money!' He played—and won every cent they had! Then very casually he counted out the amount he won from each man and returned their money. The men sat slack-jawed. 'This will teach you fellows not to invite a stranger to sit in on a poker game,' Father told them." Darcy smiled and added, "He is quite a man with card tricks, this Father Gathy."

Later that winter I watched this Belgian priest manipulate cards, pull rabbits out of hats, and work magic that made the eyes of Yellowknife bulge in wonder. Very soon I realized how fortunate I was to be stationed with a brother Oblate who had such a saga of northern experience and talent in so many fields of endeavor. In his twenty-five years of priesthood he had been a pastor, a musician skilled in half a dozen instruments, and now a chaplain in the armed forces of Canada. Here in Yellowknife he was one of the pioneers, the Father who had sympathetic ears for troubled souls, regardless of their creed or their misshapen lives.

After I had made the rounds of the mines and met the personnel, Father Gathy took me to the Indian village six miles from town, out on Yellowknife Bay. There I met the chief and arranged to come the first Sunday of each month for Mass. The Oblate Brothers from our mission had built a small single-story log cabin at the village as a combination chapel and mission house. Father Leo Mokwa had lived here for the summer months during the late thirties, administering to the spiritual needs of the Indians.

Half of the Yellowknife Indians lived in log cabins, the rest in tents perched high on the rocks. Fishing was good at the entrance of the bay, for I noted that most fish racks were well stacked.

"You like trout fish, Father?" the wife of the chief asked, handing me a ten-pounder. I accepted with a smile of appreciation. Father Gathy thanked her in a flourish of her language that brought a blush to her tanned face.

In the weeks that followed, a number of Indians came to St. Patrick's at Yellowknife when they learned I could understand a little of the Chipewyan language. They smiled when I spoke, but they could understand because it was similar to their Dogrib tongue. After an English sermon one Sunday, two young braves came rushing into the mission with a new light of interest in their dark eyes.

"Do you know Father Gilles?" one of them asked. "We like him. He was here for Easter last year. We can understand him because he speaks clear English like the other white men around town."

That was my pass key. When they learned that Father Gilles and I were friends, the first English-speaking missionaries they had ever met, I was in their social register! They must have had visitors from Fort Smith who brought news of my work, and their moccasin telegraph system certainly was operating. By the middle of December more than fifty Indians came to the mission, pointing to bad teeth. A short conference with the local doctor established the required license to attend to these fellows, and it was while working on a Dogrib Indian's tooth that I got my first dose of information on the trouble between the Indians of Yellowknife Bay and the miners.

"Father, why are these white people rushing into our hunting lands for this gold? Have they no homes, no families? Have they no gold in their country?"

"They come for gold for the same reason that you move to new trapping grounds for fur—to make money," I answered.

In co-operation with the Royal Canadian Mounted Police we succeeded in solving personal problems and keeping peace between Indians and the miners. As the winter came upon us the settlement grew quiet and normal.

Even though Yellowknife is two hundred miles farther north than Fort Smith, I found little difference in the weather. That winter we had some forty-below-zero weather after freeze-up came in November. I noticed the shorter days, with only a couple of hours of light in December, especially on my dog-sled trips to the Indian village. By the time I had my team and supplies ready after Mass it was about eleven o'clock when I started out. It took the better part of an hour and a half to cover the rough ice trail to the village, and when I made the end of the line, handshaking everyone from the chief down, staked out my team, and unloaded my supplies into our mission shack, I had to use the gasoline light to read my Office.

The short winter days made flying difficult for the bush pilots, who kept contact with half a dozen mines within two hundred miles of Yellowknife. They had about five hours of daylight, usually spending the early morning hours in darkness warming up their ships for daylight take-off. I envied those fellows flying in the smooth air overhead while I bumped over the ice behind my dogs. But one advantage I did have was that I could travel at night. I often left the mission at five in the morning to arrive at the Indian village for Mass at daylight.

These good people needed help to prepare them for that inevitable boom of progress that breaks the barriers into most of the world's frontiers. I felt needed here and I liked these good, simple, honest people. Little hardships were forgotten when I saw their smiling faces.

In mid-January, when the ice in Yellowknife Bay had become thick enough for snowmobiles and trucks, Allen came to the mission one morning when the thermometer read thirty-five below zero. "What do you say about a lumber hunt?" he asked. "The ice will hold my light tractor." We made plans, deciding to search for the lumber on the north shore of the lake, up Rae Arm. Allen figured it should be up there, and in one pile, because we had interlaced it well. I thought it was probably high on the beach, maybe on the rocks, because the storm had raised the lake level.

99

We took Allen's caterpillar tractor and two sleds. One was for the lumber, and we lived in a caboose on the other. I planned to say Mass in the caboose every day and even hoped to do some missionary work among the Dogrib Indians from Fort Rae. They often frequented this country and I knew they would welcome a priest, since most of them were Catholics.

We followed the north shore of the Yellowknife River through the islands. Occasionally we found some stray planks and boards, but we traveled miles before we came upon the big tangled heap of lumber—probably twenty-five thousand feet, Allen estimated. Splashing, icy fall waters had covered the lumber with ice, and zero weather had glued the boards together.

We pulled some of the larger pieces apart with the tractor and smashed the ice with hammers and ax. The whole mess looked like a giant beaver home. Loading about five tons aboard the sled, we returned to Yellowknife. Allen made several trips on the new ice and salvaged almost half of the lumber. We had enough to repair the old mission and even a few heavy planks for new benches. In the spring I planned to do some carpenter work when the sun came back with heat and more light.

Work among the Indians and miners was interesting, and just when I began to remember their first names a letter came from the Bishop, asking me to visit the Bear Lake pitchblende mine some three hundred and fifty miles north. Father Gathy briefed me on Eldorado, as the mine is called, and arrangements were made with the mining company to fly me there in one of their planes.

There was no sign of life from the time we took off at Yellowknife until the plane crossed the rocky hills near Port Radium on Great Bear Lake. As soon as we stepped out of the plane I heard the solid thump-thump of the big diesel engines at the mine.

The pilot, Al Caywood, introduced me to Ed Bolger, the mine manager.

"Welcome to our ice caves, Father," the short, serious-faced fellow said, slipping off his glove and pulling back his parka hood, uncovering a shock of close-cropped white hair. "You may as well bring your bag down to my bachelor quarters on the bay shore. I'm not only tired of living alone down there, but I'm afraid of getting *bushed*. I'm beginning to talk back to myself."

Before I had a chance to unpack, he took me on a whirlwind

tour of the mine. I met the men at work in the mine under the lake and in their machine shops hewn out of the solid granite rock. Dressed in a rubber suit with a hard hat and a miner's light, I had a queer heavy feeling in my stomach as that elevator dropped away into the bowels of the earth. Within the last three hours I had been four thousand feet above the earth—now two thousand feet into the earth.

"You can make a daily visit here," Ed shouted into my ear above the squeal of the winch and the rattle of ore cars. "The men will be happy to see you and to talk about their families. When accidents happen and fear digs its claws into a man he likes to air his problems."

The ride up was slower than the descent, and I breathed easier when we saw the light of day again. Our next stop was the cracking mill, where the ore was broken down into half a dozen grades and the muck rock separated from it. It was a maze of belts, wheels, crushers, shimmy tables, and noise that started my ears ringing. It was a relief to get outside in the cool air and survey the place from the recreation hall.

The offices and most of the living quarters were built on the rocks a hundred feet above the lake, and a network of stairways and catwalks took us back to the lake level.

"We just installed a new Clark diesel electric plant." Ed began opening the door to the engine room. From here on he just pointed. The noise was too intense for talking. A half dozen seven-foot-high diesel engines chugged away on their concrete bases, and two mechanics in white coveralls were up on a steel platform, working on one of the cylinder heads. The new engine was gray and bigger than the others. Jumping needles on a dozen gauges were the only indication that it was operating. Ed picked up a long screw driver, placed the sharp end against the engine block and the other end to his ear, and then put the screw driver to my ear. The noise transmitted was like the rumblings of deep thunder or like a living monster with a mighty powerful heartbeat.

My quarters were modern and comfortable, with steam heat, and I ate with the officers at the mine mess hall. For daily and Sunday Mass I chose the recreation hall and set up my altar on the pool table. Some men attended each day, and on Sunday many non-Catholics came to pray and sought advice on problems that arise wherever men work in dangerous places.

A good many of my evenings were spent playing cribbage with Ed Bolger and getting a first-rate history of Port Radium.

"Remember the young man who served your Mass this morning?" Ed asked one evening.

"Joe LaBine, if I remember correctly."

"Yes. He's the son of Gilbert LaBine, who made this strike of pitchblende."

Ed related how Gilbert and his partner, Charlie St. Paul, had been prospecting in this area when Charlie became snow-blind. The year before, Gilbert had made a quick survey of the area from a plane. It looked most promising. He took good care of Charlie, making him as comfortable as possible in the tent with a supply of wood and grub handy, and then went out alone to look around. From that plane ride, Mr. LaBine remembered spotting a yellowish-gray streak among the rocky shoreline, and on May 16, 1930, he found it.

"Gilbert couldn't believe it was pitchblende. The find was so surprising, the first in North America!" Ed said, getting up from his chair. He went to the shelf above the fireplace and brought back one of the pieces of rock from the collection.

"This is the stuff. It's not pure *pitch*, but feel the weight of it," he said, handing me the rock. It was coal-black and as heavy as a chunk of iron.

"If I broke that with a hammer, the center would be light gray. As soon as it is exposed to the air it oxidizes and turns black."

Slowly I learned the whole saga of events that had set this mine in operation. Gilbert LaBine had found a treasure, but it was buried in forbidding Arctic land over a thousand miles from the nearest railroad. He went back to Toronto and told his brother Charlie about the find, and the brothers, who had been adventurers in mining since their teens, put their heads together to get backing for this new venture.

"Many were too skeptical to invest in this new undertaking, but there was one person who had faith in God and in her sons, especially when she heard from Gilbert that he had found something that could cure cancer," Ed Bolger emphasized one evening. "That person was the saintly mother of Charlie and Gilbert," he added, bowing his head. "God bless her. If there ever was a person who could get through to God with prayers, Father, it was her.

"Three years of promoting by the boys, added to that special help of Ma LaBine, resulted in raising $300,000 to sink a shaft at

Port Radium and open the world's largest radium refinery at Port Hope, Ontario. There was enough left to start the Radium Line, the transportation company that brought the first steel boats to the Mackenzie River. A small airline was also started to fly in the weekly mail and other necessities, to transport any emergency accident cases to the hospital at Edmonton. As soon as the refinery began production, the price of radium dropped from $70,000 a gram to $25,000. A little rhubarb broke out with the Belgian syndicate, which until then controlled the market, but because of the great humanitarian need and through LaBine's efforts, the monopoly was broken. In 1940, when the war closed the European markets, the mine was shut down. Research continued at the University of Chicago, where Gilbert had sent tons of high-grade ore. Then very suddenly in 1942 the Canadian Government asked Mr. LaBine to reopen the mine—with the big noise that more radium was needed. Only Gilbert and a few top men in Canada knew that the tons of pitchblende were yielding great quantities of black oxide of uranium—requested by the government for wartime needs." This was really the essential ingredient in the atomic bomb!

Little did I dream at the time Ed Bolger and I plied our wits on the cribbage board that the United States was actually making the atomic bomb from the material mined at Bear Lake. The Canadian Government had already expropriated the mine in 1944 and had asked Mr. LaBine to manage the Crown Company, now known as Eldorado Mining and Refining, Ltd.

I remained at Bear Lake for Easter services and then returned to Yellowknife. The weather was spring-like in early May, and I had the urge to do some repair work on the old mission house. During the winter Father Gathy and I had sized up the place and decided a new altar could be built in the mission, where we could say Mass instead of lighting a fire in the church on weekdays.

On this particular day—one I can never forget—the sky was overcast and there was a below-zero zip in the air. A sandy drift of new snow covered the lake ice when I returned from saying Mass at the gold-mine camp that morning. If anything, the weather had turned a little colder during the afternoon and I slipped on an extra sweater under my coveralls before going about my work in a small shack behind the mission. So many things had to be repaired now that we had some lumber. Allen McDonald had given me some three thousand feet from what remained on the barge after our ill-fated lake crossing. With an electric motor from our mission at Fort Smith and an old bench saw from Resolution, I built a power saw to cut the frozen lumber.

I started a new fire in the shop and worked away. Having just returned from Eldorado, I began to think of that vast stretch of country and how easily and quickly we covered it by plane. Twice on the return trip I spied dog teams crossing lakes, and I was thinking of those people living in that isolated wasteland in a world where life depended on their ingenuity and on God. Then, like a bolt of lightning, the saw went *zing!* In a second a sliver of wood drew my right hand into the whirling blade and clipped off my right index finger. The sharp, jagged teeth ripped through my glove, skin, tendons, and muscles of the middle finger too.

Shocked and jolted, I held my bleeding hand close to my old work parka and poked about in the sawdust. There it lay, the finger that had been consecrated to God just five years ago. How would I finish my work? There was so much to do. My hand did not pain too much. The thoughts that flooded my mind pained more. I ran to the mission and called for Father Gathy.

When he saw my bleeding hand, he exclaimed, "*O mon Dieu! O Notre Mère Marie! Quel accident!* What have you done?" He grabbed his jacket as he ran out of the mission, looking for transportation to the hospital at the Consolidated Mine two miles away. I went to my room for something to make a tourniquet. Blood came freely now. I found a towel and tied it around the upper arm, just above the elbow, with one hand and my teeth. Then I wrapped a clean towel around my hand, pulled my heavy caribou hunting parka on, keeping my hand inside, and started for the hospital on foot. I figured that whatever transportation Father found would catch up to me.

The cold dry air revived me, and determination forced me over the snow and out onto the lake. The pain was severe now and began to make me nauseous. My feet slipped from under me again and again, and I fell into the tangled icy willows along the lake shore. A little rest was so good, but I knew I had to keep going. Never before had I realized how pain can tear a man apart. My knees were actually shaking, and it was just a little cut on my hand that caused all this.

I found it difficult to keep my footing. I slipped again, climbing the hills, and landed against a stump. Feeling cold, I loosened the tourniquet and let the warm blood run over my hand. It felt better and I was off again, weaving like a drunken man. At last I reached the hospital. I held onto the railing with my left hand, climbed the four steps, and pushed against the door with my shoulder. It was frozen shut, as often happens in the North when a building is warm inside. I heaved against the door, but it was solid. I put all my weight into the effort and it gave way finally and I fell in—flat on my face. My next recollection was a mysterious voice, and then I saw a face.

"You gave us an awful scare, Father," a nurse said, holding my head. "We picked you up and thought you had been shot or knifed! Here, take this pill and a little water. You will have pain."

She told me I had been unconscious for four hours or more. Dr. Oliver Stanton, the mine physician, had rushed me to the emergency operating room and performed the necessary surgery. I noticed the huge bandage on my hand.

"You're very lucky," the nurse assured me. "In such an accident you might have lost the entire hand. Father Gathy has been here with you, and he told us you were working with a power saw."

"Well, well, our patient is awake." Dr. Stanton, with a worried Father Gathy behind him, came into the little room. "I removed the stump of bone from the index finger and made a heavy skin pad," the doctor explained, pointing to my hand. It looked as though I had on a white boxing glove.

"I am not too confident that you will be able to use the middle finger," he went on. "I had quite a time sorting out the tendons and nerve ends. Then I set the fractured pieces of bone in the metacarpal joint of the middle finger. Just the same, you're a lucky fellow. You could have had a stump and a hook like our friend, Mr. Johnson." This was a prospector we both knew who lost his hands in a dynamite blast.

I heard him say that if no infection or other complications set in I would probably keep the middle finger but might require more surgery at some future time to tighten the tendons.

Mining accidents were a specialty in the office of Dr. Oliver Stanton. Certainly he was no stranger to mangled hands, and I had all the confidence in the world in this man who had left the comforts of Outside to help his isolated fellow men.

After three days in the hospital at Yellowknife I was flown to St. Joseph's Hospital at Fort Resolution in a Canadian Pacific Airlines DC-3 piloted by Archie McMullen.

"*Bonjour, bonjour, mon Père,*" Father Riou, the Superior, greeted as I left the plane. "We are all so sorry to hear about your accident, but thank God you still have your hand."

I looked for Father Gilles, but there was no sign of him in the group that had gathered. When I asked Father Riou, he informed me that Father Charles had left for Fort Smith a few weeks ago to take up his new duties as vicarial bursar.

All the school children were there, crowding in close to have a look. The good Grey Nuns were there too, keeping the children in line, and these wonderful Sisters gave me a warm welcome to the hospital.

"Hello, Father," a high-pitched voice shouted over the crowd. Waving both arms in welcome was a dear old friend, George Pinsky. "You come and ride in my truck cab, Father." He took me by the arm. "It's warm in there. Sorry to hear about the accident," he added seriously. Then, smiling and putting his powerful hand on my shoulder, he said for all to hear: "You look good, but a little thin. You need a good rest here in our town."

Some of the children piled in back with Father Riou, and off we rattled over the hard snow to the hospital.

George Pinsky and his wonderful wife, Mary, are just a couple of special people among Northerners. Some forty years ago, at the request of Bishop Breynat, George settled in Resolution and opened a small store. The old Bishop saw honesty and kindness in the benevolent character of this trader. Most of all, George possesses a sympathetic understanding of the Indian people. For years he dog-sledded furs out to Edmonton and barged his few supplies north in the spring. People along the river began to know and like this rangy six-footer. Kindness to everyone was his trademark, even to those who were jealous of his success or stole his furs and supplies and tried to give him a bad name. But George forgave them. He is too much of a man to hold a grudge. Now his two wonderful children, George, Jr., and Bernice, who started their school days at the mission, are continuing their education Outside and are a credit to their parents.

Although George and his wife do not belong to the Catholic Church, they certainly are Christ-like in their goodness, and I feel deep pride to count them as very dear and true friends. The long evenings during my convalescence at St. Joseph's Hospital were shortened by their delightful visits. Dr. Joseph Riopel, the Indian Affairs Medical Director in charge of the hospital, and a neighbor of the Pinskys, usually came with them. Marie Riopel and Mary Pinsky always managed to surprise me with some new creation from their kitchens. People such as these typify the hospitality found in the North.

Sister Margaret Lachambre, R.N., would awaken me about seven-thirty in the evening in time for my visitors. It seems I could sleep sixteen hours daily those first weeks, and the sound of the wind and the rolling waves lapping the lake shore acted like a double-strength tranquillizer.

Sister Margaret, with a three-year stretch in a tuberculosis sanitarium, realized the healing power of a cheerful visit, and through her kindness I learned more about the Grey Nuns and Resolution.

"We are praying with hope that soon our Canadian Foundress, Mother Marguerite d'Youville, will be canonized a saint." Sister Margaret produced a photo of the great lady. "I will leave this on your bedside stand so you will remember to ask her to beg our Lord for the grace of a quick recovery."

The faith of these Sisters always amazes me. I feel certain that more souls are being pointed in God's direction by their wonderful lives than we can imagine.

After a week I began to take walks in the old fort, and visit the Indian families, the Hudson's Bay people, Pinsky's store, and the Royal Canadian Mounted Police. Sergeant Bill Kennedy and his wife were very sympathetic and faithful visitors. I can still hear Mrs. Kennedy saying, "Don't try to eat that blueberry pie with a fork left-handed! Use a spoon!" And I recall dabbing a few purple spots on her white tablecloth.

Most of my time was spent down on the wharf, watching the fishing boats come and go. Often the high rolling waves heaved over the wharf's edge and made me realize this was Great Slave Lake. The strong west wind could get a seventy-five-mile-wide handhold on that one-hundred-and-fifty-mile stretch of blue water. Some twenty-five rivers fed water and fish into the lake. That year, 1945, was the year when commercial fishing began. Working out of Hay River, seventy miles west of Resolution on the south shore, the fishermen seined for firm seven-pound whitefish and forty-pound trout.

I recall the season of 1944, when a special survey was made by the Fisheries Research Board of Canada on Great Slave Lake. Word went around that commercial fishing would take all the fish out of the lake and the Indians would starve. Actually the survey was carried out to prevent such a catastrophe. The research party found that in certain parts of the lake there was such an abundance of fish that cannibalism resulted from lack of food! Commercial fishing opened with forty-two fishermen and a catch limit of two million pounds. Investigations continued, and in 1951 and 1952 three hundred and five licenses were issued and the quota was increased to nine million pounds. Only seven million pounds were caught in 1952, however.

The new highway from Outside through Grimshaw, Alberta, to Hay River on Great Slave Lake in 1948 made transportation of fish more economical than air freight and tractor train. Now trucks haul fish from Hay River to Chicago on a weekly-run schedule. In January 1952 a long-distance record was made of thirty-two hundred miles from Hay River to New York City. The truck left Hay River on the eve of January 3 and arrived in New York City on the eve of January 8! Today ninety per cent of the fish is shipped to the United States.

Presently there are two packing plants on the lake, one at Gros Cap on the north shore, fifty miles south of Yellowknife, and one at Hay River on the south shore. Fishermen operate in temperatures of sixty-five degrees below zero on this 11,400 square miles of frozen lake 340 miles south of the Arctic Circle, in some forty snowmobiles. This is really ice-fishing. One day I went out with the Brothers of the mission to look at the nets and got myself into a mess of work. Winter fishing is quite a task, especially digging that seven-foot hole in the lake ice!

"Years ago this used to be the gateway to the caribou country," George Pinsky told me one day while I sat on the counter in his store and admired the oil lanterns and kitchen wares hanging from the ceiling. "Now it is the haven of fishermen, but they still look for Indian clothing. Everyone used caribou-skin parkas in the old days. They wouldn't look at my store parkas and coats. And you know, Father, I still use a caribou parka. They're so much warmer and lighter. Only bad thing about them is they shed their hair in a couple of years and lose their warmth."

Being with the Fathers and those grand people at Resolution, I gleaned a real history of the place. The lake was named by Samuel Hearne and Peter Pond, explorers in the late 1770s, after the Slave Indians who lived around it. About seventy years later, in 1858, the first missionaries visited the settlement, but not until 1912 was the mission firmly established.

"You should be here in February to get a real good idea of Resolution, Father," Sergeant Kennedy told me one day while I was out for a walk and stopped to admire his famous dog team. "Last winter I had those huskies on a patrol just east of here when the mercury slid to sixty-five degrees below zero! I had to change leaders every half hour. Their eyes were freezing open!"

From our mission *Chronicle,* recorded daily by the Father in charge, accounts of exploits caught my eye: *The Brothers had to chisel eight feet through the ice this morning to look at the fishhooks. They caught twenty trout. The temperature today is fifty-eight degrees below zero.* Setting hooks under the ice is the Indian method of trout fishing. The Oblate Brothers get the forty- and fifty-pounders deep on the floor of the lake during the cold days of January and February. Our mission and boarding school practically lived on fish in those days. Now we manage to offer the children half buffalo meat and half fish. Some years we are able to raise potatoes that last until Christmas. This is a real treat.

Father Riou was a steady visitor and walking companion. Life in the North had flowed through him for almost fifty years, and his solid fatherly point of view often brought my own problems into a more resigned focus. I had come from a country of speed, efficiency, and automation. He accepted the slowness of life in the North country and contented himself with being a strictly dog-sled and canoe missionary. He taught me a few needed lessons and slowed the rhythm of my excited youth to a more mature pace.

"How could a fellow be so careless with a saw?"

"It was an accident, Father."

"Well, there are accidents, and then there are times when thought and prudence change the word to *carelessness.*" He looked at me over his glasses, which were always sliding down his nose. Then slowly an understanding smile crept into his blue eyes.

"I know how careful you are and how often you cautioned others about these new power tools and engines. I really believe it was an accident, and since it was, always remember that it could have been your arm! It is just a scar in the mission battle of the North." A mood of recollection sent his gaze far away. "I recall one very serious accident that happened when I was down on Lake Athabaska. It happened to Bishop Breynat. The Bishop froze his toe, and gangrene set in before medical aid could be reached. We had no planes in those days to fly us out of the woods to a hospital, so Brother Ancel took off the Bishop's great toe with a straight razor. It was a case of surgery on the kitchen table at Chipewyan Mission. And the patient lived and walked far enough to become an archbishop. So you never know, my boy." He patted me on the head. "The ways of the Lord are His ways." He made me feel so ashamed of my thoughts of self-pity.

One evening while still in the hospital I had barely completed my Particular Examination for the night when Father Riou came in for a visit. That Examination is a personal thing with all religious, when they measure themselves hour by hour through the day to see how they have fallen in their human weakness from the example of the Master. Certainly I was guilty that night of imperfect resignation to the will of God. I was restless, with the throbbing in my shoulder, and the mental picture of being useless in the missions with this crippled hand depressed me. The heavy bandages had been removed and my middle finger was healed but immobile!

"You look as dejected as one of my Indians returning from a two-week moose hunt empty-handed," Father Riou said, shuffling into my room.

I told him my reasons, and he took a chair and said with a serious air, "That's a good feeling. It will limber up the muscles of your humility. Perhaps now you will do much greater and more important work for our Arctic missions than you ever dreamed about. God has His ways of teaching all of us, and especially in making us realize we just have to depend upon Him and not too much on ourselves. Oh, I didn't come to preach to you, Father," he went on, slapping the arm of my chair. "We all get discouraged once in a while, and crying on some soft shoulder helps us poor human beings." There was a sparkle in his eyes. They were still young, but his weathered face and his wild white beard branded him a veteran trooper of God. Even his cassock had that aged greenish tint, dappled with "Joseph's coat of many colors" from grease off the children's hands. They always crowded around him, climbed on his knee, eager for new stories—and that little piece of hard candy he always carried for "those who were good."

Father Riou was a wonderful brother priest to me during those recuperating days at St. Joseph's Hospital.

"Remember what I told you?" he said, standing on the dock as I shoved off in a boat for Yellowknife that August. "When you begin worrying about yourself and the handicap of your injury, just think of the man with no arms." He waved a good-by blessing, and I feel its goodness today as I think of him still bringing happiness to the patients at our Fort Smith hospital.

Chapter Seven

IN early August of 1945 I returned to Yellowknife and got back into action. My right hand was very stiff, especially the third finger, so Father Gathy carried the load of manual labor around the house. We had just worked out a good system when "Anyone home?" sounded at our front door. It was the Bishop, rapping on the door with his episcopal ring, as was his custom. I knew that voice and went to meet him with my apron on. I had been baking bread. "I see Father Gathy has been teaching you how to bake," he said with a big grin. "It smells very good, especially since my last meal was breakfast at Coppermine."

"You come from the Arctic coast?" Father Gathy asked, coming in the back door. "I just heard the word Coppermine," he said, kneeling and greeting the Bishop.

"Mr. Boffa flew me down on a Canadian Pacific Airlines plane. We came non-stop."

"I'll get you a little something to eat," Father Gathy began, backing toward the kitchen. "Father is a good cook, but his hand is a little sensitive around the hot stove."

The Bishop examined my finger and, seeing it sticking straight out, said, "I'm afraid you will have trouble with that in cold weather." He seemed very concerned. "Several of our missionaries have lost fingers or injured their hands, but they still do wonderful work. Only thing about your hand is that rigid finger," he added, rubbing his chin in thought. "It will freeze so quickly, you won't realize it. That could be very serious."

I was beginning to have thoughts I did not like. Did he mean I was through in the North? No doubt his keen eye noticed my worried look and he said quickly: "You'd better come south with me and see if a little surgery will not mobilize your finger. If you can move it you can keep it warm and still do great work in our missions." He gave me a fatherly look of encouragement. "Better pack your bag now, we will leave for Smith early tomorrow. I will tell Father Gathy about our plans."

I had often heard of the sudden changes that could follow the Bishop's visit, but never in my wildest dreams did I imagine this would happen to me. An hour ago I was baking bread; now I was packing my bags for home. That evening I wrote to my family, and the following afternoon we were flown to Fort Smith, where I ran into my old friend, the professor *pratique.*

"When I first heard of your accident, the news was a shock," he said, examining my hand. Then with a light in his eye he added, "As soon as I learned it was your right hand, I was relieved. Your trigger finger is still in good shape!"

I finally caught up to Father Gilles, who introduced me to a few new Brothers and added: "We have a very special guest at the mission who is most anxious to see you." And even as Charlie spoke, voices were lowered and I felt someone poking me in the back.

"*Bonjour, mon Américain!*" It was Archbishop Breynat, now retired these past two years. His voice was low and he sounded tired. He expressed regret that I had injured my hand but added with a wink at Father Gilles, tapping his cane against his right shoe, "Every good missionary leaves a part of himself with the people he loves." And for just a moment the lines deepened around his brown eyes and he seemed to be thinking back over his fifty years of missionary life. I was not aware of the implication of his words until he said: "I hope you find a better surgeon than I did years ago." Clearing his throat—and his mind of those unfortunate incidents—he asked: "What about all that movie film I gave you three years ago? Did you record any good scenes from our mission?" Age left his face now as he stroked his thinning white beard. When I assured him that I had over three thousand feet of film on the North he smiled, nodding. "*Bon, bon.* When you get to New York City, try to have a good film made so we will have something up to date to show our good benefactors."

For ordination I had received a sixteen-millimeter movie camera and brought it along into the North. When I asked the Archbishop if I could keep it to take a few pictures for my folks, he not only granted my request but gave me two thousand feet of film and the green light to take human-interest pictures.

After a day at Fort Smith, I left with the blessing of Bishop Trocellier and Father Mansoz. Archbishop Breynat traveled as far as Winnipeg with me, and as I boarded the train for the East he said, "Come back North as soon as your hand is healed and try to bring more American Fathers with you."

Before leaving the North, I had had word from my doctor in New York City to come for surgery as soon as possible, so my visit home was a happy occasion, though limited. I was away to the big city and St. Clare's Hospital, where I met my friend, Dr. Vincent Healy.

"Welcome to the South, Father." He smiled, getting out of his office chair and stretching up to his full six feet. His hair was white and his eyes clear blue. He had the tailoring and the sure movements of a man who knew what he was doing.

After chatting awhile, Mother Alice joined us. "We have a special room for Arctic missionaries. Come with me, Father," she said, motioning me to follow down a long, wide corridor. "This will be your room." She opened a door with a half curtsy. "I hope you don't find it too warm after your life in those Eskimo snowhouses," she said, smiling and removing the spread from a hospital bed.

The room was big, with a fine easy chair and even a radio. Sister left me to unpack my bags and get settled. What a change this was from the quiet North. Bells seemed to be ringing every few minutes in the hospital, and from a small opening in my window came the pulsating noises of a living city. Ambulance sirens screeched like wailing banshees, auto horns sent up a variation of honkings that sounded like a large congregation blowing their noses; and, drowning out these petty noises, were the deep-voiced bellowings of the ocean liners coming and leaving New York.

"Anyone home?" came a voice behind me as I looked out the window. "I'm Father Andrew Watkins, the chaplain," a priest in the brown habit of a Franciscan introduced himself. I told him who I was, where I had my roots, and that my uncle was Brother Salvador, a Franciscan. That broke the ice. When he learned I also attended a Franciscan College, St. Bonaventure in St. Bonaventure, New York, he said, smiling, "How did you ever escape the clutches of the Friars and wind up in another congregation? One of our spiritual directors must have slipped up someplace."

Father Andrew was five feet six inches of solid good humor, always coming up with a new story or a joke to brighten the outlook of the patients and charge the atmosphere of the sickroom with lightheartedness and new hope.

After blood tests and X rays, Dr. Healy operated on my hand, rebuilt the joint of the third finger, and checked me out of danger in the pasture of my room to heal. Friends in New York realized my active life in the Arctic would make the days of convalescence seem endless, and they shortened them with timely visits.

"There is a special visitor for you, Father." Mother Alice came rushing into my room one morning, quickly adjusting the covers.

"Well, well, the Eskimo is back! Welcome home." It was His Eminence, Francis Cardinal Spellman. He blessed me and squeezed my left hand. "Sister tells me you lost one of the fingers I consecrated at your ordination," he said, looking at my bandaged hand. I told him about the accident and he expressed his regrets and added: "Perhaps that is just a gentle nudge from the good Lord to direct your life in some special work for the missions."

The Cardinal was interested in a firsthand account of Arctic life, and before he left my room that day his keen eyes spotted some boxes of film stacked on a small table.

"Are these pictures on the Arctic?" he asked, walking over and examining them. I explained that I had taken a few feet of film on life in the Arctic missions at the request of my Superior and that as soon as my hand healed I would try to build a small film.

"Our people have a very hazy idea of life in that far country," His Eminence commented, and asked to see my films. He was most enthusiastic, and as the Episcopal Director of the Society for the Propagation of the Faith, the Cardinal called his national director, Monsignor McDonald, and arranged a meeting. Then things began to happen fast.

At the suggestion of His Eminence, the Society sponsored the film under the title of "Arctic Missions of the Mackenzie." Mr. John Primi of Primi Productions in New York helped with the arranging of sequences. Slowly a story of life in the far North began to unfold in Technicolor.

My doctor advised a temperate climate for a few months, and that gave me time also to attend the ordination and first Mass of my brother Edmund. By a strange coincidence, the ordaining Bishop was His Excellency, Arsene Turquetil, a retired veteran of almost half a century in the eastern Arctic Eskimo missions. During his last year in theology at the Oblate College in Washington, D.C., Ed took some special classes at the Catholic University, bending his efforts in a study of the Portuguese language. Edmund studied the South American portrait of the Catholic

Church. He learned of the Oblates of Mary Immaculate, who first went to Uruguay and Paraguay in 1925 and later in 1935 in far-off Argentina. A direct appeal came in 1945 from the Archbishop of São Paulo in Brazil. Fifty-two million Catholics had only a handful of priests to lead them to God. The wise old Bishop of the Arctic, who really looked like a prophet with his long white beard, must have known more than his words revealed.

During his visitation of the parents on the afternoon of Father Ed's big day, June 3, 1946, the ordaining Bishop said with his hand on my father's shoulder: "I want to thank you in the name of all the Oblate Fathers for another son. And don't you fret now," he added with a sympathetic eye on my mother. "We will see to it that this one is sent to a little warmer place!" From his talks with my brother, the old Bishop knew Father Ed's aversion to cold weather.

While Father Edmund settled down to enjoy his first summer at home in seven years, I continued to splice film. Father Timothy J. Mulvey, O.M.I., assisted in knitting together a script, and Cardinal Spellman went before the camera, adding ecclesiastical prestige with a classic introduction.

Official orders came from Rome in September for Father Ed, and I was fortunate enough to see him off to the Brazil missions. A few weeks later our film on the Arctic was completed, and after Christmas I began a lecture tour for vocations that kept me on the road for fourteen months.

I was very happy when the following telegram came from the Bishop at Fort Resolution: "Please come to replace Father Maurice Beauregard at Aklavik." In two days my good-bys were said and I returned to the North country.

"Father Beauregard was helping to carry a casket downstairs in the hospital when something went wrong, and he ended up with the casket on his head and a fractured skull," the Bishop explained when I arrived. "Take the first plane you can get to Aklavik and replace him until Father Biname returns from Belgium."

The first plane, I discovered, was in about two weeks, so I joined the Oblate community at Resolution and made my annual retreat. Father Lucien Delalande, a twenty-year veteran missionary among the Eskimos, was the retreat master.

During those nine days I not only recharged my spiritual batteries but also took on a cargo of Arctic lore that tailored me for work among the Eskimos. The flight north over that fresh white land made many dreams come true. I wanted to reach the smiling Eskimo and learn the secret of his carefree spirit of happiness. Our plane stopped to refuel at Simpson, and at Norman Wells we changed to a smaller ski-equipped single-engine Norseman, and I was lucky enough to sit up front with the pilot, Captain Stew Hill.

"This is one of the clearest February days we have had this year," he said while the engine warmed up at the edge of the airport. "You'll get a good idea of the country and especially the mountains. If you should get cold in this thirty-below-zero weather, just give me a shout and I'll turn up the heat," he concluded, putting on his earphones.

We took off and climbed to forty-five hundred feet to clear the hills just north of the Wells. Now I had a real picture of the true Arctic wilderness. Under us, white frozen lakes cut patterns in the dark patches of spruce. To our left, the winding Mackenzie River lay sleeping under the anesthetic of winter. To the far west, the serrated horizon of the Rockies glistened silver and gold as the southern rays of the sun ricocheted off their icy shoulders.

"Over there where you see those white chimneys of smoke is the town of Arctic Red River." Captain Hill pointed after an hour and a half aloft. I looked, but the only sign of life was heat smoke. The people were turning up their fires for suppertime. It was nearly six o'clock.

About the time the stars—our street lights—began to shine through the knotholes in the blue-black floor of heaven, Stew pointed to the yellow candlelight flickerings of Aklavik.

"The Peel River makes a hairpin turn down there, and the settlement is on the inside curve," the pilot shouted in my ear, banking to the right. "Your place is there"—he pointed—"that big red brick school." I saw some children out in the yard as he spoke. Another sharp bank and we leveled off and came down with the skis rumbling on the hard-packed snow of the river.

"Those drifts are like cement tonight," Captain Hill called to me, looking ahead, serious and intent on his business. "They must have had a blow here today. When I was here four days ago Brother Beauchemin had this runway nice and smooth. He has a small caterpillar tractor and pulls a scraper he made with old pieces of scrap iron from the Wells. It does a good job," Stew added, taking off his earphones.

When our plane finally stopped at the edge of the river, I was glad to jump out and stretch my legs. I heard barking dogs, looked up, and saw two teams of galloping huskies heading right for me. Up into the plane I scrambled. Regardless of my experience with sled dogs, I was taking no chances.

"Forget something, Father?" Stew asked, putting his logbooks in their case and smiling when he heard the dogs. Hesitantly I told him I had forgotten my camera, but he guessed otherwise! "They do a lot of barking, those Eskimo dogs, but they will not bite you." He smiled and jumped out.

When I saw a man take the lead dog by the collar and drag him away from the plane, I climbed down slowly. About a dozen people flocked around us, but their breathings of steam in the forty-below air veiled their faces. I could not tell whether they were Eskimos or white.

"Welcome to Aklavik." A tall, heavy-set fellow came up to me in a muskrat-skin parka. When we shook hands, I remembered those dark eyes and that square jaw; it was Father John L'Helgouach, who had been Superior of the mission on my brief visit in 1944.

We gathered my bags and hustled off the wind-swept ice to the mission, where I met Father Adam and Brother Beauchemin. It was a warm and very clean two-story house covered with galvanized tin.

"This will be your room," Father Adam said, taking my bags into a room to the right of the main entrance. The chapel was directly in front of the entrance, and there were two rooms to the left. "I sent word asking the Sisters to have a little supper for you," he added, sniffing a pinch of snuff and brushing a few grains of tobacco out of his heavy black beard.

Father Adam was of medium build, hardened from constant exercise of daily mission chores. He introduced me to the Sisters and a wonderful broiled whitefish supper that was relaxing after the excitement of the day.

Later I went to the second floor of the small forty-bed hospital to visit Father Beauregard. Despite layers of bandages around his head, he worked up a smile. We spoke briefly, for he tired easily, and the doctor wanted him to conserve his strength for the air ride south in the morning.

It took about a week to find my way around the mission, the school, and the hospital, and a good month to get acquainted with the children, the patients, and some of the townspeople. Slowly

I met the Eskimo families who came to visit their sick relatives. Many came out of curiosity. Most of them were smiling, simple people who spoke a few words of English. When Father L'Helgouach or Father Adam spoke to them in Eskimo, they raised their eyebrows, registering new and keen interest, proud to hear their language spoken. Soon I learned that the majority of the Eskimos in the west, especially around the delta, spoke enough English to get by in the store. They learned it from the early explorers, adventurers, police, traders, and especially working at odd jobs during the summer for various transportation companies.

January and a good part of February were dark months, with only three or four hours of daylight. I spent most of the time indoors, not because it was dark and thirty-five below zero outside, but mostly because I had a lot of desk work. Hospital and school reports, writing sermons and letters kept me pinned down. When the days grew brighter, Father L'Helgouach took me on short jaunts through town and I got a good ground picture of "the City of Western Arctic."

Aklavik is just over forty miles inland from the Arctic Ocean and about the same distance east of the foothills of the Rockies. It sits smack in the middle of the wide three hundred square miles of the Mackenzie delta. Trappers, traders, Eskimos, and Indians for five hundred miles around have their sights on Aklavik for news, food, and a haven for their children and those who become ill. This main western branch of the Peel River is just one of the many veins of the Mackenzie River funneling its muddy waters into the cold blue Arctic Ocean. The settlement buildings begin with some Eskimo homes built of logs, a few tents, and then our large boarding school. The red-roofed buildings of the Hudson's Bay Company and the Army Signals are on the bend of the river. On the west bank of the Peel River the Royal Canadian Mounted Police have their barracks, followed by several private traders. The west end of the town is flanked by the yellow buildings of the Anglican mission.

Certainly this town has a good beginning and a good ending, regardless of its cosmopolitan population. There are Eskimos, Indians, English, Irish, Canadians, Swedes, Norwegians, Poles, Germans, Russians, and Americans in this town. The great attraction, regardless of its nature, is the pot of gold at the end of the rainbow—muskrat pelts. Aklavik and New Orleans are the greatest "rat" producers on the American continent! Prospectors, too, drift down for that "hidden gold lode somewhere in the mountains." Others come to escape the responsibilities of family life or to seek refuge with a new love far away, they think, from the laws of civilized society.

Here I found the people who make their home up in this snow country, the Eskimos. Where did the Eskimo come from? First of all, looking at this stocky, well-rounded fellow with dark hair, slanted eyes, moon face, olive skin, and broad features, most anthropologists conclude he is a Mongolian from the cradle of the human race, Asia. Also, because the continent of Asia and Alaska are separated by only some thirty-five miles at the little and big Diomede Islands, these people could easily have crossed into Alaska. A free translation of Aleutian, meaning *the path by which one comes*, adds practical certainty to the belief that the Eskimos came from Upper Mongolia. The Eskimo is a happy, smiling fellow with a rough exterior. Like the Chinese and Japanese, he does not wear his feelings on his sleeve, but the passions of love and hate run deep and silent in his loyal soul. "Have faith in an Eskimo and he will have faith in you," Father Delalande said.

The earliest whale hunters, over eight hundred years ago, found Eskimos on Greenland. Samuel Hearne found them on his long trek from Churchill, Manitoba, to the mouth of the Coppermine and back in the summer and fall of 1771. John Rae found them when he finally came across the remains of the Franklin expedition on the shores of northern King William Island. And Alexander Mackenzie met these nomads of the Arctic after his long epic trek down the Mackenzie in June and July of 1789. Father Peter Fallaize met them in 1923 on the Mackenzie delta when he came to look for a suitable place to build Aklavik.

I will always remember the first Eskimo I ever met. His name was Billy Trasher. By any measurement in the Arctic he was a large Eskimo, standing over six feet tall in his mukluks and weighing over two hundred pounds. Life ran strong in Billy Trasher, and all those who knew him remember him for his blustering enthusiasm. He could outwork any man on the delta—and he could outdrink him too—"if the devil has his way," as he would say. Billy would flex his arm muscles and boast: "You see me, Bishop? Still power enough to have number-two wife and half a dozen children. I have seventeen now! Good, eh?" And he would pound his chest. Usually he came with loud hellos and vigorous hand-shakings, excitedly telling of his prowess as a trapper or a rough trip on the Arctic Ocean. Then, like a whirlwind, he was off again, laughing, waving, and hustling his children ahead of him. From the days of his conversion and first marriage, Billy was a champion of the Catholic Church, and woe betide the poor fellow who said anything derogatory about the missionaries and especially the Sisters. He would do almost anything short of murder for Sister MacQuillan, who became both an advising and understanding mother to him and his family.

Then came a night I will always remember—a night I saw Billy Trasher and he was not laughing or standing tall in his polar-bear-skin mukluks. I had been in my room that evening, working later than usual, when Tommy and Peter, two of Billy's sons, came bursting into the house.

"Pa is sick. He cannot move his leg or his right arm. He cannot even talk good! Will you come?" When I asked where Billy was, they spoke in unison: "We brought him with our team. At six this morning we left our place and drove all day through the blizzard on the delta. Pa is shaking and very cold."

I slipped quickly into my parka. Eskimos gathered around the sled near the mission opened a path for me. Two men stood near the dogs that lay panting and sniffing the air for food scent.

Then I saw him. It was Billy all right, but his fire burned low. He even tried to smile through his one good eye. The other eye drooped shut. His body was jammed so tightly in the carryall of the dog sled that I had difficulty slipping my arm under him.

"You take him under the knees and we'll lift him gently out of that sled," I called to Brother Beauchemin, who was just coming from the mission.

We carried Billy into our little hospital while the Eskimos stood watching, their dark eyes glistening with sympathy. Here was their hero and their leader, a great Eskimo, who had piloted our icebreaker through the Arctic pack for twenty-two years and forged ahead on many a hunt. He often stood with high pride in his flared nostrils to see white men imitate his galaxy of antics at work and play.

Now he was helpless. Fatigue and pain made his age show through the hard facial features chiseled by the north winds. His sagging mouth struggled to form words to thank Sister, who gently made him comfortable. His good eye shifted like a rolling black pearl as he tried to express the thoughts that must have filled his soul. Above his corrugated leather-skin brow a wild mane of coarse, knotted black hair lay twisted and shaggy on the smooth white pillow. The corner of his lower lip hung downward, exposing a few yellow chipped teeth.

"There is no doubt, Father, that our friend Billy Trasher has suffered a severe stroke," Dr. Ward confided in low tones. "Time and good care may enable him to walk again, but it will mean no rat season for him this spring. That right side is almost lifeless now," the doctor added, laying Billy's huge callused right hand comfortably on the covers.

The doctor realized the importance of the spring hunt to people of the delta, and especially what it meant to this big Eskimo. Billy had a big family to look after, and the results of spring ratting meant that they either lived or starved for the next year.

But spring came with birds, boats, and botflies, and Billy continued to rest. His faithful wife, Alice, ran the trap line and fed the children. Very slowly he moved his fingers, his toes, then his arm and leg. Sister Marie Lemire was his angel of mercy. She mustered her strength and taught him how to talk and even how to walk again. She massaged his flabby muscles and poured new courage and strength into his soul with her wonderful smile, which could blast its way through tears. Her sincere prayers and determined efforts had the old sea pilot up and walking for midnight Mass on Christmas in less than a year after he was stricken. We all knew Billy made the chapel, because never before did Tommy and Peter sing with such loud, deep voices. The big Eskimo heard them, and hot tears of gladness splashed down his cheeks as Sister Marie squeezed his hand and chewed on her lower lip to be brave. His speech came back, too, and even though his lower lip is lazy, he can throw enough authority in his voice to keep the family in line and get off a loud greeting when the Bishop arrives. Again I can agree with Brother Mike Dabrowski: "It takes a lot to kill a man." And Billy Trasher is a real *Inuk* (man above other men).

In Aklavik, I found men and women spearheading a frontier—twelve hundred in all, including the Eskimos. There were the traders, for people must eat and build in order to live; the Royal Canadian Mounted Police, for men are human and err the world over. Doctors and nurses came to heal and comfort the suffering. And with these came men and women of God, the missionaries. The Anglican missionaries were the first on the scene to build a church, a hospital, and a school. They had help from the government, as we did some five years later, but nevertheless it took zeal and personal sacrifice to brave this Arctic frontier. Many fine men and women have emerged from the Anglican school, and their nurses and hospital supervision have sent a good many Eskimos to their homes well and happy.

Our own Roman Catholic mission was really established by Reverend Father Trocellier, who later became Vicar Apostolic of the Mackenzie. With Brother Beckschaeffer he erected the first log-cabin mission in 1926, planned and built the boarding school, and opened the hospital. The building was just completed that August in 1931 when Charles and Anne Lindbergh landed at Aklavik on their round-the-world flight. They were intrigued, on their tour of the mission, to find such a well-equipped little hospital and especially to visit the huge icehouse some twenty-five feet deep in the permafrost.

When I arrived in January of '49, the mission was a growing concern, with over eighty children in school and forty patients in the hospital. Father J. Adam acted as chaplain at the hospital, and Father John L'Helgouach attended the Eskimo section of the parish, since my knowledge of the language was limited. Thirteen Grey Nuns of Montreal taught in the Immaculate Conception boarding school and took care of the nursing at the hospital. Since August 1925, when three Grey Nuns came to Aklavik with Father Alphonse Duport, these Sisters have devoted themselves to the formation of the future citizens of the Arctic.

The wireless men had a small radio station at Aklavik, and with the aid of their time and knowledge we enlarged it and set up a broadcasting studio just off the school chapel. It was my intention to broadcast not only news from that station but also a solid Sunday sermon. By mid-February the new station was set up and each Sunday the entire afternoon was spent on the air! Through the kindness of friends back home I received a number of records and musical tapes, especially western folk music, which the Eskimos loved.

The Anglican mission also had an hour broadcast from their All Saints Cathedral, and many a family enjoyed Canon John Montgomery and his high English wit.

I found that the little radio station did reach out into the shacks and tents of the delta people wherever these "rat trappers" had the wherewithal to buy a battery-operated radio. Most of them had a set by June 1949, and the influx of children into our school that September told us we were getting out into the delta homes. Instead of traveling with a dog team and visiting a family here and there and living off fish and muskrat meat, now I could reach all the people at the same time. If a missionary traveled constantly he might be able to visit all the people of the delta once a season with a dog team in winter and by boat in the summer. But by visiting only twice a year it would take many years to deliver instructions sufficient to warrant a knowledge of the Church! The result? Years of traveling, years of literally carrying the cross over those frozen rivers and bug-ridden bogs of summer to reach the people. Radio was the answer, and is the answer today, in that land where distance is the wall between ignorance and knowledge.

At Christmas time we had a special program, with the children sending their greetings home by radio. The Sisters prepared them well and even coached them in the final message over the air. Then there was a patients' program, when a sick wife would speak to her husband and children in her own language for as long as fifteen minutes. We had a special news bulletin of "Outside" news for five minutes and local news for twenty minutes. Whenever a new family came into town, they would come to the mission with news of the people in the immediate vicinity of their camp and also with news of families with whom they visited along the trail, news of the condition of the trail, of how much overflow was on the river, and, too, of how many muskrat push-ups they saw on the small lakes they crossed.

Spring at Aklavik is rubber-boot time. Even the Sisters had to use them to go from building to building before "Operation Sidewalk" went into effect in the spring of 1950.

One Monday morning two Brothers and two hired men went into the slender timber some forty miles south of the settlement and slashed down one hundred and fifty logs from six to ten feet long. "Anything that will make four-by-fours and two-by-sixes or larger is what we are after," I had instructed them. On Tuesday noon they were back in Aklavik with the logs. Roy Wright from Edmonton ran a sawmill in those days and offered his expert hand on the blade toward our project. Some ten years before, the local government medical officer, Dr. Livingston, had received hay for his cow in bales with a good amount of wire on them. This wire kept the mill running for a day, and by Thursday noon we had a pile of sawed spruce, sufficient for three thousand feet of sidewalks! Friday and Saturday were spent cutting the sleepers, four-by-fours, in eight-foot lengths. We dipped them in a mixture of tar and boiling fuel oil, a kind of homemade creosote, and the following week the new walks were laid and the Sisters and nurses could promenade in their ordinary footwear.

Early spring comes in mid-April. The sun throws more heat each day, softening up the snow and melting it down to the frozen ground. By noon the roofs are dripping and the bare spots of earth are greasy. At night they freeze again. This process continues until all the white stuff of winter turns the ground of Aklavik to greasy gumbo. The empty tin cans, the lint and dregs of a long winter's living come to the surface as the snow melts.

Usually by the first week in June all the bets are down on the river-ice pool. From early February, when the first muskrats are sold, money is laid on the barrel head, betting on the day, the hour, and minute when ice in the great Mackenzie River will move. One year a teacher in our school hit the jackpot of three hundred dollars. It is a safe gamble that the ice will move out of the river between the first and the tenth of June. And following the ice comes the first of the summer river boats. This adventurer, known as the "banana boat," ordinarily comes from deep in the Liard River at Fort Nelson, where supplies are trucked in over the Alcan Highway. There is no sleeping in Aklavik when this boat arrives with fresh fruit, tobacco, and a stack of mail-order parcels from the T. Eaton Company. Orange rinds and gum wrappers announce the arrival of summer, covering the ground at the Hudson's Bay store and thinning out the farther one goes away from this "horn of plenty."

At the large mission of Aklavik our staple fare consisted mainly of fish and reindeer meat. Beans and rice replaced potatoes after our supply from the southern missions of Good Hope and Norman ran out in February. Some of the missionaries eat raw fish and raw meat when traveling among the Eskimo camps, but I cooked or roasted my food whenever possible. The raw meat and especially the raw fish did not agree with me. Hunger sometimes forced me to eat a little, but I did not find it palatable.

Eskimos eat great quantities of meat and fish, raw and dry. From the time they are able to swallow food—meat and fish given to them from the mouth of their father or mother—they have become accustomed to this fare over the years. Very often they eat not only raw but even decayed fish. On the hunt I have watched

Eskimo men and women bite into warm caribou meat. What they cannot get into their mouth they cut off with an upward stroke of their knife. Often I expected to see the tip of a nose missing, but my friends were too dexterous with the knife.

When the ice was thick enough to support the D-2 caterpillar tractor and two sleds, Brother Beauchemin made the run to the Reindeer Station, ninety miles east on the Mackenzie delta, for our quota of meat. "Reindeer" has long been a magic word that brings gladness to youthful hearts when sounds of sleigh bells and Santa Claus herald the coming of that joyous season of Christmas. For Northerners, in Alaska and the western Arctic, the reindeer means joy too, but in the more solid and realistic sense of something to eat. They are not classed as wildlife like the buffalo and the caribou but are semi-domesticated.

These brothers of the caribou are actually not native to our America. Between 1891 and 1902 some twelve hundred and eighty reindeer were brought into Alaska from Siberia. Food and weather conditions were most favorable, and by 1936 Alaska had six hundred thousand reindeer. But depletion of winter ranges, wolves, poor herding and management practices, and loss from mixing with migrating herds of caribou shaved the herds down to around twenty thousand.

After careful investigation and planning, the Royal Commission of Canada, foreseeing the success of the project, decided to purchase a herd of reindeer from Alaska. Arrangements were made with an Alaskan reindeer company to deliver a herd of three thousand deer to a range on the Mackenzie delta, and Andy Bohr, a veteran Lapp herder, started the drive with the help of several Eskimos in December 1929.

The saga of cattle drives from Texas to the railroad at Abilene, Kansas, has been the subject of a thousand western thrillers, but never had a drive taken six years! The Southwest has its drought and dust and rustlers, but the Arctic has its killing cold and its bleak, white, lifeless desert. Andy Bohr nursed his "skiing cowboys" and his limping reindeer over mountains and muskegs; lost bawling cows and calves in swollen rivers and running ice; and spent weeks and months hunting for range for the hungry, footweary deer. Finally, after four years, he arrived in Canadian territory.

New problems arose in moving the herd across the wide, flat, soft Mackenzie delta. Two years he fought quagmires, mosquitoes, and then wolves and breaking ice. At last, with the new sun of another spring, the hardest and longest drive in the history of the Arctic was over. He had started with three thousand deer, but only two thousand three hundred and seventy arrived for the newly built corrals at Kittigazuit on that memorable March 6, 1935.

The new range was northeast of the tree line in the lichen and moss tundra. Three Laplanders and their families had been brought from Norway in 1931 to train the Canadian Eskimos in the handling of reindeer herds. By 1933 the Reindeer Protection Ordinance was enacted, and a sixty-six-hundred-square-mile area on the east side of the Mackenzie delta became a reindeer reserve. Some twenty-five miles from the ocean, in the shelter of the Mackenzie River and in the western lea of three-hundred-foot hills, buildings were erected for the Reindeer Station. This was, and still is, the headquarters for the staff and equipment, such as boats and now a snowmobile.

The government devised a plan to make herding the deer attractive to the nomadic Eskimos. After a little investigation into the trustworthiness and background of an Eskimo who decided to become a herder, the government would give him eight hundred animals, on the condition that once the herd became self-supporting he would return to the government half the original number of animals. The remainder of the herd would become his personal property. But, like all new projects, reindeer herding suffered during its first years. In one case a schooner sank, wiping out two families and leaving their herds unattended. Today, after disease, nutritional troubles, famine, and wolves, there are over three thousand reindeer in two good-sized herds. The roundup takes place in September, and three hundred fifty to four hundred deer are killed to supply meat for the Roman Catholic and Anglican schools and hospitals.

When Brother Beauchemin returned from the Reindeer Station he had the meat from seventy deer piled high on his sleds. Thanks to Andy Bohr and to the dozen and more Eskimos who are now experienced reindeer herders, we have meat for our school and hospital. The set routine of a herder's life is not the most appealing thing to the nomadic Eskimos, yet they like to eat and they love deer meat! Circumstances of personal recovery, such as the low ebb of the fur industry and the increasing herds of reindeer on their new 17,900-square-mile range, have gently nudged over half of the Eskimos in the western Arctic to try this "cowboy life."

In January of 1950, while I was in charge of the mission at Aklavik, I made a pastoral visit to the camp at Kittigazuit. Brother Camille Claeys came with me to serve Mass and for a little rest after his two and a half months of isolation at our fish camp out on the Mackenzie. We flew over the Reindeer Station, and later, inland, the pilot, Mike Zubko, pointed to a herd of deer. A dozen small dark spots drew my attention. They were dogs tied at an Eskimo herder's camp in an arroyo.

"That is Guy Amigoituk's herd," Mike shouted in my ear over the purr of the engine.

Guy had graduated from our school the year I arrived at Aklavik. His little wife Therese was ill with tuberculosis at our hospital. Mike circled the tent, and Guy waved for all he was worth. He would be happy now, realizing that someone remembered that he, Guy the herder, was out there on the white tundra.

This trip was the culmination of almost two years of gentle prodding by Mike to get me off the ground. "You can't appreciate a lot of nothing until you see it," he used to say. "Wait until I get you out over the barren lands."

Now we were out over that treeless, white, rolling country. The only way I could tell it was rolling was that the light from the southern sky made an outline of shadow in the deep valleys and cut dark, definite lines along the high banks of rivers. The country was fascinating, but being aboard this little plane, listening to its song, gliding effortlessly over this rugged country, reawakened my desire to fly. I followed Mike's every movement. He was calm, alert, and sure. Years ago I had known him as an airport mechanic in Yellowknife. Now he owned two planes and operated the Aklavik Flying Service. We were flying in his Cessna 170, the passenger plane. His Waco was the fish-and-meat cargo ship.

"There's the Kitty tower. It's not easy to see against this snow," Mike indicated with a toss of his head.

He is a chunky pretzel of a fellow who can twist and climb over an engine or a load of freight with the agility of a cat. Fatigue is foreign to him. "There comes Mike, there goes Mike," the school children would shout. From early morning until long after midnight, when the nights are days in summer, Mike was zooming in with Knute Lang and a load of fur or taking off with a load of mail for Tuktuk on the Arctic coast. And this was the Arctic coast, twenty-five miles west of Tuktuk! Mike flew low over the steel-domed huts of the camp and we landed quickly and smoothly on the river icestrip.

"Nice, eh, Father? Someday we will have a smooth field like this at Aklavik," Mike beamed as we taxied to the waiting snowmobile. A canvas-wrapped bulldozer and a road grader sent up steam from their exhausts as they rumbled past, dragging scrapers and rollers over the hard snowdrifts.

"Surprised to see all this activity in the middle of nowhere?" Mike asked. "Wait until you climb the hill," he added before I could reply. Stories and news of this "Kitty Camp," as the Eskimos called it, filtered into Aklavik, but I was agog and so was the Brother at what we saw.

"So you are the sky pilot who has been telling us those retread jokes this past year," one of the Royal Air Force sergeants laughed, pumping my arm as though he were going to pull it out by the roots.

"He is giving you the business, Father." The tall, crackly-voiced CO leaned toward me. "We enjoyed your radio programs, especially the local news and stories. I hope you will give us a few talks while you are here, Father," he added. "Even though I am a good Presbyterian and over sixty-five per cent of the men here are not Catholics, they will nevertheless appreciate a good injection of spirituality." He smiled.

Three men had been detailed as a reception committee and whisked us aboard a warm-cabined snowmobile. On the way up the seven-hundred-foot hill to the camp I saw Mike take off, veiled in a white miasma of swirling snow. He promised to return for us in four days.

Captain Evans, the well-groomed lanky commanding officer in Royal Canadian Air Force blue, pointed out a few of the special buildings during our two-mile ride to camp and billeted us in a Fiberglas-insulated canvas igloo. During supper with the men and that evening he briefed me on "Exercise Yellowbeetle."

In 1947 the United States Army and Air Force, in conjunction with the Canadian Army and Air Force, built a series of defense or detection Loran (long range) stations in the Arctic. Assorted magnetic disturbances and violent storms were a barrier to effective communications systems. Low-frequency Loran stations were built at Cambridge Bay, on the southeastern tip of Victoria Island, at Saw Mill Bay, on the southwest shore of Great Bear Lake, and at Kitty. They formed a kind of right-angle triangle, with Kitti-gazuit in the right angle. Better aid to air navigation was hoped for, as well as more efficient communication for the defense of the Dominion and the United States.

That first evening Brother and I enjoyed a movie in the large twin igloo recreation hall, and I was formally introduced to the men. Next morning I was very surprised to find nearly the whole camp at Mass, including the commanding officer. Later that day we had our curiosity satisfied when an Air Force sergeant took us on a special tourist tour of Kitty.

All the buildings were of a temporary nature, consisting of igloos with corrugated sheet-metal roofs, and Fiberglas-insulated tents with wood frames and plywood floors. Machine shops, ware-houses, powerhouse, garage and barracks, and radio operations building were all resting on wood cradles on the permafrosted ground. The focal point of these bases at Cambridge, Saw Mill, and Kitty was a huge 650-foot steel tower that stood on four eight-foot-square concrete feet planted twenty feet in the frozen ground. Over six thousand barrels of oil and gasoline covered the ground around two twenty-thousand-gallon fuel-oil tanks perched on the highest sand hills near the river.

On the second day of our visit the CO called me into his quarters. He had a serious business air about him. "Exercise Yel-lowbeetle is completed and this Loran equipment is found want-ing, since we have the more effective radar. And, Father," he added confidentially, "this entire camp might go on the auction block of War Assets to the highest bidder. Your poor missions on the Mackenzie River and on the Arctic coast could use most of this material. My advice to you is to get a bid in on it."

That was quite a formidable plum he dropped in my lap. It stunned me. I stammered, telling him I didn't have the faintest idea how much to bid on this large and varied amount of sup-plies and equipment. But I agreed with him that we certainly could use it.

"As far as arriving at a fair bid price"—the CO scratched his ear meditatively—"I can detail about ten men to take inventory of the remaining stock. From the lists they make, we will be able to judge just what is left around here. This may take a few days, Father. Could you spare that much time?"

I assured him that nothing short of a couple of broken legs could prevent my being here and that furthermore Brother and I would help the men in making that itemized list. I sent a wire to Mike Zubko to delay his return until he heard from me.

Could we use that material? It would be a bonanza for the realization of missionary hopes! There was food of every kind, from dehydrated carrots and onions to canned Virginia hickory-smoked ham. Stacks of fir lumber lay half buried in the snow along with barrels of gasoline and oil. There were bulldozers, trucks, power plants, and bathtubs. Tools of every description for plumbing, carpentry, and engine repair.

After three and a half days the inventory was completed, a bid placed, and Mike came on two hours' notice. We climbed aboard, and the CO said "Bon voyage" with crossed fingers. On the way to the airstrip he confided with military sincerity that he would like to see our bid honored.

Without delay Mike took off, and when he reached two thousand feet we saw the big red ball of the sun in the southwest. It was a very clear afternoon, and when we passed the Reindeer Station I could even see the muskrat push-ups with their tiny black caps of weeds and husks of a winter's feeding. Brother's keen eye picked out familiar spots like his fish camp and several Eskimo homes on the delta. The flight gave me a very clear picture of the location of Aklavik on that west branch of the Mackenzie, the Peel River.

After Will Rogers displayed the last rope tricks of his life to the Eskimos on his visit in the summer of 1935 he described Aklavik in his usual witty manner: "Sorta reminds me of that lonesome piece of pork usually found in a can of pork and beans." As our plane began to descend and slim stalagmites of smoke marked our northern town, I was inclined to believe the Oklahoma cowboy humorist.

During the last days of ratting season in May and early June, the spring waters raised the ice on the lakes, and migratory birds and water fowl winged north under the midnight sun. Warm flower-scented breezes rolled gently down upon us from the western mountains, delta Eskimo families arrived for their children when vacation days began, and the people of Aklavik just strolled about jingling "rat money" in their pockets, relaxed, and soaked up the sun.

July 4 passed quietly without a firecracker or a skyrocket, and I was just paying my daily duty to God in chapel when bedlam broke loose in the yard.

"The Bishop's boat! Look!" the children screamed. They were running out of control down to the riverbank, tall Sister Claire close at their heels, her arms in the air with futile efforts to corral her fledglings. There was only one course of procedure now: meet the boat. I noted a new face as the *Fatima* docked.

"This is Father Biname," the Bishop said immediately after I kissed his ring. "He will replace you here at Aklavik. I have some other work for you." He smiled and went to meet the children, who began to climb all over him.

I shook hands with the new, tallish missionary, and his big work-built hand made my fingers crack. "It's like old home week coming back here." He grinned. "I built that school with Father Trocellier and planted the first garden in these parts." Then he was enveloped by the children and the people who knew him.

Fifteen years of dog-mushing, battling blizzards and a blazing Arctic sun on the bright snows had leathered his face and thinned his hair. Still there was a spring in his walk and the brightness of zeal in his blue eyes. Aklavik Mission would have a good pastor. He knew the people and their language and he knew how to work with his hands.

"You will come on the Arctic coast with us this summer aboard the icebreaker, the *Lady of Lourdes*," the Bishop confided that evening when all the shouting was over. "I want you to see our missions among the Eskimos since we will visit all of them, delivering supplies. Perhaps you can find some good material for another motion picture."

This was adventure, and I loved it. August 10 found us one hundred and eighty miles east of Aklavik at Tuktoyaktuk Mission, on the Arctic coast, loading the last of the personal baggage aboard the *Lady* for the Arctic trip. About nine-thirty that morning the Bishop and I had just left the warehouse for the boat with a box of altar linen for the Fathers when a young man came running toward us, waving a yellow paper.

"Here is a wire for you, Father," he panted. "Glad I caught you before you sailed."

I thanked him, tore open the telegram, and read:

YOUR BID FOR THE CAMP AT KITTIGAZUIT HAS BEEN HONORED BY THE CROWN ASSETS. PLEASE BE READY TO PLACE MEN IN CHARGE WITHIN FORTY-EIGHT HOURS. CONTROLLER OF CROWN ASSETS OTTAWA ONTARIO.

I must have looked a little pale. "Bad news?" the Bishop asked.

"No, Bishop. I believe it is very good news. You recall mentioning the hope of having that huge stack of lumber on the beach as we passed the Army camp at Kitty a few days ago? Well, read this." I handed him the wire.

Now I would have to tell the Bishop I had bid on the camp as a mere speculation, never dreaming it would fall into our lap for the paltry sum of twenty-five thousand dollars, when it was worth almost a quarter of a million! I learned why later. I had bid on the entire camp and not on just the items we could use immediately. This total sale saved the government thousands of dollars since it did not have to brochure the entire amount of supplies in order to put them on sale.

The Bishop looked very surprised and concerned. "How much did you bid? Two hundred thousand dollars? And why didn't you tell me about it the other day?" He was just a little excited.

"I didn't mention it when we passed the camp because I never dreamed my bid would be honored—and because you had enough other problems to worry about. Imagine, I bid only twenty-five thousand dollars for the entire camp, including the buildings!" The Bishop's face softened. He was very pleased and overwhelmed.

"That is what I call a real bargain. Let us go to the chapel and thank God. Believe me, I will throw in a special prayer for those Canadian and American Army people," he added, pointing toward Kitty.

Our trip on the Arctic coast with the *Lady of Lourdes* was postponed for a special trip to the Army camp. The Bishop placed Fathers Biname and Franche in charge with three Brothers and five laymen from our Aklavik mission, and the tremendous work of moving almost five hundred tons of supplies began. Father Franche loaded his schooner, returned to Tuktoyaktuk, and made the supply trip to the Arctic missions.

The Bishop asked me to assist Father Biname with the first loads of supplies and return to Fort Smith aboard the *Sant' Anna*. "I will meet you there in about three weeks," he said as the *Lady of Lourdes* chugged away, her hold and decks stacked with barrels of fuel oil and cases of supplies.

The purchase was a great boon to our missions, and because of this landslide we were able to enlarge the Immaculate Conception boarding school and build a warehouse at Aklavik, plus a church at Tuktoyaktuk. "Kitty" became a name of bounty all along the river, for the missionary Brothers received tools, a caterpillar tractor in two of the missions, a truck in one place, and two huge fork lifts in another. It took three years to distribute these varied effects, and even as this is written the tractors, fork lifts, and tools are still being used.

A day after our return to Aklavik with the first load of supplies I sailed south on the *Sant' Anna* and relaxed for the first time in over two years. Reverend Jean Colas was also aboard, Paris-bound after thirteen years at Arctic Red River Mission, some ninety miles south of Aklavik. Our spirits soared into holiday gear all the way south to Fort Smith, where the Bishop surprised us by his presence.

"I was just lucky to catch a plane going south from Coppermine," he beamed when he saw us. "We had zero weather there during the last three days. For a while I had visions of spending Christmas up there," he added, relighting his pipe.

Ever since I had left Aklavik, my curiosity kept nagging for news of just what was up that purple sleeve. Now he tipped his hand.

"I would like you to accompany me to Ottawa this year as my secretary," he began that evening after calling me to his room. "More and more the affairs of health and education between the government and our missions necessitate the writing of good English letters. Besides this, I would like you to lecture for vocations," he added in a very somber tone. "Many of our missionaries are getting too old to travel. We need young men who can stand both the rigors of the country and the many problems that are cropping up in these new settlements."

This was quite a change from the mission work at Aklavik, but the Bishop had both his reasons and the authority to place his men where he willed. Down deep I really felt that he wanted to get me away from the cold of the severe winters because of my tender rebuilt right hand, but he never alluded to it. We had a plane ride to Edmonton, and Father Colas accompanied us aboard the train for Ottawa.

The Bishop had to make a business stop in Toronto, and I decided to telephone home. Buffalo was just over the line and I wanted to surprise the folks.

"I have been trying to call you in Edmonton," Mother said. "There is a Monsignor Scheckelhoff trying to reach you from

Toledo, Ohio." She gave me his telephone number, and after a little news of home I called Toledo.

"You are a hard man to find," Monsignor's calm voice came over the telephone. Then he let go with a salvo: "Do you want an airplane for the missions?"

A plane! I was stunned. Before I could recover my mental balance he continued: "I am in charge of the Society for the Propagation of the Faith here, and a friend of mine by the name of Robert Lehman of Rising Sun, Ohio, saw your film on the missions and decided you could get more use out of his plane than he does. It is a four-place Aeronca sedan—perhaps a little small, but better than that dog team you have been mushing these past ten years. Well"—he hesitated a moment—"don't just stand there, say something!"

"I'm speechless, Monsignor! That is the best news I've heard in years. Just a minute until I talk with the Bishop. He happens to be right here." A few words with the Bishop, and I saw a new light come into his eyes.

"If you fly the plane and take care of it, tell Monsignor we will accept it."

"Bishop, it will be a pleasure to fly that plane for our missions." If he only knew how I loved to say those words!

"That's fine. I am happy that you accepted. It will not be easy. Now inform Monsignor Scheckelhoff that we will see him in a few weeks after my business in Ottawa." The Bishop motioned me toward the telephone.

"We will accept the plane, Monsignor. The Bishop and I will be coming to Toledo as soon as possible after the meeting of Canadian Bishops in Ottawa."

"Great news. I realize what a giant step this is for the Bishop. Welcome to Toledo! *Bon voyage* and God be with you," he concluded.

That telephone call opened new horizons for the Mackenzie. We continued on to Ottawa and I wrote letters and helped the Bishop, but everything seemed secondary now. My thoughts and dreams were of flying. With a short stop-off at Buffalo to relay the good news to my parents, we drove to Toledo and met Monsignor Raymond Scheckelhoff.

"Your Excellency, I feel God has blessed our work when such a great moment as this comes true," Monsignor began when he met the Bishop. "For these many years I have spent my priestly life always hoping for a great gift to appear from some understanding person. Two weeks ago I sent one of my assistants to show the film you gave us, 'Arctic Missions of the Mackenzie,' to a congregation in Rising Sun, Ohio, Father Allen McCartin, who spent his early missionary life among the Zulu tribes of South Africa. That's the story, your Excellency," Monsignor Ray concluded.

The Bishop expressed sincere thanks and asked about meeting Mr. Lehman. Monsignor Scheckelhoff arranged a meeting for us, at which the Bishop expressed his thanks, and I arranged a time when we could meet to transfer the ownership of the plane. The little Aeronca was in Florida at the time.

"The Jesuit Fathers supervise just about the best flying school in the country," Monsignor advised the Bishop. "It is Parks Air College of St. Louis University in East St. Louis, Illinois."

We discussed a few other details connected with the Air College, and that evening, at our Oblate house in Toledo, the Bishop agreed to send me to Parks. "You will be able to live at our Oblate house of St. Henry's in Belleville, which is just a few miles from the field," he concluded.

I wrote a letter to the dean at Parks, applying for admission in early November and requesting a reply at our university in Ottawa. The following day we motored to Toronto and spent the evening with the Oblate Fathers, who were overjoyed at the news.

On the way to Ottawa next day we discussed the future possibilities of reaching the people in the hidden recesses of the large Mackenzie Vicariate, and the Bishop predicted great things for our people now that we had a plane. We could fly the sick to our hospitals and the children from the hinterlands out to our schools.

In a week the reply came from Parks and the Bishop sent me to school with his blessing and advice. "Try to take a special course in navigation," he said, shaking my hand. "The North country has no roads or railroads to follow."

On the trip to Belleville I practically rode a magic carpet. The prospect of being able to help my brother missionaries conquer their most formidable adversary in that vast Arctic country—distance—was such a long-cherished dream. Now it was becoming a reality. I was trading my lead dog for a propeller!

"We will also give you a few nut-and-bolt courses that will come in mighty handy up in that polar-bear country." Father John Higgins smiled as he signed me in for classes at the Air College. "We

136

like all our graduates to become *old pilots*," the tall, rangy, white-haired Jesuit added.

That first day he walked me on a three-hour tour of the aeronautical school, and down at the hangar I met Roger Heald, my instructor. Slim but well knit, Roger had an air of definiteness and decision about him that gave me immediate confidence in his ability. Back at the office that day, I was also fortunate to meet Mr. Oliver Parks, who founded this college a few years before World War II. When he had the school organized he turned it over to the supervision of the Jesuit Fathers as the Air Annex to St. Louis University. Today Parks College sits on top of the totem pole, offering any course in aero technology.

After visiting the campus and seeing the various classes and machine-shop work ahead, I began to question my ability to absorb enough of this to qualify as a good pilot. Father Higgins must have guessed my thoughts, for he encouraged me that evening before I left for the Oblate house in Belleville. "After a week we will tell you whether or not you have the ability to become a good pilot. Co-ordination, good judgment, and especially faith in yourself will tell us the story. See you at eight tomorrow for meteorology class." He saluted and disappeared in a crowd of students.

Next morning I was at school, the first time in ten years. With labored efforts, that famous week passed. Any day I expected a call to the dean's office, politely telling me I should stick with a dog team if I wanted to live out my natural life. I felt as though I was not making too much progress. But two weeks passed, then three, and finally a month, and still no word.

My instructor took a weekend off, and we went to Florida and ferried the Aeronca back to Parks. The flight-line crew went over it and the civil aeronautics inspector, Thomas Harrington, one of the professors at Parks, stamped on the ready-to-fly label. In mid-February the weather cleared and I was called to the flight line to begin my actual flying.

Early in March, after a couple of circuits one clear day, Roger uttered those words every would-be pilot waits to hear: "You can leave me off here and continue to fly take-offs and landings until noon." And Roger Heald walked away from my plane and never looked back. I know he did it to give me confidence, and his psychology worked.

I flew in the morning and studied mechanics, navigation, meteorology, and radio in the afternoon. Sometimes I would fly at five in the morning, when the skies were clear of smog, and practice the maneuvers laid out by Roger Heald. During late March and April I did my cross-country exercises to get acquainted with navigation, and flew the Ozark hill and bush country, which is similiar to the North. It was strictly landmark contact flying and pinpoint map reading.

On May 10 I received a cable:

UNDERSTAND YOU ARE NOW A PILOT WITH A PLANE. WILL JOIN YOU FOR THE FLIGHT NORTH ABOUT THE END OF THIS MONTH. FATHER COLAS, PARIS, FRANCE.

That evening, like many others during those flight-training days, I spent with my dear friend of Fort Smith Army days, Bud Adkins. His charming wife, Ruth, and their son, Stephen, spent over two weeks sewing new wing and engine covers for my plane.

"I received good news today," I told Bud as soon as I entered his home. "Here is a wire from Father Colas in Paris, saying he will join me on the flight north."

"You see, Ruth"—Bud went over and put an arm about his wife, showing her the wire—"I told you someone would turn up to ride with Father. We were really worried about you making this trip alone. It will be your first long flight, and anything could happen," Bud said, returning the telegram. "Father Colas will be welcome here any time. Maybe he can teach Ruth some French," he laughed.

Father Colas arrived on May 25. Bud met him at the station and gave him a taste of American hospitality that Father will always remember. June 8 was D-day for me, and it came with jet speed. Bud and Ruth drove us to the airport, and the student body and faculty of Parks Air College gave us a send-off we could hear above the song of our little engine. They sang *Ave Maris Stella*, "Mary, Star of the Sea, guide them on their way."

Chapter Eight

Aircraft CF-GMC Red Aeronca sedan calling St. Louis tower. Check you leaving Air Traffic Control on flight plan to Ottumwa, Iowa, and points north. St. Louis out."

There are golden moments of happiness in our lives when the heart and soul enjoy the quiet peace of accomplishment. This was such a moment. When I replaced the microphone I glanced at my passenger, Father Colas. He grinned, a glow of pride in his dark eyes, and shouted in my ear: "This little fellow beats my dog team." He rubbed the instrument cowling caressingly.

Below us the yellow spring waters of the Missouri entered the wide gray Mississippi, and red earth fields of young corn sprouted green in the morning sun. Over Iowa and Minnesota we followed our maps, checked off the towns and rivers, and spent the night at Crookston, Minnesota. June 9 was another fair-weather day and we took off like a couple of veterans. At Pembina, North Dakota, we met the American Customs and flight-planned into Canada.

Our landing on busy Stevenson Field in Winnipeg was not exactly a three-pointer. I anticipated a little trouble with the twenty-mile-per-hour cross wind, and after a few bounces the plane pointed toward the grass mall off the black-top runway! My right-brake seal blew when I applied pressure, but luckily we did not ground-loop.

"Would you jump out and hang onto that right wing strut and guide me back on the runway to the Flying Club hangar?" I called into the ear of my passenger. Father Colas nodded while his right hand reached for the door handle.

"Leave your hat and glasses here. The wind may whip them off," I called to him as his feet touched the grass. That prairie breeze gave him quite a battle, sometimes lifting all of his one hundred and sixty pounds off the ground. He pushed, pulled, and did a good job of steering GMC down the taxi runway to the Flying Club.

"Well, well, what have we here?" a strange official voice came up behind us. "You fellows look like a couple of real sky pilots!" We turned and faced the Customs officer. "Where were you born, sir?"

"East Amherst, New York," I answered, reaching for my identification.

"And where are you going with this plane? It is a Canadian plane and you are an American pilot," he said, looking at the Canadian identification, CF-GMC.

"The aircraft was a donation to our Arctic missions and I'm flying it to our base at Edmonton. There I will take the Air Transport test for my Canadian pilot's license. If I pass, I intend to fly into the Mackenzie River country and use the plane there for mission work."

He nodded and seemed satisfied. "Are you bringing anything into Canada besides your personal gear?" he asked, looking into the plane.

"I have a box of cigars for the Bishop," Father Colas began in his Parisian brogue.

"And where were you born, sir?" the Customs officer asked, turning to Father Colas.

"Paris, monsieur."

"And how do you happen to be flying with this fellow?"

"I am an old-timer, almost a mossback in your country," Father went on with a twinkle in his eye. "I have lived in the Arctic for thirteen years and now I am returning North with Father Bill from a wonderful vacation. I guess we will be taking off soon now, eh?" he asked, hopefully probing the inspector.

"Are you really so anxious to fly North with this sky pilot, Father?" The inspector nudged Father Colas with his elbow. "I figured most of you fellows aim quite high to reach the Almighty with prayers for us poor beggars, but this is the first time I ever met a man of the cloth who dabbled in psalms and spark plugs." He laughed, pocketing his small memo pad.

"Well, so far I am still alive and we flew all the way from St. Louis," Father Jean said, pulling a box from his pocket. "I had to eat a few of these pills so I wouldn't become air-sick, but it was not his fault," he added, clamping his right hand on my shoulder.

Several people had gathered by this time and one interested mechanic questioned: "What happened out there on the runway, Father? Did you burn out a brake? I saw your passenger holding onto that right wing to keep your plane from weather-cocking." I told him he guessed right, and the mechanic grinned.

"That's pretty hard on a passenger's new shoes. Maybe you'd better roll your kite into the hangar, Father. I'll see what I can do for you."

Once again we were in Canada, the great majestic land of adventure where we both worked and lived. I know Father Colas also shared my feelings of elation for the birth of this day, the day we would fly North. And the kindness of this stranger, offering to patch up our mechanical difficulties, added the welcome atmosphere of neighborliness we needed on this air venture. That evening the Oblate Fathers of St. Boniface made us realize we were their brothers with real homelike hospitality.

A good rest and a prayer, coupled with fine weather, sent us buzzing over the prairies to Edmonton. Here I met my old friend of the Aklavik Flying Service, Mike Zubko. He was just leaving the Edmonton Flying Club hangar when we taxied up with CF-GMC. As soon as he recognized us, he ran over and hung onto a strut to help turn the plane into parking position.

"Not bad, not bad at all, Father," he began, slapping the nose cowl. "You're the last fellow I expected to see flying in here today. Why didn't you tell me you liked to fly when we were at Aklavik? I would have given you a few lessons."

I asked him to give me some lessons in float-flying and he agreed on a date. In a few days, with his help, we had GMC on floats out at Edmonton's marine base on Cooking Lake, twenty-five miles southeast of the city.

"Watch the nose come up," Mike directed, pointing toward the nose cowl and the horizon. "There will be two stages: the first when you pull back on the stick with full power, and the second, less noticeable, after you have reached a certain speed."

Mike also taught me the one-pontoon-at-a-time take-off with heavy loads. "You'll do this in warm still air when even the gulls are too lazy to make the effort to fly." He pointed toward an Arctic tern doing acrobatics overhead. "There's a kind of limit to just about everything, but most especially with a plane on floats," he insisted. "As soon as you learn the limitations of your ship and respect them, you will gain confidence in yourself and act with assurance. Experience in flying will be your best instructor. It will take time," he added seriously. "Just remember to give every flight the attention of a new adventure."

Satisfied, he signed my aircraft-journal logbook and wrote a letter to the Department of Air Transport of Canada attesting my competence to operate an aircraft on floats. I wanted the best checkout possible, because all my landings and take-offs would be on the great rivers and lakes of Canada's northland, and on the gulfs and inlets of the Arctic Ocean. Some navigation with our mission boats had given me a small idea of the treacherous sand bars and rocks camouflaged by the rolling muddy river water. Now these dangers were magnified, since it is almost impossible from the air to gauge the depth of muddy water. Knowledge and observation of the directional flow of a river, its currents, action of surface wind on the aircraft while maneuvering on floats—all must be studied and weighed before landing and taking off. A lot of this knowledge I pumped out of Mike and other seasoned pilots, and a good amount I learned, too, by jumping into the cold water and freeing the aircraft from sucking sand bars or hidden rocks. Mike also gave me some pointers on winter flying, the long engine-heating process with oversize plumber's blowpots, and the necessity of having a good-sized engine cover.

"I'll be seeing you down-river. If you have to sit down in some lake because of engine trouble, don't hesitate to call me, Father," Mike said, pushing the plane free of the dock.

His send-off was the hypo of confidence I needed on this first solo into the North. Of course I rubbed my rabbit's foot—in this case, a St. Christopher medal I have mounted on the instrument panel—and asked that patron of all travelers to keep a good eye on this novice cloud-hopper.

During that freshman year of my northern flying I know I put the fear of God in many of my missionary brothers. Frankly, I had more than the usual number of butterflies under my own safety belt.

Father Colas gave his place to Bishop Trocellier at Fort Smith, and we proceeded down-river. Instead of riding two days on a river boat and spending two hours visiting at each mission, the process was reversed. The Bishop could spend two or three days with his people instead of endless hours of riding on the river. At Good Hope, just under the rim of the Arctic Circle, big Brother Henry arrived the second day of our visit.

"Hello, Bishop! Blazen creek"—his pet expression—"this time you are visiting long enough for me to see you," the Brother puffed, kneeling in the grass to kiss the Bishop's ring. He had mounted the hill from the river, carrying a washtub half full of herring. "Usually when you come with the boat I come to town just in time to see you leave."

The Bishop introduced me to Brother. He grabbed my hand, sizing me up and down. "So you are an American! I saw the little red aircraft fly over, and from the news the Indians brought from the mission boat I figured it was the Bishop's plane."

Brother had been fishing some twenty miles upriver at the ramparts. He went on talking, telling the Bishop what a wonderful cache of fish he had, and as he spoke he bent over and began scooping the herring out onto the grass with his huge paddle-like hands. Father Robin, the white-bearded missionary of Good Hope, stood watching and laughing, happy to see Brother in high spirits.

When we reached Aklavik, Brother Beauchemin was on the riverbank to catch our anchor line. "You fellows will have to go on a diet if you expect to carry a passenger in the back seat of that little plane." He grinned, patting his well-rounded waistline. He is a stout, short fellow of over two hundred and twenty-five pounds, and he spoke the truth! At one of the river missions I had to leave all my personal baggage behind in order to take off on calm water with a full load of gasoline and no wind.

At Paulatuk, three hundred miles east of Aklavik, the Eskimos looked at our little plane with awe. Fathers Leonce and Andrew were so excited, they talked and visited with the Bishop and the people all night. I had a good rest, knowing that someone was up and about to keep an eye on the plane. Argo Bay was covered with ice floes, and the Bishop knew what quick changes could occur there in early September, so next morning back to Aklavik we flew, on to the south with the ducks and geese. I was back on the river again with the contented feeling of accomplishment, but the Creator of angels has His way of plucking the feathers of pride from a fellow. "You will learn by flying," Mike Zubko had said, and it was the truth.

There was about a twenty-mile-an-hour cross wind when I approached Arctic Red River for a landing. I tried to practice what my instructor had taught me, but the plane just fell away, about six feet above the water, and I bounced like a rubber ball.

"You fly like a molting duck, Father," Jerome Bernard shouted at me with his gravel voice as he jumped down the bank, almost crushing my hand in a greeting.

"Nice to see you again, Joe. You look well and fat too. Did you have a good trapping year?" I asked when we were anchored and the Bishop was surrounded by his people.

"No, Father." Joe hung his head. "The wolves ate over half of my marten and the early snow buried a lot of my traps just after I had them set. . . . Hard place to land when the wind blows off those high banks." He pointed and blushed a little at the ribbing he had dished out.

Jerome (or Joe as he is called) is a Loucheux, or squint-eyed Indian, from Arctic Red River, and one of the best trappers around. I learned to know him from his visits to Aklavik when he came to the school for his children. Joe is a solid citizen, with the Faith in every pound of him. When Father Levesque, the missionary of Arctic Red, needed a bodyguard, or a cord of wood carried up to his house, he knew where to find a man.

On September 7 I was flying supplies, personnel, and gear from Fort Norman on the Mackenzie to Fort Franklin, sixty-five miles east on Great Bear Lake. Cold, raw autumn weather and an occasional snow squall reminded us there was no time to lose. About twenty minutes out of Franklin on the fourth and last trip of the day my engine began to roughen up. I began a one-hundred-and-eighty-degree turn to go back to Franklin, but loss of power made me decide to pick a lake quickly. I chose one, checked wind direction, let the engine idle, and glided in for a landing. A little added power on the missing engine helped to clear the rocks on the lake shore, and we touched the water.

"Thank God," I said for both of us. Father Bernard Brown was my passenger on that trip, on his way to Norman and points south.

We climbed out on the floats and worked the plane to the east shore of the lake with our paddles. It looked free of rocks, and a patch of dark slender pines on the north shoreline gave promise of a campsite, in case we needed it.

Some fifteen feet from the shore we ran aground and I decided to have a look at the engine. Perhaps just a spark-plug wire had worked loose. Some oil had come up through the engine breather and greased up the fire wall a bit. Other than that, the engine looked normal and I found nothing loose or dangling. With the ignition off, I cranked the engine slowly with the propeller to judge the compression and any unusual noises or clangings. It cranked too easily, felt like an open valve. The spark plugs had to come out and each cylinder tested for compression.

With the tubular spark-plug wrench aboard I tried to loosen a plug. It was very tight. I applied more pressure and crack! That did it. The wrench split wide open! Now we *were* here for the night. How could I remove the plugs with a broken wrench? None of the other wrenches I had would fit.

"Guess we will have to do the Boy Scout act and camp out tonight," Father Brown began, eying the broken wrench.

We took off our shoes and trousers and gently let ourselves down into the cool water. The plane, minus our four hundred pounds, lifted free of the sand, and we towed it ashore. Father Bernard Brown, a fellow American, was beginning his third winter in the North. He had youth, a good physique, and a keen scent for adventure, so I handed him our .22 rifle and added:

"After a winter at Franklin, you should know a few friendly ptarmigan in these parts." Only a half hour of daylight remained at 6 p.m. this time of the year here near Fort Franklin, so Father went off, stretching his long legs toward a clump of spruce half a mile to the north. "I will have a fire going to give you a homing beacon," I called after him.

A few large boulders along the shore made solid tying hooks for the two mooring lines I ran from the wing struts.

This was the Bear River country, a hundred miles south of the Arctic Circle. Twenty minutes' flying out of Franklin en route to Norman should place us about ten miles north of the famous and fast Bear River. As a last desperate measure, walking was possible, but first there was my little radio. Perhaps the Norman station, which usually closes at 6 p.m., was remaining open tonight since we did not arrive according to our flight plan. Back in the aircraft, I started a radio transmission:

"*Aircraft CF-GMC—Aeronca sedan calling Fort Norman . . . Engine trouble. Down on small lake twenty-five miles west of Franklin, ten miles north of the Bear River. Father Brown with me. Landed safely. Here for the night. Need a spark-plug wrench for a C-145 Continental engine. Any station receiving this message, please relay it to United Aviation—Edmonton. Please advise Bishop at Fort Norman of our position.*"

I sent this message out five times from about six-fifteen to seven forty-five and then gave my battery a rest for later in the evening. Darkness came on rapidly under the umbrella of gray overcast, so I hustled to light a campfire. Fortunately I had kept the aluminum cooking utensils from my ration kit, most of which I had given to the Arctic coast missionaries. This was a regrettable mistake and it taught me a valuable lesson. Since then I have never left my ration box behind, regardless of the priority of pay load or passengers. With the larger kettle I strained the lake bugs out of a bucket of water and set it on the fire to boil. A dusky evening fog was rolling in over the small lake and the muskegs when Father Brown returned, holding up a small mangy-looking red squirrel.

"Quite a soupbone I have here," he quipped. "It's all I saw!"

We skinned the squirrel with care and let the kettle of boiling water take over. This was a first for both of us as far as squirrel soup was concerned. It quieted our rumblings of hunger but had a little dry taste, like soup made from dog bones. We promised never to grumble about Heinz 57, or Campbell's, or Brother Henry's soup again!

The weather was damp and, not having a tent, we removed the seats from the plane and spread our parkas on the floor for a mattress. Fortunately we had Father's sleeping bag. I had foolishly left mine behind at Norman to carry a bigger load of supplies for Father Philippe at Franklin.

At nine o'clock I began sending the message for help twice each hour, until eleven. I listened after each sending, covering my entire receiver band, but there was just the lapping of the water against the floats.

Father Bernard pulled out a rosary from one of his pockets and fingered it. "Let's beam this on St. Christopher's frequency. Certainly he should be able to stir up a little activity and point someone in our direction." We prayed our Hail Marys, and then said good night to each other, but I couldn't sleep.

Perplexed thoughts and Father Brown's snoring kept me awake for a long time. Did my message get through to Norman? How would the Bishop understand all this? Would he conclude that I was too inexperienced and unqualified, that I was jeopardizing the lives of our missionaries? Then I remembered the counsel of my professor *pratique:* "When you feel on the blue side and discouraged, just ask yourself this question: 'What would Christ do if He were in my place?' and you will receive consolation, new hope, and the right answer to your problem. Worry never solves problems, but a few well-said prayers might do the trick."

Sleep must have finally overtaken me, because the next thing I heard was the tattoo of rain on the cabin roof and a husky voice coming from the depths of the eiderdown: "Morning, Father Bill. Raining, eh?" My passenger jacked himself up and had a look outside.

We talked about the Mass we could not say on this September 8, the great Feast of the Lady Mary. It was also the birthday anniversary of the Oblates, a special day when most of us had pronounced our first and final vows. In keeping with such a great day, while the morning drizzle sprinkled itself out we said our Rosary and added a few trimmings with our Divine Office.

About seven o'clock we climbed out of the plane, had a good stretch, and tried to pick dry footing over the damp moss to the camp. The light drizzle and a very low ceiling did not help to liven our spirits. Trees and bushes dripped and sent us hunting for dry wood. Dry shavings were our only hope to get a fire going. Usually there were dead dry branches at the base of live spruce trees, but not this morning.

"We're lucky this isn't sleet." Father Bernard came back with a bone-dry stick. "Back in Rochester we have sleet storms about this time of the year. I have seen a half inch of ice snap power lines and take the branches off trees. Sleet could pack a half ton of ice on GMC in a few minutes," he continued, cutting a heap of dry shavings.

Fortunately the temperature remained about four degrees above freezing, just cool and damp enough to make the morning fire feel good. Having no bacon or eggs handy, we crushed the small leftover supper bones on a rock and enjoyed a squirrel-broth breakfast. Father Brown must have felt the pinch of hunger from the previous evening, because he picked up the rifle right after breakfast and loaded up with shells.

"I'll be back on the double if I hear the plane," he said over his shoulder, and took off into the bush.

I remained at the campsite, cut a few trees—mostly to keep busy—and spread more pine boughs before the fire.

At last I heard a plane! It was now half-past ten in the morning. The sound died away for more than ten minutes, then returned. But this time it seemed farther away. It was flying low, hunting for the spot or trying to do a let-down through the overcast. I ran to the plane and gave a shout on my radio so the pilot could get a fix on our exact position. About ten minutes later Father Bernard came running from the bush, pointing toward the sky.

"There it is, coming right for us." I was just able to recognize

147

it as an RCAF Mitchell from the Search and Rescue Division of Edmonton as the big plane roared about fifty feet over us. Thank you, St. Christopher, I prayed with a lighter heart. We were found! I climbed back into the plane, switched on my radio, and called: "GMC Aeronca sedan to orbiting aircraft. Need wrench for spark plug in C-145 Continental aircraft engine." I repeated the message four times, then turned off my radio and went out to see what was going to happen. The plane was coming in very low again, but more to the east of us, over a patch of yellow caribou moss. Down came a ten-gallon keg of gasoline. It hit the frozen muskeg and burst, sending up a spray of moss and gasoline. The keg hit a "hard head." Most of this moss was two feet deep, but a few boulders showed their bald heads, and they picked one!

The second and third kegs dropped and rolled free. They were taking it for granted that we were out of gasoline, but I still had one full tank of gas! Then another orbit, and another small object dropped with a yellow streamer attached. Father Brown ran over for it, and there was our spark-plug wrench. Again on the radio, I thanked those chaps and asked them if they had anything aboard that resembled food.

The plane orbited again and again and finally dropped a small package and a flare can, inside of which was a message: "Returning to our base at Norman Wells. Will stand by until your arrival at Norman." On one last orbit the pilot waved and they were off. Our hopes rode high! We broke open the mystery box. Whatever it was, it was hard! Father tried to bite into the blocks—they were like cement! "Oatmeal," he said. "Condensed oatmeal blocks."

We would have to cook them. But food was secondary now that I had a wrench. I went to work on the engine and before long had most of the spark plugs out. They were not burned or too dirty. While Father Brown slowly turned the propeller, I tested each cylinder for compression by placing my thumb in each spark-plug hole. Then we found the culprit. Number-five cylinder had no compression whatsoever.

"Let's work on those blocks of cement they dropped us," Father Brown began, rubbing his empty, growling stomach. "We can discuss all this over a campfire. I'm cold."

The fire was blazing and our pot was about to boil when again that heavenly music came out of the west. A plane! It was about twelve-thirty. As soon as we saw it we recognized the Eldorado Norseman with my old friend Al Caywood at the controls. After one observation orbit of the lake, down came the flaps, and the silver Norseman landed and taxied toward us. Some fifty yards from shore, Al ran aground and cut the engine. The co-pilot cockpit door opened.

"Anything we can do, Father?" It was Glenn McPherson, the chief mechanic of Eldorado Airlines, whom I remembered meeting at Cooking Lake when I put GMC on floats.

"Number-five cylinder has no compression," I called back.

We heard Al and Glenn talking, then they climbed down on the float and proceeded to take off their trousers. "I'll bring my tool kit and we'll make a check on that cylinder," Glenn called, taking off his shoes and socks.

Al Caywood reached us first. "This water is a little cool for wading," he began, his teeth chattering, as I gave him a hand up onto our float. "We picked up your chatter with that rescue plane this morning, Father, and since we were coming so near on our way to Beaver Lodge I decided to fly over and see if we could be of some help."

Glenn came with the heavy steel tool box on his shoulder, and without any preliminaries he had his hands and his nose in the engine like a hungry pup in a food bowl.

"It could be just a frozen valve and you'd better say a little prayer it is, Father. We could find serious trouble here." He rubbed his chin with the back of a greasy hand.

I had a catch-all canvas—our engine cover—stretched across the pontoons beneath the engine, just in case a nut or wrench slipped. It would save time fishing for them in that cold water.

"Did I hear you say you were on your way to Beaver Lodge?" Father Brown asked Al.

"Yes, we are, Father," Al answered. "You are welcome aboard. We're flying empty."

Father expressed his thanks and asked me if I would mind being left alone. When I assured him it was easier to feed one man than two, and less difficult taking off from that small lake without a passenger, he climbed into the plane and packed his gear.

"I wish I had more time to help you, Father," Al began, "but we have a long flight ahead before darkness sets in. Suppose we leave Glenn's tool kit with you. When you have located the trouble, just send word out on your radio. Your transmitter is working well. Someone will pick up the message and relay it for you.

I'll be back up this way in a couple of days, and if the fellows at the Bear River portage camp don't report you flying out, I'll be in to see you."

That sounded real solid to me, so I gave Father Bernard a hand with his bags. They all waded out to the Norseman, Father Brown following with his trousers and shoes piled high on his knapsack.

"Send a wire to the Bishop," I called. "Tell him not to worry, that I will be in Fort Norman in a few days." Father nodded and climbed aboard.

I watched their plane take off and streak southwest. I felt secure realizing the Air Force was standing by and that Al would return if I was unable to repair the engine. I took one last look at the plane, just a speck in the distance, and then the idea of food hit me like a heavy hammer. They must have had some grub aboard.

It was just two-thirty in the afternoon, a little late to start on the engine, but time enough for a short hunt. I anchored the plane with more rope from the wing struts to large rocks on shore in case of a sudden squall. Any weather can break suddenly in September. Back at the campsite I found our pot of cement blocks melted, and the oatmeal lunch gave me a send-off with the .22 rifle.

Bear River country is on the fringe of the Barren Lands, and that afternoon it kept its reputation. There was not a sign of life except for the odd flock of crane and geese flying south high overhead. A light drizzle began around five o'clock and I returned to the campfire to soften more of the oatmeal blocks for supper.

I retired into the plane early, while I had the light of day to say my Office. *Give us this day our daily bread* had special meaning that evening. I prayed with hope that some Indian hunting party would be along from either Norman or Franklin with a spare chunk of caribou meat in their packs.

Suddenly the howl of a wolf stiffened me alert! Slowly I raised my head, feeling for my rifle. He must be only a few yards from the plane—probably smelled the campfire! I strained my eyes, but none of the shapes along the shore moved. I watched for fifteen minutes, but there were no more sounds or movement.

Before deep sleep came I half dreamed about those early days and the men who made this part of the country history. Little Fort Franklin was built by George Back and Peter Dease in 1826, the headquarters of Sir John Franklin's expedition, searching for the Northwest Passage and exploring the Arctic coast line. When this entire company of one hundred and five souls were lost, rescue parties looked ten years, spending over four million dollars, before Dr. John Rae learned of their fate from the Eskimos of Pelly Bay in 1854. Searching parties explored the entire Arctic and new maps were made.

Among the adventurers at the turn of the century was Father Petitot, a gifted man who could put his thoughts on canvas or translate them into the language of the Indians. Possessing a gay personality, he made friends quickly, loved traveling, and drew accurate maps of all his voyages. His map of Bear Lake was in use until the air maps were made.

Thinking of this lake, my empty stomach grumbled for one of its tasty trout. Now I knew it was hunger and not worry that was keeping me awake, stimulating my imagination. I imagined Bear Lake was the footprint left by a prehistoric monster as he pushed up mountains of rock on the lake shore. Around its five great arms, forty rivers fed this tenth largest lake in the world. Yet only one eighty-mile-long river is the spillway for this 11,170-square-mile reservoir into the Mackenzie.

My next recollection was of being cold. I tried to snuggle by pulling up my knees in the sleeping bag. Five o'clock, my watch read! I must have slept. It was still dark. Focusing my eyes, I saw frost on the inside of the windows and opened the door a crack. Ice had tatted a lace collar on the pontoons and along the shoreline. Now I saw the stars winking down at me from a very deep blue morning sky.

Hungry and cold, I dressed and sauntered over to the camp-site. A fire would feel good. The wet and frozen wood tested my patience, but after twenty minutes I had a fire for good company. I kept my rifle ready in case some early-rising spruce hen decided to investigate the extraordinary movements around there.

The bush country was stiff that morning, and trees creaked with frost-tightened muscles. While I stood warming my back, I thought about the big day that lay ahead. What would I find in that cylinder? Could I repair it? When the fire came really alive and began to radiate heat, I went to the lake and cracked the thin ice for water.

Walking back to the fire, I could almost smell camp coffee coming to a quick boil and running down the sides of the can. But I had to make do with oatmeal blocks! They weren't bacon and eggs, but they were better than straight water. The previous evening I had chipped a tooth in my efforts to gnaw off a few bites for supper.

With my hunting knife I pared away at the blocks but eventually pounded the oatmeal to a pulp on the rocks with my trail ax. Added to the boiling yellow muskeg water, they tasted more like pussy-willow buds than porridge.

I tried to keep alert for the slightest movement, hoping that game of any kind would come around for a visit. An odd flock of black ducks went overhead, and my mouth watered as I thought of the juicy mallards we roast on the open fire during the fall duck hunt down Chipewyan way. But whenever I began to feel sorry for myself my thoughts always returned to those poor Indians. This was their life. Certainly they must have discouraging moments too, when starvation and sickness visit their camps. I was not ill and I had oatmeal blocks. This must be God's way of giving me a more realistic picture of their poverty.

In a short morning prayer, while returning to the plane, I asked the Chief Pilot of us all to make the Bishop understand that this was not directly my fault. "Work is a blessing," he often said to the Brothers. Now I tried it for size. First of all, I made a kind of platform with poles under the engine by sinking two of the gas kegs for a foundation. With this I could reach deep into the engine and work freely.

It took two hours to skin down the engine of exhaust stacks and other accessories before I could get at the cylinder itself. About one-thirty I removed the cylinder, slowly uncovering the piston. There it was! A hole the size of a half dollar right through the piston head. Compression? It had burned through and even cut into the aluminum behind the top piston ring.

What had caused this? Overwork? Gasoline? The gas I used had been refined at Norman Wells that very summer. I had not overworked the engine, nor had I run it short on oil. Perhaps the ignition? A spark plug on one side of the cylinder could have been missing. This would have placed all the load on one plug and could have caused the damage.

Normally, on all aircraft engines, there are two spark plugs to each cylinder, one on each side of the piston head. I took the serial numbers from the piston and cylinder, since the inside was badly scorched, too, and decided to order the entire assembly.

Back on the radio, I wired out, hoping that the same fellow who had intercepted my message would have his receiver open today. "Aircraft CF-GMC on forced landing north of Bear River twenty miles out of Franklin. Need number-five piston and cylinder for a C-145 Continental engine. Please contact United Aviation Edmonton." This message went out on the hour until 5 P.M.

I had been tinkering on the engine since eight that morning, with two drinks of soup at noon, so I beat it off into the bush with my rifle and an anxious eye for game. Twenty minutes away I heard the chirp of a squirrel. Slowly I turned in his direction. He stood on his hind legs, rubbing his forepaws, a foot away from a small jackpine. I raised the rifle, but missed him. He was off like a shot from one tree to another, and I after him. The moss was almost two feet deep in the bush and I began to puff and heave like an old brewery horse.

At the edge of a spruce growth I found my squirrel up a lone scrub pine, and my next shot brought him down. Without delay I was back at the campsite skinning my catch for the pot. He was a fat little beggar and even smelled good raw! I separated the hindquarters for breakfast and dropped the rest in the pot. While it cooked, I watched for more game. Geese flew over very high, but nothing else. Slowly I drank the squirrel stew-soup. It was delicious and pine-scented, giving me a warm feeling. Jerome Bernard, my Loucheux Indian friend from Arctic Red River, told me he lived for weeks on these little "red devils." Now I began to believe him. "When I get sick of the pine taste," he said, "I just cut up a muskrat or a piece of fox meat. It tastes like a real Arctic mulligan, Father." Well, if Joe could live on squirrel soup, so could I, and there must be some muskrats around the lake too. Tomorrow I would look into that.

Aboard the plane, I sent out more calls, giving the numbers and parts I needed, all the while keeping my rifle handy in case some duck decided to land nearby. The lake was very shallow and too small for fish, as I had discovered the first day. Usually fish is a good stand-by when caribou and small game are scarce. I started my evening Rosary with the best of intentions, but the angels had to finish it. I fell asleep.

September 10 was a clear day with the sun just painting a smudge of rouge on the lip of the horizon when I awoke. While getting dressed, I said morning prayers and wandered over to the campsite and started a fire. The hindquarters of the squirrel were dry and black, but they softened in the boiling water and added a special flavor to the last oatmeal block. It was quiet and the smoke spiraled that morning—just the right atmosphere for a moose or caribou to walk out into the clearing. But I saw nothing after standing a full hour like a statue near a tree.

Back at the plane, I lay the gun handy, checked and cleaned the magnetos, and removed the spark plugs on the other cylinders and cleaned them. I drained the oil into a gasoline keg and washed out the crankcase to make certain no bits of metal remained. Next I drained all the gas from the left-wing tank and cleaned the gas pump and all the lines.

About one-thirty I made another fire, warmed up some "light squirrel soup," and was just about to have my dinner when out of the west came the drone of a plane. In a few minutes I saw it flying low and recognized it as the Canadian Pacific Norseman. After one orbit it landed and taxied toward GMC. I waded out, waving the pilot to stop because of the shallow water. He did. It was Captain Stew Hill of Norman Wells.

"Climb aboard, Father," he shouted, giving me a hand. "I came as soon as we received the package," he continued, climbing back into his plane over the baggage. He told me that Moe Lynn at Fort Wrigley, one hundred and twenty miles south of Norman, had received my first message and relayed it to Edmonton. The Royal Canadian Air Force rescue plane was the result. And Mr. Lynn again picked up my message about the broken cylinder and relayed it to United Aviation in Edmonton.

Archie McMullan, a Canadian Pacific Airlines pilot, told Stew this morning that Phil Brochu of United Aviation had removed a cylinder from a similar engine the previous evening and had taken it to the airport after ten o'clock that night in order to make the weekly flight north to Norman Wells this morning. The DC-3 landed just after twelve at the Wells, and Stew took off as soon as the mail and parcels for Norman were aboard his ship. Stew was digging away at the baggage. "Phil flew a few miles up in this country, Father, and he knew how anxious you were for that cylinder." He handed me the package.

"Well, Father, I must get along," he began in his usual business-like manner. "If you run into any snags, just give Moe Lynn a call and I'll be in to give you a hand."

I turned the Norseman manually by the floats, pointing it down the lake for a take-off. The engine coughed, came to life, and then Stew was away for Norman with the mail, dipping his wings in a final salute. As I watched the plane the thought of food hit me again. He must have had at least a candy bar aboard! Receiving those spare parts had made me too excited to think of food at that moment. I hurried to my plane, unwrapping the precious cylinder. A note from Phil Brochu expressed his regret on my forced landing and offered any possible help. In fifteen minutes I was fitting the new piston and cylinder in place. It was a slow process there over the water and my hands were red, stiff, and clumsy from the cold. By five-thirty I had the cylinder back on the engine and replaced the manifold and other parts. A half hour later I saw the chance of getting into Norman that evening, so I quickly gathered all my gear aboard and made preparations to test the new piston.

I primed the engine by cranking it with the propeller and then turned on the switch. Asking Our Lady of the Airways to make everything right, I swung the prop. It sparked into life on all six cylinders.

Aboard the plane, I let it warm up slowly, watching the instruments until every one responded normally, then gave it the check list. Everything functioned as it should. I cut the switches, checked the engine for possible oil leaks, tailed the plane about, and climbed aboard. Evening was running into night. A light drizzle began to roll off my windshield and darkness was settling over the country when I eased the throttle ahead and GMC moved forward. Her motor had a clean, compact, sweet sound.

With a short prayer to St. Christopher I set the flaps, did a take-off cockpit check on the short taxi downwind, turned, lifted water rudders, and poured on full throttle for take-off. GMC was on the step in less than a minute, and the floats broke from the water with a few hundred yards to spare. It felt good to be in the air again.

Twenty minutes off the lake, I saw the radio tower lights of Fort Norman! They looked so alive and comforting. Flying over Mount Charles, I noticed the blinking lights of the portage village on Bear River, and ten minutes later I was over Fort Norman on the Mackenzie River. My landing lights picked out the channel on the dark rippling water, and then the floats were clucking the waves. It was after six o'clock, so I knew the radio station was closed and decided to call in and see the fellows later that evening.

I taxied into Bear River for overnight moorings and drove toward shore. Several barges and a tug were anchored in the river, and the odors of cooking food smelled so good. I found a solid embedded tree for anchorage high on the shore and tethered GMC for the night. The bank is a few hundred feet high on the Norman side of Bear River, and that evening it seemed as though I were climbing Mount Everest. Nearing the mission, I spotted the Bishop through the window as he sat at the familiar little table saying his Office. When I opened the door he jumped from his chair in surprise and threw his arms around me. Bishop Joseph Trocellier was a big man with an even bigger heart, and the joy of his goodness spilled out in tears as he welcomed me home. I slipped into the chapel to thank God for being alive and also for having a most understanding Superior.

"Come into the kitchen," the Bishop said, taking me by the arm, "and I'll cook you something. You must be hungry."

Brother Medard, one of the famous Latreille brothers, welcomed me to his kitchen domain. "I have soup, *en masse*. Come sit here by the stove where it is warm, Father." He pulled out a box.

I had to give a play-by-play account of everything. The Bishop was at the stove, cooking with Brother, and between them they turned out the best-tasting dishes I have ever eaten. That caribou steak with good carrots and mealy potatoes—it was a feast!

Our Bishop was a practical man with vast experience in the North. He realized how the inevitable will happen, especially when we are a little off our guard.

Never again did I fly the Arctic without a complete tool kit and my emergency rations. I was learning by experience. Before retiring that evening I entered this cryptic log in my flight journal:

Flight log on Aircraft CF-GMC September 10, 1951. Fort Norman, N.W.T. Landed here at 7 P.M. in light rain from Fort Franklin after a three-day delay on small lake with engine trouble. Note: Squirrel soup is bitter! P.S. Always carry rations and tent.

Chapter Nine

THE Bishop had only a taste of the advantages of a plane that summer of '51, but it was enough to convince him that flying was the answer to transportation in his million-square-mile vicariate.

"A larger aircraft is needed that will carry at least fifteen hundred pounds of supplies or six passengers," he suggested to his council back at Fort Smith. Then he explained how delighted his missionaries were in those far outposts when he could spend at least a few days with them and how they appreciated even five pounds of potatoes! Without hesitation the suggestion was accepted. GMC was put on the auction block and a larger plane was purchased. Fortunately we found a used Norseman that fitted our budget, and I arranged to have it flown to Parks Air College in East St. Louis.

The plane was in good condition, except that it needed a good three-bladed propeller to get it off the water on floats with a heavy load. Remembering a dear friend who had been a pilot in his younger days, I made a quick trip to New York City and rapped at the door of Cardinal Spellman.

"How much does such a constant-speed propeller cost?" he asked, smiling, after listening to my plea in his usual calm manner.

When I explained that I had located one in Texas for a thousand dollars, he uncorked his pen and wrote, saying: "I hope this will carry you and all your passengers safely over millions of miles of those Arctic wastes. Be a good priest is all I ask," he added, handing me the check with his blessing.

Back at Parks, I worked once again with my instructor, Roger Heald, learning the maneuverability and mechanics of this larger plane. During January of 1952 the new identification letters, CF-GTM were assigned by the Department of Air Transport in Ottawa, and with the aid of Parks' best shop men, a complete inspection check was carried out on the ship. The students even

157

waxed the plane, and its bright orange and blue trim sparkled like new when I flew it off the field, bound for Edmonton in late February. Engineers at United Aviation in Edmonton replaced my wheels with skis and put a winter front on the engine while I untangled the web of red tape wrapped around an imported used aircraft by Department of Air Transport regulations.

Then came that memorable Saturday, March 8, a day of high adventure, rifle-quick decision—and sobering humility. Brother Charest met me at the chapel door after Mass with a telegram.

HOPE WE CAN EXPECT YOU SOON TO FLY BUFFALO MEAT TO RESOLU-
TION. HOSPITAL AND SCHOOL ON FISH DIET FOR PAST THREE WEEKS
BISHOP TROCELLIER.

For several days Edmonton had had snow squalls and foul weather. Even the day Captain Bert Birch of Canadian Pacific Airlines gave me a checkout on skis, we had a ceiling of only seven hundred feet. I pocketed the telegram and called the airport for weather along the Edmonton, McMurray, and Fort Smith route.

"We have a storm center, just over Lesser Slave Lake, that is throwing showers of snow over McMurray and Embarras Portage," came the voice over the receiver, "but there is a possibility of clearing by noon. Give me a call around eleven o'clock, Father."

At breakfast I alerted my three passengers. Brother Michael Dabrowski, a hard-working veteran of twenty years in the North with the endurance of a saint, and a man with hands that fit a thousand tools; Brother Antoine Petrin, another man of the North for over two decades, who also could wear the badge of many trades; and last the novice, Brother John Dougherty, a gangling six-footer on his first adventure. The first two men were returning after a medical checkup in the East. All three promised to be ready by noon, and Brother John came along with me to load the aircraft.

First we picked up a heap of sundry small packages which had accumulated for the missions all the way to Aklavik since freeze-up. Then we loaded four fifty-pound tins of dry milk, some electric wire, one case of celery, and one case of lettuce.

On the previous day, Friday, after a thorough radio check and full wing tanks of gasoline, I had taxied to a grass take-off strip on the south side of the airport in front of the Royal Canadian Air Force hangar—the assigned spot for ski-equipped planes. I had refilled the wing tanks and was assured that this was an ample supply of gasoline for a Norseman to fly to McMurray. I had a 105-gallon belly tank and was advised to leave it empty, that there was plenty of fuel at McMurray. GTM was ready for her maiden voyage North.

Later in the morning the weather office gave me a ceiling of three thousand feet at McMurray and v.f.r. (visual flight rules) clearance to make the flight. Father Fournier drove us to the airport, and by 1 P.M. we were all aboard, with a lunch box for Brother John from the Sisters.

"His first flight and all, you know, Father," Sister Superior said with motherly concern.

I started the engine, let it warm up, then tried my radio to reach the airport tower for taxi clearance. I tried several times, but there was no reply! It was hard to understand. The radio had been inspected and tested the day before, and for a minute I thought of going across the field and calling a technician to check it. But time was of the essence now. If I delayed an hour I would have to cancel the flight. Wires had been sent and all was ready. I looked at the tower and saw a green light flashing, and naturally figured it was for me and that they had heard my call. Must be a loose tube or some loose connection in my receiver, I thought. This could be quickly repaired in McMurray.

My bold decision was made. I pushed the throttle forward. The snow was new and very sticky. We barely moved with full power. I taxied the full length of the field and returned to take-off position to pack the snow. After a run-up and magneto check I "poured on the coal," and the Wasp strained every muscle of her six hundred horses to get us up to flying speed and off that sticky runway. I held the plane low to gain speed, it took fifteen minutes to reach our four-thousand-feet altitude. Brother Mike smiled when I trimmed the plane for level flight. The ceiling was unlimited and the wind only ten miles an hour from the northwest, so I breathed a little easier.

Over Lac la Biche, after an hour's flight, the radio trouble nagged me again. I turned it on, manipulated all the switches, but no luck. This was the halfway mark to McMurray, and twenty-five miles farther, over the settlement of Wandering River, I switched to my second wing tank of gasoline. Brother Mike kept a constant check on the gas gauge, now under his wing. I was tempted to follow a seat-of-the-pants direction along the railroad rather than my compass over that heavy-timbered country, but the warning gremlin of my instructor kept a steady tattoo in my ear: *Whatever you do, keep on course despite what you think. After half an hour or so, if you don't find check points on your route, do a 180-degree return to your base.* In half an hour, however, we saw the windings of the Christina River, and at two forty-five I could see the low hills on the south side of Anzac, some thirty miles from McMurray. It looked as though the first leg of our flight would soon be history, when Brother Mike bellowed in my ear, pointing at the same time to the northwest: "There's a fog coming."

It did look like fog, but I knew it was heavy snow. We had been flying through very light snow for the last few minutes, but Brother Mike was not accustomed to seeing snow while in an aircraft and did not notice it. We cleared the hills to the flat country west of McGregor Lake, and the full fury of the storm was upon us. I let down to about a hundred feet over the muskeg country and could barely see the treetops! My engine began to run a little rough, and I immediately closed the carburetor heat shutters. Snow had built up on a fine screen over the air scoop and was slowly closing it. We flew on course for a few minutes, but the storm grew worse. Brother Mike touched my arm and measured with his fingers that we had three inches of gas left in the tank. The snow was causing me to use a very rich mixture, but we had enough for a good forty-five minutes of flying. Then I thought of those McMurray hills and our low altitude. My forward vision was zero! There was just one course of action: land on the first clear prairie. I could not risk the lives of these men, even though we couldn't be more than ten miles away from McMurray. There it was—an all-white prairie sliding beneath us! I flew the length of it, orbited, and took a downwind run. It looked good.

"We will land here, Brother," I said in his ear. "I can't take a chance on this storm."

Turning on the upwind landing leg, I eased off on power and touched down. It was like landing on foam, so soft that my passengers did not realize we were on the ground until I taxied to the edge of the bush in snow three feet deep. When the engine died, we heard the roar and whine of the storm. It rocked the ship!

"Thank God we are on the ground," Brother John called from his seat in the tail of the plane. "I was dog-sick. Did you order this up special to initiate me into this North country, Father?"

"No, Brother, but you have a brilliant idea there. I'm sure it was ordered by God to give me a second initiation into this country!"

I tried the radio again, but it was dead. We checked the power terminals and other connections and found all seemingly intact and tight. In the meantime it was getting cold inside the ship and the storm seemed to be getting worse. Certainly we had to remain at least overnight, and in that case there was just one course of action. The thick green spruce shelter a hundred yards ahead of us gave me a warm feeling. Thank God the passengers were safe and the plane was undamaged. Slowly tension released its grip.

"We will make camp here at least for tonight," I told my passengers. "Before you leave the plane make certain you have on all your storm gear and just move slowly. We have plenty of time."

Brother Mike helped to cover the engine. His leg was stiff from arthritis and he limped, but never complained. I cut a trail into the spruce. It was a relief to find shelter from the cold wind, and in a few minutes I had a fire going. Brother Dougherty was a tenderfoot and Brother Petrin was just recovering from illness, so I asked both of them to remain aboard the plane until Brother Mike and I made camp. We used one of the wing covers for a tent and tied it down with quarter-inch manila rope. Silently I thanked Henry Krug of Kitchener, Ontario. "You will find many uses for this" was his prediction when he gave me the coil of rope.

With an eight-foot-long campfire throwing out heat, I left Mike in camp to keep watch for sparks that might blow on our tent and burn it, and returned to the aircraft for my two passengers. Brother John was cold. His hands were balled up in his mitts and his teeth chattered. He was eager to move toward the fire.

"You'll freeze your lungs gulping this twenty-five-below-zero air. Walk slowly and breathe easily," I cautioned.

Brother Petrin knew a woodsman's life, but his health had cracked six months before this trip. He had recuperated at home in northern Quebec and was still on the mend. Camping in the woods among the Slave Indians of Fort Resolution was his life, and he did things from force of habit.

Our tent was a lean-to affair with the long red fire for a front door. We cut spruce boughs for a floor, banked snow around the ends and back of our shelter, and cut a supply of wood for the night.

"What are we going to use for food?" Brother John asked.

"We have two hundred pounds of milk aboard for you." Brother Petrin smiled, wrinkling his face at me in a big wink.

I took Brother John in tow and we brought the ration box from the plane. He needed exercise to get warm. Brother Petrin made soup from one of the half dozen packets of dehydrated soups in our kit. After sandwiches from Brother John's lunch box, we enjoyed tea and some sweet biscuits for dessert. When the passengers were fed and comfortably warm, I made a final check on the aircraft, locked the rudder, elevator, and aileron controls, then joined the Brothers for an evening Rosary.

To keep warm, we crawled into our sleeping bags, and one by one my passengers drifted off to sleep while the gusty northwest wind ran its giant fingers through the tops of the spruce. I dozed, but only at intervals. My thoughts raced back home, down North, and back to Edmonton again. Certainly this was a situation for sitting under the worry tree if ever there was one. I began my Rosary again and tried to concentrate on the Mysteries.

Brother John awakened me. "My feet are cold," he said, shivering. I told him to remain in his sleeping bag while I stirred up the fire. Again I dozed, and again added more logs—until the gray light of morning at 6 A.M.

The trees still arched their backs against a good fifteen-mile-an-hour wind. I went to inspect the plane, and my path of last evening was drifted over and frozen solid. My wing thermometer read thirty below zero. Then between gusts of wind over the long prairie I heard the chugging sound of an engine. I listened again. It was the airport electric plant. Of course we were downwind, but I estimated we were no more than seven or eight miles away. A gasoline check assured me there was plenty to fly us into McMurray. Plans began to formulate while I walked back to camp. The snow was too deep to attempt a take-off with both passengers and baggage, so my better sense told me to make two trips into the airport and split my load.

Back at the fire, I found Brothers Mike and Antoine up and melting snow for the morning meal. It was Sunday morning. We could not say Mass there, even though I had my Mass kit, so we all said the Rosary while breakfast cooked.

Around 9 A.M. the wind began to stir up the white dust on the prairie into another blizzard. We cut more wood, warmed ourselves by the fire, and Brother John kept us in a gay mood with his expressed desires of food and colorful descriptions of appetizing dishes.

I did not let on that I had heard the airport engine that morning, for I was afraid it might give someone the idea to try to walk out. That would really put me behind the "eight ball" as far as Air Regulations were concerned. A pilot, like a ship's captain, is responsible for his passengers. Whenever a plane is forced down, especially in the North, all passengers must remain at the ship. There are many reasons for this regulation. The food, if any, will be at the plane—and an aircraft can be spotted much more easily than a man or woman walking. With our fire throwing heat and the Brothers drinking tea, I decided now was the time to lay down the law about trying to walk out. They all agreed to remain in camp.

"What if we run out of grub?" Brother Petrin questioned. "Then one of us would have to walk out or at least try to save the others!" I assured Brother we had food for ten days.

To put muscle in the regulation, I told about a man who had become impatient and left his ship, John Bourassa. I had met Johnny in Yellowknife on a day when other pilots were pumping him with questions on his exploits as a Pathfinder pilot for the Royal Air Force. He had done plenty of flying and had had some close calls. Two days later he was missing on a flight for a local airline from Bathurst Inlet, Northwest Territories, to Yellowknife. From his notes we learned a faulty battery was the real cause of all his trouble. Fog forced him to fly so low over that undulating glacier-ditched country in the wild Barren Lands that finding check points was impossible. His magnetic compass was all but useless there, and he dared not land and stop his engine for fear he could not start it again. So he flew south by the seat of the pants. More than a week later his plane was found some three hundred miles southeast of Yellowknife, but Johnny was not there. He had grown impatient and decided to walk in, his notes said. The plane was not damaged. He had come as far south as his gas permitted, but far to the east of his course. To this day, after one of the longest and biggest air-search and rescue operations in the history of the Royal Canadian Air Force and private pilots, no one has ever heard or seen any sign of John Bourassa.

Brothers Mike and John agreed and saw the wisdom of remaining with the plane, but Brother Petrin commented: "Many people believe John Bourassa is still alive. It was April in the Barrens and he should have been able to find plenty of game like rabbits, ducks, geese, and caribou. They begin their northern trek about that time." Then he added seriously, talking half to himself, "Of course I would not like to battle those hungry wolves at night, nor those mosquitoes." He knew the life of the Indians, this Brother.

The blizzard corralled us at the fire throughout the afternoon, and between tea and "frozen malteds" Brother Mike gave us a rundown on the childhood days of this country. We learned that the Athabaska River, from Athabaska Landing some ninety miles west of Lac la Biche, was the first avenue into the Canadian Central Arctic. By oxcart, and later by railroad, supplies were moved in York boats and barges over the Athabaska River, the lake, and down the Slave River into the northland. The Hudson's Bay Company and other trading companies, free traders, Mounted Police, and missionaries, all moved north over the waterway to Smith Landing. Here sixteen miles of rapids on the Slave River forced the travelers overland. In 1911 Inspector Fitzgerald of the Royal Canadian Mounted Police died on a trip from the Upper Peel River into Fort Yukon, and from 1916 Smith Landing has been known as Fort Fitzgerald. These accounts of the early voyagers and their struggle to gain a toe hold in this bleak country put my passengers in a reflective mood.

About four o'clock it began snowing heavily and the wind sent powdered snow down through the spruce. An extra squeeze on the ration box that evening resulted in a cup of rice soup apiece with tea and pilot biscuits. When darkness came the wind died slowly, and by nine o'clock we saw the shivering stars in thirty below zero.

"It's my turn to keep the fire going. You fellows have a good sleep," Brother Petrin said, slipping on his mitts and picking up the ax.

I was tired and slept soundly, with the happy thought of a clear day coming up and our departure.

"It looks as if Brother Petrin left camp," Brother Mike said, waking me with a twist of my toe. "Your flying jacket and my boots are missing."

That news was electrifying. I was up and dressed very quickly and examined his tracks going north out of camp. They were already frozen! He must have left camp at about three that morning. My watch read five o'clock. Now I had a real worry. Brothers

Mike and John fed the fire and we had breakfast before it was daylight.

There was no wind. It was clear and twenty-five below zero, just what we had been waiting for. Brother Mike and I went out to the plane and started our gasoline blowpots burning nicely under the engine tent when the buzz of an aircraft engine sounded just behind us. I looked outside and saw an aircraft taxiing up to us. Inside were Bert Birch and Glenn McPherson, his mechanic.

"We brought you a little gasoline, Father," Bert said, jumping out of his Norseman. "Thought you may have run short because of that flash snowstorm last Saturday afternoon." I told Bert I had enough to get into McMurray, though I had used more because of running with full carburetor heat and rich mixture. "You picked a very good landing field, Father," Bert went on. "It must have been rough in that storm. I'll take some of your passengers and fly your kite out if you like." I accepted the offer gladly since Bert had just checked me out on skis. I had plenty to learn about deep-snow landing and take-off procedure.

We started breaking camp, and then a Royal Canadian Air Force Search and Rescue Mitchell was orbiting over us. Brother John started an excited gallop all over the place, trying to retrieve parachuted grub and snowshoes. I had to slow him down for fear he would freeze his lungs or his hands and face. In a matter of half an hour we had the supplies aboard both planes. Then another plane landed! This time it was Bert Bury from McMurray Air Services, Ltd. He taxied up with his little Stinson Voyager.

"Gosh, Father," he beamed, "you are sure making headlines."

"We spotted the plane on our trip in this morning," Bert Birch cut in. "This is directly on the Canadian Pacific Airlines' route north," and he went on to say that he was going to fly my plane off the heavy-snowed prairie. Mr. Bury immediately offered to fly him back to the prairie to bring his own ship out.

It felt good to see such generosity from my fellow pilots. They were men who realized that a few miles ago they too were freshmen in this North country.

I started the plane and rode along as co-pilot as Bert Birch flew it off the prairie. We were in the air five minutes when I spotted the airport.

"You sure were right on course, Father," Bert said, leaning toward me. As we flew I searched the area for a man on foot or for a track, but saw nothing. A dozen people flocked to the plane when we taxied up to the airlines' office.

"How are you? Did you fellows get hurt? Are you frozen? How about a story, Father?" There must have been six reporters, all asking questions at once. Then Father Joseph Turcotte elbowed his way to me.

"How about a cup of coffee, Father Bill?" he said, pulling me along to the Department of Transport kitchen. "I notified the Bishop all is well," he continued. "The radio and newspapers really gave you headlines. Right now you must be starved," he added, pushing open the door to the kitchen. Brothers Mike and John did not need urging when it came to the beans and fresh-buttered toast. I was just halfway into a bowl of soup when one of the officers from the Royal Canadian Air Force Search and Rescue Squadron sat down beside me with a mug of coffee.

"Are all your passengers here, Father?" I took a swallow of coffee, more for courage than for clearing my throat, and told him about Brother Petrin leaving camp. He scratched his head and a look of concern spread over his face. "That's serious, Father. We will have to search for him and I'll have to wire Edmonton that this rescue operation is not complete."

I emphasized that Brother was a veteran Northerner. Nevertheless, he proceeded to carry on his routine regulations when a passenger is missing. The rescue team spoke of making parachute drops and of returning to the spot where we had had the forced landing. Two men fully equipped and towing an aluminum toboggan with medical supplies, emergency rations, and sleeping gear would be put on the Brother's trail.

When the rescue officer left, one of the reporters took his place next to me and kept up a steady barrage of questions. Had I filed a flight plan out of Edmonton? Had I received the latest weather report? How much of an overload did I have on the plane? Why did I land on that prairie? Did I run out of gasoline? What were my plans for the future? I left the questions just mellow for a moment, because the cook came in with a steaming dish of lovely brown beans.

"Would you please excuse me while I take on a little fuel?" I asked the reporter nearest me. He nodded and kept questioning Father Turcotte about us.

I suppose we looked like story fodder with two-day-old beards and slept-in clothes. With a passenger missing, the affair took on added color. Suddenly the sound of a plane on the airport drew all the reporters outside. Bert Birch had returned from the prairie with his plane and was being dispatched on a charter trip to Chipewyan Lake. Brother Henry and his brother Philip Latreille joined me for a last cup of coffee and then helped refuel GTM. We arranged the baggage on board for a flight north to Fort Smith in the morning. Everything was ready except our missing passenger, Brother Petrin.

The Air Force Search and Rescue team and Bert Bury in his private plane combed the eight-mile area, and at about four o'clock Bert spotted Brother in a clearing. He radioed the airport, and the Department of Transport radio radioed the rescue plane. In short order the big twin-engine Mitchell zoomed low over Brother and dropped a food parcel. When the team returned to the airport they reported a successful drop but added, "That Brother just kept walking. He paid no attention to the food we dropped!"

A rumor slowly spread that my passenger was in a state of shock and hysteria and that he was going on, probably snow-blind, trying to reach help. I knew this was pure conjecture, since Brother Petrin certainly must have heard the gunning take-off of aircraft engines that day at the airport and directed his steps accordingly.

I made a thorough check on the aircraft and asked one of the government radio men to have a look at our wireless set. He brought a tube tester aboard and in fifteen minutes found the tube that had caused the trouble.

Then at exactly four-thirty Father Mercredi came to the airport in a taxi and handed me a telegram:

DEPARTMENT OF AIR TRANSPORT EDMONTON ALBERTA. PLEASE RETURN TO EDMONTON TOMORROW MORNING ABOARD THE ROYAL CANADIAN AIR FORCE SEARCH AND RESCUE PLANE. BRING YOUR PILOT'S LICENSE AND REPORT IMMEDIATELY TO MY OFFICE. K. S. SAUNDERS, SUPERVISOR OF AIR TRANSPORTATION.

Storm clouds mounted in the back of my mind. I handed the wire to Father Turcotte, who read it quickly, a worried look on his face.

"We'd better send a wire to the Bishop immediately and explain the situation," he confided quietly. "He will be expecting you tomorrow." With a heavy heart I wired the Bishop, with thoughts of Resolution and fish menus plaguing me as I did so.

The fog of evening laid its heavy breath just below the top

branches of the spruce, and still there was no sign of Brother Petrin. After supper at the airport kitchen Father Turcotte and I walked the roadway between the edge of the woods and the airport. Surely Brother should be making an appearance soon. I realized that walking in deep snow was tiresome and that Brother would have stopped often to rest. So we waited, anxious for a sign of him, and discussed the events of the past two hectic days.

"Every hour the radio gave us news with all kinds of probable happenings," Father Turcotte related. "Brother Henry was very concerned and even wanted to go and look for you. He was sure you had made a landing on the Athabaska River in that storm."

We walked until seven-fifteen, when we heard the rattle of bushes just behind us. We turned, and there was Brother Petrin! Like a jack rabbit, he jumped over a windfall jackpine out of the bush and onto the trail.

"How are you, Brother?" Father Turcotte asked, running up to him.

"Just fine, but I need a smoke and something to drink. I'm thirsty," he puffed. "Sorry I left you, Father," he added apologetically. "I was too far to return when I heard the planes this morning. I wanted to help." We walked and talked our way to the kitchen. Word got around fast, and reporters flocked around and pumped questions at Brother. He smiled all his answers, nodded, and kept eating. He had suffered no ill effects from his trip.

We returned to McMurray that evening and I sent a wire home, assuring the folks I was very much alive. The mission was crowded with friends, concerned about our safety, but we retired early.

Tuesday morning I offered my Mass in thanksgiving to God for the services of His man of the road, St. Christopher. Certainly without him we would never have found that prairie. A few hours later, aboard the Royal Canadian Air Force plane bound for Edmonton, I spotted our camp and even the case of frozen celery we had abandoned. The rescue men aboard the aircraft were quiet, either reading or sleeping, so I had time to think and pray. One thing that gnawed away at my normal tranquil conscience was my carelessness in not filing a flight plan. The more I thought about it, the more serious and grievous a misdemeanor it seemed to be. Why had I acted against my better judgment? Was it pride?

At 11:30 A.M. we landed at Edmonton's Municipal Airport and I went immediately to the Air Transport supervisor's office. This

Fort Smith in late April. (Mission in center photo.)

LEFT: Brother H. Sareault, pilot and captain; on the pilothouse of the mission boat, *St. Anna*, at Fort Wrigley on the Mackenzie River. RIGHT: Oxen pulling wood sled in Resolution.

The *St. Anna* on the wide Mackenzie.

Bishop Fallaize with Fathers Biname and Griffin, sailors on the Arctic Ocean.

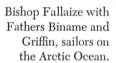

Slave Indian summer home at Fort Wrigley

Bishop J. Trocellier
with some of the Rabbitskin
Indians at Fort Franklin.

Bishop J. Trocellier and
a Slave Indian trapper
at Fort Liard.

Brother R. Mahe
at the graves of
Father Grollier and
Brother Kerney
at Fort Good Hope.

Providence Mission and river ice breaking up.

Brother H. Sareault with a moose at the edge of the Mackenzie River.

Father Rioux, chaplain of the *St. Anna,* saying Mass.

Father A. Mansoz, the professor *practique,* Father Leising's first superior at Fort Smith.

Brother George Mrugalla
running the nets for
whitefish at Aklavik.

Father F. Labat,
pastor of St. Therese
Mission at Fort Franklin,
Great Bear Lake.

Bishop Trocellier and Fathers Grias and O'Toole with Granie
(a grand old Rabbitskin Indian) at Fort Norman.

Bishop Trocellier and Inspector Henry Larson, R.C.M.P.,
the Mountie who sailed the Northwest Passage.

Father Leising
in dog-trail gear
at Fort Smith.

Grey Nuns and Reservation school children.

Fathers Leising and Colas ready to go North; Fathers Mooney, Higgins, and Jensen wishing them *bon voyage*.

Father Leising making a winter pre-flight check on the CF-GTM.

Fathers Leising and Levesaue
with Joe Gully
at Arctic Red Mission.

Fathers Leising and O'Toole planning a flight north.

Father J. Franche and one of his prize
Huskies at Tuk Tuk.

Father Leising in dog-trail gear, visiting
Indian camps.

Father Leising and Brother Crenn assisting Grey Nuns aboard the CF-OMI at Fort Smith.

Sisters Bourke and St. George, Grey Nuns, aboard the CF-OMI.

Reverend Sister Paulett Fortier, R.N., with her dog team, visiting the sick in Indian camps.

Father Henry and Father Leising at Gjoa Haven.

Father Leising with a group of Eskimo boys at Gjoa Haven.

Father Leising broadcasting to the Eskimos of Aklavik,
with Father Colas operating the radio station.

Father Leising at the controls of the CF-OMI.

Father Leising and Brother C. Claeys—winter flying in the Norseman GTM.

Most Reverend
Paul Piché, O.M.I.,
Vicar Apostolic
of Mackenzie in the
Northwest Territories
and Titular Bishop
of Orcisto. Appointed
March 21, 1959.

was a tense moment. As soon as I saw Mr. Saunders walk out of his office toward me I sensed something serious was brewing.

"What were you trying to do here on Saturday?" he began. "You made a very dangerous take-off, far too low over the city. No doubt you had an overload on your plane."

"The snow was sticky on the runway," I tried to explain.

"Then you should have lightened your load," he continued. "And of course you omitted filing a flight plan."

Here I had to admit my guilt, and I felt just like the publican in the Gospel. "To top off the picture," he went on, "you allowed one of your passengers to leave the aircraft. Now I don't like to do this, but I am forced to ground you for one month. Please give me your flying license."

"Could I postpone this grounding until May first?" I pleaded. "We have some forty tons of buffalo meat to fly to our mission hospitals and schools."

"No, I'm sorry." He shook his head. "You will have to hire a pilot to do that job."

With labored movements I handed over the license I had worked so hard to gain. Mr. Saunders must have read my thoughts.

"Don't take it too hard, Father," he said, walking to the door with me, his hand on my shoulder. "I have acted and judged you as lightly as I possibly could. You look tired. Why not take a good rest? This month will pass quickly and you will be a better and wiser pilot when you fly again."

"Can I fly my plane back to Edmonton?" I asked.

"I'm afraid not. I know you also have a valid American pilot's license, but under the circumstances it would make a better impression on the younger pilots if you had someone else fly your ship back. I'll find someone and call you, Father," Mr. Saunders said, and I left his office.

That was a black day for the ego and a happy day for humility. I returned to the Oblate Fathers' house and retired to the chapel to talk the whole thing over with God. The wisdom of those famous words of Father Eugene Dooley, our moral theology professor, rang out loud and clear: *With ordination all powers do not come!* I said my Rosary, asking Our Lady for the grace to act wisely, retired to my room, and wrote a letter to the Bishop with the latest news.

"Flying Priest Is Grounded," the headlines of the evening

paper spilled the news. My brother Oblates gave me a gentle ribbing about trying to give Brother John a rough initiation ride, and
then consoled me with the idea that I needed a rest.

"The Bishop will be able to hire another plane to get that buffalo meat out to the missions," Father Fournier, the Provincial, assured me. "This is just God's way of telling you that none of us
are indispensable."

I appreciated the phone calls from fellow pilots most of all. It
was like healing oil on my wounds. *Don't let it bother you, Father.
Remember, it is better to have a red face with a few scars of
humiliation and live to be an old pilot than to die a bold smooth-
faced young cloudhopper.* These men knew how those last ten
minutes in that storm could tie knots under a pilot's safety belt.
They knew a month of time can be lived in seconds of a pilot's
life, like an engine sneezing on a take-off!

More experience would have alerted my attention to those long
blanks between radio stations, especially at that time of the year
when the weather was so changeable. Any reason I might have
used to make that flight necessary was no excuse for my carelessness that day. I was wrong and I had to admit it. I had not
weighed every article of baggage and I know there must have
been at least two hundred pounds of overload. This would not be
cause for concern since it would not affect either take-off or flight
under normal conditions. But on fresh, soft, sticky snow even a
few hundred pounds less might have made a difference. My take-
off had been low, but I followed the twin railroad tracks out of
town, just in case a faulty engine did force me down. Yet rules
of safety had to be respected, and this experience certainly would
sharpen my attention.

The following morning at my Mass I asked for special grace
from God to use good judgment in the future, to swallow my pill
of pride like a man, and always to double-check on the weather.
It would take added courage to meet the fellows at the hangar,
and I wanted to meet them and admit I was wrong.

After lunch that Wednesday, Mr. Saunders called and said he
was sending a pilot over to see me. It was Walter Katcher. We
arranged to fly to McMurray on Thursday.

For the last few weeks I had had light heart pains and severe
backaches, so this seemed an appropriate time to see a doctor for
a thorough physical check.

"You'd better ground yourself too, young fellow," he said after examining me. "You must have had some severe mental and physical strain these past months. Your blood pressure is too high and your general health is a little run down. I suggest you ask your Bishop for a month of rest."

Again I went home to the quiet of the chapel, thought the whole situation over, and wrote to my Bishop, including the doctor's report and advice, saying that I would await his answer at McMurray.

Thursday morning my relief pilot and I were aboard CPA's DC-3 daily flight for McMurray. Father Turcotte met us at the airport with the Brothers, expecting me to fly north. When he learned the latest news from Edmonton, we all returned to the mission and my new pilot found a room at the Franklin Hotel. I saw Captain Don Grey of the Canadian Pacific Airlines before leaving the airport and asked him to check out my relief pilot, which he promised to do first thing in the morning.

That evening I met some newcomers who came North for the Shell Oil Company. "We have a drilling crew at work just a few miles from where you were forced down, Father," one of the men spoke up. "Our men told me they thought they heard a plane on Saturday and reported it to us yesterday."

This was certainly a consoling thought, and it is typical of the helping-hand philosophy of the North. Many people of St. John the Baptist Mission came to shake hands. I began to relax again.

Friday morning the mail brought a reply from the Bishop. I will always treasure that letter. It was packed full of understanding. He assured me that Father Gilles, our bursar, would engage a plane from Yellowknife to fly the meat to Resolution and to the other missions. "Take a rest and have your plane ready to fly in June," he advised.

Father Turcotte was happy on hearing the good news and drove me to the airport with Brothers Henry and Philippe. One of the Grey Nuns was also along on this trip to Edmonton. As soon as I saw GTM my heart began thumping. It had been moved. The engine cover was off and so was the engine cowl. Coming close, I saw my hired pilot under the plane with a rag. Then I noticed that the whole ship was covered with oil in the slip stream of the propeller. Father and the Brothers went over to see what had happened to the plane and I took Sister in the airways' office, for it was some twenty-five below zero that morning. Opening the door, I saw Captain Grey and Glenn, pacing and smoking.

"What happened, Don?"

"One of those close shaves, Father," he began excitedly, and related the story. When he arrived Walter was in GTM, warming up the engine. Naturally he thought I was there or had given Walter special instructions. After the warm-up, Wally came in and said he was set for the checkout flight. Don climbed aboard, did a pre-flight check, and took off.

"Just when I was bringing the r.p.m. back to two thousand from the climb, the propeller seals blew oil!" Don went on with gestures. "I did a quick 180-degree turn and set the ship down, opening my safety belt as we touched the runway. I thought sure we would burn and I would have to abandon the plane. Your St. Christopher certainly was on the job, Father," he smiled, "or we were just lucky!"

I explained to Don that the GTM had a twenty-gallon oil tank and that it took a half hour run-up to burn off the gasoline used in the oil dilute.

"Walter thinks the propeller seals were old and just blew out," Glenn commented. "Wait until he hears about that big oil tank."

I was at a loss for words and thanked Don Grey for bringing GTM down safely. Before a pilot flies a strange plane, he must be checked out in that ship to familiarize himself with instruments and specialized equipment. It's no problem. That twenty-gallon oil reserve on GTM was what fooled Walter. He had been accustomed to an eight-gallon tank.

"I'm sorry, Father, for this mess," he said with sincerity, and I could see the poor fellow was suffering with humiliation.

He had tried his best to clean off the oil in that below-zero weather and his new parka was ruined. I asked him to come into the office and get warm. His hands looked frozen. A quick look at the plane told me we had real work ahead of us. Oil was splashed even over sections of the wings, the entire fuselage, and over the whole tail section. Icicles of hardened oil hung from the engine fuselage and armpits of the wings.

"Use our Herman Nelson heater, Father." The airline agent pointed at a pile of snow from which two canvas tubes protruded. "We don't use it except in cases of emergency. If you cover the plane with your wing covers and get some heat on it to melt the oil, you should be able to clean it in a day."

The heater he suggested operates with gasoline and is a hot-air stream fed into the work with canvas tubes. I talked it over with Father Turcotte. He asked the two Brothers to remain at the airport to help with the cleaning while he returned to McMurray with the Sister.

Walter and I worked with the Brothers from eleven that morning until four in the afternoon, without so much as a thought for lunch. We had to remove the entire engine cowling, the wing panels, farings, and rudder sections. Everything had to be washed in cold gasoline. It was 5 P.M. before we had GTM clean and set for a test run. I started it with caution, after a good heating, and ran the motor for a half hour. A check after the run-up assured my hired pilot that not a seal leaked! I taxied the plane for a circuit of the airport and put the nose bag on for the night. Walter was relieved and happy that all was in readiness to fly in the morning.

That evening I wrote home, telling my folks the latest news and that I would spend the next month assisting our procurator, Father Charles Gilles, in Edmonton. The next day we flew back to Edmonton, this time on a flight plan.

That one week made major changes not only for me but for the Bishop and the Provincial of the Grey Nuns. Both had planned several changes in mission personnel. These had to be postponed, all because of my carelessness. My morning meditations at St. Joachim's little chapel centered on the future and planted new and firm resolutions in my soul to act with prudence and sound judgment for the remainder of my flying days.

That night in the quiet of my room I wrote in my personal logbook: *Flight log on aircraft CF-GTM Norseman, March 15, 1952. Edmonton, Alberta. Arrived in Edmonton at 11 A.M. today after a week of blizzards, a forced landing near McMurray, rescue, and finally a rest. Lesson? Always check the weight of pay load, gasoline, and FILE A FLIGHT PLAN.*

Chapter Ten

"I'LL have four Sisters ready with their baggage to make the flight north to Fort Chipewyan," Mother Lachambre called me one day in early June of 1952 from the General Hospital in Edmonton. She was Mother Provincial of the Grey Nuns of the Far North in those days, and her problem was changing personnel during the short summer. Each year when the eight schools under the supervision of the Sisters closed their doors for vacation, the pupils were not alone in their eagerness to frolic free of the classroom. The teachers, too, looked forward to a breath of fresh air, a change, or perhaps a visit home. Now that we had a plane Mother Provincial had plans.

On June 10, the Feast of St. Margaret, I flew north with Mother Margaret Lachambre and her four new Sisters. This flight to Chipewyan began a summer that was to set a precedent and firmly established the idea of air transportation in our missions. The young Sisters took keen interest in this big country—like young birds on their first migration flight.

We stopped at McMurray for fuel and lunch. Father Turcotte rushed the Sisters over to see his new school, where they may teach someday, while Brothers Henry and Philippe rolled gasoline barrels and helped me with the refueling.

"How did you like landing in this small snye here at McMurray?" Brother Henry asked when we were down at the plane. "Too many hills and a little on the short side for me," he answered before I could think of a good reply. "I like a good long stretch of river to land on, as we had at Good Hope. Wish I were back there," he added, looking north. Brother had just returned from a rest at his home near Montreal, and the Bishop had asked him to help out here with the building of the new church.

The landing snye at McMurray is a challenge to any pilot. I was certainly no exception. From the day I overheard one of the pilot's comments at Cooking Lake, I have respect for its hazards:

"If a fellow can land and take off safely at the snye, chances are he has made the grade as a bush pilot."

The Aeronca I used to have was small enough not to give me a problem. With a normal load it took off in half the length of the runway. Now, with the Norseman, my courage was beginning to feel cramped. Landing was simple enough. I had no cross wind and a light load. Take-off with five passengers, baggage, and fuel was beginning to give me that strange light feeling of fear. I took just enough gasoline for our flight, plus the forty-five-minute reserve, buckled in my passengers, and asked Brother Henry to begin communications with our mutual friend, St. Christopher.

There was just a slight leaf-flickering breeze when GTM came about at the very end of the snye. Silently I said my usual three Hail Marys for a safe trip, asked our Lord to forgive my past offenses, made the Sign of the Cross, took a quick look at my passengers, and eased the throttle to full travel. The Wasp worked up a powerful growl, and just after the midway mark we were skimming over the willows, slowly rising above the twisting channel of the Clearwater River.

At one thousand feet I began to breathe again. I'm sure now that Brothers Henry and Philippe had had all their spiritual equipment operating. I could see them waving from the little dock after we circled the settlement on our way north.

My passengers pointed to boats and barges down on the Athabaska River and kept my "co-pilot," Mother Margaret, from her prayers with their questions, like real tourists. I elected Mother Lachambre to ride up front because I knew she was past the stage of airsickness and I felt she could even assist me with the flight maps.

After an hour and fifteen minutes we circled Fort Chipewyan and landed on the calm bay in front of the mission. By the time I taxied up to an anchored barge, the rocky shoreline was lined with townspeople, children, and the Sisters. Because of the shallow water, Father Mousseau had directed the Brothers Veillette and Crenn to anchor the flat-decked wooden barge for our floating dock. When the aircraft was anchored, Mother Provincial asked if she could spend the rest of the day at Chipewyan. We agreed to set the departure hour for Smith at nine in the morning, and everyone began to make noises like visitors.

Brother Crenn unhitched his bunch of keys and opened the door to my gasoline cache. Since the spring of 1950 I had prepared for these flights throughout the Mackenzie by sending aviation gasoline and oil to all of the missions. Up to now my visits to this old settlement had been touch-and-go, and Brother Louis Crenn was just the live history book I was after. After fifty-three years of climbing around those rocks, this calm, observing, sharp-eyed little Oblate Brother ought to know what he was talking about when he commented: "This airplane makes just as great a change in our transportation as the outboard motor did up here around the lake years ago."

He was fascinated with everything about the plane and asked many questions. The motor, and especially the propeller, intrigued him. Hydraulics was his pet admiration. The automatic changing of the propeller blades, to keep the motor at a constant speed in light or heavy air, "is almost like a living thing," he marveled. While GTM had her drink of fuel and oil, we rowed back to shore with the skiff Brother built, and he took me on a tour of Nativity Mission.

Brother Crenn took me up on the high rocks east of Holy Angels School and pointed out the potato field, which had been a lake before Father Faraud drained it. The new brick school, built by the Brothers in 1945 and '46, the church, the Fathers' house, the warehouses—all sat firmly on the granite rim of the bay. We could hear the water south of town as the swells came up out of the blue lake and washed the gray, sparkling granite rocks.

"This is shotgun country in the fall." Brother pointed to a flock of gray geese. "Some of them spend the summer over on Lake Claire, but they all take this road south in October." Brother Sareault told me later that this talented Brother Crenn was a "real artist with a scattergun."

On our return to the house we came to the dog kennels. I could see now that Brother Crenn's first love around the place was his dogs.

"That dog has a wolf strain in him." Brother pointed to a coal-black, sharp-eared fellow with a wagging tail. The canine had a long red tongue that dripped saliva as it ran over sharp-fanged teeth. Brother related how he had bred the dog's mother with a half-wolf dog owned by an Indian at Rocky Point on the lake.

"When Blackie was a pup he was so wild we had to snare him, but he trained well," Brother commented. "Funny thing though," he added. "A fellow has to have a harness or a chain in his hand to get anywhere near that dog."

From handling my own team I recalled how eager the dogs were to get into their harnesses in the fall. On cold days they would cringe from the frozen straps, and often in spring they would slink away to nurse paws that had perhaps been injured by the ice. Brother explained how he made moose-skin boots for his team, cutting small holes for the toes to pass through, so they would not cut their feet on glare ice.

"Here is Brother Sareault's great leader, Duke," the old Brother said, opening the gate. What an elephant of a dog! He must have weighed almost 175 pounds! "Some dog, eh, Father?" Brother patted his shaggy head. "He is part St. Bernard."

When I was in the hospital years ago in Resolution, Father Riou, who used to be in charge of Nativity Mission, often spoke of Brother Louis Crenn and his dogs. Now I knew why. Father related that when the weather was not stormy the young fellows would gather around the mission on Sunday afternoons just to watch Brother line up his team and leave for the Goose Island fish camp across the lake.

That evening I sat in the recreation room with Father Mousseau and all the Brothers, listening to the news of the past winter. They were all very enthusiastic about the plane. They realized now how quickly I could gather all the children for school in the fall from two hundred miles around. Such encouragement from my Brother Oblates sent me off to bed without worries that night.

The sky was clear in the morning, and my passengers were ready and waiting on the dock to climb aboard GTM. Practically the whole village came out to see us take off. The new Sisters snapped pictures of the settlement, and a little way along the route, when we spotted a herd of buffalo, I thought they would jump out of the plane!

When I fly over this country my thoughts always return to Mike Dempsey, the old ranger. This used to be his back yard. I remembered the story of a very unfortunate accident when we approached Fitzgerald.

On one of my many visits there, I read in the mission records about the time young Father Brohan asked Father Bremond to paddle him across the swift-flowing Slave River to have a better view of the rapids from the east bank. It seems that, after Benediction, Father Lefebvre, a visitor from Fort Smith Mission, accompanied the Fathers and a group of interested Indians to the riverbank. Father Bremond had learned his canoeing from the

Indians, so he took the stern. They dug their paddles deep and pointed the canoe upstream. The Indians watched with concern. They knew what this twelve-mile-an-hour current could do to a broadside canoe—but the Fathers reached the opposite bank safely, and after a good look at the rapids they climbed back in the canoe. In midstream a swift eddy turned the canoe broadside! Father Bremond dug his stern paddle deep and righted it, but a nervous movement on the part of the young rider capsized the canoe in a flash! They were sucked under by the swift current. Paralyzed with fear, Father Lefebvre and the crowd on shore could do nothing. Some of the Indians rushed into the river with a canoe but found nothing. It was the first great tragedy in those pioneer days.

Flying over Fitzgerald with my gay young passengers, excited and amazed by these boiling rapids below us, I thought of the two Oblates who also came to look but never returned to tell what they saw. The radio towers, three miles from town, came in sight and soon we were circling the settlement. It was then I noted the huge hole in the ground across the street from St. Isidore's church. Tractors and a few dozen men were at work preparing the foundations for the new General Hospital. I usually fly over the mission to pry one of the Brothers loose from his work to get a truck to meet the plane a mile away at the waterfront.

Those rapids of the Drowned at Fort Smith look a lot more dangerous from the air than they do from the ground. My passengers were suddenly very still, and Mother fingered her rosary, with an occasional glance at the scene below us. The airport gave me a wind of twelve knots from the northwest, which meant I would have to fly low over the rapids to approach my landing area. When I turned off of my base leg on the home stretch, even my co-pilot made an extra Sign of the Cross. Once we swooshed on the water, they all found their voices. The Bishop himself headed the group of well wishers on the dock, eager to see his plane finally arrive at Smith. All the Fathers and Brothers from the mission and a dozen Grey Nuns were there. Brother René Berric stretched up to his full six feet, hooked a powerful hand on the wing strut, and leaned back to ease GTM into the dock. Ropes were attached quickly, and my passengers stepped off the plane into their new mission field.

When the greetings quieted down, everyone had to have a look inside the ship, and the Bishop was first. He tried the seats for size, including the co-pilot's seat, but chose the one behind it.

"I like to watch the proceedings when we fly." He smiled, try-ing on the spare set of earphones. "Maybe I could help with the charts too. Thirty-one years around these parts should give me a kind of honorary degree as an amateur navigator." He winked at me as a Brother climbed aboard.

It was Brother Camille Claeys, who seemed a little nervous at the Bishop's words. He had spent many years working with the Bishop on the boats around the shallow rivers of the delta at Aklavik and was no doubt remembering those occasions when the Bishop, relieving him at the helm, had touched a few sand bars. But the Bishop laid a friendly hand on his shoulder and said, "Brother, perhaps you would like to have a little rest from that galley on the boat this summer. How would you like to fly with us and help with the gasoline?"

Overcome with emotion, Brother Claeys said, "This is some-thing I've dreamed about for so many years." When he looked up at me, his gunmetal-gray eyes were shining with a new light. I knew I would have a devoted assistant.

During the next three days Brother Cam and I built a dock for the plane and a small oil shed on the waterfront. Evenings I worked out a schedule of flights with the Bishop for his visita-tion of the vicariate and wrote letters to the mission posts, ad-vising them of our approximate time of arrival. His Excellency also wrote that I would make special flights for supplies and per-sonnel changes. Our plans included, first of all, a visit to the mis-sions on Lake Athabaska.

Early on the third morning after GTM arrived, the *St. Gabriel* from Fort Resolution reached Smith with my old friend, Father Riou, on board. The Brothers had come for their year's supplies stored at the Smith warehouse. The Bishop met Father Riou with this announcement: "You are just the fellow I'm looking for. I need a good preacher for the Indians at Fond du Lac."

"Fond du Lac?" the old missionary said, surprised. "Why, I have to go back to Resolution when our barge is loaded in five or six days. It will take longer than that . . ." His voice trailed off as he thoughtfully combed his beard with his hand. "You mean I will fly with you in your new plane?" he asked, his eyes brightening.

"Can you be ready to leave after dinner?"

"Oh yes." Father Riou pulled a dusty beret out of his pocket. "I'm ready to go now."

After midday dinner there was a procession of the two mission trucks down to the river, and the Bishop performed the very simple ceremony of blessing the aircraft. Brother Claeys, decked out in clean coveralls, had every window in the plane sparkling. The Fathers and Brothers gave Father Riou a solemn send-off, and the Grey Nuns sent along a special box of bonbons for his good people. Included was some hard candy the children always expected. I flight-planned directly to Fond du Lac, Saskatchewan. The weather down on Lake Athabaska was like ours, sixty-five degrees in the shade, the wind at eight knots from the east.

Father Mowka, the tall, silent, smiling Superior at Fort Smith, raised his hand in blessing when I pushed the throttle forward and moved away from the dock against the current of the rapids. GTM slowly gathered speed, and with a loud one-minute groan of her powerful engine we were in the air. Father Riou was as gleeful as a youngster at his first circus. He pointed out the buildings of the settlement to the Bishop and then sat shaking his head in wonder at the mist rising from the rapids below us.

For a hundred miles southeast on our route the country was rocky and sprinkled with lakes. Scrub jackpine, poplar, and birch grew in small patches and in river valleys, and there were no signs of people. In an hour we came to the Athabaska lake shore, and the Bishop picked out the first tents of new Goldfields (Uranium City). Our plan was to stop here on the return to Fort Smith. I followed the north shore of the lake, with its smooth granite hills and deep bays, and Father Riou began to feel at home. For twenty-five years, without a vacation, he had been the missionary of Fond du Lac. Yearly he would come along this lake shore, over the ice with his dog team, to Chipewyan for a visit and confession. This trip was bringing back a lot of memories.

When we arrived at Fond du Lac on the eastern end of Lake Athabaska, I flew over the settlement and saw a few people, but no signs of a black cassock. My intention was to land in the bay west of town, into the east wind. On the downwind leg, over the town again, everyone seemed to be out and moving toward the bay. There was just a little ruffle on the blue water and our landing was a very smooth one. I saw Father Charlie Gamache now, standing on a rock and waving his arms. We approached slowly. Twenty-five yards out, I stopped the engine and coasted in. When

I climbed down on the pontoon with a rope, the people became suddenly very quiet. Even the dogs were propped on their front legs along the shore, waiting—thinking maybe I had a fish for them.

At twenty feet I tossed a line to Father Charlie. He caught it and gave it to one of the men behind him. GTM eased into shore. Father Gamache was smiling and shaking my hand in a grip that was used to the ax and the oar.

"I see someone moving in the plane besides the Bishop," he commented after we met, while making the lines fast to rocks. "Anyone I know?" he asked.

"Father Riou," I answered in a low voice, but not low enough.

A buzzing began among the people, and soon the air was alive with loud hellos and waving and shouting. When I opened the door of the plane and Father Riou stepped onto the pontoon, there was a sight I'll never forget. He waved, then raised his hand and blessed the people. They all fell to their knees, silent, and crossed themselves. The Bishop came out, and quietly the people flocked around, knelt, and kissed his ring.

"Did you see Brother Labonte?" Brother Claeys asked as the crowd moved off in the direction of the mission.

I pointed toward the lake. Brother was coming with the skiff for the baggage. He knew that the Bishop would not come without a few hundred pounds of potatoes for his "caribou eaters." We also had a case of eggs and even a half case of oranges for them. When the skiff arrived, the Brothers took over and I went up to the church and said my Divine Office.

The Bishop spent two days at Fond du Lac, confirming over thirty-five children and giving them their First Holy Communion. Father Riou preached to his people in their language, visited their tents and log-house homes, and met all the new arrivals since his leave-taking twelve years ago.

This mission among the Chipewyan Indians at Fond du Lac was given its first resident priest, Father Albert Pascal, in 1875 by Bishop Faraud. Since then the Oblate Fathers have administered to the people in this area, and the majority of them are a credit to the missionaries. They make their living hunting, trapping, and fishing, and live the same quiet life their ancestors did a hundred years ago.

I flew the Bishop and Father Riou fifty miles farther east to our mission at Stony Rapids. Father Perin had his people gathered at the dock to greet the Bishop and their friend, Father Riou. This mission was officially opened in 1941, the summer I helped Father Gamache build the little church. Many of the people remembered me and came to show off their families. They were happy, they said, to see the Bishop with a plane. Now he could come and see them every year instead of once every four years.

After our two-day visit we flew west to Camsell Portage and a visit with Father Brown and the Cree Indians of Black Bay. Here the Bishop learned of the great influx of prospectors and the uranium rush that was going on thirty-five miles away, just north of the old town of Goldfields. Father Brown and some of his prospector friends had built a fine little log mission in sheltered Camsell Portage Bay. There the people gathered and brought a dozen of their children to be confirmed by the Bishop on his first visit to their little community. This tour of the missions on Lake Athabaska was the beginning of a wonderful summer of flying for GTM and her crew.

The great event that year was the celebration of the one hundredth anniversary of the founding of St. Joseph's Mission at Fort Resolution. Father Robert Haramburu arranged a grand feast, and the people came from five hundred miles around to visit their alma mater. On the day before the feast, Brother and I flew to Fort Vermillion in the Grouard Vicariate, one hundred and fifty miles southwest of Smith. Archbishop Breynat, Bishop Routhier, the Vicar Apostolic of Grouard, and Bishop Coudert, the Vicar Apostolic of the Yukon, had arrived there by auto and were waiting on the riverbank when we arrived.

"I had a telegram from Bishop Fallaize saying he would arrive in Smith today. Did you see him?" the Archbishop questioned as soon as I climbed up the bank.

"Not only did I not see him, I didn't even know he was coming," I replied.

I was very happy at the prospect of seeing Bishop Fallaize. It was over seventeen years since our last meeting back in Newburgh. A tall white-haired priest came over to us and the Archbishop introduced him as Father Joseph Habay and asked:

"Would you have a corner in your big orange plane for this slim fellow? He doesn't weigh much," he added, looking at Father Habay over his glasses.

I assured him we could juggle our load to put him aboard. He was grateful, smiling, and joined the others, who went for their baggage.

We took off for Fort Smith at three-thirty. Father Habay waved at his brother Oblates as we flew over the eighty-four-year-old mission post and the little white hospital. This country had been his dog-sled run for over twenty-five years. Now he was looking in retrospect as we flew over Vermillion Chutes and the little cluster of houses where he had said Mass so often for his Indians at Jackfish Creek.

In an hour and fifteen minutes we were landing at Fort Smith, and when I saw the group of people down at the river I knew Bishop Fallaize had arrived. After my passengers were safely on shore I went to meet my old friend. As soon as he saw me coming up from the plane he started toward me with his white cane. He was totally blind in one eye now and wore thick-lensed glasses.

"I see you have come to our Mackenzie missions. It's so good to see you after these many years," he greeted me as I knelt and kissed his ring. The plane spelled progress in our apostolic work and he looked forward to a trip to the missions down-river.

After supper that evening we continued our flight, adding Bishop Fallaize to our passenger list. Brother Claeys gave him the co-pilot's place so he could get a good look at the country, and especially at Resolution. When we circled the lake settlement, Bishop Pierre Fallaize strained his good eye for a lasting look at the place where in 1931 he had been consecrated by Archbishop Breynat.

There was a line of people from the church to the landing wharf to welcome my ecclesiastical cargo. As soon as our plane touched the dock—boom! went the cannon, a relic of early Indian treaty days and now used only on very solemn occasions. The feast had officially begun.

When our passengers were safely on the large wharf and the barrage of cheering that greeted Bishop Fallaize died down, we breathed easily again. Brother took a couple of rags and went to work under the nose of GTM, cleaning the grime and engine droolings of oil from the day's flying, while I went into the ship to fill the logbook. I was inside only a few minutes when a muffled call of "Help, help!" sounded in the bubbling water under the plane. I went out quickly on the float. A group of Indians were standing on the wharf, laughing like mad! Bubbles were coming up under the plane.

"It's the Brother. He slipped into the lake, Father."

Just then two legs came to the surface and clamped themselves around the crossbar between the floats. Then Brother's head came to the surface, still bubbling and spouting. "Help, *pot fur dumma*" (a Flemish expression meaning nothing in particular).

I reached down and caught hold of his legs and pulled him to my side of the plane float, out of the water. His always neatly combed hair was dangling like corn silk over his eyes, and he spouted water from his nose and mouth.

"I slipped in the lake, *fur dumma*," he said, disgusted with himself. The boys were splitting their sides with laughter, which did not help matters.

Poor Brother must have been rushing to finish so he could join in the celebration and slipped on the oily crossbar. It could have been disastrous had he bumped his head. Actually there were only four feet of water there at the time, but Brother was too excited to sound for the bottom. When he got his breath and a good look at the situation he began to laugh.

That was the only swim Brother had during the entire summer. He was extra careful on those oily crossbars after that experience.

Bishop Fallaize rode the co-pilot's seat down-river and met all his old friends. At Aklavik, when the Eskimos heard he was in town, they came from all channels of the delta to meet their great friend. He decided to remain there and visit while we flew out on the Arctic coast. We would stop for him on our return upriver.

With the exception of four days of fog at Tuktoyaktuk on the Arctic Ocean, we had wonderful flying weather. The Bishop met his people and had ample time to listen to the problems of his missionaries.

For the first time we flew several trips from the Arctic coast into Aklavik with Eskimo children for our boarding school. When the Bishop promised to return the children in the spring by plane, the majority of the parents were most willing to see them go. GTM became a winged school bus, stopping at river junctions, small lakes, and wherever people lived. Their door opened for the Bishop and they offered the best they had. Often they asked me little favors, like stopping on my return trip with some ammunition or tea. Never before had the Bishop made such a complete visit, and in just one month! When I flew south that autumn he realized the value of air transportation and began making plans and schedules for winter flying.

184

In answer to a request from the Father General in Rome, Leo Deschatelets, the Bishop sent me off to fly Father Paul Drago on his canonical visitation of the Keewatin Vicariate.

After my final landing that autumn of '52 at Cooking Lake, Alberta, I entered the following log in my flight journal: *Arrived from McMurray this afternoon, completing a summer of 17,000 accident-free miles. I feel sure that one passenger who never left the plane was St. Christopher!*

Chapter Eleven

OUR MEAT SUPPLY WILL BE EXHAUSTED IN ANOTHER WEEK. REQUEST MISSION AIRCRAFT TO FLY IN FISH FROM MOUNTAIN LAKES. FATHER DELALANDE.

"Sounds as though he could use a few tons of that buffalo meat we have in the warehouse," the Bishop commented when I returned the wire to him.

Throughout December, with GTM shod in her skis, Brother Cam and I had flown meat to Fort Chipewyan and Resolution missions. We had just returned from a Rae trip in January when the Bishop handed me the above wire.

"There is a low west of Providence around Nelson in British Columbia," the Fort Smith radio men told me when I flight-planned out the following morning. They expected I would just miss it, but the flight log tells the story: *January 22, 1953. Fort Providence. Our flight originated at Fort Smith this morning with 1800 pounds of frozen buffalo meat. Icing conditions forced us to land here at Providence.*

"It was snowing so heavily we didn't see Providence at all," Brother Cam told the Brothers in the recreation room that evening. "Did you hear our motor?"

"Yes, I was splitting wood near the bush when I heard a plane to the west of town," Brother Gosselin answered.

I could hear Brother Camille Claeys talking excitedly in his high-pitched voice, relating the events of the day. My room was just off the large upstairs recreation room, and the interior walls of this old log mission are paper-thin. Brother Cam was riding co-pilot for his second season and knew most of the flying lingo.

"We followed the west bank of the river because it was on Father's side," Brother Cam was saying. "I saw treetops fifty feet below us sometimes! We were flying very low because of fog and snow. At Mills Lake we began picking up ice, and I saw the anxious look on Father's face." Brother lowered his voice, but I could still hear him. "Father was trying to decide whether to turn back or continue. All this time I had noticed he advanced the throttle slowly until it was almost full forward. Then, pointing the wing at the ground, we turned and followed the islands and the left bank of the river until I spotted Providence."

"Did you see the small pine trees Brother Gosselin and I planted?" Brother Marchessault asked in his clear tenor voice.

"Yes, they're a great help in feeling our way down to the snow. I believe we ran over a few of them," Brother Cam added with a chuckle.

The Mackenzie River at Providence usually freezes too rough to land on, and the Brothers always mark a runway in the blue creek snye north of the settlement.

After I completed my log entry and said my Office for the day, I joined Father Denis and the Brothers.

"That load of buffalo meat you brought today, Father, looks like real tender beef," Père Jean Denis began with a broad smile. "Perhaps it is a special tender lot you picked out for the hospital patients at Simpson," he said with a little sparkle in his eye. "I am happy that storm made you land here, Father. Providence is a real orphan. They all seem to pass us by." He cleared his throat and asked, "Are you going to leave the meat here?" I told him we would if he needed it—and of course he did.

Father Denis is the Superior at our Sacred Heart boarding school at Providence, and the eighty boys and girls there know him to be a man of few words—but plenty of action.

"I am anxious to hear about the buffalo hunting in the modern manner," Brother Gosselin said, tilting his chair back against the wall and lighting a cigarette.

I explained how the government built a large corral at the Hay Camp, thirty-five miles south of Fort Smith, and herded the buffalo into it that were selected for the fall kill. They were all surprised to learn that from two hundred to five hundred were slaughtered annually. I explained that the meat was shipped throughout Canada and some of it even to the United States. The Brothers liked the idea of having the meat all packed in boxes and boned. Now they did not have to struggle with two-hundred-pound pieces and cut their hands on broken pieces of bone.

"I'll add a little something special to this evening." Father Superior got up from his chair. "Such a fine load of meat deserves a treat. Here," he said, handing his keys to little Brother Marchessault. "Go down and bring up a bottle of our oldest wine and a box of cookies. I'm sure they will appreciate a little internal warmth after their long cold ride today."

That brought contented comments all around. Brother Charboneau put a few more pieces of jackpine in the big box heater and Brother Gosselin asked: "What's all this noise among the Indians about the government allowing open season on buffalo, Father?"

My only comment was that Wild Life Service men believed a limited open season would preserve some of the feeding areas, especially the winter ranges. Today only Indians, Eskimos, and persons with a general hunting license can shoot buffalo.

Usually on our stopovers the Brothers and even the nuns are eager for news. Some mighty interesting evenings follow like the one we spent at Providence.

On our next attempt out of Smith we reached Fort Simpson with sixteen hundred pounds of buffalo meat. Six flights were made to lakes one hundred miles northeast of that settlement for over four tons of whitefish. There are many mouths to feed at St. Margaret's Hospital. When the hospital was first opened in 1916 by the Grey Nuns, Fathers Andurand and Moisan had to go two hundred miles south to Great Slave Lake with the Oblate Brothers for their fish.

Brother Cam and I spent ten evenings at the Sacred Heart Mission of Fort Simpson and eavesdropped on some of the stories of the old times. In the winter of 1905, eleven years after the mission was founded, Father Edward Gouy performed some amateur surgery, using his pocketknife to remove the frozen big and little toes of Father Moisan.

Sir George Simpson, governor of the Hudson's Bay Company, had stamped his name on this island settlement where the Liard joins the Mackenzie, and until 1886 it was the freight center of the company. Actually Fort Simpson is geographically in the center of the Mackenzie District, and in March of 1921 it was the center of air news. The first airplanes had arrived then and one had a few ruffled feathers when it landed on the hard drifts in the field behind the mission. Brother Henry Latreille ran out from the workshop just in time to see the other ship land on the snye. Next day the plane on the snye developed engine trouble and the propeller and part of the undercarriage were used to repair the first plane in the field. When it attempted a take-off on the rough snow the machine rocked up on its nose and shattered the propeller. Walter Johnson, an engineer on one of the Liard River boats and a handy man with tools, offered to try to make a propeller.

The pilots were skeptical. They knew the balance and stability required. Walter was determined and chose some good oak dog-sled boards from the stock of the Hudson's Bay Company, and Father Gouy offered him the mission workshop and tools. The Brothers helped him and the wood took shape. Brother Henry made some glue out of moose bones and old moose skin. They clamped the boards together, let it dry well, then bolted it to the machine. Brother Henry watched it fly the plane off the field, and his glue was holding. Actually the ship flew out to Edmonton via Peace River Crossing. Eight years later the first air-mail service was established, and today there is semi-weekly service from Edmonton.

The eighteenth of March during the winter of 1953 was an overcast day, and Brother and I had decided to do one of those bad weather day chore checks on the aircraft. About one-thirty in the afternoon Mr. Essex, chief ranger of the Buffalo Park, came to the mission with a telegram. We had completed our work at the airport, where it was some thirty-five degrees below zero and windy. My room was cozy and warm and I was set for a good afternoon of work on the books and mail when Father Gilles called me and I met Mr. Essex.

"We just received this emergency wire over the ranger radio system from the 5th Meridian, some hundred and fifty miles southwest of Smith, Father," he said, handing me the telegram:

MY BOY FELL ON A POINTED STICK AND IS DANGEROUSLY ILL WITH A DEEP WOUND UNDER HIS LEFT ARM. COULD YOU SEND A PLANE TO BRING HIM TO THE HOSPITAL? PHILIP MANDEVILLE, RANGER.

"Pat Carrey is out of town with the Beaver aircraft, Father," Mr. Essex pleaded, "and you are our only hope to save this boy's life."

Looking out the window, I could barely see across the river, a mile or so to the east. But there was still a good five hours of daylight.

"I'll try, Mr. Essex, if you accompany me. You know the cabin's location and the country."

"Thanks, Father. The weather is not the best, but if necessary we can follow the Slave and Peace rivers." He was happy. I asked for two nurses. Sisters Bonin and Simone Lapointe were chosen to accompany us with some medical supplies.

"Well, this is one trip I am happy to miss, Father," Brother Beauchemin commented on our way to the airport. "You may run into some ice with those low stratus clouds." By two-thirty the engine was heated, our passengers were aboard, and we taxied downwind on the edge of the airfield and took off.

"Fort Smith radio to Norseman aircraft GTM," came buzzing in my earphones.

"GTM to Smith radio loud and clear, over."

"We have your flight plan, Father, but thought you should know our latest Smith weather. Balloon ceiling reads 300 overcast and possible icing. Temperature thirty-four below zero. Winds west at twelve miles per hour. Light snow. Altimeter 29.01. Please keep your receiver tuned in for us, Father, and we will relay any further news to you."

Glancing back at my two passengers, I caught poor little Sister Lapointe with ashen face and droopy eyes, reaching for an emergency cup. Sister was a cracking good nurse, but every time she stepped on a boat or a plane she became ill.

Checking my instruments, I read 250 feet from the ground. The ceiling was bearing down on us. In fact, I saw huge patches of it falling on the tree line to the west. We followed the Slave River south over the Hay Camp and then did a cross-country portage west-southwest, with a compass bearing on Point Providence on the Peace River.

My next check on the altimeter gave me 150 feet! I tooled around some hills, and once we found ourselves a dead-end street! The valley I followed began to climb into the hills that were topped with a heavy ceiling of fog. I thinned out my propeller pitch and added a little throttle to do a tight 180 about-face. Twenty minutes of playing tag with the hills and low stratus brought us to Peace River—a level white highway with dark spruce-tree guardrails along its banks. We all breathed again. Regardless of how low the ceiling pushed us, we could always land on the river. The blue leading edges of the wings were now white with a quarter inch of rime ice, but nothing to worry about.

Sister Lapointe had recovered and was talking into Sister Bonin's ear and pointing at the snow-covered country flashing beneath us. Often the trees on the high riverbank were level with our wings. At three-thirty Mr. Essex became anxious, searching the bank, then he pointed excitedly.

"There's the cabin on your side, Father."

I picked it out, snuggled in the tall poplars high on the river-bank. Now for a landing spot. In such leaden light, through the foggy lens of high drifting snow, it is very difficult to measure levelness. I circled and came down to twenty-five feet on an inspection sweep of my intended runway. Little trees on the bank made depth perception easy; the packed snow looked smooth. After an orbit we landed on the river in front of the cabin.

Philip Mandeville came on the run, sliding toward us down the bank, a slender, quiet man with the agility of a red squirrel. The Grey Nuns had groomed and molded him at Holy Angels School in Fort Chipewyan and predicted great things for him. He did not disappoint them. Today he holds the post of chief park warden and is an example to all his Chipewyan brothers.

"It's sure good to see you, Father. My boy is very sick." Then he saw the Sisters and his eyes brightened.

I asked him to prepare the lad quickly and told him I would be up at the cabin for him in twenty minutes. We had only two hours of daylight left and I had to make the most of it.

After a quick inspection check on the plane I went up to see the family. The young lad was conscious but very weak. Patches of red blood on the bandage of his wound spelled out real danger. He was hemorrhaging. Philip carried him part way down the hill and I took him aboard the plane. The Sisters made him comfortable and warm in my sleeping bag.

At four-thirty we left the river ice, and there was no change in the weather conditions. I had asked Philip to advise Smith, via the Buffalo Park radio relay system, that we were on our way, and a lucky thing I did. When I tried to contact Smith for a return flight plan I could not hear even the beep of their radio. The weather conditions had blanked my radio.

Sister Lapointe assured me with a smile that the patient fared well. I followed the Peace River to Point Providence and then cut overland northeast to the Slave River. At Murdock Creek the ceiling lifted to four hundred feet. The weather was improving. I was further relieved when the sound of the Fort Smith radio came crackling over the earphones. I gave them my position and estimated time of arrival at Smith as forty-five minutes. Mr. Essex smiled contentment when he saw that we had radio contact. He knew that now I could use my manual direction-finding audio-loop radio to locate Smith, regardless of weather.

Near the demi-charge rapid I spotted a dog team on the Slave

River. The driver was breaking trail on snowshoes, and he waved as we flew low over the poplars on the riverbank.

"Looks like your missionary from Fitzgerald." Mr. Essex leaned toward me, lifting the earphone off my ear.

This was our native Chipewyan priest, Father Napoleon Laferte. Twenty-two years ago he was ordained a priest and served not only the little town of Fitzgerald but also the families living along the Slave River. Father Laferte is a hard worker and model among his people. He slashes down timber for his winter fuel supply and takes two months of long grueling trips deep into rocky barren country to the east, visiting his people. His mechanical hobby has resulted in a number of vehicular contraptions, all dog-powered, that bring him to Smith over the sixteen-mile-portage road during the summer months. "I have to feed my dog team all summer, so they may as well earn their keep," Father Laferte remarked once when I questioned his canine-powered car with a pickax drop for a brake.

Mr. Essex tugged at my sleeve and pointed down. We were directly over Father Laferte's little mission at Fitzgerald. I called Smith radio and gave them our position. They cleared me to land, advising that the runway lights would be turned on. I requested transportation and asked for landing clearance. We landed at just 6 P.M.

Our little patient was very weak but still breathing and conscious when I handed him to Mr. Essex aboard the car bound for the hospital.

The doctor examined Jean Louis and gave him immediate attention. It seems the lad had fallen on a sharp-chopped willow stump and punctured his left armpit to a depth that just missed a lung. That evening Dr. MacRae assured me he would live, now that the hemorrhage was stopped. There was no serious internal injury. This good news was a tonic after such a day of hazardous flying, and a real consolation to realize we had saved a life with the aircraft.

When breakup came in late April and closed our winter flying season, the Bishop handed me his June and July schedule. One glance at it told me the aircraft was really taking root in the scheme of mission activity down North.

192

Chapter Twelve

O N June 3, 1953, GTM flew north out of Cooking Lake to Fort Smith for a new season.

"This year I have another assistant for you, Father," the Bishop began when I arrived. "Brother Claeys is needed at Fort Norman, so I am assigning Brother Herman Beauchemin to help you as a mechanic on the aircraft."

Brother Beauchemin was no stranger. He had been stationed at Aklavik with me, and I knew that I had a willing and able assistant. Before our first flight he made it clear that he had no intention of learning how to fly.

"You do the flying and I'll handle the gasoline, oil, wrenches, and maybe say a few extra prayers when we run into bad weather," he said with a little chuckle.

And fly we did, into every corner of the Mackenzie. For three weeks we had the "flying school bus" in the air for ten hours a day. Over two hundred and fifty children were returned to their homes on small lakes and along the river. Brother Stanislas Szczepaniak and his men were building St. Patrick's School in Yellowknife that summer, and practically every week special supplies were needed. The Bishop and Father Provincial made a complete tour of the entire vicariate and more than thirty Grey Nuns were transferred to new posts.

In late August a forest fire threatened our sawmill twenty-five miles north of Fort Smith. We were called back to our base and flew eight trips through dense smoke and dangerous live sparks to haul in men, pumps, and hose that saved the mill. The heat and smoke caused one of the cylinders on GTM to throw oil, and we were in the process of changing it at the Fort Smith waterfront when the Bishop forwarded a telegram he had received from Father Lapointe at Coppermine:

FATHERS METAYER AND TARDY AND FOUR ESKIMOS DEPARTED FROM

READ ISLAND ON AUGUST 10 FOR COPPERMINE. STILL NO SIGN OF THEM. THEY MAY BE LOST AT SEA. COULD YOU SEND OUR PLANE TO SEARCH FOR THEM?

My assistant became very excited and anxious. "Are we going back to the Arctic coast?"

"Yes, Brother," I answered, fitting the manifold clips in place. "Suppose you were lost up there. Naturally you'd expect the mission plane to come and look for you."

"Yes," he mused hesitantly, "but it's very dangerous up there this time of year. Those west winds really churn up the ocean."

"We'll take all the precautions necessary," I pacified him. "And we won't travel unless the radio station gives us v.f.r."—visual flight rules clearance.

We completed our mechanical work on the ship that day, and on August 31 the weather station gave us clearance but added: "There is a front moving into the area of Hottah Lake southeast of Great Bear Lake. You may outfly it since it is moving slowly." The Bishop and Brother were my passengers on the flight north to Yellowknife, where we refueled. Yellowknife radio gave us another v.f.r. clearance on a 350-degree heading north to Eldorado and also the same warning about the slow-moving front from the Rockies. The Bishop had quite a list of supplies to purchase from the mining commissary for the coast missions.

"They will expect some fruit and fresh vegetables since we come from the south," he said, giving me a list of over seven hundred pounds.

About two hours out of Yellowknife, around the Hottah Lake area, we ran into patches of fog, the forerunner of the front. I had to detour through a couple of valleys, reaching Bear Lake east of the hills at McVicar Arm, and then followed the south shoreline fifty feet above the water, east to Eldorado Pitchblende Mine. The fog was rolling on the water when I landed, and we realized that was an RON (remaining overnight) for that day. There is a good harbor for the plane at the mine and it was a worry off my mind. I had been chaplain here during the war years of 1944 and 1945 and knew my way about the place.

Harold Lake, the mine superintendent, put us up in a very comfortable apartment, "especially built for the accommodation of our visitors," he said, taking the Bishop's bag.

Bishop Trocellier was puffing after climbing up the rocks

when we finally reached our room. "It was worth the effort," he said, looking over the ultra-modern apartment. We had steam heat and a wonderful bathroom with a tub and shower. To me this is still a high luxury in the North, at least as far as our missions are concerned. So many other high-priority duties have preference over the comfort of a good bath because of heating and plumbing costs.

We took our meals in the mine officers' mess hall at the regular times, but the Bishop started a good half hour before the appointed time, "so I can take my time on those million steps," he panted.

September 1 was out for flying both in Eldorado and Coppermine. I liked Eldorado not only for its modern accommodations but more especially for the radio facilities. Four times that day I had the weather from Coppermine and around the country. A complete picture such as this is most informative, especially since we were going into a zone with limited radio communication. Despite the consolation of an authentic weather report, the Bishop was uneasy and paced constantly.

"Will this fog ever lift?" he asked, pacing the floor the morning after our arrival. "I dreamed last night that the Fathers and the Eskimos burned in their boat at sea. It's possible, too, you know," he added, stopping in front of Brother's chair.

"I believe they are still safe in some small bay on the river," Brother Beauchemin commented confidently. "They just ran out of gasoline."

September 2 turned out to be worse than the day before. The wind changed during the afternoon, and I made another trip to the radio station. A friend of mine from Resolution days, Sergeant Bill Hall, was in charge of the radio at Eldorado at the time. As soon as I entered the station I realized some unusual news had come in.

"Tell your Bishop he need not worry so much. His men were spotted on August 31 by an Air Force Canso and they are all alive! Coppermine radio just relayed the message to me," Bill said as he handed me the wire.

This was wonderful news, and I ran back to the apartment and told the Bishop. He put his arms around me, and hot tears of joy spilled on my face.

"Let us kneel and thank our Blessed Mother," he said in a choked-up voice. I told him they had been spotted near Harding

River on the Arctic coast and that the east wind was increasing at Coppermine and the fog was lifting.

"Tomorrow we will go and get them," he said to himself, and dug into his pocket for his rosary. "Go back and see if there is more news. Perhaps that Air Force plane will return and rescue them." The only news I had was of the weather, and it was good. Even the east was clearing.

"Better make a check on your aircraft, Father," Bill Hall cautioned. "The wind velocity is now forty-five miles an hour from the west and increasing."

My trip down to the docks was well timed. A swell had developed in the bay, and the constant bobbing of the plane had badly chafed two of the ropes from the port float ballards. I changed these and padded the new ones with old rags.

That evening we met the McGuinnis brothers from Vancouver and learned about shipping on Great Bear Lake. The pitchblende of Port Radium is 1660 miles from Edmonton by water, rail, and truck, and another two thousand miles to the refineries in eastern Canada. By the end of June activity begins on Bear Lake with the breakup, and by the first week of July the first boatloads of ore are trucked over Bear River portages and up the Mackenzie.

Alan McGuinnis was then captain of the *Radium Gilbert,* a steel-constructed diesel-powered tug that towed the barges laden with pitchblende 170 miles to the Bear River portage docks, returning with oil and supplies to keep the mine in operation. Alan's brother is a pilot on a wooden lake schooner, the *Great Bear.* It runs from the mine forty miles to the airport at Saw Mill Bay, carrying passengers, mail, and fresh foodstuffs. During winter, snowmobiles and cat trains run the mail and supplies from the airport to Eldorado.

August and September are busy months at the mine, and crews often work around the clock. Alan left us at 9 P.M., when word was sent up to him that the barges were loaded. We retired early, for we expected an active day ahead.

September 3 began with rain, fog, and wind, and the Bishop was very quiet, too quiet. I knew he was boiling inside and expected an eruption of some drastic decision any moment. My morning weather report was due from Coppermine at ten o'clock, and Brother waited patiently with me at the radio station. I couldn't see the hills twenty miles to the north across the bay from the mine.

"Ceiling two thousand feet at Coppermine, Father," Bill Hall announced, pulling off his earphones. "But I don't know the fly-ability of this stuff we have around here. It may be clear after lunch, since the barometer is constantly rising."

Bill was correct in his assumption. The rain drizzled on, but the skies cleared sufficiently for us to make a take-off. I flight-planned for Coppermine via Dease Bay and Dismal Lakes region—a kind of dog-leg. Dense fog covered the September Mountains to the east, which is our usual route to Coppermine. Actually this same fog held us down to one hundred feet over the water all the way across the lake to Dease Bay. We flew over the cabins of Fathers Rouvière and Le Roux in Dease Bay. I worked into a pass in the Coppermine Mountains that put me over Dismal Lakes and then the skies opened and gave us clear flying with two thousand feet into Coppermine. We landed at 2:30 P.M., and Father Lapointe was there to catch our mooring lines.

"Bill Hall told us you were on the way," Father called to me. "I have the gasoline ready to refuel, if you intend going after the Fathers today."

Jumping ashore, I told him my real concern was general weather conditions in the area of Coppermine and asked Brother and Father Lapointe to start refueling. After giving the Bishop a hand to come ashore, I took off for the wireless station.

"I have been working every station since you landed, Father," Jack Foley told me, taking off his phones as I entered the station. "From all indications, this weather is as good as it might ever get!"

The barometer was steady. Everything pointed to a stationary ceiling of at least two thousand feet. Jack Foley, who was radio supervisor and manager of the Department of Air Transport's weather station at Coppermine, promised to keep his receiver open for our frequency during this flight. I told him I would leave as soon as GTM was refueled and call in my flight plan. Back at the mission, I informed the Bishop of our definite plans to try a rescue trip that afternoon. He was very happy. He agreed that Brother and I should make the trip alone, for he knew his extra weight might mean difficulty taking off on the sea.

"Better take a little grub and a few kegs of gasoline along just in case you can't land where they might be," he advised. "You can always drop the food and kegs of gas to them. Perhaps Brother was right about them running out of gasoline."

We loaded three kegs of gasoline and some food and took off

from Coppermine at 3:30 P.M. in light rain. I flew across Cape Kendall on the west shore of the Coronation Gulf. The skies were dark in the west. We followed the shoreline to Basil Bay, then changed to a north-northwest course to take us over Stapylton Bay. From Stapylton, I planned to begin searching the Arctic coast line to Inman River. Heavy fog banks forced us down to three hundred feet above the rolling gravel country, but I remained on course. Fifty minutes after take-off we flew over the swells of Stapylton Bay. Long white-collared rollers foamed on the golden sandy coast line, but there was no flotsam or jetsam. We gave special attention to small bays and orbited over the river mouths to make certain they were void of life. On a calm day the Fathers could have maneuvered their boat along the coast to any of these places. Finally, there was Harding River! This was our goal. We circled twice but saw no boat. I made two orbits and searched out the hidden canyon walls a mile upriver. Nothing!

I pointed to the fuel gauge. We had twenty minutes of flying left before the engine began to burn our going-home gasoline!

"We are now at Harding River and have found no trace of a boat so far," I informed Coppermine radio. "I will search the coast for another twenty minutes and then our fuel supply necessitates a return to Coppermine." I had a "Roger" from Jack, and we flew on west.

The next river was a small one called the Hoppner. We approached it from the sea, and Brother pointed.

"Look! It's a boat! There they are, Father!"

I flew low over four frantically waving men. Two others were in their boat. Now came the moment I dreaded to think about— landing in the sea. Huge boulders broke the surf along the shore, and the mouth of the river looked far too shallow for a landing or even for taxiing. I made another orbit over the small bay just east of the river mouth. It was sheltered from the east wind by a kind of peninsula jutting out into the sea. That would be it. I called Coppermine and informed the Bishop that we had located the men and that I was attempting a sea landing to effect their rescue.

I had my eye on the sea ever since we left Stapylton Bay and noted that very often there were spots where the water was absolutely calm. I looked for one now. The wind was southeast, offshore, so I went out to sea on a kind of downwind leg. A little to the southwest I saw what I was looking for. Luckily there was no ice here. Before Brother had time to get worried, we were on the

Arctic Ocean, riding the waves. Sliding down in the troughs of rollers, our wing tips cleared the smooth rounded crests by only one foot. No time to linger here. We swung into action. Brother eased over the side of a float into the cold, salty water, but he never flinched. Like a walrus, he thrashed through the waves and waded ashore with a line. I dropped anchor and kept watch on the aircraft as we had planned. Should our anchor drag, I would start the engine to keep the plane off the rocks. One puncture of the floats here could mean a long walk!

I instructed Brother to ask the Fathers and Eskimos to come aboard immediately and leave their belongings aboard the boat. Time was important now, both for the safety of the plane and in order to arrive at Coppermine before darkness set in. I knew it would be difficult for them to leave their few belongings, but the safety of their lives and ours was at stake—plus one airplane. The little boat was anchored almost a mile into the river, which would have meant at least another hour to gather their effects, especially since their feet were too sore to walk rapidly. One Eskimo could not walk. He was on all fours. With a few years of experience behind them, the Fathers realized the great chance we had taken to land in the sea. They came one by one along the rope to the aircraft, Father Metayer first.

"Thanks, Father, you have saved our lives." He was breathing hard as I pulled him from the cold water onto the float of the bobbing plane. His face was drawn and his eyes lay deep in their sockets. I told him I was sorry he had to wade out into this cold water, but he understood the situation. I had an old coverall aboard and he had carried his parka over his head.

"Good thing you didn't try to land in that small channel. It's very shallow. We broke our rudder there, trying to leave the other day," Father Metayer said, his teeth chattering. I noticed then that his feet were bleeding through his moccasins.

"Falla, give me a hand," I heard behind me. It was Frank Kudluk, and right behind him Wallace Goose and James Minorana. I helped them up on the float and into the plane. They carried their parkas and trousers above their heads. From the looks of their emaciated bodies, we had arrived just in time. I could count their ribs! They just entered the ship when Father Tardy and Jack Goose followed, with Brother close to his heels. Father Tardy just squeezed my hand. His gratitude was beyond words. Ropes and anchor were coiled aboard quickly and I fired up the engine. In five minutes it was heated.

I asked the passengers to come forward as much as possible for the take-off. They were all life-belted and instructed in case of emergency. I taxied free of the jutting peninsula, waited for a calm spot to appear in front of us, and gently eased the throttle forward. GTM climbed on the step, kissed a few high crests, and we bounced into the air. What a relief! Brother was smiling and patting the instrument panel. I contacted Coppermine radio.

I climbed to two thousand above a thin layer of evening mist, but with good ground contact. There was a high overcast, which advanced eventide and darkness by half an hour. It would be a twilight landing. I began to visualize the reefs and sand bars, the radio towers and rock hazards at Coppermine. At least one light would be burning. The Hudson's Bay boat, the *Fort Hearne*, was riding at anchor in front of the settlement, and her masthead light would be burning. I called Coppermine again and requested it, just in case, giving my position as forty miles southwest of Stapylton Bay. Coppermine wired back that a misty moon was on the way up and that my request would be honored, "plus a few other candles burning in the window!" I could hear other voices at the radio station, indicating a little excitement there. Father Metayer touched my shoulder and pointed down. The Eskimos spotted something, and all crowded along the portside windows.

"We saw three caribou," Father Tardy called into my ear. That reminded me of the grub the Bishop had asked me to store aboard. I mentioned it to Father Tardy, and in short order eggs and sandwiches were popping into hungry mouths. I cautioned them to eat slowly, and very little, since their stomachs would be rebellious, and I did not want them to suffer retching pains. At least they were shelling the hard-boiled eggs! At Bathurst I once saw a hungry Eskimo pop a whole egg into his mouth, crack it, eat it, and take out the shells as we do fishbones!

We flew over Basil Bay and Cape Kendall, and Brother pointed out the red signal blinkers of the Coppermine radio towers. His face beamed relief. Evening was fast sliding into early night, and I realized there would be difficulty in judging depth perception. Ten miles away I spotted the winking candles of Coppermine. There was the dark hulk of the *Fort Hearne* and on the masthead —the light! That was it. I could land alongside the boat, using that light as my guide. When we circled the settlement I noted lights near the water's edge. They firmly fixed the picture of the shoreline in my mind, and I planned my landing strip along the boat.

About fifty feet above water I switched on our powerful landing lights and flew the plane on, touching the water some thirty feet off the starboard bow of the *Hearne*. Flashing lights from the boat signaled a welcome, and I blinked our navigation lights in thanks. There was a chop to the bay that evening which made it difficult to see the sand bar just north of the mission dock. Bishop Trocellier often cautioned me about that reef and told me it had been an island when he was stationed in Coppermine in 1931. I taxied past the mission, turned, and pointed GTM at the shore.

Almost the entire population of some eighty people waited to catch the rope when Brother expertly flicked it from the stern of the pontoon.

"Well, I see you are alive, Brother," the Bishop needled him.

"Yes, Bishop, I had to wade ashore with the line. I am still cold and wet on the outside but very dry on the inside!"

That broke the tension of the moment. Among the three of us—the Brother, Bishop and I—this remark recalled an incident of the previous summer. On one of our trips into the Liard country a few of the Army lads who had been on a surveying crew there gave us a hand to moor the plane in the fast twelve-mile-an-hour water, and one of the fellows fell in. He was rescued immediately by one of his buddies, but the Bishop, knowing that the boys might be on the dry side up in that neck of the woods and that there was even the possibility of a cold for the lad who had fallen into the water, motioned Brother to get him a bottle of scotch for the poor chap. "Gosh, Bishop," Brother had replied, "I'll fall into the water for a bottle too!" So when the Bishop called back to Brother there at Coppermine, "We have some good hot tea to warm you up," a flash of humor lit his episcopal eye. He knew if there was one thing Brother could not stand, it was tea!

"Welcome to Coppermine," Father Lapointe called to the two Fathers, who had come ashore. There was the traditional accolading and handshaking and words of sympathy and joy for the lost who had returned. Out of the crowd emerged a tall Northwest Mountie, and in one of his long strides he was on the float.

"Congratulations on the sea landing, Father. It must have tied a few knots in your belt!" I admitted it did.

Sergeant Harold Heathcock, Royal Canadian Mounted Police pilot, knew that country and the risk of an Arctic Ocean landing. We share the honor of having the entire Arctic for our flight beat. Jack Foley from the signals also came aboard. While filling out my logbook I gave them a rundown on the flight.

Father Lapointe and the Bishop had outdone themselves in preparing a sumptuous supper for the eight of us, and during the meal we pumped the whole story from Fathers Metayer and Tardy. About ten Eskimos came in quietly during the meal and sat around the stove, smoking and listening.

On the eighth of August the two Fathers and four Eskimos had boarded a thirty-foot sea-fishing boat at Holman Island, two hundred and eighty miles north of Coppermine. With fuel and food for a week, they set their course for Read Island, one hundred and eighty miles south, off the coast of Victoria Island, and arrived there two days later, taking on more gasoline and fuel. The Fathers and one of the Eskimos, Jack Goose, had decked in the boat and built a low cabin on it to keep dry and out of the wind. They also had a fifteen-foot mast with a leg-of-mutton sail, an eight-foot boom, and even a four-foot jib.

On the twelfth they set out for Liston Island, due southwest. That same afternoon they passed the island three quarters of a mile off starboard. Curious seals were breaking water all around them and seven were shot and stowed in the hold of the little boat. With seal meat aboard, the Eskimos were happy. Regardless of the weather or a camping place, they had food. Toward evening the entire crew began to take note of the fact that the horizon of Lambert Island had remained stationary, just a little larger than a popping seal head, for the last two hours. Some invisible anchor was dragging. Father Metayer remembered the time, and then it dawned on him. They were caught in the Gulf tide.

Battling the strong current until three in the morning, they came within two or three miles of Lambert Island, but a strong southeast wind breathed a dense fog over them and they lost sight of the island.

Father Tardy said, shaking his head: "As long as I live I'll never forget that night adrift on the Arctic Ocean in the wind, the fog, and the rain. We ate seal meat, drank a little water, then said the Rosary. The wind whistled so over our little boat it almost blew the Hail Marys out of my hearing! We had to hang onto the seats, and I remember when Frank Kudluk went flying in a heap in the corner with his seat board wrenched out but still clutched in his hands."

About five in the morning, the curtain of fog lifted and they saw land, which appeared to be about two miles away. Land to Northerners means caribou and fish—a real treat after all that seal.

Approaching the coast line, they all agreed it did not look like Victoria Island. They noted black hulks of what appeared at first to be rocks. On closer examination they turned out to be oil drums. Perhaps even some gasoline. A little creek flowed into the sea there, and they anchored and ran over to examine the drums. Empty! The wreckage of a boat was strewn along the shore and, of all things, they found a huge ship's compass. The compass they had on board and even this big one kept hunting and were not trustworthy.

Jim Minorana, who had been quiet, suddenly came to life: "And they were going to leave that place when I saw a caribou! We all went to shoot it except Father Metayer, who started a fire and got fresh water boiling. But we had to walk far inland. The caribou saw us and ran over into the hills." They finally caught up to more caribou and at last cornered three of them in a ravine and shot them.

They returned, laden with meat and tired after a four-hour walk. Father Metayer was waiting with water boiling. He said he had found some ice nearby on the bank of the little creek that made some very tasty drinking water. They cut chunks of the meat, and with some onion flakes they still had among their boat supplies managed a very tasty caribou stew.

"With a fresh bone marrow for dessert, we all felt warm and good again and decided to sail away along the coast," Father Metayer said. "We thought we were going west, but actually we were going east!"

At about four that afternoon they spotted a little river running into the sea, and it was a real harbor. The Fathers and Jack Goose decided to go for a walk along the shore and see if they could spot something familiar. In one hour they came to a cabin on the bank of another river. The decision was instant and unanimous. They all trudged back to the boat, climbed aboard, and shoved off for their new home. The little boat entered the river with ease and the high bank afforded a good shelter from the wind and the rolling sea. They scrounged some scraps of wood and managed a fire in the rusty maw of the old ship's stove they found in a corner of the cabin. After another satisfying meal of caribou and seal stew they pored over the maps in the waning light and planned a new course of action. After much argument and discussion they decided they were on one of the rivers west of Coppermine.

"Next morning was our first chance to say Mass, after a good sleep in the old cabin," Father Tardy took up the story. "It was August 15, the Feast of Our Lady's Assumption, and we needed her help. We erected an altar with boxes from the boat."

They sailed what they figured was northwest, always hoping that around the next point they would see the islands lying north of Coppermine. A fair wind pushed the little boat along at a good seven knots for two hours before the sea became rough. Long swells raised them on high crests, then dropped them out of sight of land into deep troughs. When they realized a real gale was coming out of the northwest with fog creeping over them from inland, they struck out for shore.

A V cut in the high coast line was really a river entrance. This was a lifesaver both for themselves and their boat. Black boulders blocked a direct route into the river, but after passing it they noted that it entered the ocean on a dog-leg to the east.

"I said we sailed along the coast," Father Metayer began, "but we actually used our motor all the time. Now as we came about and chugged up the entrance to the little river, our engine died. Out of gas! We had to use our oars to pole the boat the rest of the way into its harbor." The high banks formed a shelter of rocky ledge under which they tucked the bow of their little boat.

That night the sea smoke was so thick they could not see the opposite bank of the little river. After supper over the primus stove, they spent the night in their boat, which was very cramped, but they said their Masses there next morning with extra-special fervor.

Thinking they were no more than twenty miles from Coppermine, they decided to walk there for some gasoline. James Minorana, Jack Goose, and Father Metayer started out with a small compass, binoculars, .25-.20 rifle with twenty-five rounds of ammunition, and a camera.

They found the country far from level. It was full of gullies, ravines and bogs, rivers and high craggy rocks. Their sealskin boots got wet and it was just like walking on oily, sea-mossed stones all day. At three that morning, August 17, the skies burst their seams and they were awakened with buckets of pouring rain. They walked east, and about one o'clock Jim ran across some ptarmigan and killed five of them. There was no wood anywhere and they were so hungry they ate them raw—even to the hearts and livers. While eating they followed a good-sized river, too wide to cross, and found a bed of soft moss. Temptation got the better of them, and they took a rest. But not for long. Again the rains came and they climbed up on the high rocks to get out of the mud and the slippery, sharp rocks that cut into their moccasins and feet.

From their perch on the rocks, Jack Goose spotted a patch of blue sea, and it gave them new hope and courage to walk on. At nine that evening they reached the bottom of a deep bay. Jim found an old rusty jam can and used it to boil a small duck he had carried for two days. It was good, especially the broth, when they strained the rust out of it with Father's handkerchief! They sat there until almost midnight and rested, but the rains came again and chased them back toward the boat. For two hours they trudged along the shore of the ocean. Then in the early dawn of August 18 Jack shot two ground squirrels. They stopped and made a big fire of driftwood on the shore where a boat had been wrecked, and cooked the squirrels in the rusty pot. But no one could eat the meat—they were so hungry that as soon as they tried to eat they became sick.

They began walking at five in the morning, when the rain stopped. Footsore, they made little progress and decided to send out a call for help and said the Rosary. About eleven o'clock that night they reached their boat. Jack could not walk on the deck; his feet hurt so much, he crawled.

For the next three days they rested, and on August 23 they all decided to try to take the boat under sail into the deep bay they had found. But the wind pushed them on the rocks before they cleared the river's mouth and broke the rudder. Working and straining, they finally waded ashore and towed the boat back to the river harbor and spent all the following day fixing the rudder.

On August 25, Wallace, Frank, and Father Tardy decided to try their luck walking. With a small tent, a little grub, field glasses, and the rifle they walked along the coast, taking note of everything.

"The only living things we saw the first and second days were ground squirrels or siksiks," Wallace commented. "I told Father Tardy I would walk parallel to the coast, but about two miles inland, with the rifle. The chances of spotting game there were much better. It was on the afternoon of the twenty-seventh that I spotted three caribou and shot them."

That evening they found tent rings of stone on the ground, the remains of an old camp, and a little farther on a caribou-skin tent and a little torn book that had one word written in it, a word that gave them the key to their position. The word was Akuliankattak, or Stapylton Bay. Now they knew their boat was at Hoppner River, twenty-five miles west of Harding River. The next morning they decided to get back to their boat and tell Father Metayer of their discovery. The return trip was difficult because of the heavy packs of caribou meat. Back at the boat, they had a good rest and decided to sail for Bernard Harbor when the weather turned fair.

Then, on August 31 they spotted the Canso aircraft from the Royal Air Force. The plane came through a hole in the fog and circled for forty-five minutes, dropping ration boxes and cigarettes.

"We knew you would send your plane for us when you heard we were lost," Wallace said to the Bishop. "We remained close to the boat after that."

Ordinarily there are only ten or fifteen Eskimo families around the settlement, except over Christmas and for a few weeks during June and July to trade their furs. Most of the Eskimos in the area live from twenty to a hundred and fifty miles away at deltas of small rivers, where they can net fish for themselves and their dogs. Around the settlement they would starve. But that summer the Department of Transport was erecting new quarters at Coppermine and employed about twenty Eskimos to feed lumber and building material to the carpenters from "Outside."

During early September, when the Arctic salmon come down the Coppermine River to the sea, the entire settlement, including the Mounties and the missionaries, moves twenty miles south to Bloody Falls on the Coppermine River for their supply of fish. The run is on from a week to ten days. With nets and trident spears the Eskimos have fun and a feast on fish. They cache them in stone pits for the long winter. Father Lapointe and the Royal

Canadian Mounted Police have a screened shelter to store their catch and to protect it, not only from a few flies, but especially from sea gulls and dogs, and to allow the air to dry the catch thoroughly. The natives like their fish rotted, so they pit them and mark the caches with stone cairns.

That evening, as the Eskimos entered the little house, I could smell decayed fish. It has a very special odor, one that permeates their clothing—they never lose it, like a high-priced perfume. After the last visitor we had to open doors and windows to air the house before stretching out our sleeping bags on the floor.

"Father, come and see the plane," Brother called to me, poking his head into the room. "There is quite a wind coming up from the east and the waves are getting higher."

September is a wild month for wind in the Arctic, and Coppermine was no exception. The Mounties' twenty huskies tied along the shore were sending out eerie howls into the night when we approached the sea where our aircraft was moored.

"There's a sandy bottom here," Brother explained. "I went out into the water with my waders and inspected for sharp rocks and found just gravel."

Rollers four feet high were cracking over the heads of the floats and rocked the plane back on its heels. We put four lines to shore and an extra-heavy stern line for added safety.

"I'll stay here and keep an eye on the aircraft while you have a rest, Father," Brother offered. "You must fly tomorrow, because I know the Bishop is very anxious to attend a meeting in Edmonton in a few days. I overheard him explain to Father Metayer."

Brother kept his vigil, and before I zipped into my sleeping bag at midnight I wrote in my flight log: *We returned to Coppermine this evening after a landing in the Arctic Ocean near Hoppner River, where we rescued two missionaries and four Eskimos who had been lost twenty-three days.*

Again I was grateful for the privilege of being able to help my brother missionaries. All the physical and mental strain of the last few days were melted by the warm gratitude that flowed from the hearts of the men I had brought back home. Here was the source for renewed strength and courage to fly another day.

Chapter Thirteen

ON December 23, 1953, our winter season for flying was officially inaugurated when I flew Brother Henry into Fort Smith with a cargo of fresh fruit and vegetables. The Bishop called the Brother from McMurray to help with the painting and decorating of the new St. Ann's General Hospital. Unfortunately we had a chinook the following day and, of all things, rain. The temperature shifted from thirty below zero to thirty-eight above! On Christmas Day it dropped again to twenty below and covered GTM with a thick cellophane wrapper of ice. Brother Beauchemin and I worked three days to melt that skin of ice off the delicate fabric wings and fuselage.

Again letters and a telegram came asking the Bishop for meat at Fort Rae, and on January 2 we left Fort Smith to start a busy winter. We were refueling at Yellowknife when Father Ebner brought us the sad news of the death of Father Mansoz on January 4. He had passed on to his reward quietly in his sleep, I learned a few days later. I was to miss him very much, especially for his sound fatherly advice, yet I realized now that he was close to our Chief Pilot in heaven he could give an extra tug on the sleeve of the Almighty when we needed it. And several times that winter Brother and I called out for help.

After our supplies and personnel flights were completed we took the Bishop up on the Arctic coast for a winter visit with his missionaries and people.

Our trips went smoothly until April 3, when we were one hour out of Coppermine, en route to Bathurst Inlet. We ran into very light snow showers, and Father Louis Le Mer, who was up front with me, thought it was fog. He was on his way to build a mission at Cambridge Bay.

"This is mighty rough country. The rocks tower to two thousand feet and even higher," Father shouted into my ear, pointing out of the left cockpit window.

I must admit that the visibility was a mite poor. He had reason to be disturbed. The light snow was heavy snow now. I went down to three hundred feet above the Arctic Ocean ice along the coast line. Here I could gauge my depth—or height, as the case may be—from the dark patches of ice that were broomed clean by the mighty winds. At Cape Barrow the continental land comes to a kind of point, rising mountain-like into the Arctic Ocean. As we rounded the cape the visibility went to zero. I descended to fifty feet to keep on contact.

"Look, rocks ahead!" shouted Brother.

I dropped the left wing and did a tight 180-degree turn. The ice and snow looked smooth and I was now flying upwind. That was it. I decided to land while we were all in good health, and in half a minute the heels of our skis were licking the ice. GTM finally stopped, and fine snow blew in through door cracks.

"*Merci au Bon Dieu!*" Brother rejoiced. "I don't mind rocks when I am riding a bulldozer, but they make me a little nervous in a plane!" Making the Sign of the Cross, he opened the door and stepped out on the ice.

"I stopped in this bay on my dog trek to Coppermine some three months ago." Father Le Mer pointed to the huge granite rocks to my left. "There were a few Eskimos camped here then, but I don't suppose they are here now. Would you like to have a look?"

I told him I would like to, but first I had to radio Coppermine and inform them about the weather and of our forced landing. I had talked to the police at Coppermine before leaving and they had informed me that if Sergeant Heathcock and Inspector René Belec of the Mounted Police arrived today they intended to push on to Bathurst Inlet. I didn't want them to run into this weather.

Brother dug out the engine cover and I began tooling the radio. In less than a minute I had Coppermine and told them there was a possibility of spending the night here but that we would push on to Bathurst if the weather cleared. I arranged to call them in two hours.

Father Le Mer and I stepped from the plane and left the Brother and the Bishop on guard. It was only twenty below zero, but that wind felt as though we were facing a blizzard of ground-up razor blades. We walked toward the rocks.

"When I see those rocks it will give me an idea just where we are in relation to my old snowhouse." Father trudged on. His breath was freezing a beard on the fur of his parka hood.

I marveled at this man. How he could find a spot the size of an igloo in this vast white blank wilderness was a miracle of at least the second class. Of course in twenty years a man is at home in almost any country, and Father Louis calls Coronation Gulf home. He is a solid man both in frame and in faith. Visitors, regardless of their beliefs and their work enjoy his company and regard him as God's official ambassador. He has the respect of the natives too. He can eat a piece of raw fish or seal with them, but he doesn't like it any more than I do. He does it because they would feel offended if he refused. He knows their language and customs as well as they do, yet he does not live like a native, nor does he act like one. His philosophy is *not to come down to their way of life* but to elevate them *to our way of living.* Essentially Father Le Mer is a teacher. Like Father Mansoz and Bishop Fallaize, he believes and realizes that the great barrier between the Indians and Eskimos and ourselves is knowledge. A trained intellectual way of life, with God as the Master and Father of us all, will make a difference. To many of those people, life is just luck or fate.

We came to the high rocks I spotted in landing and Father began a survey of the land and sea about us.

"I was camped over there." He pointed to the northwest, where a deep saddle in the spine of stone arched up from the Arctic Ocean floor. We went down on the ice again and leaned into a wind that really made a fellow's eyeballs smart. We bucked it with our backs. We put our shoulders into it, until they smarted from the biting cold. Indeed the winds could dictate the movements of men in the Arctic. Eskimos say so, and we who live here know the truth of their saying. Father began thumping on the snow with his feet when we came to the saddle.

"Here it is." He pointed to the hard snow.

There was no visible evidence that an igloo existed there. The snow was smooth. He took his hunting knife and began to carve the snow. He must have seen a skeptical look on my face and decided to prove his point. In five minutes of digging and cutting, a block of snow fell away like a barrel head, leaving a black hole. He lay on his belly and motioned me to look too. I lay down and shaded my eyes from the light to see into the pit.

"That was where I had my bed, on that snow shelf, the

'iglurtin.' And there was my primus stove on that block of snow." It was a small round hole in the snow, very much like the kind some animal would make to shelter itself from the cold.

I had been in many Eskimo igloos, but always when people had been living there. This was a dead one, never again to be lived in. When a snowhouse is abandoned for a few days, the snow freezes into a kind of ice and it is impossible to warm it again. Ordinarily a snow block is porous and breathes. But when it freezes it loses this quality of insulation, and a man would freeze to death in such an abandoned igloo.

We started back for the plane with the wind at our backs, and it was a short hike compared to our coming to the igloo. Aboard GTM we checked our time as 3 P.M.

"How about some coffee?" the Bishop asked, holding out a cup from the two thermos bottles Father Lapointe had prepared for the trip.

About three-thirty the storm blew itself out and the landscape began to develop. "Look at those rocks, Father." Brother pointed to the south. The sun glistened off high granite cliffs a good thousand feet above the sea.

"We'd better fly while this good spell of clear weather lasts." The Bishop looked anxiously out of the window. "My feet are getting cold sitting here."

When the aircraft is in flight I can use the gasoline heater, but not on the ground. So the ship had cooled off and, not having walked, the Bishop began to feel some of that twenty-below-zero air that crept into the plane.

We lost no time. Brother had the engine cover off and folded, and I started the engine. After ten minutes Brother hopped out, sat on the snow opposite each ski, and gave them a good kick with his two feet to loosen them, like a wrestler freeing himself from a head scissors, then quickly took his place in the ship. We turned and taxied over the landing tracks. After a silent prayer and a Sign of the Cross, we tailed about and gave our sky horse the spurs. It zoomed aloft quickly in the crisp, boisterous air. At five hundred feet we turned on course, still climbing, on a heading for the bottom of Arctic Sound.

I could see the delta of the Hood River and the black gorge cut in the rocks to the south by Wilberforce waterfalls. It was a black thread on the white cloth of the land. My altitude registered twenty-six hundred feet now. To the south there was a gray-white blanket at about five hundred feet slowly moving our way—more snow. Beneath it the landscape was almost in darkness. High mountainous hills soared above us to the southwest. We left the Sound; the gravel heights rose to one thousand feet and ledges of rocky cliffs clutched at us.

In twenty-five minutes on this southeasterly course I was over Bathurst Inlet but could not see it. I could distinguish the rocky hills to the right and left and to the south of us, but I could not make contact with the terrain beneath us. We descended to fifteen hundred feet into blowing snow. This was too hard on the eyes and also on the lungs of our Wasp. So back up to two thousand feet again, and there I had a very good look at the landscape, the visible hills above the snow line. In three orbits, I selected a spot void of hills. I began a descent into the swirling snow. There were objections voiced, I learned later, but that was to be expected. My altimeter read one hundred feet when I leveled off and hunted for contact with the ice. It came so slowly that it was painful. My eyes burned, darting from the instruments to that blank whiteness. Then I saw blue ice! My altimeter read seventy-five feet. It looked so good I did a slow pylon on it, just to keep it in sight and examine the area. I descended to fifty feet above the ice, and with definite clearance in that area I could see black cliffs to the north. I leveled off and streaked for them. In less than a minute we were there.

"This is the delta of Bathurst River," shouted Father Le Mer, pointing to the flat country beneath us.

Now we had something. I banked to the left and followed what I knew was the sand bar. It was one huge expanse of immaculate white snow. Then Father spotted the settlement. I was flying directly at it below the level of the buildings, which are fifty feet up on the riverbank. I elevated to three hundred feet to be in a position from which I could see the lay of the land and easily clear the radio antennas of the Hudson's Bay Company. It is very difficult to see a thin pole from the air, and at one hundred and forty miles an hour it is particularly hard to dodge one with over three tons of airplane!

Two tiny figures were moving toward what I supposed was the riverbank shrouded in snow. On the second orbit of the place I saw they had stopped and were waiting for me to act. Now I knew they were marking the definite shoreline by their presence. Then I spotted the gasoline drum, exposing about two feet of its red cheek against the snow. A check on the wind, a little flap, and off throttle brought us down on Bathurst River in front of the mission. I checked in at just 5:15 P.M.

"Hello, hello," called little Father Menez with his parka hood back and a smile cracking his cold red face. He spied Father Le Mer and was jubilant. Father Louis had administered this little fellow's baptism into the big-league Arctic coast mission field, and there was a special brotherly friendship established.

As a novice in the North during his apprenticeship at Fort Resolution, Father Menez always introduced himself on the Bishop's visit with: "When am I going up to the Arctic coast missions, Bishop?" And the Bishop would size him up and smile, no doubt thinking that he would make just a healthy bite for a polar bear. He is only five feet two and about a hundred pounds. Father Menez was a little thinner than usual but overflowing with joy to see us. The manager of the "Bay" was there also, and he immediately invited all of us to share his bachelor meal at the post. Right then and there he and Father Menez had a short pointed conference. Result?

"We will have dinner at the mission," Father beamed at the Bishop and the manager. "He will bring the duck," he said, pointing to the Bay man.

This was a golden leaf in the book of social relations which I am sure the Bishop loved to see. He always worked with the men at the Bay. Often in years gone by there had been missionaries and Hudson's Bay men whose bigotry or nationalistic tendencies set up barriers of real enmity that were a discredit to our civilization. No wonder a native would throw up his hands and give up trying to understand our social problems, for that is really what it amounted to. Anyone who sets himself apart as being just a little better than his fellow man does not do very much thinking on the whole philosophy of life. Just who, how, and where we are born is one choice we do not have. The manager of the Bay was not a Catholic, but he was and is a real gentleman.

Brother and I busied ourselves refueling GTM and tied it down for the night. Fathers Menez, Le Mer, and the manager hauled the mail and other sundries up the hill to the mission. The Bishop kept near the stove, thawing out his cold feet.

The Bathurst settlement of Burnside is located on the south shore of the Bathurst River where it fans out into the inlet. The land rises above the sea some fifty feet, and on the crown of this highland are five buildings—one belonging to the mission and four to the Bay. Since the middle thirties this little settlement has been a terminus of Eskimo boats in summer and dog trains in winter. Even the Eskimos deep inland make the long trek northward to buy needed supplies and trade their furs. Before these posts were established some of the natives traveled as far west as Coppermine and even into the Great Bear Lake country to buy supplies. In the middle thirties, too, our Oblate missionaries established a mission post here. It was new ground, a new language dialect, and a new tribe of Eskimos, primitive in thought, manners, and customs. I met them a few times during my visits there in the summer, but now I anticipated meeting new faces.

The little mission at Bathurst follows along the same pattern as all the other missions of the Arctic coast. The entry is a room some twenty-five feet long. To the right there are two rooms, Father's private room-office and one for visitors. A third door leads to the kitchen. At the end of the long room are sliding doors, and behind them the altar for Mass and religious services. When the doors are closed the large room is a combination sitting-dining room. When a lot of company comes, resulting in an overflow of visitors, it is used for a dormitory. There is a small upstairs or garret that is utilized for storage of freezables. If the missionary is fortunate enough to have a 32-volt wind charger and a dozen wet-storage batteries for light, his batteries are always stored in the attic. When Dr. Melling and I visited the mission in the summer of 1955, we slept with the batteries. Most of the foodstuffs for the year are also stored in the garret.

That evening we had supper in the large room, since there were six of us. Father Menez was jumping up and down like a grasshopper and making a track on the brown, shiny linoleum to the kitchen. Ordinarily Brother Beauchemin served the meal and did the cooking in these small missions, but here at Bathurst, Father Menez had his own methods. "I know where I've stored things in my cupboards," he said. "You will mess them up."

That touched off a good-natured attack on Father Menez by Brother and Father Le Mer. The Bishop felt it required the ministrations of a good referee and, being a fair cook himself, threw a little salt-and-pepper comment into the stew. The Bay manager and I finally rang the bell to end the round when we walked out of the kitchen with the steaming baked trout and the rest of the meal ready to eat.

214

The dinner conversation had a very wide range. Father and his friend were starved for news and, along with Brother's comments on the cook, we just about missed the thumping of feet on the outer porch. Father Menez was up in a flash to see who the visitors were. We could hear coughing and talking outside, and in a few minutes we left raisin pie to greet two Eskimo families who were total strangers to the Bishop and myself. One was Catholic and the other was Anglican. The men, women, and children came to shake hands. They looked emaciated. The children had that look about them that comes from being deprived of food for a long time. Saliva drooled from the children and the two men. I noted the women swallowed too. They must have been without food for days, and the sight before them was evidence of their wildest dreams come true. To an Eskimo, and even to a white man, any settlement means first of all food. Everything else takes second place when a man has been deprived of food for a long time.

"They have been starving for many days," Father Menez almost whispered to us. "I will give them some dried fish I have upstairs." He asked us to get cups and give them some hot tea, then disappeared upstairs.

One of the men sat near me on a bench by the wall. Brother gave him the tobacco can, and he rolled a cigarette. His caribou parka was bald in spots and his trousers had patches on the knees. The hair on his parka front was matted with drippings. The shoulders were rubbed clean of hair, and the caribou skin was roughened from packing heavy loads. Father called him Jimmy—I never heard his last name. Jimmy was not a tall man, but squat and well muscled. The heat of the room made him strip off his outer parka, and as he did everything came with it.

Eskimos usually wear one parka with the fur next to the skin and one with the fur out. He peeled his slipover shirt from the parka and put it back on. Normally, Eskimos do not use any kind of shirt. He had a grizzled-looking chin and upper lip with hairs about as sparse as the trees in the Barrens—a few here and there. After about ten minutes sweat dripped from the hair at his temples. Coming into this warm room from twenty-below weather was too quick a change. His nose had been bubbling sweat from the moment he entered the room. His nostrils were fanned out and flat, as though someone had bashed him on the nose. Whether or not Eskimo noses are flattened from the constant rubbing—the Eskimo method of kissing—is a debatable question.

Jim's mukluks were made of caribou skin, but they had sealskin waterproof soles. The inland Eskimos make the legs of these boots from the tough neckhide and the soles of the forehead skin of the caribou. Often, too, the skin from the front part of the leg is used to make the leg of the mukluk. Jim had two white strips of caribou-belly skin decorating the lapels of his parka, and a cuff and waist strip of the same white skin.

The Eskimos on the Arctic coast ordinarily make the entire mukluk out of sealskin, with a sole of ugiuk, or square flipper sealskin. These last much longer and are far more durable, especially for wet weather, than the caribou-skin footwear. The best caribou skins for making clothing are from the autumn hunt.

The ladies were busy with their children, at least the two babies of some eight or ten months. A little boy of six stood by the Bishop and a little girl of five stood by her mother. She looked a little shy. The babies began to cry as soon as the Eskimos had entered the house, but it was not just for food. They stopped crying when each mother pulled her child from his nesting place in the artigi, an oversized hood on the back of the parka. It was far too cold on the trip to take the little ones out to change them, and after they were dried and clean the babies gurgled contentedly and then hunted for food.

Ordinarily the Eskimo mother has the bottom of the artigi well padded with sphagnum-type moss. On the first opportunity she cleans up her child. Dermatophytosis, a skin disease, sometimes covers the entire body of the children. Before the advent of our civilization infant mortality was so high that the Eskimos were a dying race. Even today, in many isolated places, infant mortality is high.

Our conversation was centered around them. The women were conscious of their disheveled hair and as soon as the babies were quiet they smoothed it back and tucked it into their parkas. Compared to the men, they were clean. These people had been alone and away from other human beings for so long that a kind of fear had built itself in their very characters. About all we could draw from them was a "yes" by the raising of their eyebrows or a "no" by a wrinkle of the nose.

We who are in constant touch with our fellow men have built up a kind of turtle-back skin. We go where angels fear to tread and say hello to total strangers. We ask directions. We speak to strangers as though we have known them all our lives. Isolation, regardless of what kind it is, creates a mystic yet real wall of fear. Anyone penetrating that sanctuary is a stranger and a potential enemy. A monk in his monastery or a nun in her cloister is isolated somewhat like these Eskimos. Some of these detached people actually fear contact with the world.

There are more cases than I like to mention of men who went North to seek a fortune in furs and were made "mad trappers" by the isolation. For a time they eagerly awaited the day they would go to town for supplies and for news of Outside. Then, the longer they were alone, the less they cared about meeting people. Finally, in the loneliness of their minds, they developed a persecution complex. Every trader was trying to cheat them. They became suspicious of every visitor and finally began shooting at everyone they saw. Either they committed suicide or the Royal Canadian Mounted Police had to track them down.

Most of the Northerners, the missionaries, Hudson's Bay people, and the Royal Canadian Mounted Police use the term "Outside." It can be defined as a term used by people of civilization who find themselves in an isolated area, out of easy contact with their fellow men. "When I get Outside," usually prefaces how, when, and where a fellow will celebrate. "Outside you will find this kind of pipe for me, Falla," an Eskimo will tell me. "Outside you have beautiful churches, you have plenty to eat, and even some kind of yellowish drink that makes a man feel happy." "Outside" to many Eskimos means a place of plenty.

When soldiers are away from home during war their thoughts, their dreams, and their desires are to come back to the wonderful place called home. It takes absence to create appreciation, as their greatest desire is to return—"just to kiss the good old soil," to be within the borders of their native land.

So it is with a normal individual of our civilization when he finds himself within the fastness of the vast, faceless Arctic. He may have his work to do, be it to manage a store, to preach the Gospel, or to trap fur. If he is balanced with good judgment and a sense of values, when his task is done he awaits that glorious day when his face points southward toward home. Miners are fired with the "pot-of-gold" idea and missionaries with the zeal for souls. Regardless of their aims, however, they are human beings with a desire for social life, for the music in the voices of their loved ones.

Ever since the days the first explorers penetrated the North, the natives have been fascinated by white men. Whenever a boat arrives or a plane lands, even today the people flock around it. The natives stay a little distance away, and the whites of the settlement as close as they can get to the new arrivals.

This little boy at my elbow, with big eyes for food, is a veritable representative of his people. Even the father and mother, regardless of their frequent acquaintances with us, pressed as close as their shame and bashfulness allowed.

Everything about us fascinates them. They watch our reactions when we speak to each other. Our eyes, our lips, and our gestures hold their attention to the point of imitation. I have watched young Eskimos in their late teens move their lips trying to follow the movements of the Bishop as he spoke. Once I saw them burst into laughter at some simple gesture Father made with his hands to express himself. The tones of our voices must be real music to them, since they can sit for hours and listen to conversation, often in a language they cannot understand.

Our clothes, too, are intriguing, especially buttons—and parka zippers. Most of their clothing is made to fit without buttons, zips, or hooks. A leather thong around a man's waist serves to hold his pants from falling down. His parka is a pullover affair with holes for the head and arms. Drawstrings are sewn into a neat hem around the top of their mukluks, and often this is tied above the knee. This latter practice is more in keeping with the custom of the inland Eskimos. Years ago they used to make their mukluks to reach above the knee like our high-top rubber boots.

Our meal at an end, Brother set the table with jam, some bread, tea, and hot beans. Father Menez asked the people to come and eat.

"These people have been boiling their skins for the last three days," Father Le Mer whispered to me. "They started from the Back River, north of Garry Lake, over two weeks ago, and one of the older men died on the trail. Jim told me that one night the old fellow just walked out into the storm and they never saw him again. Then she has been sick," Father indicated, looking at Jim's wife.

Her eyes were baggy and set in deep, dark yellow pockets. She had a dwarfed mustache. Her raven hair was twisted in every direction. She kept pushing it out of her face and tucking it into an imaginary bun at the back of her head.

One of the women had been chewing some fish and I saw her put her mouth on that of her baby to feed it. Lack of food had made it impossible for her to nurse her child. The men ate with gusto, and a steady stream of fish grease dripped from their grizzled chins. They gave each mouthful of food about two chews and then lowered their chins, threw their neck muscles into play, and swallowed hard. About every five swallows they gulped down a cup of tea—not a few sips! This was indeed a banquet. After the bean bowl and the fish plate were empty the men had a few pieces of bread and jam. They ate quickly, as though fearful the food would be taken away from them. When the teapot was empty the women cleaned the table and washed the dishes, with their little ones slung on their backs. The men sat and smoked and smiled. About 9 P.M. two other families arrived and Father Menez gave them food and tea.

"They come to the mission whenever they are in the settlement. Perhaps someday they will ask about God and receive His grace of the Faith," Father Menez told me quietly, looking at them with kindness and hope.

The late arrivals had just about reached the bottom of the second kettle of tea when the Bishop told Jim he was glad to see that he had come for Easter. "It is one of the great feasts of the Catholic Church, if not the greatest," the Bishop emphasized.

"To say it true, Bishop," Jim began haltingly in English, "I was not going to come this far north, but we had nothing to eat and could find no caribou for over three weeks. We know there is always something to eat here," he said, rubbing his stomach and smiling at the other Eskimos.

"We are happy to share with you our few rations," the Bishop continued. "I hope you will remain for Easter now that you are here."

"We will stay if the Falla gives us something to eat." This was shouted from one of the late arrivals in the kitchen.

"Falla can give you a little grub, but you must dig holes in the ice and net some fish for your dogs," the Bishop answered just as loudly, so all could hear.

"Will you give us some nets, Bishop?" Jim pleaded in a milder tone.

Father Menez said he could let them have two nets. He joined the Bishop with two of the Eskimos and a fresh can of cigarette tobacco. The men rubbed their hands together, smiling at each other. It had been a long time between smokes, and here was a half pound of tobacco!

"Thank you, Falla." Jimmy spoke out for the rest. "We are happy to stay for a while if we can find food for our dogs and our families. It's bad time of the year in the Barrens. The caribou are still in the south. When they come north in late May and early June they are not fat."

Jim was proud of the mission. He was proud now, in front of the other Eskimos, that he was an official member of the Church. He looked around at them with assurance, as much as to say: "You see, these fellows treat me right!" And he puffed away on a cigarette almost the size of a short fat cigar. He had used two cigarette papers to make it.

"We are happy to help you when we are able and when there is a reasonable need of help," the Bishop began. "I do not give you food and nets and anything else just to try to make Catholics out of you. I want you all to realize that. To be a Catholic takes more than a full belly and the assurance of food. It takes a real Inuk!" A wave of seriousness spread over the gathering. The Anglican Eskimo leaned over and whispered to Jim, and Jim cleared his throat.

"Bishop, for a long time many of the men have asked me this question, and now this man asked me. Why are there different churches at Coppermine and why do the other ministers come here in the spring and again in the summer and ask us to join their church? We have many small gods, but really only one big God, Kaila. Are there many gods and many churches?"

The Bishop relit the stump of his often-lit cigar and answered with a twinkle in his eye, "That is a very good question, Jim. Just as truth is one, there is but one true God. That question of many churches? Well, let me ask you this. When you shoot at a caribou, where do you aim?"

"I shoot to break his back or his neck," Jim replied, looking at the other men. And they waved their hands at him, as if to say, "That is not the place to hit the caribou."

"What part of the caribou do you shoot at?" The Bishop directed his question at the one who was doing the most guffawing at Jim.

"I shoot at heart," the man said with finality, pointing to his heart. "He will run a little, maybe, but surely he will die. If a man shoots at the spine and is a little too low or too high, he will lose the caribou." And an argument began between Jim and the other fellows with plenty of gestures.

"All right, all right now, Jim. I will now answer your question on why there are many churches." Silence followed the Bishop's authoritative voice. "As you see, in the question of shooting a caribou, you have a different opinion from your friend here. Who taught you to shoot a caribou in the backbone?"

"My father," Jim replied quickly, "and he was the best hunter in the Barren Lands!"

"And so you follow the method that your father taught you. But, Jim, you can see, too, how there might be other and better ways to shoot a caribou. Perhaps if your father had known about them he would have taught you." The other Eskimos were nodding their heads in approval.

"As you see now, there is a question of which way is the best. Do you believe it is better to shoot at the heart, especially when there is great need of food, since there is a greater chance of killing the caribou that way?"

Jim rubbed his chin and looked on the floor a full minute before replying. "Yes, I think now it might be better. If the bullet does not hit the heart, it will surely tear a hole in the lungs and the animal cannot breathe."

"So, Jim, let us return to your question of different churches. When I was a boy my mother and father taught me to pray and attend church with them—just as your father taught you to hunt and make a living in this unusual country. My parents belonged to the Roman Catholic Church and I was naturally brought up as a Catholic. Later in school I studied religion and learned about the many different churches in the world and how they all began." The Bishop stopped a moment to relight his cigar, and Jim reached for the tobacco.

"For many years I used to ask myself the same question you asked me just now. Why are there many different churches? Why not one church with the same teaching, if they all pray to and worship the same God? I read and studied and prayed to God for many years for the right answer. One truth began to stand out like a mountain. The Catholic Church, no matter where I found it, always believed and taught the same truths! And of all the other churches, not two of them could agree. What one would teach as true the other would teach as false. Finally my reason and the faith God gave me pointed out very clearly that the true Church must be the one that has always been persecuted and ridiculed more than any other, and whose founder was even murdered on a cross! The founders of all the other churches never aroused enough envy with their greatness as to have their fellow men crucify them. And what proved to me beyond any doubt that I was in the right church was the fact that Jesus Christ was the only founder of a church that ever arose from the dead! By this He proved that He is truly divine and truly God. None of the other founders of churches ever arose from the dead or healed the blind and made the lame walk, because they were men like you and me, Jim."

"Well, Bishop, if this is such a sure thing, why don't these other white men understand this too? They study like you and some are smart too," Jim asked.

"Jim, some of these other white men don't understand for the same reason that you did not understand about shooting a caribou. Their parents taught them the religion of their family and so they follow it today. Perhaps they have had no chance to learn about all the other religions. Perhaps they think that what was good enough for their parents is good enough for them. Perhaps they were too busy about making a living to think about religion.

"The other reason for many different churches is this," the Bishop continued. "Very often I found the laws of God and the Church very strict, but I also found them to be just and good laws that made me feel better for keeping them. Now you know that any great organization has laws. The Royal Canadian Mounted Police is an organization, and you realize that it not only has laws for the people here like yourselves but also for the policemen too! Now the laws of our church are strict and good, but some men thought them to be too strict and decided to found a church with a few softer regulations and some easier rules. They used some of the laws of God that they liked, but not all of them! They put aside the hard laws, like no divorce and that the Holy Father, the Pope of Rome, is the lawful successor of St. Peter, the Vicar of Christ. Many men founded churches with rules they liked. So we have today many different churches always trying to find easy ways to reach God, *but not God's way to reach God!* Jim, that is why I am here and why I decided to be a priest and a missionary. When I learned for sure that Jesus Christ gave us the true Church, I decided to spend the rest of my life pointing out the road to my fellow men like you and your friends."

The Bishop put his hand on Jim's shoulder. "Jim here studied very hard with our missionaries, Fathers Cocola, Adam, and Le Mer. He learned about the Catholic and then about the Anglican Church. He learned that a man cannot make a judgment as to whether one is right or not unless he studied about both. With the grace and light of God he has accepted what he found to be the truth and joined the Catholic Church. That is not to say that he found all falsehood in the Anglican Church, but rather that he did not find all of the teachings of Christ in it. Some are lacking, as is the case in every other church except the Roman Catholic Church founded by Jesus Christ. They have taken a few teachings of our Lord suitable to their convenience of life. If these churches accepted all Christ's teachings, they would be all in the same church as you are, Jim. It takes a big man to admit that he can be wrong, and a great man to abandon his beliefs of childhood and accept those which he finds to be true according to his sense of righteousness—just as he will now aim at the heart of a caribou when hunting instead of aiming at the back." The Bishop looked at Jim, winking.

Jimmy looked around at the other Eskimos, and his chest swelled in justified pride that he really had intelligence, regardless of the fact that his friend knew a better method of shooting caribou.

The other man was encouraged, now that the Bishop had in effect patted him on the back for his hunting methods, and decided to ask a question that was building up a head of pressure. "The Falla tells us not to use bear claws for luck when we hunt seal and not to carry the wolf foot when we hunt caribou. Yet he carried a medal on his neck all the time and he prays to statues and pictures." He pointed to Father Menez, as if to accuse him of a crime.

Very slowly the Bishop reached into his pocket and took out his wallet. Every eye was upon him. Carefully he unfolded a faded piece of paper and a news clipping with a photograph.

"This is the last picture I have of my mother. She was so good to all of us children," he began, but his big heart would not let him go on. The Eskimos gathered about him and looked at the picture of a little old lady and then sat silent. He restored the picture to its hiding place and blew his nose.

"Most of you remember your mother too, so I am sure you understand and excuse me. That picture reminds me of so many

223

good things my mother told me and taught me. And one of them was to have devotion to the Mother of God. Since I could talk my first efforts were to say 'Hail Mary full of grace.' Father Menez carries a medal on his neck to remind him that he should pray to Mary, our heavenly Mother, and ask her, since she is very close to God, for protection and help from our Creator to live a good life. When Father kneels to pray before a statue of the Blessed Mother, he does not adore her, but he speaks to her, asking for favors from her Son, Jesus Christ. A statue or a picture of her reminds him to pray to her, just as the picture of my mother reminds me of all the good things my mother taught me when I was a boy."

Many of our evenings are spent in this fashion when the Bishop visits the missions and his people. He delights in meeting the people and in talking over their personal problems with them. Most often the Eskimos air their difficulties in public, since their neighbors are aware of them anyway. Naturally, if they have a personal problem and ask for a private talk the Bishop readily takes them for a walk or to his room—if he has one! Most of the Eskimos are very friendly toward the Bishop and recognize him as a great leader and a man from whom they might learn something, whether they are Catholic, Anglican, or "not very much of any religion."

That evening at Bathurst, while the conversation seesawed and the wind squealed eerie calls of the killing cold of the Barren Lands, a thermometer just outside the window read twenty-two below zero. That was cold for April.

"The wind is beginning to develop muscles," Brother Beauchemin called, coming over to my side of the room. "Perhaps we should have another look at the tie-down lines on the plane. They could have worked loose." He is always conscious of the ship, and I needed no further prodding to slip into my parka.

Swirling snow dusted us the instant we stepped outside. Descending the hill from the house to the river and the plane, we both noted that the wind had shifted to the southeast. Our ship was moored on the ice in the protection of the high bank, with the few buildings of the settlement acting as a windbreak. We could retire without worry. After that gulp of cold air we zipped into our sleeping bags in the attic of the little mission and went to sleep to the sound of the wind doing a strange solo on the stovepipe.

Chapter Fourteen

SPRING fever seems to get into the blood stream of every Northerner, and big Brother Henry is no exception to the rule.

Ever since his fishing days at Good Hope, Brother always begs Father Superior at Fort Smith for permission to spend a week or two at Salt River in the spring to restore the mission larder with a fresh supply of fish. It is only twenty miles north of town and accessible by road. Brother Joseph Brodeur usually makes the trip by truck. All the fishing gear is loaded, with Brother Henry sitting on top of the load to keep an eye on his precious equipment while they bump over the rough road. Once settled in his bachelor camp in a tent, Brother Henry sets his nets and visits them as often as twice daily, catching suckers and whitefish.

Early in June of '54 I had just arrived with GTM for the summer season when Brother Henry returned from his spring fishing. That first evening we all gathered in the recreation hall to hear what kind of season he had had and were regaled with stories of his experiences, which included bagging a four-hundred-pound black bear—to say nothing of lots of fish. We always enjoyed Brother Henry's stories. They took on a new flavor at each sitting, and his realistic telling of them kept us in peals of laughter. He would wiggle his beard and flash his eyes, clap his hands, and his voice had boom and power. Often the Brothers teased him with questions and tried to sidetrack him. He just shook a mighty finger in their faces and continued. Besides his stories, we all enjoyed eating the firm whitefish he netted and dried or smoked. The hospital patients loved him for "bringing home the bacon," their favorite dish.

That summer I had the pleasure of flying Brother Henry to a new mission, Uranium City, on Lake Athabaska in northern Saskatchewan. Brother Larocque came along as the chief carpenter to build the new church of St. Barbara.

Prospecting in this area had begun in 1944, and by 1948 over three thousand surface showings of pitchblende were recorded. Underground work began in 1953, and Eldorado started production of uranium on the northeast end of Beaverlodge Lake. The Beaverlodge Local Development area was established by order and council that year, and a district was town-planned by the Saskatchewan government. The settlement is centrally located some seven road miles inland from Bushell Landing on Athabaska Lake. The residents and miners four miles away at Eldorado or twenty miles away at Gunnar can easily utilize the services offered in town. A site was suitably located on the western rim of the settlement, and the old Goldfields mission house was moved on it. The church at Goldfields was moved also, but a brush fire destroyed it early that spring and the Catholics appealed to the Bishop for a new church.

Being short-staffed in Brother carpenters, the Bishop engaged Burns and Dutton Construction Company from Edmonton to do the cement foundation work. Brother Larocque did the interior woodwork finishing, while Brother Henry helped with the painting.

The summer of '54 was unusually warm, and many forest fires burned over thousands of acres, creating a real sub-Arctic smog. Brother and I were happy when the winter came to clear the air.

It was well on in February, after our buffalo meat had reached its respective places, that we had the news of a visitor. Father John Drouart was coming from Rome as a representative of Father General, who every six years sends a canonical visitor to all the missions of the Oblate Congregation throughout the world. This is the opportunity for the missionaries to air their views on mission work and for the visitor to get an idea of each missionary in respect to his personal life and apostolic work. Such a visit may be likened to the co-pilot check ride to which every good pilot subjects himself annually. Characteristics might develop that can take the sharp edge off an efficient pilot. The same goes for a missionary.

The days were growing longer around the twenty-fifth of March when our rangy, jovial visitor arrived at Fort Smith. Bishop Trocellier had delayed his winter visit of the missions so that Father Drouart could accompany us. On this trip he would have an idea of the vicariate before his official visitation began later in the spring.

Dressed in Father Mousseau's wolf-skin parka and beaver mitts,

Father Drouart had the cut of an adventurer as he stepped aboard GTM. Now he would have a look at new country and meet his brother missionaries. This white wilderness was quite a contrast from his last assignment. Just a month and a half ago he had been in hot, steaming Laos, climbing the mountains of Indochina!

Now, down the wide Mackenzie and over the mountains we flew, and he loved every mile. Evenings we listened to his lively stories of other lands. For fifteen years he had been Superior of the scholasticate in Rome and a student of the catacombs. The Indians and Eskimos sat in rapt attention while he described those underground crypts and explained the significance of the carvings on those miles of mysterious passageways.

When we arrived at Tuktoyaktuk on the Arctic coast Father Drouart complained of nausea and loss of appetite and retired about an hour after our arrival. The Bishop was deeply concerned and wondered if the great change in climate had affected him.

On Sunday morning Father said his Mass, but by ten o'clock he was back in bed with a fever of 103! Aboard the plane in my medical kit I had some acromyocin capsules. I gave him four, then one every three hours. He ate a little at five o'clock and went back to sleep. His temperature was almost normal. We said special prayers that evening for his speedy recovery. He slept until four in the morning, when through the thin wall separating us I heard his groaning. I took his temperature—103 degrees! This was serious.

"I believe the wisest thing to do, Father, is to fly you back to Aklavik and get you under a doctor's care as soon as possible. You have more than a cold and more than fatigue."

"I feel awful causing you all this trouble. Perhaps in a day or so I could continue on with you."

I told him that I would consult with the Bishop after Mass and then we would decide definitely. Later His Excellency took one look at him and whispered to me: "Do you think he can even travel to Aklavik? That fever is mighty high to expose him to thirty-five-below-zero weather!"

I admitted there was danger involved. But I figured the odds were less if we wrapped him in a sleeping bag and took him to a hospital rather than let him remain here without a doctor's care.

There was no question of weather. The sun was up and a light drift sifted over the blizzard-hardened drifts. Brother Beauchemin went under the engine tent with his gasoline blowpots, and Father Franche, director of the mission, dashed off a few short letters and packed the mail sacks. He is also postmaster there, the most northern post office on this continent.

The Bishop and I prepared Father Drouart. We dressed him as warm as possible in heavy wool underwear and caribou trousers and parka. Father hitched up his dog-team ambulance to make the mile dash to the plane with our patient zipped in my eider-down. Our patient tried to smile, but his eyes were glassy with fever. A handful of Eskimos had gathered to see what all the ac-tion was about on Sunday morning. Three of them gave us a hand lifting Father aboard.

At exactly eight-thirty we were airborne and flight-planned for Aklavik with the Bishop aboard as flight nurse.

"We will keep our receivers turned up for your transmission CF-GTM on mercy flight to Aklavik," the Aklavik radio informed me.

This special attention was appreciated about fifty miles out of Tuktoyaktuk when the ground drift hazed over our flight path. Visibility was less than five miles on the Mackenzie delta. Some-where under the gray-white lens of drifting snow was the hospital we were looking for. Familiarity with that area and a careful eye on the check points, plus the guiding hand of St. Christopher, brought us safely into Aklavik at nine forty-five.

Many hands came in sympathy to assist Father Drouart to the hospital. He had left in such a gay mood just a few days before. I advised the doctor of the medications we had administered at Tuktoyaktuk. He registered surprise when I told him how Fa-ther's temperature returned to normal five hours after the antibi-otics were administered and how it mounted again each evening about six o'clock with chills and nausea.

"Those are strange symptoms for a fever in this part of the world," the doctor mused.

"Do you think it advisable to fly Father to Edmonton?" Bishop Trocellier asked.

"No, Your Excellency. If there is any immediate danger I can have an aircraft here in a few hours from Norman Wells or Fair-banks," the doctor assured the Bishop. "You have come so far to visit the missions on the Arctic coast, it would be a shame to go south without seeing them. You should be in Coppermine in about five days. I will send you a wire on Father's condition," the doctor promised.

That was the deciding factor—along with the promise of clearer weather—in establishing our flight east that day.

"We have over three hundred pounds of mail for Paulatuk. Would you also have room for two hundred pounds of potatoes and a hundred pounds of cabbage and fresh carrots?" Father Ruyant asked as we were leaving the hospital.

When I assured him we could carry them, he was happy. "I'll have them ready in half an hour," he said, and hustled off.

Father Max Ruyant, a trim six-footer from France, is the director of our largest Eskimo mission school and hospital at Aklavik. He spent six years on the Arctic coast at Stanton Mission, near the mouth of the Anderson River, and learned not only the Eskimo language but the know-how of life among these northern people. The Eskimos like Father Max because he is always ready to listen to their little troubles and help them when he is able.

After a short conference with the Bishop we set one o'clock as departure time for Paulatuk. After our lunch I stopped by the kitchen to pick up a special box of cookies and cake baked by Sister Rachel Deschênes for the "bachelors of the coast." Our sleeping bags had been preheated over the hot-air register at the mission, and we packed the vegetables, a big thermos of coffee, and the special box in them.

By half-past twelve the Eskimo children and four Sisters from our boarding school at Aklavik and some thirty people of the settlement gathered around the plane for our departure. We were in the air at exactly one o'clock, when I checked out on a flight plan from Aklavik to Paulatuk. Weather changes are sudden and drastic up here on the roof of the world, but that day when we climbed above six hundred feet of fine powdered drift snow, GTM entered a clear pale blue sky. The rolling tundra country east of the Mackenzie looked cold and sinister beneath the film of gray-white drift. It reminded me of white whale or porpoise swimming ten feet below the surface of the cold blue Arctic Ocean. I often see them on our August flights with the school children.

On the winter flight our course was tight and beelined over the undulating faceless country. I picked out the wide ravine of the Anderson River and saw the speck of black that was our mission at Stanton, forty miles to the north, built in 1937 in honor of Father William Stanton. Now he was looking down on both of us!

Soon the smoky mountains roughened the lip of the horizon, and there we saw the bending Horton River bulldozing its way through the mountains to the Arctic Ocean via Franklin Bay. Pulling my arm for attention, Brother Herman pointed to the shadowed country beyond the Parry Peninsula. I followed his finger, and the hills on the south shore of Darnley Bay were leveled and lost in the horizon. Strong winds and blowing snow! This was a storm! Below us I could pick out the heavy blow of the drift as it covered some patches of blue ice and then left them exposed again. A check on our gasoline supply assured me we had enough to return to the cabin at the mouth of the Anderson River. I had a cache of two fifty-gallon steels there for emergencies of this kind.

That dark mass of cloud was coming toward us like an evil thing, and Paulatuk was under it. For a whole year Fathers Leonce Dehurtevent and Andrew Vermaut had been living in anticipation of this visit of the Bishop. They would be very disappointed if he did not come this spring. We just had to give it a try.

I made a descent to five hundred feet above the sea to clear the ripple of rocky hills this side of Argo Bay. As GTM leveled off we entered the black shroud of drifting snow. A close check on my instruments and time gave me an estimate of ten minutes to put me directly over the mission! I was mindful of those twin pipe aerials the Fathers had erected. They constituted my most dangerous hazard, so I kept a little to the right of the course and descended to a hundred feet. Nothing was visible below, above, or ahead of us.

I glanced at Brother and noticed that a rosary had appeared in his hand. His eyes were glued to the instruments. My time said we were close, so I elevated to seven hundred feet. Now to the southwest I saw the drift sweeping off the Hornaday River hills in a thick white curtain. We were directly over the mission. I began a slow descent in a kind of downwind run.

"There is the Grotto," the Bishop called out excitedly. "It just flashed by under your wing, Father."

That magic word "Grotto" released a lot of tension. Another orbit and my orientation was fixed and complete. On our final approach we were down to fifty feet. When the Grotto flashed by again I turned out more flap and let GTM down until her skis rumbled over the corrugated, cement-like drifts of the bay. We slowed down quickly in that wind and came to a stop as soon as the tail ski touched the snow.

I quickly turned up the flaps and added power to turn and taxi toward the mission. It was impossible to turn. The wind on my air speed registered fifty-five miles an hour. I was afraid it would catch a wing and turn the ship on its back. Deep inside me I was thanking God for the safe landing in that blizzard. I left the engine idle a minute to allow the skis to freeze and anchor us.

"You cannot turn?" The Bishop tapped my shoulder.

I cut the engine just then and told him I was afraid of wrecking the plane if the wind caught it broadside. He understood now, for the roar of the whistling wind was loud and powerful. Like giant claws it ripped and clutched at the plane, lifting the tail two feet off the snow and plopping it down again. We shifted some of the baggage to the rear of the plane to keep the tail quiet and give the Bishop a little room to stretch his legs.

"When Brothers Beckschaeffer and Kraut carried those rocks over ten miles of tundra in 1936 and '37 and built them into the most northern Grotto of Lourdes in the world, I am sure they never meant it as a guiding beacon to Paulatuk, even though it does stand fourteen feet high!" the Bishop commented, rubbing a cold foot with the boot off.

"I didn't see a soul near the mission," Brother said, unbuckling his safety belt for action. "Perhaps they couldn't hear our engine above the storm."

"You have good eyes to have seen the house," the Bishop said. "I looked but saw only blowing snow."

"We are a mile or more out on the bay and it will take them almost an hour to dress and walk here," I added, zipping up my parka.

Brother jumped out, and a gust of wind blew him down and whipped off his cap. He looked into the storm, but it was gone. It must have taken us a good twenty minutes to manipulate the cover over the engine. Snow was blowing into it and I was afraid, what with the melting because of the heated engine, it would freeze into a solid block of ice. The skis were holding fast—frozen on the hard snow. Usually the friction of landing warms the ski bottoms and we taxi on poles to keep them free. Our little tail ski was still lifting and breaking free, but we had to go into the plane to warm our freezing faces.

"Let's bury the tool box in the snow under the tail with a rope attached. It will make a good anchor," Brother suggested, and it sounded like a practical idea. We attached the rope to the box in the plane, and circulation came back into our faces.

"Here, take my good cap, Brother," the Bishop said when I told him Brother had lost his cap in the storm.

We ventured out again, and digging the hole for the tool box tested our patience. With Brother as a windbreak I succeeded in burying the box. We stamped and packed the snow and were about to re-enter the plane when Brother called excitedly:

"Polar bear! Look!"

I turned quickly, reaching for my hunting knife.

"Hello, Father! Welcome to Paulatuk!" It was Fathers Leonce and Andrew in their polar-bear parkas and pants. Brother really had a scare.

We all climbed aboard. There were a lot of excited greetings, for it had been over nine months since they had seen any of their brother missionaries or had had any mail or news of their families.

"Our Lady of the Snows must have guided us through that terrible storm," the Bishop said, brushing off some snow that had blown in on him. "St. Christopher must have known the love you have for good potatoes!" he added with a playful tug on Father Leonce's frosty beard.

"Are we far from the mission?" Brother asked, still puffing from his battle with the wind.

"About a mile," Father Vermaut answered, then added: "If we walk close together, holding onto each other's parkas, we can walk there in half an hour."

The Bishop was happy to move after the long trip and his extended wait in the cold plane. "I may have to rest a little on the way with this oversized heart of mine," he said, pulling on his heavy wolf-skin mitts, then suggested: "I believe it is the best plan to go and hitch up your dog team to fetch all the baggage. We must not lose time, either, if you don't want your precious cabbage to freeze."

Thirty-eight below zero gave that fifty-five-mile-an-hour wind saber teeth. Luckily it was on our backs, yet I could feel it needling the calves of my legs and cutting into my back through my windproof parka. A few hundred yards from the house deep hard ridges of drift ran off the east shore of the bay, some of them four feet deep. We had to watch our footing, especially the Bishop. A fall on one of those cement-like drifts could fracture a leg. The dogs set up a howl even above the wind when we approached the house.

"There are no people here just now," Father Leonce puffed,

brushing the snow from his parka in the little porch. "Some may have heard the plane and they will be here tomorrow. Our people never travel in a storm of this kind."

Some forty Eskimo families inhabit the hilly country around the mouth of the Hornaday River at Paulatuk. They fish, trap white fox, and have plenty of seal meat for their dogs. During the long winter they live only in snowhouses. In summer they live in tents. The mission house, built by Fathers Biname and Griffin in 1935, is the only dwelling in the entire area. When we arrived in the two-story house, the soft-coal fire had burned out, although the stove was still a little warm. Father Leonce went into action with some newspaper and the coal pail.

"It will be good and warm in half an hour," he said, blowing on the coals to start a flame. This was a wooden frame house, without insulation, and the sub-zero winds drove the cold into it.

I asked Father Vermaut about the availability of my two steels of aviation gasoline. "I want to bury them, one under each wing," I told him, "and use them for an anchor to keep the ship from blowing away if the wind should increase. I won't rest tonight until I know the plane is safe."

He assured me we could haul the gasoline out on one trip and while Brother and I anchored the plane he would bring the baggage to the mission with his team.

"You can all go to the plane for the supplies," the Bishop said, pulling off his coat. "I will get these fires going and start something cooking."

The Bishop had not forgotten his days on the Arctic coast. He realized every helping hand counted now, as it did back in 1930 when he first landed fifty miles north of this spot at Letty Harbor with Fathers Biname and Griffin and Brothers Beckschaeffer and Kraut on the first trip of the *Lady of Lourdes*. They lived in a sod hut then, not a clean frame house like this one.

Father Vermaut dug out his sled and hitched his team while the three of us loaded the gasoline. Fortunately the barrels were standing near the mission and not buried in the hard snow. Unlike the light basket-type Alaskan sled, this was a heavy Komatik type, built with heavy pieces of three-by-eight-inch fir planks, eighteen feet long, and for runners, two-by-fours of three-feet lengths were notched every four inches and lashed on with rawhide thongs of ugiuk sealskin for decking. It was a sturdy sled, to run the wind-packed drifts and ram through rough ice hummocks over the pressure ridges on the frozen sea.

"We will use just five dogs," Father Vermaut puffed, steam blowing from his parka hood. "If I use more I cannot control them alone on this short trip."

The white, squat huskies leaned into their traces and we pushed and rocked the sled to break it loose and start the load moving. The wind acted as a brake on the hill in front of the mission, easing the sled onto the frozen Arctic bay. Our dogs scratched and clawed the ice, and the huge sled creaked and squeaked like a dry wagon axle as it eased over the sharp white ridges. The dogs picked up the scent of fish and food aboard the plane, and they began straining and yelping, their bellies almost dragging on the ice. At the ship we rolled off the gasoline and loaded the bulging sleeping bags of vegetables and mail, and the Fathers were away with their treasured cargo.

Brother and I dug shallow pits, tied a rope on the 350-pound anchors of gasoline, and rolled them in. We packed snow over the gas drums, made the ropes fast to the wing struts, and tightened the rope from our buried tool box to the tail ski. During the process of anchoring, we made several trips into the plane to rub the cold out of our hands and faces. That wind had the sting of a million wasps. For added security, we wrapped another twenty feet of quarter-inch rope around the engine covering, to keep it from whipping and working loose in the gale during the night. Father Vermaut returned for us with his dog team as we finished our tie-down.

At the house we carried our personal baggage into the porch, then helped Father unhitch his team and tie them on the chain-anchored dog line for the night. Husky dogs never see the inside of a house. All they howl about is for more food, not because they are cold or lonesome. When they have eaten, they curl up with their faces tucked under their tails and their backs to the wind. Soon the drifting snow all but covers them and acts as a wind-break. They sleep until some strange scent or noise awakens them.

After hanging our outer snow parkas in the porch, we carried our precious vegetables and mail into the warm room and closed a heavy caribou-skin-padded door on the wind and the cold. The aroma of roasting caribou came from the kitchen at the end of the big room, and the house was good and warm now.

"Everything is cooking." The Bishop pointed to the huge pot on the stove. "We can say our Rosary, and fifteen minutes of adoration will just about bake those potatoes," he added, opening the oven door and testing the potatoes with a fork.

After a wash-up we retired to the chapel upstairs and Father Leonce began the Rosary. I had so much to be thankful for that day, and a very special favor, the speedy recovery of Father Drouart at Aklavik. Brother Beauchemin knelt on the stairway. Every ten minutes he went to fire up the stove with native soft coal, a lignite type that burns quickly.

In true community fashion Father Superior tinkled the bell at the appointed time and the lid was off the beanpot. Chunks of caribou meat, beans, and carrots floated in brown onion-flake gravy, and the aroma dilated our nostrils. Baked potatoes done to a turn and a round browned loaf of Father Leonce's bread topped off the table. It looked good, smelled delightful, and tasted delicious!

"Now, just a minute," the Bishop cautioned. "I have some special soup for this occasion," and he lifted a large aluminum pot from the back of the stove. "Here, Father," he said to Leonce, ladling out a generous portion of his famous cabbage-onion soup. "This is just what you need after all that work in the cold weather."

We all had some, of course, although I took only half a ladle. It isn't that I don't like onion-cabbage soup, but our good Bishop likes a very generous amount of fat added—to "stock it up a little," he says.

We worked our way into the meat and potatoes, and I was after a second small piece of meat when we all heard the porch door open. It was not the wind; there was a stamping of feet. Father Vermaut went to investigate.

"Welcome, Joe," we heard him call out.

It was Joe Trasher and his wife and two children, whom I knew well from previous visits. They came in, blue from the cold.

"I was camped at the bottom of Argo Bay when you passed over, Father," Joe said, pulling his parka over his head. "You were flying so low we thought you were going to hit the mountains."

Having only one table, Father Leonce told Joe we would finish our supper, then he could take over the table with his family. Ida, his wife, began to unfold herself, slipping off her artigi. Out came a little baby, who immediately began fighting for his supper. As his mother nursed him, the other little boy just stood there with all his clothes on, watching us with large eyes and swallowing. He was cold and evidently very hungry.

To all the sixty Eskimos of this area the mission at Paulatuk was a haven of kindness, food, and shelter. Mr. and Mr. Joseph Trasher were one of those families. Address? The Barren Lands, Paulatuk, Northwest Territories. Joe is an Eskimo with a slight Caucasian mold to his features. He speaks both English and his native tongue. Occupation? Trapper. Age? Forty. He is the oldest son of the famous Billy Trasher, the *Inuit,* or the Man among all central Arctic coast Eskimos. Joe had met Ida Gruben of Paulatuk during their last year at the Aklavik boarding school and after their marriage decided to leave the Mackenzie delta and try Ida's country, where white fox were plentiful and brought a fair price. His first year in that country Joe fell on a sharp rock and cut his knee returning from his trap line, the accident leaving him with a limp and a bowed knee.

After ten minutes of talk he limped up the stairs to the chapel. Joe was not trying to make an impression on us. His entire life has been good and wholesome. He has been true to his family, to his friends, and especially to his God. Joe is the first to realize he is far from a saint or a perfect man. Like his famous father, Joe can drink and eat too much at times and even tell a few off-color stories. But he has a conscience. He recognizes his faults and tries to correct them. This fact alone is enough encouragement for any man of God to continue his work of bringing God to man, and man to God.

About half an hour after the arrival of our visitors we set the table for them. Mrs. Trasher spent at least ten minutes washing herself and the baby in Father Leonce's room, then called her other son in for a scrub-down.

Keeping herself and her children clean is probably one of the greatest tasks of an Eskimo mother. During the long winter, especially when traveling, it is almost impossible to wash. Even washing in a snowhouse means extraordinary effort! There is the melting of ice or snow for water over a tiny primus kerosene stove. Some families still use the hollowed-out soapstone seal-oil lamp. For this the Eskimo has to find a good piece of soapstone about two feet long, a foot wide, and six to eight inches thick. He begins the slow process of carving a long trough in it, actually making a stone pan. Into the soapstone lamp or stove he pours seal oil, throws in a chunk of moss for a wick, and lights it. A dark red flame burns slowly, sending out black soot over the white dome of the snowhouse and also over everyone in it. A kettle or pail is suspended above the fire, and snow or ice is melted for water. Sometimes soup is made from old bones—a matter of two or three hours' work! Then comes the moment of actual stripping down and bathing. Even the idea itself feels cold, and it is hardly ever done. Towel baths usually bridge the gap between the non-stinkers and those who really smell.

Twenty-five years of education have filtered through the primitive habits of a few, and Joe and Ida headed the list.

"I have been hunting these past five days and feel a little dirty, Father." Joe smiled, rolling up the sleeves of his sweat-ringed, once-gray shirt. "Will it be okay if I use your room and basin to wash up a little?" Father Vermaut nodded and gave him a fresh towel.

The little five-year-old boy had no sooner sat down than he reached into the big pot, grabbed a fistful of meat, and stuffed it into his mouth. His mother quickly wiped off his hand with a piece of newspaper and slapped it good. He looked around to see if we noticed, bowed his head, but did not cry. Joe made the Sign of the Cross, and the boy's little red hand did the same. Then, like the real mother she is, Ida ladled out the meat stew with one hand and patted the crying baby on her back with the other. Before sitting down, she worked the baby around to her breast and held him with her free hand, so he could eat with the rest of the family.

"Your bread is real good, Father," Joe managed with half a mouthful.

This was a delicacy, since Eskimos seldom bake anything but bannock—a sour-dough biscuit—if they have any flour. Summer supplies of flour last only a month at the most, so most of the time it is a question of eating straight fish and meat.

We left the family to their meal and joined the Fathers in the main room. During our supper the question of mail was often mentioned. Now the pressure of suspense reached the breaking point. They were opening the mail sacks with expectancy. As they read parts of letters, gleaning news highlights and glancing at the end to see who had written, they questioned us to elaborate on items they ran across in their mail. After the long and full day I retired to the little chapel to catch up on my prayers. I must have dozed off, for the next thing I knew Father Leonce was shaking me alive.

"We will have night prayers now. The people are coming upstairs."

I heard many feet and soon knew why. Another family had arrived. It was Eddie Gruben, his wife, and their two children. The Bishop had had them in our Aklavik boarding school in the late thirties, along with Joe and Ida, so they were all old friends.

After the evening prayer Bishop Trocellier stood before the people and spoke to them like a father.

"My dear children of the Arctic coast. We had a difficult time coming here today, but I know you suffered more than we did to make the trip from your hunting grounds. When you heard our plane you quickly packed your meager belongings, hitched your dogs, and came, leaving the older people in charge of the camp. You do not live in a land of plenty, yet I know you love your country and you love each other. Most of you I have instructed and baptized. Some of you I had in school and had to use the strap when you were bad boys and girls. I remember when a certain young lad put a baby muskrat in a young lady's desk, maybe to prove to her he was a good trapper!"

A few eyebrows went up and smiles broke out under some sparkling black eyes. There was one red face, Joe Trasher's. The Bishop smiled and so did Joe, bashfully.

"I ask you one favor tonight, my dear friends," the Bishop went on. "Even though it is impossible for you to come to church often because of the nature of your country, there is one thing you can do to keep yourselves close to Almighty God. That is, to be faithful to your prayers, especially your Rosary. Say it every day. Be charitable to all the members of your family and especially all those who are not members of the Catholic Church. 'See how those Christians love one another,' the pagans of ancient Rome used to say about the early followers of our Lord. Make this charity a mark of your character that will set you apart. Make it shine like the midnight summer sun, lighting the way to our Lord. Obey the laws of God and the laws of your country. May God bless you and keep you safe and well." And the Bishop blessed us all.

Father Leonce arranged for all the people to spread their blankets downstairs. Ordinarily the people would build snowhouses, but the hour was late and there was room for all. We made our beds on the chapel floor, where a set of double sliding doors closes off the altar from the rest of the room. Brother Beauchemin and the Bishop had the far corner to themselves.

They snore! About twelve o'clock Father Vermaut grew tired of telling me stories of the hunt and his exploits in the coal mine and dozed off to sleep.

These two men of God, isolated on this tongue of land jutting out into the Arctic Ocean, have given up so many of the ordinary pleasures we enjoy to bring God to these Eskimos. During the six weeks of summer life was bearable, but these long unending winters!

Father Vermaut had told me how he and Father Leonce had to hurry with their fall fishing that year because of the early freeze-up in the Hornaday River. The fish run had started in mid-September, and for five days they caught over eight hundred good salmon trout. Then a week later the ground was white and frozen. That night the river began running ice and they had to remove their nets or lose them. Four days later they walked on the river and set their nets under the ice, difficult because of the swift water. Using a pole eight feet long, they chiseled holes in the ice every eight feet and passed the pole under the ice from one hole to the next to thread the net across the river. All this cold hard work netted only a hundred and fifty fish in a week. So they packed up their gear and came home. After fish for so long, the vegetables were a treat.

Father Leonce, sleeping so soundly beside me on the floor, had not tasted the luxury of vegetables in many months. It was impossible to fly many of these delicate freezables in during the winter, but I promised myself that next summer I would surely bring this little mission a load of potatoes. Listening to the whining of the wind, I drifted off to sleep.

The delicate tinkle of an altar bell gently awakened me. One of the Fathers was already saying Mass. Light streamed in the upper room and, glancing about, I quickly noted I was the last sleeper. All the others had their eiderdowns packed. I dressed quickly. Heat came from the floor register, with cooking odors and muffled voices of children. By the time I was washed and dressed and had said a few prayers, the two Fathers and the Bishop said their Masses.

Father Leonce asked me to say Mass for the people. As I vested I heard them mounting the chapel stairway. For a moment my thoughts went to Aklavik and Father Drouart. I would have an intention asking God to cure him of whatever sickness or virus he had.

Then I started my Mass, offered for these good souls of the high Arctic. These few brushed shoulders with our civilization and learned to know our God. The modicum of knowledge they absorbed and the grace of Faith they had really changed their world. They were living now for that future life with God, which offered everything they longed for here on earth.

Chapter Fifteen

BEFORE leaving Paulatuk, Father Leonce confided to the Bishop that he was suffering very much from acute hemorrhoids. Since our plans were to fly south from Coppermine after visiting the other missions, the Bishop had Father pack his bag. Father Vermaut would remain alone for a few months.

After two days of weather the storm blew itself out, and we flew northeast to Holman Island. Fathers Metayer and Tardy, the Hudson's Bay manager, and one Eskimo family were on the ice to welcome the Bishop. Our visit was short because of good weather and because Father Metayer was ill with stomach trouble. He also joined us, leaving Father Tardy in charge of Christ the King Mission.

When we arrived at Coppermine there was still no word from Aklavik on Father Drouart. "No news is good news," the Bishop said, and we flew east to Bathurst and Cambridge missions in wonderful weather and returned to Coppermine. Now we did have news!

BROTHER GEORGE SERIOUSLY INJURED IN ACCIDENT ON TRACTOR. MUST BE FLOWN TO EDMONTON SOON AS POSSIBLE. PLEASE WIRE IF GTM WILL COME. FATHER DROUART HAS MALARIA FEVER BUT DOCTOR HAS IT UNDER CONTROL. FATHER RUYANT.

"Looks like our plans change a little," the Bishop said, handing the wire to Father Leonce. "You'd better check the weather conditions. If there is a possibility of getting through to Aklavik, wire Father Ruyant."

It was late on Monday of Holy Week when we returned from Cambridge Bay and received this sad news. While Father Lapointe prepared supper I went to the wireless station. Our available weather reports came from Port Radium and Norman Wells. Radium was enjoying a high, cold and clear. The Wells had winds and snow showers from the outskirts of a front flowing over Good

Hope in a northeasterly direction. By tomorrow it would be well on its way over the Arctic Ocean, leaving me a clear flight path. I sent a telegram to Father Ruyant that we would leave in the morning for Aklavik.

The Bishop was happy with the weather picture, and bags were packed and preparations made for the long flight in the morning. Father Lapointe had another passenger for us. A ten-year-old Eskimo lad would come along for school. This was his first opportunity to go, since his people had just arrived from the north for the first visit in nine years.

The Tuesday-morning weather at Coppermine was quite a picture. A white fuzzy sun was just visible through a haze of falling ice crystals, and a heavy layer of dark stratus hung low over our anticipated flight path. It was anything but CAVU—ceiling and visibility unlimited. A wind of about twelve miles an hour rolled a thin screen of snow dust over the ice and rocky country, reducing the visibility to some eight miles.

After our Masses and a healthy serving of beans and fish and good coffee, we geared ourselves for cold weather. It was thirty-four degrees below zero. When Brother Beauchemin was installed with the gasoline blowpots to heat the aircraft, I walked up to the radio station for a final check on the morning weather picture. A new front had developed in the last twelve hours, moving southeast over Eldorado on Great Bear Lake. However, the Department of Transport gave me clearance on the northwest coastal flight, and I flight-planned a Coppermine to Aklavik trip with a two-hour refueling stop at Paulatuk. We have quite a gas cache at Paulatuk, thanks to Father Franche and our Arctic schooner, *The Lady of Lourdes*. Without this cache such a flight would be impossible.

Back at the mission, our departure became definite with the latest weather report, and we started the procession of baggage to the aircraft. Our passengers now included the Bishop, Father Leonce Dehurtevent, Father Metayer, and the young Eskimo lad. Our baggage load was four hundred pounds, plus rations for ten days and a sack of a half dozen Arctic char trout for Paulatuk.

By eight-thirty GTM was ready for life. We started the engine and heated our oil. After a day's flight, when the oil cools off to about twenty degrees centigrade, we start the engine and give the oil a two-minute dilute. This adds about a gallon or more of gasoline to the oil, depending on the below-zero weather. In the morning, after a gasoline-pot heating of the engine so that it will turn over easily by hand, we use the battery starter and run the engine slowly, until the oil temperature reaches forty degrees centigrade. The revolutions per minute are then stepped up to sixteen hundred for eight minutes. This will boil off the gas from the oil and give a true reading of the oil pressure. If this procedure is not followed on an oil dilute, there is the danger of blowing the gas-thinned oil through the propeller seals. This has burned many an aircraft and caused plenty of unnecessary labor.

After the pre-heating and engine run-up we loaded passengers and baggage, wished Father Lapointe a joyous Easter, and took off on the three-hour flight to Paulatuk. Aloft, we circled the town for altitude, climbed above the layer of ice crystals and ground drift to four thousand feet, and leveled off on a west-by-northwest course.

About an hour out of Coppermine the ground drift became so dense we often lost contact. In this barren country, rocks and valley shadows take the place of trees to mark the land. There is a terrible rawness, an emptiness about this white void, that can nauseate a person. I like to keep flying contact here just in case my engine decides to rest a spell. At least then I have a chance to choose a fairly level terrain to glide down to earth. The south side of rocks is usually black and bare of snow because of the sun at this time of the year, and they are a great aid to navigation. Far ahead, above the high ground drift, we could see the glistening domes of some of the Melville Mountains.

After two hours aloft we were over the mountains and rough terrain. Most of the low country and the valleys were obscured with drift. Ahead of us wisps of smoky stratus began to appear, and in a matter of minutes we began picking up the dreaded ice. I tried climbing over this layer of cloud, but the ice formed so rapidly on all leading edges we began losing altitude even with added power. My windscreen iced over and forward visibility was reduced to a "white-out." This all happened in a matter of minutes. I turned and headed back to where I saw those mountain peaks and black rocks we had passed some ten minutes ago. Perhaps we could melt off our load of ice. I flew for twelve minutes, and Brother began tapping my arm and pointing down. Jagged black rocks were flashing by one hundred feet below us. My altimeter read twenty-five hundred feet! These were the tops of the Melville Mountains. I thinned out my propeller pitch for power, added a little flap, and began a wide orbit. Slowly I descended fifty feet. On the second orbit I saw a level spot void of boulders. Thank God we were not icing up any more. As it was, we must have added a half ton to our load. On the third orbit I spotted our runway and made a wind check. One more turn to inspect it well, and then we took a low pass at it, ten feet off the deck. That was it. Wisps of snow or ice-crystals almost blinded us as I flew downwind for my base-leg turn.

Some of my passengers became a little anxious as they surmised what was about to happen. I told them to hold on tight as I turned upwind and made the final let-down. A good wind helped slow us down, along with full flap, and before we realized it our skis were rumbling along that wonderful snow. The landing was exciting, since it was in a strange and new place, even though I had made many like it on lakes, rivers, and prairies these past three years. We glided in and out of a five-foot dip that was obscured by the drifting snow, but our guiding angel kept us clear of all those jagged, frost-busted rocks. Once GTM stopped we all breathed easier and sent thanks to God for a safe landing in this desolate place. I had been saying Hail Marys ever since we began icing, a habit I had formed while driving my car.

Fathers Leonce and Metayer decided to take a walk and see this new country. Perhaps they could recognize some of it. I cautioned them not to lose sight of the aircraft. With poor visibility and no sun, even an experienced man could get lost.

Brother and I covered our engine, hoping with the Bishop that in an hour or so we would be able to continue our flight on to Paulatuk. Meanwhile I began to work my radio, sending out a call to Norman Wells, Coppermine, Aklavik, and Eldorado. My receiver was blanked out by the weather, so after a ten-minute try I decided to preserve my battery.

To pass the time and satisfy our hunger, Brother dug out one of our gasoline blowpots to melt some snow for tea, and I opened our ration box. Over a good cup of tea and biscuits we decided to wait one hour. If the weather was still out we would dilute our engine oil and build an igloo for the night.

As always, fuel is one factor that takes precedence even over food on a landing of this nature. We usually add an hour of extra fuel on such a trip, but an emergency landing and take-off always consume more fuel than anticipated. So we decided that the weather had to be excellent for good altitude to take new bearings and fly directly to our destination.

At two o'clock the weather was about the same, and my passengers were beginning to feel the chill of this thirty-below-zero weather. The best answer to this was a good snowhouse. After diluting and re-covering the engine, we set to cutting snow blocks, blessing Father Menez for the huge snow knife he had given us at Bathurst Inlet. The aluminum shovel I had to clear the skis on mornings after a storm was also a godsend. The two veteran missionaries set to work as though it were a routine procedure. Back at Coppermine I had built two igloos with Brother just for practice, so with our combined efforts the snowhouse took shape quickly. We decided to use our tent for the roof instead of the usual dome of snow, to prevent dripping when we started our gas stove for cooking and heating.

By four-thirty we had the Bishop and the young lad inside, out of the weather, on a warm carpet of polar-bear skins. We had four aboard, and they made excellent insulation from the cold. Father Metayer went inside with the Bishop, to prepare the evening meal, while Father Leonce, Brother, and I built the low, long entrance tunnel to our igloo.

At six o'clock Father and the Bishop had some good hot soup ready and boiled Arctic salmon trout with beans. A little shifting and adjusting had to be done to wedge everyone into the snowhouse, but, once inside, it was cozy. Knives and other utensils were poked into the hard snow, and candles in snow niches provided plenty of light.

During supper the conversation drifted to polar bears and Brother Beauchemin, who is a loud snorer. We usually kid him about it and he rides along. Evidently the Bishop had talked this over with the other Fathers and they decided to put Brother on the spot. The general consensus was that he sleep in the entrance tunnel, to keep guard over the igloo. Brother objected vehemently, on the grounds that he would be polar-bear fodder. With very convincing reasons Fathers Metayer and Leonce persuaded Brother to make the sacrifice, especially for the sake of the Bishop. He finally agreed reluctantly, but only on the condition that he could have my gun beside him. At this the Bishop decided we had carried the story far enough. Seriously he thanked Brother for his bravery, then told him that only small polar bears, if any, ever wandered this far from the Arctic Ocean.

After we said our Rosary and night prayers and zipped ourselves into our sleeping bags, I retraced our course from Coppermine about five times. Finally I assured myself that we were exactly on the summit of the Melville plateau, some fifty miles inland from the Arctic Ocean and about ninety miles from Paulatuk. I had fuel for one hour and forty-five minutes, so my decision now was final. I would not proceed on course over the mountains, just in case I might be twenty or thirty miles off course. That could spell trouble because of the fuel situation. Instead, I would fly due north to the Arctic coast, then follow it, regardless of how low I had to fly, all the way to Paulatuk. That was the safest way, especially since there was a Dew Line station at Pearce Point, sixty miles this side of our mission. That decision was relaxing and I had a good sleep.

About six o'clock a light westerly wind began to ruffle the roof of our igloo. We all heard it and started our good mornings. Father Metayer moved the block of snow covering the tunnel, and the loud snoring of Brother put us all in good humor. At our laughter Brother awoke and immediately assured us he had had a very bad night dreaming of polar bears.

It was Wednesday morning of Holy Week, but the Bishop decided our place was too cramped and cold to say Mass. He led the Rosary and morning prayers. The weather was about the same as the night before except for the wind, which we all predicted would clear up the skies. Our aircraft was covered with about two inches of hoarfrost, over the ice, which had to be cleaned off before any attempt to fly. But first things first. We had coffee, frozen raw fish with biscuits and jam for breakfast. In our cramped quarters that took an hour. We had plenty of water and coffee, too, so this was our main course. The young lad ate a piece of raw fish, half a biscuit, and a chunk of chocolate.

Breakfast gave us new life, and we set to work cleaning the aircraft. I cut off about two feet of our refueling hose and fitted it over a broom handle to beat the ice gently from the wings. We had to be very careful not to damage the wing fabric. With a rope over the wing and a man on each end whipping it back and forth over the surface, we removed the frost.

Almost every winter morning we have to utilize this rope routine. The least amount of frost or snow on the wings of an aircraft disturbs the flow of air over the surface and results in a loss of lift.

The Bishop and Brother concocted a thick soup with fish, beans, rice, and plenty of powdered milk. While it cooked, Brother found some onion flakes and added them for seasoning. With steaming hot tea and pilot biscuits this made a tasty dinner.

"The wind has died down," Father Leonce commented, looking up at the tent.

"Maybe we will have snow. The sky looked gray and ready for something," Father Metayer added.

I went outside, and it was snowing "Hudson Bay blanket" sized flakes. The orange wings of the plane were changing color!

"Guess we don't fly anyplace today," Brother said, coming up behind me and pulling up his parka hood.

We gathered some fresh snow for tea and went back into the snowhouse. When I mentioned the possibility of another night here because of the weather, the Bishop suggested another Rosary —for clear skies.

I knew he was thinking of Brother George, suffering at Aklavik, and also of Father Drouart. He was so anxious to get there. To make sure we could not fly, we all crawled out to have a look. The snow was still falling. About four inches of fluffy feather-down snow had covered everything.

"It might be a good idea," Father Leonce began, "if we anchored the plane tonight. Usually after a calm like this we have very strong east winds."

I could imagine what strong wind would do to this light snow. Taking his advice, Brother and I dug pits under each wing to the rock. Under one wing we buried the tool box, with a half-inch rope attached to the wing strut. And under the port wing we buried our gasoline pump, with another rope attached to the wing strut. For the tail anchor we buried two suitcases, with ropes leading out to the rudder ski. I secured all the controls and tied the engine cover snug, to keep it from flapping and ripping in the wind.

We dug some fresh granular snow beneath the surface of the drifts for our water supply, took six fish and our emergency ration kit, and a five-gallon can of gasoline into the porch of our snow-house and slid a huge block of snow across the entrance. Now we were all snug inside. The temperature had risen a little outside since the snowfall, only about twenty degrees below zero now! We left our porch section of the house open, and Brother Beauchemin sat on the ration box there and began preparing the fish for supper.

The Wednesday before Holy Thursday is one of our four fast days of the year in the vicariate, and a boiled fish supper was in order. While there was still light—it was just after six o'clock—we all decided to pray our Divine Office for the day. That took almost an hour, just the time Brother needed to put supper on. His stove warmed the snowhouse and we could eat with warm hands and warm food!

The Bishop spoke again of Aklavik, and the suffering of Brother George and Father Drouart was never far from his thoughts. Then as usual whenever he spoke of suffering he recalled Coppermine and how the early missionaries had suffered to bring the Gospel to the Eskimos. He was on that subject when Father Leonce asked:

"Bishop, I would like to hear a firsthand account of the early days at Coppermine. When I came North I heard many different views and versions. Whatever did happen in those days?"

"I was far from Coppermine when I heard the first news," Bishop Trocellier began. "Those were the days of European unrest, before the first great war, and I was attending preparatory school when the Coppermine story appeared on our bulletin board. All the students at St. Giorgio's College in Italy became interested. Naturally when I came North in 1921 I asked many questions, and Father Alphonse Mansoz gave me a very clear and true picture of events. He was active at the mission of Fort Smith, the news and nerve center of the North, and he learned the whole story."

"Where did the first Eskimos and missionaries meet?" Father Metayer asked.

The Bishop related how Archbishop Breynat, by some moccasin telegraph, had heard that a group of Eskimos came annually as far south as the north arm of Great Bear Lake to meet some of the Hare-skin Indians of Norman. This meeting seemed a God-made occasion to have a missionary meet these strange Arctic coast peoples. The Bishop also recalled another meeting of Eskimos, back in 1860, on the Mackenzie River with the Loucheux Indians. The Indian men were out hunting when the Eskimos came, raped and killed the women and children, and burned the camp. When the men returned and saw what had happened, they hunted down the Eskimos at Separation Point and killed them. Father Grollier acted as peace officer in '61 and stopped the sniper warfare that existed between the Indians and western Eskimos.

"What about those two French Canadian missionaries?" Brother asked. "Bishop Fallaize told us at the novitiate that the first missionaries to work among the Eskimos were Fathers Lefebvre and Constant Giroux. Isn't that true, Bishop?"

Bishop Trocellier agreed it was.

"Fathers Lefebvre and Giroux made the first attempts to Christianize the western Eskimos, even up to Richards Island on the Mackenzie delta, as early as 1890," Bishop Trocellier continued. "They found these Eskimos to be an entirely different race of people from the Indians. They were stubborn in their ideas, very materialistic, so when Archbishop Breynat saw the opportunity to get a toe hold in the eastern Eskimo group he sent Father John Rouvière to the meeting in the Great Bear Lake region."

As the Bishop spoke, I noticed the tent roof sag heavy with snow. Father Metayer lit the primus stove both for a little heat and to melt snow for tea.

The Bishop continued to tell us that when Father Rouvière arrived in Dease Bay on the Great Bear Lake, two hundred miles east of Fort Norman, he found the place abandoned. All indications pointed to the Eskimo trek east, up the winding Dease River, and Father John followed it by canoe while his dogs went along the shore. When it became too shallow he continued by foot for three days and finally found the Eskimos. To his surprise, they were very friendly and asked him many questions. He decided to spend the winter there at Lake Imerenick (now Lake Rouviere), some fifty miles east of Dease Bay, and built a small cabin from stunted trees in the area. By September 17 he said his first Mass there, his diary stated, and after October he lived alone. The Eskimos all returned to the Arctic coast.

"What did he eat?" Brother Herman asked, rubbing his stomach and grinning.

"His diary told us he fished with three nets he carried along from Norman," the Bishop went on. "He put up fish on a stage for dog feed and shot some fat caribou on their way south. When the days grew light again, in early April of 1912, Father Rouvière trekked by his homemade dog sled to Norman. Here he took on fresh supplies and a new assistant, Father William Le Roux. Father Ducot was at St. Theresa's Mission at Norman at the time, and he outfitted the two adventuring missionaries. They left around mid-July of 1912. A month later they were at the cabin on Lake Imerenick. They found no Eskimos there, so they returned to Dease Bay where fishing was good."

As the Bishop spoke, Father Metayer made some more soup and passed it around. While soup call was on, we learned how the missionaries spent a full winter studying the strange new language of the people from a few notes made by Father Rouvière. They waited patiently in the spring of 1913, but no Eskimos came. A new cabin was built and supplies of wood were stored during the summer, but still no Eskimos came. Determination to reach these people with Christianity decided them to go and live among the Eskimos. Father Rouvière sent a letter out to the Bishop with a trader that August and stated that he and Father Le Roux were going into the Coronation Gulf country, where the Eskimos made their home.

The Bishop relit his cigar, holding it over the flame of the primus stove. "Then, silence. There was no news for almost two years."

"What about the Father at Norman? He should have notified the Archbishop that these men did not return and that he had had no word about them." Father Metayer became concerned.

"The Archbishop did receive letters from the Father at Norman and also from Fort Rae," the Bishop replied. "He was so concerned about his men that in the spring of 1915 he asked Inspector La Nauze of the Mounted Police to look into the situation."

The Royal Canadian Mounted Police found nothing but ruins at the Imerenick Lake cabin and returned to spend the winter in Father's cabin in Dease Bay. About the end of April 1916, when traveling is at its best, the police pointed their dog team toward the mouth of the Coppermine River. They met families of Eskimos but received only evasive answers until they asked the direct question: "What happened to the two white men?" And then news of the whole story tumbled out. With the remains of Father Rouvière's diary found later, plus special information supplied by an explorer in the area, Darcy Arden, the complete story finally came to light.

Early in October 1913, Fathers Rouvière and Le Roux had left the Dease cabin, spent a few days at Lake Imerenick, and continued east over Dismal Lake to the Coppermine River. Some Eskimos, including two by the names of Sinnisiak and Karmick, accompanied the Fathers to show them the route. It took them about twelve days to make the hundred or so miles over the rocky country, and Father Rouvière's entry in the diary indicated they were at the site of the present settlement of Coppermine about October 22, 1913. He also stated that some families left when the missionaries arrived. Father Rouvière misunderstood and was very disappointed. He thought they had left because of the priests. We know that the Eskimos had to leave the settlement to find something to eat.

Fishing was very poor at Coppermine that fall, and the people were hungry. Consequently the few provisions brought along by the missionaries disappeared quickly. Later Father Le Roux's gun was missing, a serious thing in such a country, where without the means to kill game or protect oneself against wild animals a man could not survive long. Father Le Roux recovered his gun, only to face danger from an unexpected quarter. Karmick, a man he thought to be a friend, tried to kill him, but an old Koeha stopped him. This wise old Eskimo knew his people. He advised the missionaries to go back south and return in the spring, when a better spirit existed in the camp.

So the Fathers packed their sleeping bags, Mass kits, and the few supplies that remained. They hitched their four remaining dogs to their Komatik sled, and old Koeha even accompanied them almost to Bloody Falls on the Coppermine River and then left them to go alone.

"I know the shapeless uniformity of that land." The Bishop spoke in a meditative mood. "The first year I was a young missionary at Coppermine I went out one day to visit a family who lived in that same area, and on the way home I fell often and finally became lost. There was no sun and no shadows, just a hard white faceless land. Fortunately for me, a friendly Eskimo family came along. Those poor missionaries must have had a lost, outcast feeling that day, alone and with almost no food left."

Our Bishop was a most sensitive man, and he could not go on talking. Tears came and he brushed at his face. This happened often, too, when he preached on our Blessed Mother. The Bishop cleared his throat, made himself comfortable by stretching out his stiff leg, and continued.

"From the best accounts, we learned that on their third day out two Eskimos, Sinnisiak and Uluksak, joined the Fathers. They had two dogs with them and told the missionaries they were going to meet some of their people coming from the south. In fact, they helped the two Oblates to pull their sled up the steep foothills of the September Mountains. The first night the Eskimos camped alone, but the fourth night all shared an igloo built by the natives. On the fifth day Father Rouvière, just thirty-two years old, started out, breaking trail with his snowshoes. The two Eskimos followed him, helping the dogs with the sled, which was guided by Father Le Roux, who was only twenty-seven. A high wind came up and started a real blizzard. The Eskimos talked together and came back, as if to confer with Father Le Roux. Sinnisiak made a motion to loosen his belt, pleading a necessity of nature. Seeing the situation, Father Le Roux turned his back and looked away. In that instant Sinnisiak pulled out his knife and stabbed the missionary in the back. Father Le Roux screamed and tried to run toward his partner, but Uluksak was on top of him. He pleaded with Uluksak, but the Eskimo stabbed him in the heart and in the stomach, killing him!

"Father Rouvière heard his yell, turned, and ran back. It was too late. He saw Father Le Roux fall. Then he saw Sinnisiak pull Father Le Roux's gun from the sled and take aim at him. He headed toward the river and the first shot whined over his head. The second hit him. The two Eskimos ran to him, and Uluksak knifed him in the side. Sinnisiak ran back to the sled for the ax and cut off Father Rouvière's legs and arms while he still breathed and moved his lips. Uluksak killed him, cut him open, and took out his liver, and the Eskimos ate it, hot and bloody.

"Then they threw Father Rouvière's body into a ravine near the Coppermine River," the Bishop continued with difficulty, "and went back and also ate Father Le Roux's liver. Eskimo medicine men of old believed that eating a white man's liver would give them eternal life. These natives most probably shared those beliefs."

"How did you learn all the details of those murders, Bishop?" Father Leonce asked.

"I heard it from the murderers themselves," the Bishop replied and continued: "Well, when their brutal work was finished, they gathered the cherished gun and ammunition, returned to Coppermine, and boasted that they had murdered the white men. Uluksak was eager to tell every move he made to outsmart the Kabloona—white men."

The Bishop went on to say that the following day some Eskimos went to the place, six hours' walk south of Bloody Falls—in all, some twenty miles from Coppermine—and found the dogs still in their harnesses attached to the heavy sled. Old Koeha was along that sad day and admitted that he felt ashamed. The other Eskimos, who had no worries or thoughts about the dead, helped themselves to all they could carry away. Even after three years, a Royal Canadian Mountie who accompanied the inspector in 1916 found the sled and a human jawbone near it. The Eskimo who led the police to the scene of the crime pointed out the ravine where Father Rouvière's body lay buried under six or more feet of mud, ice, and rocks. Respectfully this lawman had two crosses made at the Royal Canadian Mounted Police barracks in Coppermine, carried them to the spot, and erected them in memory of the two brave men who died there.

I recalled seeing the crosses the previous year when I flew supplies from the Eldorado Mine on Great Bear Lake into Coppermine. They were on the west bank of the Coppermine River.

The Eskimo murderers were tried in Edmonton in 1917. A jury failed to convict them, and a new trial was held in Calgary, Alberta. This time they were convicted and sentenced to death, but the Bishop appealed to the Minister of Justice on the grounds that they had been driven to murder by hunger and an uncivilized desire to possess the goods of others. Their sentence was reduced to imprisonment at the Mounted Police cell in Fort Resolution on Great Slave Lake. After two years the Bishop interceded on the strength of promises by the two men. Paradoxical as it may seem, they promised to help the missionaries for the rest of their lives and make amends for their evil deed.

It was just after five in the morning when Father Leonce awakened me. "The wind is blowing very hard," he said, brushing the frost from his beard.

I didn't have a beard, but there was a white halo around the top of my sleeping bag. We were all covered with an inch of powdered snow. The wind hooted and howled. Granulated snow salted our tent roof, and a loose rope end beat like a drum roll. Everyone was awake now, even the little Eskimo boy, whose name I learned was Noel. We were all outside in a matter of ten minutes, and I had never seen such a storm. The wind must have been blowing at least fifty miles an hour. Fortunately it was a southeasterly, as Father Leonce had predicted, and only sixteen degrees below zero.

"The plane anchors are holding," Brother shouted in my face.

"I tied one end of the flapping engine cover, and all seems well, except we have about five inches of snow inside the plane!"

It was a cold ordeal to wash that morning. Out there we just scoop up a handful of snow and rub our hands together until it melts. By the time my face was washed I was cold! Fathers Leonce and Metayer had quite a time with their beards icing up. I don't think much water ever got through to their faces. Back inside our igloo, we dusted the fine snow from our clothes, bedrolls, and bearskins, and the Bishop reminded all of us it was Holy Thursday. While we said our morning prayers Brother tapped the pot of melting snow. It was cold inside, despite the heat from the primus stove, so we kept tucked away in our sleeping bags, except for Brother Herman, our chef. Fish was on the menu again, but breakfast was eaten in a meditative mood.

My passengers were settling down to the stark realization that they were in the isolated Melville Mountains! The excitement of the trip and the landing in such a strange place were over now. I began to see the question in their eyes: "Will this fellow ever manage to fly us out of these bald, lifeless wastes?" If they could only have followed my troubled thoughts and seen the knots and butterflies under my safety belt when I was deciding on a landing in that glacier-scraped country. Right now the problem was weather. This storm was beginning to bother me. I realized we had food for another fifteen or more days, but it was more than just food. What would the long delay do to Brother George at Aklavik?

"Have more fish, Father?" Brother cut into my meditation.

The boiled salmon char tasted good. After a second cup of coffee we said our Divine Office while Brother went outside to inspect the plane. I followed him in an hour. The wind had blown itself down to about ten miles an hour. This was beginning to look like a break. Brother was sweeping out the ship and had all the gear stacked in the tail section.

"There was six inches of snow in here," he mumbled, grunting and working away. At the least effort Brother grunted, and we all kidded him about it.

Powdery snow, still swirling in the air, reduced visibility to a mile at most. The thermometer on my wing strut read sixteen below zero. It was a good sign. I noticed, too, from my altimeter reading that the barometer was rising.

"It looks like we fly tomorrow," I called to Brother. He heard me all right, and his cold, red, unshaven face cracked in a smile from ear to ear.

"I'm getting just a little sick of this diet of fish," he said, coming up to me. "What should I make for dinner?" And he answered his question before I could speak. "We could boil that little sack of white beans. It's only about two pounds." So we had the beans for lunch, with hard pilot bread and tea.

The Master of storms had administered the *coup de grâce* to the mighty wind, and in its final gasps we decided on a walk to have a look at our surroundings. The two Fathers took the .22 rifle and went to climb the ridges to the west. Our visibility had stretched out to about three miles now. Brother and Noel and I went east over our landing path. I took my 306 rifle. After examining our "landing field" I realized how fortunate we were to have landed unscathed in that place. Brother was pointing to some black four-foot-high boulders.

"St. Christopher must have rolled them out of our path. And look down there." He motioned ahead. "Why, it's over a hundred feet deep, that ravine! And we just missed it by only fifty feet!"

I assured Brother I had seen it on my downwind pass and actually used it as a marker to land. He looked at me, scratched his head, and made the Sign of the Cross.

We walked around the area for an hour, climbed some rocky hills, and searched for a better take-off stretch to the southeast. Around four o'clock visibility was almost five miles, and the overcast became patchy. Tomorrow would be the tee-off day, I thought to myself, walking toward the plane.

It was after six on Good Friday morning when someone stepped on my face and jolted me awake! Noel was just escaping through the outside door when I looked to see whose heavy foot had so rudely disturbed my dreaming. The view outside made me grab a quick second look. Was that really a star out there? Thank God! Clear weather today. Brother also snorted in his sleeping bag and sat bolt upright when Noel crawled over him.

"You awake too, Father?" the Bishop's froggy voice croaked. "No wind today. I can see clear through the door. We will fly. I was thinking of that poor injured Brother George. I hope he is still alive and not suffering too much."

While slipping into my mukluks I assured the Bishop that there was a doctor at Aklavik and that he would give Brother the very best of attention until help arrived.

After our morning prayers and one more look at that clear weather we swung into action. Brother and I untied our engine cover, let it drop to the ground in tepee fashion, and started our blowpots. We made breakfast and heated our engine at the same time. The wing thermometer registered only eighteen degrees below zero and there was no wind. During breakfast it seemed as though the angels were ahead of time with their Easter confetti. The sun was coming out of the east and the snow crystals in the air began to sparkle. Everyone was in an excited mood.

At ten o'clock patches of blue began to brighten the sky. Our hopes and ambition to get moving kept everyone active carrying our gear near the plane. We thoroughly inspected the ground over which we had to turn with the aircraft and made a careful examination along our take-off runway for rocks that could break our skis.

At eleven-thirty the engine was warm and our propeller turned easily by hand. Brother and I went over the entire ship, checking for damage of fabric breaks by the storm, and then started our engine and heated the oil. New zest surged into everyone when our Wasp fired into life. The Bishop and the Fathers folded the tent and the bearskins. We ran the engine for fifteen minutes to boil off the dilute and heat it thoroughly. When the oil temperature read forty centigrade I cut the switches and we proceeded to turn the plane. Brother attached a rope to the tail ski, and with all hands straining on the rope we did a one-eighty turn. We replaced the seats, loaded the baggage, and Brother was folding our engine cover when the Bishop said:

"Let's ask Our Lady of the Snows for a little help to get us out of these mountains." And he took off his cap, leading us in three Hail Marys.

At exactly twelve-thirty, when our engine ran itself good and warm, I made the Sign of the Cross and eased the throttle forward. We began to move and that ravine came at us fast, but our air speed reached sixty, and just a light tug on the stick and we were airborne. It felt so good. We were off for the Arctic coast. I did not reveal my plan to the Bishop and other passengers until we saw the coast at one-fifteen. They were happy and much relieved to see familiar territory. We had often flown along the coast line in very bad weather.

Ice crystals filled the air, but the sun continued to cut through them, giving us good visibility. Flying at fifteen hundred feet, we spotted a landing strip on the ice at one forty-five, where a crew of DEW personnel were unloading a plane. That was Pearce Point, some sixty miles from our mission and gasoline. I checked my tank, and estimated another forty-five minutes on it, and we needed only twenty-five minutes of good flying to reach Paulatuk. Some twenty miles from our destination we flew into overcast and I went down to three hundred feet. Father Leonce spotted caribou as we skimmed the Hornaday River delta and then pointed out his coal mine to the Bishop. The gas was getting really low when we landed at the mission.

The flying time was one hour and forty-five minutes. My watch said two-fifteen, but at Paulatuk it was only one-fifteen. We had gained an hour, so before we left the ship we decided to refuel as quickly as possible and fly to Aklavik that afternoon.

Father Vermaut and all the people who had gathered at the mission for Easter were greatly surprised to see us. With the greetings over we told Father Vermaut of our need to refuel immediately and continue on to Aklavik. He said he had left our gasoline on the beach last autumn to hide it from poachers who might stop at the mission when he was absent and help themselves. Now it was buried under quite a depth of snow.

"I know just about where it is," he said. "I'll ask some of my Eskimos to help me dig it out. It won't take long."

Our passengers went up to the mission, where the Eskimos were glad to meet and talk with the Bishop. Meanwhile Father and I found a steel bar, a half inch thick and twenty feet long, which he had ordered to reinforce his dog sled, and began to probe for gasoline. Father Vermaut indicated just about where the fuel was located. After the fourth try, with all but six inches of the bar buried and no results, I laid a pattern on the snow and we began looking over every square foot. At three-fifteen we touched steel and the men began digging.

"Come in and have something to eat now," the Bishop called. I let the men dig.

The drifts were like cement and had to be axed and picked. Four men dug furiously and found a steel drum at four o'clock. One came running to the house to tell me about it. But before I had my parka on Father Vermaut was at the door. "Never mind, Father. It is fuel oil."

That let the wind out of our sails, and I decided it was too late to attempt the three-hundred-mile flight to Aklavik that after-noon.

"We will spend the night at Paulatuk," I informed the Bishop, and he understood. "By the time we find gas and refuel it will be perhaps another hour."

Brother and I diluted our engine and anchored the ship. Then the Bishop called us all to the mission and announced that since this was Good Friday and since we were now in no rush, we would all come for the Stations of the Cross.

After supper we continued to probe and search. Ten-gallon kegs of oil, fifty-gallon steels of gasoline for the boat, and even empty steels were uncovered—and all under some fifteen feet of packed snow! They had a system working now. A huge tunnel was being cut, following the beach, some thirteen feet beneath the surface. The hard snow was cut in blocks, and a chain of men worked it to the surface. Close to nine-thirty the aviation gasoline was found. The pit was too deep to roll the steels out, so we pumped them into drums on the surface. By eleven o'clock, GTM was refueled and Father called the weary men to the mission for a well-earned meal prepared by His Excellency.

That night Father Leonce graciously gave me his quiet room and unpacked my sleeping bag on his bed. He said the people would be visiting until all hours and he wished to remain with them. I gave him my air mattress for his bed upstairs whenever he decided to retire, and went to the chapel. It was close to midnight and after night prayer I began to feel weary from the strain of these last days.

During the Stations of the Cross that evening, I recalled the story of another Good Friday eighteen years ago, the story of a wonderful bass voice that had sung in this very chapel. It all began back in 1937, when Archbishop Breynat was making a visitation of his missions. He had a small Waco aircraft in those days and a daring pilot by the name of Louis Bisson. Brother Sareault, who related this incident to me, was co-pilot.

Foul weather forced the Waco down in Darnley Bay, some twenty miles from the mission. Mr. Bisson sent out a call on his radio and Father Lesage received it at Norman. From Norman the message was relayed to Aklavik, and from Aklavik to Father Griffin at Paulatuk. He and Father Biname had a small set there in those days, and at eleven o'clock at night he received the message. Early next morning he left a note for Father Biname, who was away with the dogs at the coal mine, and started out on foot for the plane. In midafternoon he arrived and found the Archbishop in a tent and Mr. Bisson and Brother working on a damaged tail ski.

Ingenuity and a few tools repaired the ski, and they were about ready to leave when they spotted Father Biname coming with his dogs. When he arrived his poor dogs dropped in their tracks. Forty miles they had come at full gallop! Father Biname was tired and hungry. They had the teakettle boiling soon, and along with a lot of fast conversation they began to eat. The Sisters from Aklavik had given the Archbishop a box with some pies that were separated by pieces of paper. Father Biname was so hungry and so excited he ate pie, paper, and all!

Father Griffin started out with the dog team and Mr. Bisson took off a half hour later. At nine o'clock that evening they were all together at the mission and the Archbishop suggested the Stations of the Cross because it was Good Friday. They mounted the stairs to the chapel. Father Griffin, with a rope holding his pants up and a torn old brown sweater, was the cross-bearer. Father Biname, in his short cassock, bearskin mukluks, and coal dirt still streaking his face, said the Stations. Then, transcending all this excitement, they lifted their hearts to God, and when the Archbishop heard the sweet strong voice of Father Biname ring out clear and true above all these earthly trials as he sang the *Stabat Mater*, it was too much for him. He wept, sobbing out the great paternal love he had for his missionaries, who gave so much.

Holy Saturday morning, the weather was clear, and we thanked God as we attended the Bishop's Mass in the little Paulatuk chapel. Six Eskimos came with four children. I always enjoy a stop-over here. The people are especially friendly and so cooperative in helping us with freight and gasoline chores. During my thanksgiving after Mass, when the aroma of coffee and frying meat drifted upstairs into our little chapel, it added to my feeling of contentment and security. I thought of the men who pioneered this place in the mid-thirties.

There was Father Delalande, a Parisian full of gay piety, yet a man who breathed fire wherever he preached! And Father Anthony Biname, a Belgian full of energy, with "it's got to go" spirit of progress, yet a man of solid faith! And with these there was Father Thomas Griffin, the reticent, hard-working, steel-nerved Texan who could fight the helm of a schooner through pack ice on a cigarette diet or spend months in an Arctic coal mine on a retreat with God! With these priests two Brothers, Beckschaeffer and Kraut, worked side by side. They left a lasting impression not only with their building of the most northern Grotto of Lourdes on this continent but also by their example of kindness and understanding that still remains in the hearts and minds of the Eskimos here. Brother Kraut was the musician and a mechanic who could repair anything from busted engines to broken legs! Boulata, as they called Brother Beckschaeffer, will always be a legend. His stories of the Bible and his work live from mouth to mouth and camp to camp over the years. The people loved him, respected him, and recognized him as a true man of God.

A loud rapping on the stovepipe startled me from my reverie. Breakfast was ready, that rapping said, and I was up to it that morning. Eskimos sat on a bench near the wall, smiling, as I came downstairs. Two little boys, about four years old, caught my cassock and pulled me toward the kitchen, pointing to a table steaming with coffee and a big pot of beans. Food means so much to these people. They wanted me to join the others and eat quickly so they would have a turn at the table. Usually when only a family or two visited the mission and had very little food, goodhearted Father Leonce invited them to the table after the Father's meal. And these children knew that.

"Looks like a real flying day, Father," the Bishop said as I entered the kitchen. The smell of burning soft coal gave the house a lived-in atmosphere. I was about halfway into my plate of beans when Father Vermaut said:

"Excuse me, would you please make room on the table for this meat pot?" He stood holding a huge cast-iron kettle. The outside was charred black from open-fire cooking, and spurts of steam came from under the heavy cover. The two little boys crowded near him, sniffing at the escaping steam and meat odors. "This caribou will give you strength to fly right to Aklavik," he said, lifting the heavy iron lid. I thanked Father and left the food for those who looked as though they really needed it.

It was after nine when Brother and I geared ourselves for the twenty-below-zero weather and began to heat our engine. A fifteen-mile-an-hour south wind had come up with a white, cold-looking sun, and powdery drift ran over the surface of the land and the sea. Father Leonce was not well that morning, and Father Vermaut assisted him to the plane with his dog team.

"Here is one of my prize catches of river trout," Father Vermaut said, reaching into his sled. "It weighs almost forty pounds. Never can tell, Father Bill, you may have to build another snowhouse between here and Aklavik. This will taste good!"

I thanked Father and packed the big fish aboard, realizing he spoke the truth.

"Here is something I almost forgot about. Your friend David Bernard left it for you." Father pushed a folded bearskin into the plane. "He came a few hours after you left on your way east two weeks ago. Here is a list of things he would like you to get for him." He pulled a folded brown paper from his pocket.

Dave Bernard was a good Eskimo who had lost his wife. His daughter and son attended our Aklavik school, and David and I had an understanding. I needed a few polar-bear pelts for my benefactors in the south, and he needed ammunition and tobacco.

Our engine was warm about ten-thirty and I started it to dilute the oil. The Bishop and my other passengers came down about ten minutes to eleven, and we took off. GTM climbed to one thousand feet, then we turned and flew over the mission. Father Vermaut and a few Eskimos waved us off to Aklavik.

Over the Smoking Mountains I saw the Horton River snaking north. Its high banks and golden sand bars glistened on the white snow. My magnetic compass did the usual amount of erratical dancing, but the young April sun turned the rocky ridges black, and their arching spines along the northern horizon made contact navigation possible even in this white country.

Little Noel pointed to the scrawny trees guarded by long jealous snowdrifts. He shouted in Eskimo, "Look, many small people down there." It was the first time he had ever seen trees!

Two black ribbons lay ahead, two bands of trees curved like a chain of mountain climbers on the white snow. Soon the land fell away and the valley of the Anderson River lay like heavy-textured white mercury, squeezing banks of sand into high golden hills. Southward, slim icicles of white tundra cut into the dark verges of the timber country. Wind and sun lifted snow lids on blue-eyed ice patches over Sitidgi Lake. To the northwest was a rippled sky line of the serrated Arctic coast, the Tunumuk Hills, and the Reindeer Station country.

Little Noel was having a field day, jumping from one window to the other to see everything. Then as quickly as a cloud shades the sun, our aircraft was flying over the dappled Mackenzie delta with its rivered network of veins and arteries. The hard-top lakes and rivers are all in formal black and white at this time of year, their spruce trees trim. Ahead of us, white spires of heat curled into the cold blue sky. It was Aklavik.

One orbit over the town, and people channeled to the river where I was to land. Over a hundred children from the school, the nuns, missionaries, and townspeople came to see who was arriving on the mission plane. After the mechanics of landing I taxied toward the crowd of people, fearful that some excited boy or girl might run toward us into our propeller.

Crowds like this always remind me of the ski plane that skidded out of control into a flock of children at Fort Chipewyan back in 1937, killing two of them. Noel was not excited. He was frightened stiff! He had never seen so many people. When I left the ship he followed, hanging onto my parka.

"How is the Brother?" I asked Father Max Ruyant, who came out of the crowd.

"He is anxiously waiting for you, Father. The doctor has been with him almost constantly."

"And Father Drouart?"

"Much better. His temperature is down now, but he is weak."

I thanked God that we were not too late. When our passengers and well-wishers left the area of the plane—all except Noel, who still hung to me—Brother and I diluted the engine and covered it. I wanted to talk to the doctor first of all, to find out just when Brother George could be moved south. After that we could act definitely, getting southern weather data and advising Simpson of our refueling stop at the airport.

I joined the Bishop at the hospital and saw a man suffering. Poor Brother tried to smile.

"He is in great pain, Father," the doctor said. "I give him a hypo every three hours, but it lasts only about two."

"When do you think he will be able to be moved south?"

"I believe we can have him ready by Monday, Father." The doctor looked toward Sister St. George for approval. "It is almost a miracle that this man lives."

The doctor told us that Brother George had tried to release a snagged cable on the rear hoist drum of a D-4 bulldozer. The ton-and-a-half blade was suspended by the snagged half-inch wire cable, and whatever he did released it. The flying cable caught his left arm, broke it in at least five places, and cut through muscles, almost twisting the mangled arm from its socket and cracking his collarbone. He could have been decapitated or cut in two in the wink of an eye. The doctor had cauterized every torn blood vessel and it was now a question of major surgery.

The doctor was a young man, sent North for experience as a general practitioner, and he seemed overworried about this case. Personally, I was relieved that Brother still lived. Across the hall I looked in on another patient.

"Thanks for flying me here," Father Drouart said softly through his fever-cracked lips. His face and eyes were lemon-colored, and a familiar smile played around his eyes. "The doctor said I'll be fine in about three weeks. I'm having a good rest."

After lunch Brother Herman and I refueled our ship, took out the seats along the starboard cabin wall, and replaced them with our portable stretcher holder. The weather looked promising for a beautiful Easter, and Bishop Trocellier was happy to be here at Aklavik again, where he had been pastor for a dozen years and more, winning the hearts of the Eskimos and residents.

Bishop Trocellier liked the peace among these jovial people after seeing the horror of war as a sergeant major in the French Army in World War I. Government officials found his judgment sound and unbiased, and the Hudson's Bay Company and other traders respected his keen eye in business and his sociability. Since his consecration as Bishop of the entire vicariate we often accused him in fun of showing favoritism where Aklavik was concerned. We know part of his heart was still with the "muskrat eaters" of the delta.

Easter was a happy day with the Bishop in town, and many old friends came to see him. The evening was spent at the school, where the Grey Nuns had coached the students to give their annual Easter concert. A few of the parents and townspeople crowded into the small room, and the little scholars performed like Oscar winners, with Bishop Trocellier passing out hard candy and wishing everyone a very joyous Easter.

Monday of Easter week came in with a high barometer, and my route forecast looked good, except for Fort Smith. A new storm was due there from the west about two in the afternoon. It would be past Smith and out in the Barren Lands by the time we arrived. I made a last-minute call at the hospital and arranged a meeting with Father Drouart in June. By that time he said he would be ready to ride the co-pilot seat on GTM.

At nine o'clock Brother George was safely aboard, strapped to his stretcher. Mother Margaret Lachambre acted as flight nurse on the trip, and the Bishop rode the co-pilot seat. Brother Herman sat on a pile of bearskins along with Father Metayer, who was coming south for a medical check in Edmonton.

I flight-planned out of Aklavik for Fort Smith, with refueling stops at Norman Wells and Fort Simpson. At nine-ten we were airborne. A half hour out we ran into heavy snow and flew out of it twenty-five miles west of Good Hope. Navigation was fun here in the timbered country—especially with the added consolation of the Norman Wells radio bleep in my ear. We landed at the Wells, a three-hour flight from Aklavik, and Brother George even managed a smile when Sister fed him coffee and sandwiches from the generous personnel of the Canadian Pacific flight office. Clear weather was with us, and at one o'clock we were off again, heading toward Fort Simpson.

More and more overflow appeared on Mackenzie River ice in long dark green patches, and the ridges and mountains had black cheeks from southern exposure. Winter was losing its grip on the land. Passing Fort Norman, the Bishop pointed to a real spectacle. Bear River was open. Its fast blue water had cracked the wide Mackenzie for almost a mile, piling the blue-green ice high on the graveled shoreline.

I had heard about this strange phenomenon of the Bear River breakup in April, freezing again in May, only to reopen in June! The farther south we flew, the more evidence there was of warm weather on every lake and along the Mackenzie. There was overflow on all rivers and many were open, like the Blackwater, half a mile from the big river. We spotted the mission at Wrigley, but the airport radio informed me that Father had left for Simpson that very morning.

At three-thirty that afternoon I flew over the town of Fort Simpson and saw muddy streets. Several people, including some of the nuns, waved to us from the little knoll between St. Margaret's Hospital and the mission. The Simpson radio assured us that the airport, ten miles up the Liard from town, was still firm enough to land on with skis. My usual landing place in the snye behind the mission was covered with overflow. The airport's center runway looked firm, but ducks were swimming along the edges of it. On my downwind leg I noted several people waiting for us near some red gasoline drums. They had rolled the gas out of a cache to the edge of the firm snow-packed runway. Father Lesage and Sergeant Stan Byer of the Mounted Police hailed me over to the gas drums as we taxied in their direction.

"We made the trip through the overflow in Stan's Jeep," Father Lesage said, climbing onto a ski.

They had my wire of our expected arrival, and in half an hour we were refueled and ready to fly. I filed a flight plan while taxiing downwind and learned that Smith was just digging itself out of a real snowstorm.

At 4:15 P.M. we were airborne, and after two and a half hours of routine flight we had just passed Long Island, south of Fort Resolution, when evidence of the great storm was manifest beneath us. Westward, everything was white. To the east the trees were bare of winter. The days are long in mid-April, and the seven o'clock evening sun painted a colorful picture as we arrived at the capital of the Northwest Territories. Smith radio gave us a special welcome. Tom Aneroluk, an Eskimo operator, was on duty that evening. His excited exchange of words told me he was fighting with himself to stick strictly to business.

"See you tonight for news, Father," he signed off.

The airport was covered with plenty of new snow, for which I was thankful. This was my big worry even before I started from Coppermine. One orbit over town brought Brother Joseph Brodeur out of the house and on his way to the airport. We landed smoothly on the new snow and within a half hour Brother George was in the doctor's care at St. Ann's Hospital.

It was spring at Fort Smith—only four below zero! We would have to hurry. I decided to change from skis to wheels that night and take off at 6 A.M., before the morning sun softened the airport. Brothers Beauchemin and Brodeur worked with me until midnight, removing the skis and adjusting the wheels and brakes.

With a mere eight below zero on that wonderful Easter Tuesday, we left Smith at 6:30 A.M. on a flight to Edmonton's municipal airport, with a refueling stop at McMurray. Brother George was again under the careful eye of Mother Lachambre, who remained aboard as our stewardess and nurse.

Dr. John Melling met us in Edmonton at two o'clock that afternoon and rushed Brother to the General Hospital. X rays were taken immediately, and the diagnosis of Dr. Lavallée at Aklavik was correct. Brother had a compound fracture of the left arm, along with a supracondylar fracture, besides a fracture of the left clavicle and scapula. Three days later the mutilated arm was pieced together and put in an arm and shoulder cast.

After a summer of healing and excellent care by the Grey Nuns he was able to climb aboard GTM for her last flight to Aklavik in September. Recently, when I saw Brother at Aklavik, he pulled up his sleeve to show me his healing arm.

"Thanks to your plane, Father, I still have my arm. And look at the muscle I have developed in my greenhouse." He pointed to a lump the size of a hen's egg!

Chapter Sixteen

JUNE of '55 was smoky and hot down North. Not a drop of rain fell from the last snowfall in April until the drizzle of July 4. Forest fires smoldered, fanned up, and smoldered again. Choosing the clearest days, Brother and I flew the Bishop on his pastoral visit down in the Lake Athabaska country.

"I'll visit the other missions this fall after the rains come to kill those fires," he said when we returned to Smith. "Perhaps you could fly enough on the better days to take Father Drouart on his visit," the Bishop added.

Father Drouart arrived from Aklavik on the mail plane on July 9, frisky as a spring lamb. "Only trouble is," he confided, "I have to eat these yellow and white pills from now on." He held up a small box. Father had quite a "malaria tan," but it didn't bother his energy. "I have my bag packed, and I won't mind the smog. In fact, I must look like a piece of semi-smoked moose hide now," he laughed.

On the Smith to Hay River flight we skirted a big fire to the northeast. Fortunately a southwest wind helped to keep our flight path open, and Father had a close-up view of the fire. Fathers Dessy and Lusson were on the sandy shore of Hay River when we taxied up, to catch the mooring line and receive the Roman visitor.

That evening, Brother and I left the visitors to their visiting and climbed into Father Dessy's rowboat with our fishing poles. We had been casting for one of those Hay River wall-eyed pike for about a half hour when Brother noticed two fellows on shore calling and waving to us. They looked like wireless boys from the Royal Canadian Signals. Thinking it was probably a wire for Father Drouart, I reeled in my line. Brother Herman swung the little boat about and made for the western shoreline on the new townsite of Hay River.

"This may be more orders from the Bishop," he mumbled in

French. "Guess I won't have a chance to visit the town now." There were some fine fishing boats here and especially a new diesel electric plant. Brother had been stationed at Aklavik for ten years, far from all modern mechanical developments, and his curiosity always got the better of him in places like this.

"Here is the latest, Father." The Signals operator handed me a wire when our boat ground into the sand. I ripped it open and read:

FATHER LAPPERRIÈRE DANGEROUSLY ILL. COULD YOU GO TO RAE AND FLY HIM TO SMITH HOSPITAL AS SOON AS POSSIBLE? BISHOP TROCELLIER, FORT SMITH.

"Would you give me a weather report on the Yellowknife-Rae area? The Bishop has asked us to make a mercy flight to Rae."

"Give me a call from GTM in about fifteen minutes, Father. I'll try to get something from Yellowknife."

We shoved our skiff off toward the plane, tailed on shore in front of St. Ann's Slave Indian Mission. This certainly would change our plans of a three-day rest here.

St. Ann's Hay River Slave Indian Mission was built by Brother Boisramé in 1868, and the following year Father Gascon came as the first resident priest. The present church and mission house were built in 1930 by Brother Larocque. Slave Indians inhabit the area but spend most of their lives in the surrounding bush country. They make only occasional trips into town with fur, again for Christmas, and of course for their five dollars on Treaty Day! Chief Buggins still retains the black sombrero with a gold band, all that is left of the glory days of the Indian chief. Before entering the house I looked across the river at the modern new town of Hay River. That little river was a China Wall for this small settlement of Slave Indians.

Father Drouart read the telegram and agreed that I should go as soon as possible. It would give him time to visit with Father Dessy across the river, and here with Father Lusson. I told Father Drouart my time of departure depended on a Yellowknife weather report and hustled back to the aircraft.

The wireless station was calling when I turned on my radio: "Weather from Yellowknife to aircraft CF-GTM—one thousand overcast and smoke. Visibility three miles and light rain. Winds southwest at six miles per hour. Welcome to Hay River, Father!" the report ended.

"We will spend the night here," I called to Brother, climbing down on the pontoon. "They have smoggy weather at Yellowknife, and it's a safe bet the people of Rae are breathing a little of the smoke also!"

Brother certainly approved of waiting until morning. By half-past midnight we completed the refueling and baggage unloading and made a beeline for our beds under the mosquito bars at the mission. This was one of those "bug-and-mosquito years," as Brother Hand, a pioneer with a great sense of humor, called them back in 1869.

My alarm made a racket at 4 A.M., but Brother snored on. I shook his bed and he jumped up and looked outside. "No more smoke out there," he yawned, pushing aside the blanket we used for a curtain. Then he saw the whitecaps on the river. These were the months of the midnight sun, and here at Hay River the sun just dipped below the northern horizon for about an hour and a half of midnight evening light, but no darkness.

Brother fired up for coffee during my thanksgiving after Mass, and without delay I climbed into GTM and checked the radio station for weather. They gave me the green light! That wind must have cleared the Yellowknife area also. It was just five-thirty when Brother came along with our sleeping bags from the mission.

After take-off I filed a flight plan and pointed the Norseman out over Great Slave Lake into the north toward Fort Rae. It is usually an hour-and-a-half flight over the 150 miles to Rae, but a fifteen-mile-an-hour tailwind this morning would chop at least twenty minutes off our time. I leveled off at three thousand feet, and our flight path looked clear. The southwest breeze wrinkled the blue lake, and off to the southeast, in the region of the forest fires, a white silk mantle of haze was creeping over the land. Over my left shoulder I could still see the gray-white ribbon of the Hay River road coming into town from the south. That road had brought a big change, not only in this little settlement, but in the entire North. For the first time the treasure-trove of this new land—the millions of pounds of fish and tons of pitch-blende—had an avenue to southern markets. And in return new luxuries and adventures moved north. Almost two thousand people were living there now, perhaps just a little irritated this Sunday morning at a roaring airplane that awakened them too soon.

Now I had time to say my morning prayers. Flying the Arctic

has taught me many lessons of caution and introduced me to new ways of life. Above all, it has opened my eyes to the insignificance of man and the Almighty power of Him Who feeds the Sun. The homes, the towns, and all the creations of man are so small compared to God's mountains, lakes, and mighty rivers. Dependence on the goodness and mercy of God is no mere thought here. I believe it is the very heart of every Arctic flier's nerve—regardless of what he says he believes.

Thinking of goodness, I could not keep my thoughts from leap-frogging to Fort Rae. Ever since my first trip there in 1944 I liked those friendly people and enjoyed being tranquillized in the luxury of their restful hospitality. To me they represented that ideal of the simple life of the woods that many people visualize when they hear about the North country. Perhaps it's because Rae is just a mite off the beaten track, but I like to think it's because the people are just plain good.

Fort Rae is just sixty miles by air from Yellowknife, eighty-five by water, and a mile west of the new highway to the Rayrock Uranium Mine some forty miles northwest. Being so close to Yellowknife, this little town enjoys a few of the crumbs that fall from the table, like a surprise sack of mail or a case of eggs or oranges. Yet regardless of its proximity to the bustling mining town, Rae is still in that drowsy blinking stage of stretching after its lifetime of isolation.

At six forty-five that morning, however, when we circled the settlement, I noticed an unusual number of people gathered in groups around the hospital. Blue smoke from tamarack-stoked campfires lay over the town, and canoes were out at the nets in the bay. Ordinarily on a Sunday morning there is little activity until the High Mass at ten o'clock. I was afraid Father had passed away and we were too late.

Visibility was good, thank God. More aircraft have ripped open their floats on rocks and fishnet poles or broken their skis landing here at Rae than in any other place in the North. In 1951 I spent one day sounding the shallow bay and marked a safe landing run for floats. This morning we noticed fish sticks and nets everywhere. Usually the people keep our spot clear. Evidently they did not expect a plane this early in the season. Between us, we picked a landing strip clear of rock shoals and net sticks and set down on Rae Bay. Good old Father Lapperrière used to meet me out here on the water with the little mission boat and take the children and other passengers aboard so I would not have to taxi the two miles through the rock-infested waters. But no boat met us this morning.

Approaching anchor rock, we saw a crowd of people waiting for us. Some waved a somber greeting. I cut the switches to let the ship glide in and climbed down on a pontoon, uncoiling the tie line. Now I saw Father Amourous in the crowd, who told us that Father Lapperrière was very ill with a strangulated hernia and there were no local facilities for an operation.

I hurried over the rocks with Father to the Bishop Faraud Hospital, where the Grey Nuns of Montreal nursed the ill of Fort Rae. At the bridge over the channel Douglas Stevens, manager of the Hudson's Bay Company, met us and offered to help in any way he could. I asked him to send a wire to Smith to tell the Bishop we had arrived and that Father Lapperrière lived.

"Holy Mary, Mother of God, pray for us sinners," I heard on opening the door of the hospital—the Indian patients saying the Rosary. Sister Bertha Gaudet met us, and tears came as she told me of Father's condition. We entered the patient's room and he tried to lift his head.

"Thank God you came, Father." He strained for breath.

I explained briefly the reason for the delay, and he nodded understandingly. As quickly as possible the local doctor and Sisters prepared Father Lapperrière for his trip. I sent an Indian boy to the Hudson's Bay Company, asking the manager for his large skiff to meet us in front of the hospital. Father Gabriel Duchaussois, the Superior of Rae Mission, took me to the warehouse, where we found a stretcher suitable for the trip. It was a mesh-wire affair left over from the United States Army days in the North. When the Sisters had prepared the patient I picked him up in my arms and laid him on the stretcher. We fastened him in with straps, and four of us carried Father aboard the skiff.

People were coming from everywhere to see their beloved Father Nicholas Lapperrière. It was the most touching, open-hearted devotion I have ever witnessed. Indian canoes by the dozens paddled around us on our way to the plane, but not a word was spoken—no sound but dipping paddles and a baby's cry here and there as they rode on their mothers' backs. The older people, unable to contain their emotion, let tears spill down their tanned, weather-scarred faces.

Nearing the plane, I saw Brother had all in readiness. He

caught the bow of the boat and gently eased it along the pontoon. I took the head of the stretcher and lifted it into the doorway of the plane, allowing the foot to remain in the skiff. This put Father in a semi-upright position so he could look over the people he loved and had served for fifty years. He blessed them, and tears ran down his drawn face and into his white beard. The people fell to their knees on the rocks and signed themselves.

We arranged our patient aboard the plane, gathered our mooring lines, and waved good-by. All the usual shouting was muffled to solemn silence.

I taxied out on the bay, made the take-off checks, and looked back at our passenger. Sister Gaudet assured me with a nod that all was ready for take-off. It was just 9 A.M. I made the Sign of the Cross, sent a telegram to St. Christopher with a glance, and eased the throttle forward. The south wind made our take-off easy. At two thousand feet I leveled off to avoid the stronger winds aloft. While climbing I contacted Yellowknife radio and filed my flight plan. They gave me the usual weather report, but with south winds of sixty miles per hour at four thousand feet.

This was one of the times I thanked God I was able to fly. That look of hope in Father Lapperrière's eyes when he saw me made my pilot's wings the Wings of Hope. Looking down on the blue-clayed milky waters of Rae Arm as they boiled and washed the rocky islands beneath us, I saw the old fort. In 1859 Father Grollier had said the first Mass celebrated in this Dogrib Indian country. Rae itself was named after the famed Dr. John Rae, a Hudson's Bay Company explorer, who made it his headquarters from 1846 to 1854. Because of lack of men and material, the mission was not built until Father Bruno Roure's arrival in 1906. Father Lapperrière came a few years later. Under his able and courageous efforts the Indians of Fort Rae learned to know and love God. Their faith became as solid as the granite rocks over which they shuffled to church in their moose-hide moccasins. By the grace of God and the efforts of their pastor, they have had a modern hospital since 1940 and a school for their children. I knew why they were silent with grief to see their Father Nicholas leave. They loved him almost as much as he loved them.

Outpost Islands slid under our wings, and we were just about over the Slave delta shoreline of the lake when the slight wind shift over a low-pressure trough of air created a little turbulence. I slowed down, which usually helps, and shifted to a thousand-foot altitude. That smoothed out some of the wrinkles but not all of them. Dead ahead, the old smoldering forest fire laid a heavy smoke screen across our flight path. I called Fort Smith radio. They gave me clear weather, so there was just one avenue south —fly around the fire. It took us about twenty minutes more of flying time to make that dog-leg to the east, then south to Smith, but the air was less rough and we arrived over Fort Smith at eleven-fifty. The people were leaving church after High Mass when we flew over the mission. My wire to the Bishop had activated the right people. We were no sooner moored to our dock than Dr. Roman Lyshak was aboard examining the patient.

"We will move him to the hospital as quickly as possible, Father," the doctor said with a worried look. "His chances are one in ten thousand! With his age, and being so long overdue for this operation, I hesitate even to try, even though he still looks quite strong."

Bishop Trocellier, Fathers Serrurot and Gilles, along with two Sisters, made Father Lapperrière comfortable in the ambulance. I breathed easier now, and I felt sure St. Christopher had a hand on the controls of that Sunday-morning flight.

At two o'clock that afternoon Dr. Lyshak made his decision in the little hospital chapel. He would operate. The Fort Smith Hospital was equipped with a fine operating room and the required instruments. With financial aid from the Department of Health in Ottawa, we were able to construct a hundred-bed hospital in 1952–53. Our Oblate Brothers did the work, even to the installation of the huge steam heating system and the complex electrical wiring necessary. When I arrived in Fort Smith in 1940, Dr. Lyshak could not have performed this operation in the small hospital built in 1916. It had few requirements for a hospital—not even running water. For twenty-four years the Sisters carried the water in and the refuse out, using a shoulder or neck yoke to tote the heavy pails. Today, with modern conveniences, our hospital was ready to receive and treat patients like Father Lapperrière.

That afternoon I went into our little church of St. Isidore. While saying my Office I asked the Divine Doctor of souls to show mercy on Father Nicholas. After a young man receives the major orders of the subdeaconate in the seminary he takes on the duty of praying the Divine Office for the rest of his life. That Office includes special prayers for the saint of the day, interlaced with the Psalms of David. For over fifty years, walking over the rocky Rae country,

Father Lapperrière had prayed these very same prayers. I was just beginning Vespers when the church door opened. It was the Bishop. He motioned me to come outside.

"The operation was successful, but the doctor does not have much hope. He does not think Father's seventy-seven-year-old heart can stand this great strain."

We walked to the hospital, and the Bishop told me that Brother Joseph Brodeur and his fellow Brothers had been in the little mission chapel since the operation began at 2 P.M.

Father Lapperrière was under an oxygen tent, still in the world of anesthesia. We prayed the Rosary with the Grey Nuns. At five-thirty his eyes began to focus on us. He recognized us and smiled. Whenever I used to depart from Rae he would say, "If you get to St. Peter's country before I do, don't forget to put in a good word for a poor old Frenchman." Now I put my head under the cellophane tent and whispered in his ear, "Don't forget this gallivanting American when you meet your friend St. Peter." He smiled and squeezed my hand.

That was my last conversation with Father Nicholas Lapperrière. He slipped off into unconsciousness and went to his reward at seven-fifteen that evening. His weary heart was at rest now, and the Chief of Missionaries claimed his soul.

Dr. Lyshak assured me that even had I been able to make the flight on Saturday evening when the wire arrived at Hay River, there would have been only a five thousand to one chance of life.

"In cases like this, Father," he said, "you fly and I operate with the knowledge that our efforts may prolong a life. When I was young in this business I was afraid of death after my operations. What would people say about me? Now I realize the decision must be mine alone, since I have devoted my life to heal people's bodies—just as you have devoted yours to heal their souls."

Next day this trim, mustached Ukrainian doctor followed the procession when we laid Father Nicholas Lapperrière to rest in the little sand-hill cemetery under the pines at Fort Smith. Father had expressed the desire many times to be buried there beside his cousin, Father Mansoz. On his visits to Smith, Father Nicholas often walked to these "hills of home," as he called the little graves. There he said his Office and prayed for his brother missionaries buried beside the mist and roar of the rapids. He joined them now in the great family circle of God's hall of fame.

Later that day, at five o'clock, we flight-planned to Hay River to resume our flight north with Father Drouart. The serious visitation was over when we arrived, and that evening over a glass of Father Lusson's homemade wine Brother and I related the details of our mercy flight with good Father Nicholas Lapperrière.

Next morning when Brother shook me awake, he quickly went to the window, pulled the curtain aside and pointed. "See that clear weather? The smoke is all gone," he said in a jubilant voice. "I'll bet we're going to have clear weather for the rest of the summer."

The change was spectacular. Father Nicholas could have nudged St. Christopher to turn on that twenty-mile-an-hour-or-so south wind. For the sake of Father Drouart I hoped that spiritual nudging would continue, because now we had to fly.

Anomalies do happen, even in northern weather, as we found out. The Mackenzie River trip was smooth and routine flying, and by August first we were in Yellowknife. Arrangements were made to have Dr. John Melling join us for the central Arctic flights that summer. Through the kindness of the Grey Nuns of St. Vincent's Hospital in Toledo I had several parcels of antibiotics for our Arctic missionaries and people. Dr. Melling agreed to make the trip with us and give the Fathers a check-out on the use and dosage of these medicines. He was a pilot and a Northerner of both the eastern and western Arctic, and I asked Jack, as we all know him, to act as my navigator. He is a rugged fellow who loves the outdoors. Having hunted elk with him, I knew he would not mind sharing a hard floor with his sleeping bag.

Dr. Melling arrived in Yellowknife on August 4. The following day GTM put her six hundred horses to work and we left with a capacity load of supplies for the Arctic coast. The weather was generally good. We had a shower of snow around Holman Island, where Father Roger Buliard founded Christ the King Mission in 1937. There was a smidgen of fog at Bathurst Inlet, but nothing serious to keep us on the ground until we arrived at Cambridge Bay the last day of August.

"Hello, Father, and welcome to the end of the line," Father Louis Le Mer called. We landed in the bay in front of his new construction, and I had just climbed down on a pontoon after cutting the switches. "Better use a paddle and steer your plane into my homemade dock." Father pointed to a line of rusty oil barrels in the water. There was a natural little curve to the shoreline there. His barrels made the little bay large enough to anchor the plane by running lines to the shore. We landed and I introduced Father Louis Le Mer to my passengers.

"Someone is missing. Where is Brother Beauchemin?" he asked.

I told Father that Brother had remained at Coppermine to help Father Ovila Lapointe overhaul his boat engine.

"Too bad." He shook his head. "I was counting on him to help carry rocks for my house." Father pointed up the thirty-foot rocky embankment to his house.

"We'll carry a few for you." Father Drouart flexed his muscles. "That's just the excuse I'm looking for after all this riding. I'm getting fat."

At Father Le Mer's suggestion and with his assistance Jack and I ran a half dozen lines off GTM to huge boulders. "When it blows around here the waves break twenty-five feet high on those rocks." Father pointed to a spot a few hundred yards down the shore.

At midnight we were grateful to Father for his advice. The wind began to cut loose from the northwest in a fifty-mile-an-hour gale. Jack and I went down to inspect our tie lines. They held firm. Waves, even in the shelter of the bay, were four feet high, washing our floats and bobbing GTM like a cork. But our anchor rocks were big and the nylon ropes held fast.

Next morning there was a drizzle mixed with the wind. "It's a nor'wester." Father Louis came in, rubbing his hands. "Wouldn't surprise me if we had this for three days. And it may turn to snow!"

All that day a fog blew in, the wind gradually slacking off. Midnight of September first there was a very heavy rain. The following morning it was colder, around thirty-four degrees. The rain fizzled out at ten o'clock, but skies were dark with a very low overcast.

We had just come from our prayers after lunch when Mr. Wilson, one of the construction engineers on the Dew Line project across the bay, came to the mission.

"Our two aircraft that usually base here have been wrecked by the great storm these last two days, Father," he began. "I was wondering if you could make a flight for us when this Arctic scud thins out a little. Two of my men went on a trip with an amphibious Duck three days ago and are long overdue. Just about anything could have happened to those fellows in that blow. We may even be lucky enough to find their bodies or maybe it's just engine trouble."

I assured him we would try to find the Duck as soon as we had a thousand feet of ceiling. He agreed on the visibility required for such a mission and expressed his gratitude for our cooperation.

"We will keep a check on the weather, Father," he said, pulling on his cap. "It is too late to start today. Perhaps this fog will clear overnight."

Dr. Melling and I spread air maps on the floor and began running flight lines when Father Louis leaned over my shoulder.

"Don't believe all you see there," he cautioned. "Most of this island and the country east of us for five hundred miles is not officially mapped. Whenever you see a broken line along the indicated coast line the map is just an educated guess. Let me add a line or so to that map of yours." He took a stub of pencil from his pocket. "This is the coast line of the islands as I found it," he pointed out, drawing a solid line over what was marked as water. "I believe those fellows tried to cross this big-mouthed bay. While they were crossing it this recent blow caught them. Their machine is either sunk—or disabled on the rocky shore when they tried to come out of the sea."

Dr. Melling carefully plotted our course to that bay, but the next morning fog was rolling in off the sea like smoke off a burning pine forest. In fact, we could not see the plane from the house, not more than a hundred yards away! After breakfast Father Louis Le Mer gave us a thumbnail sketch of Cambridge Bay:

"This settlement really had its beginning when the Hudson's Bay Company established a store here in 1923. Before that time the Eskimos merely stopped here in the hope that some passing trader might be anchored, waiting out a storm, and they could get a few supplies. A small river empties into the bay a mile north of the house." He pointed. "Years ago the passing natives cached a few fish there in the fall. There used to be a lot of seal here. They are scarce now. And last year our nearest caribou was a hundred miles away."

A rap on the door interrupted Father Louis. It was Bob Cruckshanks, the manager of the Bay store that year. Bob was no stranger to me. I knew him from Coppermine. After he was introduced to the doctor and we told him what we were learning about the settlement from Father, Bob told us the story of the first plane at Cambridge.

"In 1929 one of our clerks here, Ian McKinnon, sent out a radio beep heard almost round the world, and Cambridge Bay was born to the newspaper world." Bob began rolling a cigarette and told us how in September 1929 Colonel C. MacAlpine of the Dominion Explorers started from the Pas in Manitoba, via Hudson Bay, with two aircraft and two assistants, to investigate the Coppermine mineral-ore deposits. They intended to fly from Churchill, Manitoba, to Baker Lake and then to Bathurst Inlet, with a stop at Coppermine, then on to Aklavik. Weather played its hand, and between Baker Lake and Bathurst Inlet they were lost and finally landed at Cambridge. Newspapers reported them lost, and one of the widest air searches in the history of the North began, lasting over a month and a half. Then on November 4, Ross Smythe, toying with his radio aboard a Company ship at Gjoa Haven on King William Island, picked up the message from another Hudson's Bay Company ship that the MacAlpine party was here safe and well.

"I read a few of those names in the mission history a visiting missionary wrote about Cambridge," Father Le Mer added. "During the summer of 1930 Father Trocellier came here aboard the Company ship, the *Bay Chimo*. He met many of the Eskimos and also Captain Peterson, the private trader, who had a post here."

"By the looks of things, you mean to stay." Bob smiled, admiring Father's clean new house. He examined the two-and-a-half-foot-thick stone walls. "It will take a good wind to blow this shack down," he said, patting the heavy wall.

Father had first learned of stone construction from reading the gleanings of a vanished tribe of Eskimos who lived on Southampton Island in northern Hudson Bay, from which their name was derived—Sadlermuit—from *Sagdlern* (meaning Southampton Island) and *muit* (people).

"Father Henry built the first stone mission at Pelly Bay in the mid-thirties in imitation of those native dwellings, and I have followed his example." Father Le Mer looked at his hands. We knew how this man had been working. For two years he carried stone and laid the walls of this place with a mixture of seal oil and sand.

"You should recognize the wood in those partitions, Mr. Wilson. It was scrounged, as you fellows call it, from the packing cases of the radar equipment at the site." Father pointed to a label still visible on the window frame. "My big problem, even before a stone was gathered and set, was the question of heating, and you fellows solved that with this fuel-oil stove." The square kitchen

278

range was sand-polished and sent out enough heat to keep the whole house comfortable.

"Don't forget we made a bargain, Father." Mr. Wilson winked. "We will supply the fuel and light for you here if you see to it that we don't have to worry about *heat* in the hereafter!"

When the first men arrived at Cambridge Bay to build the Dew Line site, they consulted Father Le Mer and immediately elected him as their spiritual guardian. Even though the majority of the men belonged to other denominations, they respected this man of God and invited him to say Mass at the camp.

It was after one o'clock that foggy afternoon, when the visitors left, that Dr. Melling and I decided on a three-mile walk. We were anxious to have a look at the sea. On our way we stopped under the 650-foot steel Loran tower set up in 1947 and listened to the song it always sang, wind or no wind. An elevator to ascend the tower was still in its cage, and an abandoned ten-ton walk-in refrigerator stood directly beneath the massive hulk with its heavy door ajar, revealing that it was the electrical brain and nerve center of this million-dollar radio antenna. A few steel igloos, two abandoned tractors, and the usual debris of rusty tin cans and a few thousand steel-oil drums were all that remained of Exercise Yellowbeetle, giving mute evidence of the price of experimental ambitions.

A few hundred yards from the old camp we stumbled down the thirty-foot bank of an arroyo, and there was a five-foot-high Eskimo shack built with Army olive-drab lumber scraps from an abandoned prefabricated hut. We were about to walk past when an Eskimo woman came out, walked up to us, and offered her hand.

"Hello," she said to each of us in fine English. She carried a baby on her back and kept patting it gently with her left hand. The doctor offered her a cigarette, which she eagerly accepted.

"Perhaps you could tell us about this weather," he ventured. "How long does a fog like this last around here?"

"I do not know much about it since this is really not my country. My husband could tell you, but he is working at the site." While she spoke she kept looking at me. "Now I remember you. You are Falla, the pilot of that big red plane that came three days ago. Many years ago I saw you at Aklavik and heard you on the radio."

"Yes, I was at Aklavik. And now I know why you speak such good English. You must have been in school."

"I was at the Anglican school for three years and my husband was at the Catholic mission school for two years. We met at Aklavik." We learned that she was from Coppermine and her husband from Bathurst Inlet. Poor trapping results and the low price of fur, plus the offer of work here, decided them to move to Cambridge.

"So you don't want to tell us how long the fog will last." Jack smiled, looking toward the sea. She wrinkled a well-tanned little flat nose, "no"; then she raised her thin dark eyebrows, "yes."

"I do not know," she said slowly. "If this was Coppermine I would take a guess. Will you like a cup of tea," she offered, trying her best to be a lady.

We thanked her and went on our way to get a look at the sea from the forty-foot cliffs. During our walk Jack spoke of his encounters with the Eskimos of Hudson Bay, where he acted as medical officer and agent in a spot known as Chesterfield Inlet. He saw there, as we do in the central Arctic, that some of the natives will revert to their old way of life when they return from school. In general, however, the majority show a marked improvement.

We stumbled over the rocks of Cambridge Bay until we reached the sea. Blue-green frothy water massaged the gravel beach, rolling the finer stones in a pile with each wave. As the water drained back into the sea it leveled the gravel again. Sea smoke rolled in over the land with a light on-shore wind that held hope for better visibility in the later afternoon. I judged the swells to be about two feet deep, and only an odd chunk of ice was visible. Satisfied with our observations and a little on the damp side, we returned to the warm, dry house where Father Le Mer had tea ready. We just sat down when Mr. Wilson entered.

"Sorry to disturb you, gentlemen, but I rushed over as soon as our plane landed." He was breathing heavily. "The pilot told us the weather is clearing very rapidly. In an hour we will have two thousand feet of ceiling. The aircraft is a Canadian Pacific Airlines DC-3 and is of no use to us as far as a sea landing is concerned."

We had refueled for our return to Coppermine, so I assured him we would be ready in forty-five minutes and would taxi over and meet him at the Hudson's Bay dock.

The Cambridge Bay site of the Distant Early Warning Line was humming with around-the-clock action to complete construction in time to join in the link of twenty-one airfields and sites stretching three thousand miles from western Alaska to Cape Dyer on the eastern tip of Baffin Island. Every fifty miles there is a radar station, forming an electric gill net that will sound a warning of any large-scale attack across the north polar regions by long-range bombers. There are six main sectors, each one covering about five hundred miles. A large H-type module holds administrative and communications personnel, plus heating and electrical units. Around the radome (a crisscrossed dome of waterproof plastic) are storage buildings, including a garage and a hangar. The radome houses the search radar antenna. Around forty civilians and a USAF officer staff the place. Every hundred miles between these main sites are smaller auxiliary sites, manned by twenty technicians and assistants who live and operate under a radome-crowned auxiliary. The smallest stations are known as three-man "I sites" and do not have search radar equipment. However, they do transmit a semi-radar signal that will sound an alarm at the main or aux station if any object crosses its beam.

We were now at one of the main sectors at Cambridge, where our two hundred men were working twenty-four hours a day during the short summer.

Dr. Melling and I climbed aboard GTM, taxied over to the Bay dock, picked up Mr. Wilson and his supplies, and took off to find the lost Duck. The ceiling was then up to five hundred feet, and to the west I saw patches of clear sky. We followed the course plotted by Jack, after an orbit at sea for a general survey of the weather picture. Fifteen minutes on a southeast course, I had to descend to three hundred feet above the water to remain clear of the fog which piled rime ice on our wings. We kept on course at this low altitude for forty-five minutes before I could climb into clear weather at three thousand.

As soon as we elevated, Mr. Wilson tapped me on the shoulder and pointed off to starboard, a big happy smile on his broad face. There was the Duck and two men waving up at us. I was saying a quiet "Thank God" that at least the men were alive. After a series of two orbits to gauge the wind and the swells, we bounced off two waves and landed. GTM slid into a deep trough, and a wave crest just lapped the under surface of our port wing—a little too close for comfort. With our paddles Jack and I worked the plane within calling distance of the Duck. The men seemed well as they walked and climbed over the boxes and gear. "We broke our fan belt and boiled the oil out of the engine," one of the men called to us.

"I brought a box of spare parts along with some oil and gasoline. Can you repair your engine and return to Cambridge?" Mr. Wilson called from the float. The men motioned him to send out the gear.

We had to yell at the top of our voices to be heard, since I dared not approach that bounding heap of steel with my tender-skinned pontoons. We tied a rope to the keg of oil and tossed the end of the rope to the stranded boat some twelve yards away. In this fashion they towed over the gasoline, spares, and the grub in a watertight box. Our aircraft was getting too close, so I started the engine and taxied free. We stopped and floated again, while the men worked over their engine. It would have been difficult bringing the men aboard in these heaving seas, especially if they had been disabled. Someone would have had to go swimming in thirty-five-degree water!

"There's the exhaust of their engine," Mr. Wilson called to us from his observation seat in the tail of the plane. When I looked their way the Duck was leaving a trail of blue steam on the water and coming toward us.

"Thanks a lot, fellows," one of the men called to us. "We'll head back for Cambridge and see you there about midnight."

Now came the anxious moment of take-off on those swells. The experience of another rescue with six passengers aboard and a sea take-off was under my safety belt. It helped now. I fired up the Wasp. It hiccuped a few times before breathing evenly. That cold sea was not to its liking! Ten minutes of slow orbits around the Duck and my oil temperature reached the required take-off heat. Dr. Melling called out the pre-flight check list and I followed through.

At exactly 4 P.M. I taxied upwind, worked on the uphill side of a long swell, and poured on the gas. The big three-bladed propeller bit into the cold air and we gained speed. I followed the wave in a half-moon take-off curve until air speed registered sixty miles per hour, gave a tug on the wheel, and we were airborne. I breathed again and Jack smiled contentment. It was easy returning to Cambridge Bay. The weather had cleared, giving us four thousand feet of ceiling, but we remained at one thousand until we reached the coast and followed it home.

"How much do you want for that trip, Father?" Mr. Wilson asked after we docked. "You have done us a great service and we wish to reimburse you sufficiently." I told him of my great need for gasoline in this far northern part of our vicariate and that he could pay me in kind.

"Very well. I will see to it that you receive some gasoline," he said, turning on his heel with a parting salute. And that same afternoon a huge truck came to the mission and I unloaded enough gasoline to last me for two seasons of Cambridge Bay flying.

As I taxied back to the mission dock where Father Le Mer waited for us I called the Cambridge Bay radio and closed my flight plan. My eyes and thoughts climbed the huge steel tower, and I remembered Kitty and said to myself, "I owe the Army and Air Force plenty for that prize of the Kitty camp."

During World War II missionaries aided the Army and Air Force in the South Pacific with competent knowledge they had gained with their years of experience in these remote areas. In 1952 when the idea of the Dew Line was conceived at the Massachusetts Institute of Technology's Lincoln Laboratory and the first officers went North, they consulted our missionaries on a suitable site for an airport.

Father Franche at Tuktoyaktuk spent more than a week with the surveyors, and so did Father Louis Le Mer at Cambridge Bay. The builders needed gravel for their construction and they needed the Eskimos to prepare the first ice-strip landing fields. Father received the orders from the officers and relayed the order of work to the Eskimos in their language. There was ice to be sounded and cracks to be filled with water before the heavy C-124 Globemasters landed. Eighty tons was a lot of airplane to land on the ice! Sixty planes crashed and twenty-six airmen perished in this gigantic airlift. That year Merchant Marine and Navy vessels entered Arctic waters from Bering Strait in the west, and into Fox Basin, Frobisher Bay, and Hudson Bay in the east, carrying thousands of tons of supplies.

My small share in this project was a few survey flights to check on ice conditions for the ships and to make a few mercy flights like this one at Cambridge.

Those of us who realize the vast stretches of the naked Arctic and how vulnerable it is to a transpolar air raid know that the Dew Line is a plug in the dike that keeps the boiling tide of a third world war from spilling over our land.

"I heard that of the twenty-three thousand men who worked on the Dew Line, two thousand were Eskimos," Father Le Mer related one evening. He had occasion to learn about this work from the frequent visits of the officers. During our visit he told us how the entire Line is under the operating control of the North American Air Defense Command at Colorado Springs, Colorado.

"From this map you can see that this Line is the latest link in our fifteen-thousand-mile warning loop around North America," an officer told us one afternoon, using one of Father's maps.

"The North will never be the same again," Father Louis commented when we packed our bags to leave Cambridge, and I detected a note of sadness in his voice. He would miss the quiet hard life of those pioneer days. "I think it will be good for our Eskimos," he added, helping me load the plane. "They will learn how to work and rest at regular hours. It will prepare them for the inevitable advance of civilization into this country."

Father Drouart found it hard to leave that quaint stone mission on the barren hills of Cambridge Bay. When he said good-by and blessed Father Le Mer, kneeling at his feet on the rocks, Jack and I just looked at each other. We sensed the devotion this man had for his brother missionaries who gave so much of themselves in this faraway land.

On our flight back to Coppermine we encountered heavy rain showers and fog. I left our course to follow the mainland from Arctic Bay, and our arrival was delayed forty-five minutes. A system of foul weather was moving into the area. Coppermine radio gave us wind at twenty knots from the west. The overcast was bringing on early darkness as we landed in the mouth of the Coppermine River. Because of the high waves and the difficulty in approaching the shore, we anchored in the river. Father Lapointe and Brother came with their jollyboat, a sea-going skiff, but by the time we reached the mission the wind and rain had drenched us. Father surprised us with a wonderful roast goose supper that evening, and during the next two days of weather we had plenty of time to dry our clothes.

The next morning a young Eskimo evidently heard us call Jack "Doctor" and up came his sleeve to reveal a festering boil. Dr. Melling had performed the first abdominal surgery at Chesterfield Inlet and from that time the Eskimos regarded him as a kind of superman and wanted to be operated on whenever they were ill. Men who stake their life's reputation on the twist of a knife with the limited facilities in the Arctic certainly deserve the credit of our admiration and have earned their rightful place as pioneers in civilizing the Eskimos and Indians. Their wives and children likewise make many sacrifices to follow their husbands down North, and from these lady pioneers the Eskimo and Indian women have learned the finer things of life. There at Coppermine I could see the impression that was made by Mrs. Coleman, the nurse, on some of those Eskimo women, even to the use of bobby pins!

To pass the time profitably Father Lapointe and Jack trimmed each other's hair and then the doctor opened a barbershop for the Eskimos. He had fun with their thick, matted, wirelike hair! Jack's last customer was from Winnipeg, who became very interested in Father Drouart and his travels in the various mission fields. Father explained that the Oblates of Mary Immaculate were founded by Charles de Mazenod in 1826 and since then have expanded to over seven thousand missionaries.

"What is their special work, Father?" Jack asked. "I know the Jesuits teach and the Dominicans excel in preaching, but I never heard of any special work for the Oblates."

"Our motto is 'To Preach the Gospel to the Poor,'" Father Drouart explained, telling us that Oblates work in the missions in over twenty countries in the world, including the Eskimo missions from Labrador to Alaska.

"Here the Oblate Fathers found an ideal place to put their motto to work." Father Drouart smiled, looking at the Eskimos on a bench by the wall. He talked about the mud in South Africa, the jungles of the Philippines, the sticky clay of Brazil, the sands of Japan. But when he told how the bugs and reptiles of the jungle in Laos tormented and even killed some of the people, the Eskimos scratched their dark tousled hair in wonder. I'm sure they left the mission with a better idea of the difficulties of other people, thankful for what they had, even in this impoverished land.

On the morning of September 6 great masses of stratus clouds hovered over the September Mountains to the southwest as I returned from the wireless station.

"Do we fly today?" Dr. Melling met me at the door of the mission.

"They gave me three thousand feet of ceiling, but it looks a little on the short side." I pointed to the south.

"Personally, I don't like the looks of this scud rolling over the hills—especially with those children on board, and at this time of the year there is practically no game in the country," the doctor said seriously.

I had to agree. We had three little Eskimo boys from Holman Island and a little girl from Coppermine as passengers on their way to the Aklavik school. I didn't like the idea of camping on some lake in this wild country. After Mass and breakfast Jack and I sought the vantage point of the high rocks where we could get a better look at the local weather. Jack pointed to a patch of blue sky to the west. My spirits rose when I saw it, and we decided to give it a try.

Looking down from the rocks, we could see the yellow Coppermine River fan out into the blue-green Arctic Ocean of Coronation Gulf for twenty miles around. This is one of the features that makes Coppermine easy to find. In winter it is a different story. A passing pilot has to take special precaution or he will miss the settlement. Coppermine is actually between two weather fronts, northwestern and southeastern. With the limited facilities for weather reports, a pilot has to juggle all the pieces of the meteorological picture available before making a final decision.

When the doctor and I returned to the mission Mr. Foley was there with the latest weather. "Our ceiling balloons gave us southwest wind at thirty miles an hour, at an estimated ceiling of four thousand feet. That should take you over the mountains around Dismal Lakes. Reports from Norman Wells and Port Radium indicate you should have no trouble on your flight west to Fort Franklin."

This good news sent us all to our last-minute packing. Father Lapointe prepared a lunch, and at eleven-thirty we taxied downwind for the take-off, the entire population of Coppermine waving us a *bon voyage*. We had a capacity load with full tanks of gasoline, so I took three miles downwind before coming about. Usually on the downwind taxi runs we do the cockpit checks, and Jack sang out the list and I followed through and then we were aloft. When Coppermine fell away under our wing, Father Drouart and the boys pressed their noses to the windows to get a final look at the town. I followed the Coppermine River with its high banks for about five miles to get air speed and altitude.

My new passengers loved this part of the world, where they saw mountains for the first time. The three Eskimo boys, Roy and Billy Goose and Simon Minorama, were as excited as children on Christmas morning. They were hunting from a plane, searching the rolling, rocky terrain for caribou. Our other little passenger, Angela, was extremely quiet. This was her first plane ride. She was tense and kept a firm grip on Father Drouart.

For three quarters of an hour flying was routine. Then some seventy miles out of Coppermine, over the Dismal Lakes area, the ceiling began falling in a light drizzle with patches of valley fog. Lac Rouvière was just visible to the southeast, and minutes later I spotted Lac Le Roux. The boys began to shout and point at the trees. It was too much for Angela's curiosity. She loosed her hold on Father Drouart and pressed her nose against the window with the boys.

The drizzle was fast turning into a downpour! Visibility fogged down to about five miles, and the rugged terrain was coming up to meet us and in fact we were already below many of the higher hills. With such conditions, especially the increasing fog, I decided to pick the next good-sized lake and land. We followed a canyon for three minutes, but it was a dead end. Fog covered the mountains and we did a quick bank and about-face. I flew back out of the canyon and a little farther west spotted some water sticking its tongue out under a fog bank. Once over the water, I estimated it to be a large enough area to land, even though I could not see shorelines for the thick fog and scud that rolled in off the gravel hills. We did a fast downwind run, turned, and settled quickly on that wonderful little blue lake.

Rain poured down and steam arose from the water, as though it were fed with hot springs. There was a ten-mile wind, but the waves were negligible. I stopped the engine and asked Brother to take a paddle and sound for depth. By the waves, I could tell before landing that there was at least five feet of water there.

"No bottom," Brother called back. "And there is no shoreline in sight either," he added in an excited voice. He was worried, yet relieved to have landed safely in that dense fog and rain. This was my first forced landing with Father Drouart aboard, but his spirits were high.

"I never thought I could feel so happy sitting on an unknown lake in the Barren Lands in the rain," Father commented, looking into the rolling fog. I shared his feelings of contentment, although I made no comment. My stomach had been tying knots ever since we had hit the foggy mountain passes—fog and mountains mix with flying about as well as gasoline and scotch. Hungry looks on the faces of the little passengers told me it was lunch time. One word about food, and Brother dropped the anchor. We opened Father Lapointe's surprise box of fish sandwiches and candy bars. They tasted wonderful washed down with the cold blue lake water that was sweet and good.

"The anchor is dragging," Brother alerted us just as it caught on a rock and gave a tug on the plane. Before I could tell him, Brother was out on a float sounding for depth. This drifting gave us anxiety as we ate and everyone kept on the lookout for a rocky shoreline.

"Falla, look there." Billy Goose pointed. It was the shoreline below a hill. The closer we drew to land, the more excited the children became. Land meant just one thing to them since they had visited Coppermine, and that was blueberries.

Brother weighed anchor and we drifted shoreward as he sounded for bottom with one of the paddles. Closing in on the shoreline, we noted what looked like a clear beach—that is, clear of those huge skull-shaped black boulders. When the plane ground to a stop against the gravel and stone, Brother waded ashore with the line.

"That fellow is tough. He takes to water like a seal." Jack shivered, watching him.

The heavy rain had calmed the wind and we decided to build a stone bridge from the tail of the floats to the beach. Brother and I got into raincoats and started work. The round granite rocks were heavy, but there was no danger of their cutting the soft aluminum floats. The rain thinned out to a drizzle, making the rocks slippery. We had to move slowly and carefully.

It required an hour of stone handling to make a bridge fourteen feet long and some three feet deep, but it was worth the effort, especially for children. There was no holding them once they touched land. Father Drouart and Jack had them all geared in waterproof sealskin boots and their oldest parkas so they could change to dry clothing later. Regardless of the boggy spume rolling over the ground, they spread out on a hunt for berries. It was certainly a land of plenty for the three lads, since they had known only the land of lifeless gravel sand and black rocks all their lives on northern Victoria Island.

I left them free for about an hour and joined Father Drouart and Dr. Melling for a little walk. There was no sign or trace of any kind of human habitation in the area. In all probability we were the first white men to set foot on that exact spot of shoreline. The early missionaries, Fathers Le Roux, Rouvière, and Fallaize, may have come over the lake in the winter on their way to Coppermine. Dr. Melling suggested we call the body of water Lac Drouart, in honor of our passenger from Rome. Whenever I fly over the little lake in the future I will look for the little stone bridge Brother and I built that day in the rain. After forty-five minutes the rains came again. We returned to the plane and began to plan on just what we would do if we had to spend the night on "Lac Drouart."

About four o'clock the rains tapered off to a drizzle and finally stopped. A little east wind cleared the air and in half an hour gave us the required seven miles visibility. In came the mooring lines and we started our engine. The waves out on the lake were over three feet high and bobbed us about like a gull. In ten minutes we were off and back on our flight path to Fort Franklin. It had been just a little tricky keeping on course while we turned around mountains and flew back through canyons, but Dr. Melling is a very sharp and accurate navigator, and his estimation of our position was pin-pointed correctly. Fifteen minutes after take-off we spotted Dease Bay and the river which is really the northeast arm of Great Bear Lake.

"Igloo, igloo." Little Roy Goose was pointing to the old cabin of Fathers Rouvière and Le Roux, a log building with a sagged-in roof on the shoreline of the bay. We also flew over the very spot where Father Frapsauce was drowned in 1920. He was the first missionary to follow the Hornaday River to the Arctic Ocean in 1916. There he met the famous Kris Klengenberg. This adventurous Dane records many Arctic firsts in his autobiography, compiled by Tom MacInnes, and one of them is the marriage of his daughter Etna to an Eskimo, Ikey Bolt. This couple, who live at Coppermine today, have often recalled those early days of Kris Klengenberg and his son Patsy. Besides this record in Mr. Klengenberg's life, a small bell from a Mass kit with a cross on it was found some thirty miles south of the Arctic coast, high on the Hornaday River bank, by Joe Trasher a few years ago. From this Bishop Trocellier was certain that Father Frapsauce was the first priest, and probably the first white man, to follow this river over two hundred miles to the Arctic Ocean.

Leaving the islands on the north shore of Dease Bay, we flew out over Great Bear Lake. It had some low long swells, but we could have landed in case of an emergency. We flew on course to Deer Pass Bay, with the range beacon of Sawmill Bay coming in loud and clear, and a half hour out on the lake ran smack into our horizon—a nice fat fog bank! The white stuff rolled along the water and climbed up over ten thousand feet. Our only safe flight path lay directly across the lake to Sawmill Bay on the south shore, some forty miles west of Eldorado's Radium Mine. Sawmill Bay had an airstrip now being used by Eldorado Airlines, and I was counting on a barrel of fuel and accommodations for my passengers. All these detours had dipped into my reserve fuel tank. According to my time, we would just about reach the bay before darkness set in.

In September the days are normal again for about four weeks, and when it gets dark it is night-black. I tried to contact Eldorado to inform them of my change in flight plans, but the air was dead on that frequency.

The overcast sky brought on early evening that day, and at 7 P.M., when I flew over the bay I had to use the landing lights to pick out the docks. After a safe landing and mooring, Dr. Melling and Father Drouart gathered the children to go into camp, but as soon as the boys spotted trees there was no holding them. They not only looked at and felt the trees but pulled off pieces of bark and began to chew it. Wood is not only a novelty but a highly prized luxury among these peoples. Even tent poles and canoe frames, ice chisel handles and spear handles are passed on from father to son. These treasured pieces of wood are well preserved and seldom rot in the high Arctic. They are well oiled from greasy hands and look more like ebony than white spruce.

While the doctor and Father gathered the belongings and the children, Brother and I located some gasoline and refueled. "I hear a motor." Brother stopped pumping and listened. He was right. A beat-up olive-drab weapons carrier rolled into camp. It was the caretaker of the airstrip for Eldorado. We inquired about quarters for the night and he informed us we were in luck. We loaded our baggage and climbed aboard and after a few bumps and bangs were in camp, out of the drizzle, safe and warm. There was plenty of room, so the doctor and I allotted beds to the children and began to unpack our gear.

"I will get acquainted with the kitchen staff and see what can be done in the food line," Brother said, sniffing at cooking odors that emanated from the front part of the building. We were invited to help ourselves from a veritable treasure heap of canned goods, and we selected cans of frankfurters and Boston baked beans. It was a real feast, especially for the boys. Father Drouart said he lost count after the ninth hot dog.

Next morning clear weather greeted us and we flew on to Fort Franklin, 175 miles up in the northwest corner of Bear Lake. Fortunately the lake was calm for a fine landing and Fathers Philippe and Labat were on hand to help us dock the plane. We said our Masses and then enjoyed a healthy breakfast of baked trout. The children romped in the woods and mingled with the Indian boys and girls. That day a Wardair plane landed on its way to Aklavik with three teachers. Sister Beatrice Leduc from Aklavik, Miss Margaret Poirier from Arctic Red River, and Mr. Bowerman from Franklin were all returning from a teachers' convention in Yellowknife. When the pilot agreed to add the children to his passenger list the two teachers from down-river took over. There were tears and longing looks, especially from little Angela, when they climbed aboard, but now they were in capable and understanding hands.

We continued our flight south, leaving Father Drouart at Fort Simpson. Here he could make connections with the mail plane south when his visitation was completed. For GTM with her aluminum floats the season was over. After several short flights out of Smith, our summer ended in early October, just in time to shoot a few mallards at Chipewyan, also on their way south.

Chapter Seventeen

WILL you search with your plane for the remains of Father Joseph Buliard?" Father Cochard asked me as soon as I was introduced to him at Chesterfield Inlet.

Father Buliard had mysteriously disappeared in late October of 1956 around Garry Lake. I conferred with my passenger and arranged to make a search after we returned from the flights at the northern missions.

Our flying chores in the Mackenzie were abbreviated during the summer of 1957. Bishop Trocellier farmed out GTM and myself to Father Stanislaus La Rochelle, one of the assistant generals from Rome, for his visitation of the vicariates of Keewatin and the Hudson Bay.

From July 15 to August 14 we covered the entire Vicariate of Keewatin in northern Saskatchewan and Manitoba. On August 15 we left Churchill, Manitoba, for Chesterfield Inlet.

When Father La Rochelle explained his plan of visitation to the Provincial, Father Cochard, we flew northwest to begin the official visit at Baker Lake Mission. Father Charles Choque gave us a royal welcome on August 16 in his new home—so new it still needed the touch of paint.

On August 17, the weather perfect for flying, Father completed his visit at noon, and by one o'clock we were airborne for Gjoa Haven. Two hundred miles north we had to do a little cropduster-flying over the Bock River and down Chantrey Inlet, but in four and a half hours we landed in the harbor at Gjoa Haven. Fathers Henry and Goussart could not find words enough to express their happiness. They led us up the steps into a twelve-by-twenty stone building.

"Here we are. Have a chair," Father Henry said, pointing to a box. Father La Rochelle gave it a second look, to see if it would hold him, and sat down. "We were expecting four new ones last year, but they missed the boat." Tall, gaunt Father Henry smiled and ran long fingers through what had once been a red beard. Now it was fringed with white. Father Goussart was a much younger man of only a year or more in the North. He sported a black beard and a windburned face.

We were enjoying a cup of tea and some of Father Henry's brown bread when the Hudson's Bay manager, George Porter, came in. "Nice to meet an American Father," he said in his slow drawl. "I knew a lot of them during World War I. I was an enlisted man in the U. S. Army, Father," he said proudly. George had tea with us and then he took me by the arm to meet his Eskimo wife and seven children. We had a long visit, during which I learned he was a Catholic and "praying that my wife will turn. She is such a good woman, Father," he confided.

The son of a Scottish whaling captain and an Eskimo mother, George had survived the reindeer drive from Alaska to Aklavik, and even three shipwrecks on the Arctic Ocean could not kill him! His greatest honor, he admitted, was knowing Roald Amundsen, the Norwegian explorer, who had spent two winters here in his forty-seven-ton schooner *Gjoa* and gave the place its name.

Father La Rochelle and I enjoyed our short stay at Gjoa Haven, and before leaving next morning I promised to come back and pay Father Henry a visit one of these years from our neighboring mission 250 miles northeast at Cambridge Bay.

Our next stop was Spence Bay, eighty miles northeast. There Father Leverge greeted us with sad news. The day before our arrival two Eskimo children had drowned while playing in a boat in the bay. The whole town was in mourning.

It rained that night and turned colder in the morning with overcast. Father completed his work at noon and we continued on to Pelly Bay, 150 miles to the southeast. Many of the inland lakes were frozen, and when we crossed the bay itself it was solid pack ice. Our ceiling was just high enough, fifteen hundred feet, for us to slide in over the hills. I was halfway around my first orbit of the little ice-packed bay when I spotted the stone mission buildings, well camouflaged on the rocky hillside. A river flowing into the bay from the northeast looked shallow but clear of ice. On a second orbit, two hundred feet off the water, I saw a deep channel. After another circuit GTM was safely on the water.

"There's a rowboat coming out to meet us." Father pointed. By the time I had my safety belt off, the boat had scraped along our pontoon. "Welcome to Pelly Bay," a heavy voice boomed up from the skiff as I opened my door. It came from a short stocky man with a dark silvery beard blowing in the wind. "I have an extra anchor here and some heavy rope. You must anchor your plane right out here in the wide, deep part of the bay. We have six- to eight-foot tides here and quite a few sharp rocks. Must be careful," he said, climbing on the pontoon. "Father Frans Vandevelde." He stuck out his hand and turned a pair of smiling sea-blue eyes at me. I thanked this cheerful, vibrant, colossus of Pelly Bay and introduced him to Father La Rochelle. "Better get an anchor down. Your plane will drift out in the ice with that current," Father Frans warned. He put my anchor and a hundred feet of half-inch rope in his skiff and rowed upstream.

I looped the Y hitch I had spliced on the end of the rope over the two front ballards of the floats, and when all the rope was reeled out Father Frans dropped the anchor. My hands were numb from the cold water until we had the plane safely anchored.

"You landed in the exact spot where Father Paul Schulte landed twenty years ago." Father Frans pointed to the river as he climbed up on the float, breathing hard. "The other planes landed out in the large bay. We have two or three aircraft a year in this busy settlement." He winked at Father La Rochelle.

It took three trips with the skiff to ferry us ashore, including a special case of mail from Chesterfield. When I told him about the case and its contents he nearly opened it then and there.

"This is my first mail in almost a year. I hope we will receive it more often now that the Dew Line site is only forty miles away!" Eskimos lining the shore gave us a hand with our baggage, and then came a handshaking and laughing. They were the happiest, fattest, and most prosperous-looking people I had ever met on the entire Arctic coast. The men were dressed entirely in sealskins, and the women wore long parkas that resembled a priest's chasuble. Their artigies were long in front and back and cut high at the hips, with an extra-long hood in which they carried their babies. I noted a special odor as soon as we climbed the rocks, and so, apparently, did Father La Rochelle. He sniffed and held his nose, turning an eye on the little missionary.

"That must come from my seal-blubber shed. I am so used to the smell now, there must be calluses in my nose. Did you ever see just how we keep our seal blubber?" he asked quickly. "I should offer you a kind of gas mask, but just for a few minutes it won't kill you," he chuckled. "Next year will make twenty years at Pelly Bay, and you see I am still alive." He pounded his chest. Father La Rochelle looked at me with an "I-suppose-we-must-go" look.

I followed the tour—and my nose—to the blubber shed. A good thirty feet above the high-tide mark on the rocks, we came to a square stone building nestled in a rock pothole.

"I spent three months hauling these rocks with my dogs," Father Frans explained, rubbing his callused hand caressingly over the two-foot-thick stone wall. This little Flemish Father was not a large man, but his quick, deliberate actions told me that every ounce of his hundred and fifty pounds was like spring steel. The interior of his shed was dark until he lifted a burlap sack that plugged a small opening for a window.

"Look at that!" Father La Rochelle pointed to a bloody heap of meat, then put his hand to his mouth and turned away.

"That's not as bad as it looks," Father Vandevelde said, bending over and picking up a chunk of meat. Oil and blood dripped to the floor and oozed over his hand. That chunk of meat must have weighed fifty pounds, yet he held it out like a head of cabbage.

"Here, smell it at close range." He held it up to Father La Rochelle. "It really doesn't smell so bad once you become accustomed to it. It's clean—even though it's black and bloody. One hour or two after a seal is opened it turns dark. The oil and fat get a little rancid, especially if it is exposed to the sun," he added, taking his knife out of its sheath on his belt. "Want to taste a little chunk?"

I smelled the meat and cut off a piece. It was good but very oily. Father La Rochelle just wrinkled his nose when I offered him the knife, and pointed to the door. He had had his look. Fresh air was perfume after the dank, fetid odor of the blubber pit. Yet, foul though it was, Father told us the two hundred or more seals he would cache here would be a good bank account for the Eskimos, himself, and his dog team during the long winter.

From these high rocks beside his seal house we had our first good look at the Pelly Bay mission.

"Father Henry laid the first stone and built the farther end of that long house with the dark wall back in 1936." Father Frans pointed. "The wall is dark because he used seal oil to mix his clay mortar to lay up the stone." Four stone buildings squatted on the gravel of a glacier-cut draw that sloped to the sea. The largest and longest was the mission building, with a square adobe stone tower over twenty feet high, topped by a cross. This was St. Peter's Mission of Pelly Bay.

"That is the settlement, but it's been my home since 1937, and a haven for over fifty Eskimo families around the country. Those are their tents." He pointed to the distant puffs of white high on the rocks. "During the winter, when they come for the Feast of Christmas, they build their igloos down on the ice on the bay shore." A handful of people followed us to the house, and I saw that the Eskimos were at home here. We passed only one locked door—on the food and hardware warehouse. Father saw me looking at the lock.

"A starving man has very poor judgment," he remarked when I asked about the honesty of his people. "He could come into this supply of food and waste it, or even accidentally set the place on fire and jeopardize the lives of all of us."

Cautiously we made our way down the smooth rocks and over a crushed redstone path to the glacier-leveled gravel, where the main buildings stood. Father had gathered these small redstones off the beach and spread them between two lines of granite boulders, forming a sidewalk to keep his sealskin mukluks dry. Like many of our missions, this one was built on the remains of boulders and silt left by a glacier and was constantly wet during July and August. The frost is only a few inches below the surface; consequently, the water is not absorbed and softens the fine gravel to mud. Even the waterproof sealskin boots made by the Eskimo women, who tan and crimp the skin on the toes and heels with their teeth, soak through and become damp. The crushed-stone path kept Father's house free of debris and fine sand picked up by wet boots.

"Watch your head, Father. These doors were cut low to conserve on fuel," Father Frans cautioned me. But his warning was too late. I was already holding my head and leaning against the wall when he spoke.

A kind of lean-to shed was built off the back of the house with an ordinary door, in which I entered. Inside it was night-dark, especially after the bright daylight. I had a hand out ahead of me, but before it touched the door, which was recessed on the inside of the three-foot rock wall, my head bumped into a particularly hard rock.

"You'll have a strawberry on your forehead for a week, but there's no deep cut. Guess I'll have to make some kind of a window in that porch. Last year one of the fliers from Trans Air, Ltd., really conked himself. He had to spend an extra day here resting. I think you'll live."

In a few minutes, when the fog lifted, I had a good look at the little room we had entered. It was a chapel, for I could see a corner of the altar peeking out from the drawn curtains. It was also the general meeting and visiting room, with the usual wall benches and a few chairs. There were almost forty people crowded around —visitors were quite an event for them. There was no doubt in my mind that many of these same people came here to receive the attention of Father Frans when they cut their hands or froze a foot. By the devotion in their eyes and their offer to jump and help at every opportunity, I saw that these Eskimos really loved this missionary. He was their man of hope, their doctor and dentist, their teacher, trader, builder, and fixer of things. Only twice in twenty years—in 1949 and in 1955—had Father Frans gone back to his native Belgium; and when he returned the Eskimos gathered from a hundred miles around to welcome him back.

Continually more people entered, curious and smiling. They came over to us immediately and shook hands without a word, looked us over, knelt and crossed themselves in front of the curtained altar, and sat with the others on the wall benches. This demonstration of faith was not an act for our benefit. After meeting most of the Arctic peoples, I can tell the difference between the real thing and the "see-how-holy-I-am" Christian. We have many Indians and Eskimos who try to establish a credit rating in the prayer department. Piously they attend church on Sunday morning, for a loan of fifty dollars or a few sacks of flour on Monday. These people of Pelly Bay could not expect anything in a material way; there was nothing available. But they did seek help from God. Seeing this great faith so deeply emblazoned on their simple souls meant that the missionaries who brought the teachings of our Lord to these people must have been truly holy men.

"How about a good cup of coffee and a little lunch?" Father Frans called from the kitchen. "You will have plenty of time to meet those people later."

The kitchen, about six by twelve feet, also contained Father's bed, a small table, one chair, and a queer-looking arrangement of steel drums with a spigot dripping into a funnel on his stove.

"That is my kudlik—seal-oil lamp or stove."

Father La Rochelle became interested, too, and asked how it worked.

"Well, when I learned that my fuel oil would cost over a thousand dollars to air-freight it in to Pelly from Repulse, I decided to experiment with the Eskimo fuel oil—seal blubber. I lined that ten-gallon steel drum with fire brick begged from Chesterfield." He pointed to the stove with a small funnel soldered to one side. "I put the chunks of blubber in that open half drum, and the heat of the burning seal oil melts the blubber. The stove produces its own fuel, as easy as that." He clapped his hands, then pointed to a dripping spigot near the bottom of the blubber container. "I use coal oil to start the fire. For the first half hour we notice the dead-fish smell, but the heat feels so good we don't mind a little odor."

After lunch I had a look around this famous place. Despite the icebergs in the bay and the dampness, the weather was warm at thirty-nine degrees because there was no wind. Up on the rocks, above the high-water mark, Eskimo women sat fleshing sealskins, their children playing nearby. They stood up, wiped oily hands on their parka hems, and shook hands. One little boy about two years old caught my eye. His face and hands were a mess of blood as he bit and chewed on a piece of raw liver. When I came within five feet, he began to cry hard and loud. His mother rushed over, picked him up, and proceeded to wash his face and hands with her tongue. Her work of cutting the remaining flesh and blubber away from the sealskin—fleshing—had left her a little greasy, but she was no match for the little fellow. He was actually wet!

In a kind of stone pit I spotted some Arctic salmon. The men saw my interest and pointed north to the river, so I climbed the rocks to have a look. With field glasses I could see fish traps of stone in the wide, shallow river. Four men were moving about, spearing fish. I hurried over the rocks, and on a flat plateau someone was digging among the rocks. When I approached, a strapping blond six-footer stood up.

"Gerry Vande Steenhoven," he beamed. After introductions I learned he was a Dutch anthropologist studying tribal laws among the Eskimos.

"See these tent rings?" He pointed to circles of boulders covered with moss. "I've been digging in this six-inch-deep moss and found these." He produced some chipped flint rock, pieces of ivory, and a chunk of musk-ox horn. "People were living here over a hundred

298

and fifty years ago," he commented, adding that he was staying with Father Frans and would see me at suppertime.

I went on to see the fish traps. High on the rocks, several women were opening fish, cleaning and storing them in round stone pits. Some of the caches were already covered with heavy stone to protect them from foxes and wolves. In the winter these fish would be the main source of food for these people, especially around Christmas and Easter, when they visited the little mission. Most of the fish were at least ten-pounders and some larger—the rainbow char trout of the sea.

It is not easy to spear those char. They are quick as lightning. The spearman must be careful not to plunge his weapon too deep in the water, or he will hit rock and dull the point or break the horn which holds the nails on each side of the spear. This Eskimo fish spear is a specialized weapon. Handmade, the ten-foot spruce pole is usually handed down in each family and blackened from many oily hands. At the business end is an eight- or ten-inch barbed steel prong. Affixed to the pole with sinew are two pieces of caribou horn bowed toward the prong tip. At the lower tip of the bowed horn, sharp thornlike nails slant upward toward the shaft of the spear, so that when the fish is struck it cannot wiggle free. Often handles of the spears vary for deep and shallow water. One family may have as many as six spears of various lengths. Before I left the fish traps an Eskimo woman came and offered me two ten-pound char. I accepted them with thanks and took them back to the house for our supper.

That evening, after the dishes were cleared away and the night prayers said with all the people, I asked Father Frans if there were many polar bears in this part of the North.

"The people call Pelly Bay the home of 'Nanuk, the ice bear'— or the polar bear," Father began. One of the Eskimos spoke quickly with emphatic gestures to Father. Father Vandevelde kept on filling his pipe and nodded to the man. "He wants me to tell you about Nanuk, how he comes so silently out of the Arctic night, like the northern lights, hunting for seal or a fish cache."

"Where does this white bear live?" Father La Rochelle asked.

"When the first cold weather comes to Pelly Bay, in late October or early November," Father began slowly between puffs on his pipe, "Mr. Polar Bear begins to look for some wind-packed snowdrift on a hillside. Usually he tries to find one with a southern exposure, so that he can feel the sun as long as it comes above the horizon. In a matter of minutes his powerful claws cut out a snowhouse, and the first good blow seals the entrance."

"You mean he is a hermit in this snow cell all winter?" Father La Rochelle looked at me, pulling his parka tight about him.

"When the weather is good—and Nanuk can smell good weather —he is out for fresh air and anything he can find to eat." Father Frans tapped his nose and looked at the Eskimo men out of the corner of his eye. "In midwinter, bears come out of their snow-houses and search for food. Sometimes they even raid the igloos of the people."

Gerry Vande Steenhoven had been listening intently and now asked, "When do these white bears have their offspring, Father?"

"I was here for six years before I got all the particulars," Father began. From the people he learned that by November, Tayark, the female bear, is usually in her snowhouse with her cubs of one or even two years. Both bears hibernate for a while, but the male bear does much more winter traveling than the female.

Polar-bear cubs are usually born in December—one, two, and even three in a litter every four years. They are covered with pink down and weigh just a little over a pound. It seems the Eskimos often imitate Tayark sitting on her haunches like a person sitting in bed. She leans back against the snow wall and holds her newborn in her furry paws against her broad breast. There they can feed on her milk and she can lick them without disturbing herself. If she is thirsty she gulps a bite of snow from the walls of her home. The young bears eat frequently and grow rapidly but, strangely, do not have their eyes open for almost six months. Tayark keeps her igloo clean by just scratching another hole in the snow bank and moving herself into it at least every three weeks during the winter. By March, when the light comes again to the North, she breaks through the roof of her snowhouse, then digs a small corridor on a level with the floor of her house and pushes her cubs out. They cry and try to hide between her legs to get away from the bright light and out of the wind, but she pushes them aside and hunts for lichens, plants, and lemmings beneath the snow. After a few hours they all return to the snow-house or she builds a new one for them on the spot where they have been hunting. By April the cubs are strong enough to travel, and Tayark begins the long trek north to the Arctic Ocean. The polar bear is born on land but lives on the sea. Often during this long trip, which is not a hurried one, the Eskimos run across bears, and Tayark will kill anything to protect her young.

Many of the people left the mission as Father spoke, and after nine o'clock the last of the men went off to join their families. But this did not put an end to Father's stories of his experiences.

"Two years ago I was traveling north to a place called Tom Bay with an Eskimo," Father Frans began. "We ran across the zigzag track of a bear and knew it was Atertak—'she who goes to the sea'—with her young. After a little while we spotted them, and again they disappeared in the hummocks of ice. We turned two of our dogs loose, and in a few minutes Tayark was leaping over the rough ice in high gear, alone! Superhuman efforts to follow her over that rough ice left me panting like a boxer in the last minute of the fifteenth round." He winked at me. "So we gave up and concentrated on the cubs. One of them gave us trouble and we had to shoot him. The other we took alive aboard our sleigh and returned to our snowhouse. I tied the cub outside with a seal-skin rope, and we proceeded to get a little rest. That little fellow kept squealing and crying, but we were tired and fell asleep. About three hours later I awoke and the cub was gone. He had chewed through his lashings! We followed the track, and Tayark had come within a hundred yards of our igloo when her cub joined her. We were lucky and decided to move away from that place before she changed her mind and attacked us."

"How can a bear live on that polar ice?" Father La Rochelle leaned forward with interest. "From the air, the sea ice and the barren land seems absolutely void of life. Often the ice is solid for miles. How can a bear break it?"

"A polar bear is a very keen seal hunter. In fact," Father Frans said, "the Eskimos learned seal hunting from the bear! You know the seal must breathe every few minutes. In order to do so, he makes breathing holes. In early winter, as the ice thickens, a seal will choose a good fishing ground in the sea and then make breathing holes in the ice. He does this by going from one hole, or aglu, to another, to keep the holes open as the ice freezes. He eats a little, then continues to make the rounds. One seal may have as many as ten aglus. As the ice thickens, the seal holes are often six to eight feet deep, cone-shaped with wide bottoms so the seal can use his flippers to move in and out of the breathing hole. Now an Eskimo needs the assistance of his dog to locate one of these seal breathing holes, but the polar bear can find them with his sensitive nose. A thin layer of hard snow covers the hole. When a bear locates one, he takes his position, sitting and waiting. If the cubs make noise I have seen her swat them and send them rolling." Father gave a little kick, imitating the bear. "She knows that the slightest noise will scare a seal. Finally, when the seal comes up for air, the bear strikes like lightning. The razor-sharp claws dig deep into the head of the seal, and with one yank the bear flips him squirming out onto the ice. Strange thing about those cubs," he said, his blue eyes squinting. "Even when they grow to the size of dogs they still feed on the milk of the mother, to wash down their first taste of fresh blood and seal meat."

More interesting anecdotes of life in this remote region kept Father talking until nearly midnight.

"Don't dream about too many ice bears now," Father Frans laughed as he bid us all good night.

Before blowing out my candle I noticed a huge bear skull with a full set of bone-cracking dentures. I promised myself a good look around in the morning and zipped in for the night.

"We said our Masses already and the people are still in chapel. Would you say your Mass now? It's just a little past seven," Father Frans whispered as he knelt beside me. I dressed hurriedly, had a quick wash, and after a few minutes of morning prayer on the altar step I began my Mass. The Eskimos and Father sang some hymns, and about fifteen, including Gerry, received Holy Communion. Father Henry and now Father Frans had spent themselves for these Eskimos, and the fruit of their efforts was gratifying.

Rain and murky weather continued most of the day, and it gave me an opportunity to learn more of Pelly Bay and those people who could enjoy life on so little.

In Father's rowboat I went out to the plane, made a minute inspection of the engine, and drained the gasoline sumps. Before leaving I turned on my radio receiver to get some idea of the surrounding weather from the hourly Dew Line weather report. Despite the smoky mist and rain, the reception was excellent. Back on shore I met Father Frans and went out to the net with him for our supper.

"All the net floats are under," Father pointed out. "Either we have a seal tangled in the net or many big fish." I steadied the little craft with the oars while Father lifted the net from the water, beginning at the anchor-pole float. It was a cold business on the hands. Every five minutes he hung the net on the bow and warmed his hands, rubbing and blowing on them. Some twenty-five feet of net passed before I saw his expression brighten.

"Here's a trout! Give me the stick." He indicated a short club like a policeman's billy that lay in the boat. As soon as the fish broke water Father belted it a few times on the head. The net was wound around the fish like a shroud, and Father had to be careful not to cut his cold hands on the thin, strong net cords.

He flopped a good twenty-pound trout into the boat, announcing it would be plenty for all of us. In addition we caught nine other good-sized fish. The dogs, too, would eat well that evening.

After a wonderful supper of roasted fish, while I was relaying the weather news gleaned that afternoon, an Eskimo came rushing in and spoke excitedly to Father.

"He wants me to tell you about the bear he found this spring." Father Frans smiled and told us that this Eskimo, Tokannerk, was a very successful and cautious hunter. While hunting he had found a polar bear with his head jammed into an aglu. Tokannerk approached very carefully, and to his great surprise the bear was dead. Evidently it had missed a seal with his claws, pushed his head into the narrow hole, and could not withdraw it. He suffocated. So without a shot or any mark whatsoever on the skin, Tokannerk had a huge bear to his credit. He kept the people guessing for a few days as to just how he did kill the bear.

"April and May are the best hunting months," Father Vandevelde continued. "When we spot a bear we are almost certain another one is close behind. This is the mating season. Also at this time game is plentiful among the ice floes, and a bear just eats the seal blubber, leaving the meat for our dogs—and ourselves!

"Probably you have heard that some of our people have actually battled polar bears with snow knives." Father reached under the stove and came up with an eighteen-inch ivory-handled knife. "This is really an indispensable weapon here in the Arctic." He told us that one day in December his best hunter, Nilaulak, was driving along on his sled with his wife when he spotted a bear standing on a floe of old ice surrounded by new ice. Nilaulak freed his dogs and they cornered the bear on the floe. Nanuk was afraid of walking on the new ice and just sat and fought off the dogs. Nilaulak rushed in and drove his seal harpoon deep in the bear's side. The bear growled, bit at the harpoon, and worked himself to the edge of the floe. All this commotion broke the ice floe free of the new ice, and slowly it began to tip. Bear, hunter, wife, and dogs—all went sliding into the icy water. Here the bear was master. He took a bite at the hunter's thigh, but the double-heavy caribou trousers saved his life. Nilaulak fought free, cutting at the bear's neck and belly with his sharp snow knife. He managed to pull his wife up on the upturned floe, where his dogs waited, dripping and shivering in the cold. He went to his sled half a mile away on the shore, hitched his team, and set them on a break-neck pace, to warm them up, to his igloo. It took him and his wife three days to dry out their clothing with heat from the seal-oil lamp before they could return to the bear. When he did return, he found the carcass of the bear, his harpoon—a family heirloom —on a small island, half eaten by the white foxes. He took some of the best meat, then set fox traps. Nilaulak had over a dozen foxes to compensate for his bath in the ice water.

After two hours of stories Father Frans unhooked his bright gasoline lamp and led the way into his museum. He had everything from a whale's tooth to mounted specimens of rare birds that wandered into this Arctic land of rocks. One chest contained rocks of various sizes and hues, of lead, zinc, silver, and iron. In one corner stood wood handles that had been found while traveling—handles of knives, ice chisels, handles that could be tied to stone for hammers, and handle bars for sleds, blackened from much use by greasy hands. On one side were shelves stacked with arrowheads and handmade arrows, pieces of early Eskimo Dorset-culture carvings, musk-ox horn combs, wooden and bone spoons and forks, and over one hundred pieces of Eskimo art carvings on ivory walrus tusks.

"Take this for our friend, Bishop Fulton Sheen," he said, handing me a little polar bear, the size of my fist, carved in ivory. "It will tell him in a small way we appreciate all that the Society for the Propagation of the Faith has done for us." I thanked Father, packed the little bear safely in my bag, then packed myself in a bag for the night.

The next day the weather was foggy but clearing in the west. The bay was almost free of ice. After Mass we had some of Father's good Flemish-style coffee, fortified with toast and cold fish. When our bags were packed we began our long adieu. Shaking hands with some hundred Eskimos made me realize the great privilege it was to be a missionary and to be able to reach these wonderful people. They were so very grateful.

Father rowed us out to the plane, then climbed aboard for a last good-by. Leaving this wonderful man of God and his devoted people was a little like leaving home, and I promised to return to Pelly Bay.

Chapter Eighteen

O UR flight plan to Igloolik, 375 miles northeast, took us directly across North Committee Bay. When I saw it was solid with ice for over a hundred miles of our flight, I climbed to seven thousand feet so that if need be I could choose a landing spot in case of engine failure. But our Pratt and Whitney sang an even, true, sweet song, and in three hours we landed inside the horseshoe island at Igloolik.

"This is a great day for us," Father Louis Fournier said, taking my passenger by the arm after we met his fellow missionary, Father Trebaol. "You are the first Roman Visitor in the history of our missions. That should rate at least a good dinner." He laughed, steering Father toward the mission. But before they took five steps, Eskimos surrounded the group to shake hands.

Father La Rochelle and I had decided to continue our flight north that afternoon since the weather was so favorable, so before going up to the mission house I made a post-flight check. Before our departure from Chesterfield Inlet, Father Courtemanche had assured me that Trans Air Lines had a good cache of gasoline at Igloolik. The Hudson's Bay manager pointed to the steels high on the white sand beach, and with two Eskimos I refueled GTM and made an oil check.

"The tide is still on its way up," Father Louis called on his way to the house. "How about taking on a little fuel yourself?" I needed no urging. The breakfast trout of Pelly Bay had long since burned up. Father La Rochelle turned out a juicy caribou steak, with a little back-seat coaching from Father Trebaol, who, I noticed, was packing his bags.

"When you circled over the mission I thought of Father Paul Schulte, who came here just nineteen years ago to the week," he said, showing us a picture of Father Paul's plane, the *Flying Cross*. "I helped him refuel the day he flew through here on his way to Arctic Bay to save the life of Father Cochard. The big question in those days was fuel, because Father Schulte didn't have such a large plane. His first attempt was foiled by strong head winds. On the second try he took gasoline in ten-gallon kegs, left his mechanic, Brother Beaudoin, here, and made the rescue." Then he winked at Father Visitor, crossed his fingers, and asked: "You have a fine big plane, Father. Do you have room for another passenger on your way south?" I nodded with a mouthful of caribou steak and was just about to ask where he was bound for when he said: "I'm going to that Rankin nickel mine about seventy miles southwest of Chesterfield, to look after the natives there."

An Obedience to one of the missionaries is similar to orders issued to police or Army or Air Force personnel, the only difference being that an Obedience is the will of God coming to us through our superiors.

The friendliness of the little settlement of Igloolik and the Fathers' cozy home made me want to stay and rest awhile. A kind of flat limestone abounded on the island, and the house had a solid foundation. Even parts of the walls were laid up in rock. Like most of the other small missions, it had a large entrance room that served as a meeting room and chapel. To the left was the Fathers' room and the kitchen. A curtain separated us from the children playing in the large room. Every so often they would peek in and sniff, closing their eyes, then break out into laughter.

On our way to the plane we inspected Father Fournier's project. "I'm going back to the stone age of the Sadlermuits and the Dorset Eskimos and building a new church entirely of stone," he said. "I'll bet the winds won't blow it away. When I visited Site 29 of the Dew Line a hundred miles south, the boys not only gave me some lumber scraps from the packing cases, but they also turned me loose on this pile of cement that was in excess of their needs. They said it had to be used," he added, winking at me.

"This stack of boards is worth its weight in gold." Father Louis beckoned us, lifting the corner of a green tarpaulin to reveal the remains of a hundred packing cases. "A fellow can work wonders with that good plywood if he has a little time. Next winter I expect to build an altar and some other church furniture. I'll have plenty of time when the natives are off on their trap lines." Father carefully replaced the cover and weighted it with a stone.

"When you return from the north I will show you the plans I have for this outline of a stone mission. As you see, it will be built in the form of a cross. There will be adequate room for my living quarters and even a little storeroom for supplies. I expect it will be completed in another four years—if the rocks hold out around the vicinity and if I can keep a trickle of a few hundred pounds of cement coming on the boats each September."

Father Fournier planned with the courage and stamina of his robust youth, and the grit of his determination had brushed off on many of the natives. A dozen or more were hauling rocks from the bay shore in a two-wheel cart. To project his ideas of building a house of God into the minds of these primitive peoples was a major project all its own. The actions of this young missionary were speaking louder than his words—at least as far as these material-minded people were concerned. Here was a man of God they liked. He preached with the example of his work, which is the idea every missionary starts out with when he or she enters a field of work. Too often, however, petty quarrels and envy side-track them. Desire to attain prestige and public honor by advertising themselves as sacrificial victims for the sake of the poor often ends in personal frustration. Pious protestations come from talkers of religion, but real men of God embody religion and follow the Master of Missionaries with an unupholstered cross of sincere faith. This young priest led his people by outright example and commanded their respect by his manly and Christ-like goodness.

The Hudson's Bay manager came upon me unawares with the latest on Pond Inlet weather. I had left the Fathers at the chapel site and was waiting for Father La Rochelle.

"There has been a lot of wind up there these past three days, but it blew itself out early this morning," the Bay man explained. "Ordinarily our radio communications are not so clear with Pond Inlet. We're lucky to have this timely 'sked' today."

I had not anticipated this choice bit of news and it certainly eased the tension of the flight. At two o'clock that afternoon I filed a flight plan with the Hudson's Bay manager and by two-thirty we were off with a maximum load of gasoline. Like Father Schulte, I respected those powerful winds and took three kegs of gasoline along. My intention was to leave them at Pond Inlet for a future cache in case I did not require them.

Throughout the entire summer I tried to think of all the emergency gear a fellow might need in case the Wasp decided to balk on this Baffin Island trip. With the added gasoline, mail, and some supplies for the Pond Inlet mission, the cabin was so loaded I asked Father La Rochelle to ride up front with me.

308

I am sure that if Admiral Beaufort had flown the Arctic in 1805 when he developed his scale estimating the velocity of winds he would have included the effect of wind speed on water in varying degrees. At least a moderate gale was coming out of the northeast that afternoon, of some forty-five knots or about fifty miles per hour, that certainly would have broken the branches off trees—had there been any trees. From five thousand feet I could see the wind cut off the wave crests. This slowed us down with a ground speed of not more than ninety miles per hour, which I calculated after the first half hour of flight.

We were just north of the latitude area of permanent fronts. Latitude 60 is about the center of the polar front area. Here the warm southwesterly winds meet the cool northeasterlies and form a permanent front. We were about five hundred miles inside the northeasterly cool belt. The weather report from Pond Inlet gave the wind a mere five miles per hour, indicating that we were moving north into winds of less velocity. My chief concern was gasoline for the return trip to Igloolik.

This was new and bleak territory compared to the verdure of the Mackenzie Valley and the western Arctic. Canada is such a vast country, with a topography that confuses most people unless they make a special study of it. After eighteen years of poking my nose into the remote corners of the North where our missionaries have penetrated to reach the people, and smelling out the reasons for an often paradoxical climate, I have compared my gleanings with meteorologists and arrived at a few conclusions.

I agree with the climatologists who say the weather of North America is affected by that huge inland sea, the Hudson Bay. This cold body of water pulls the Arctic more than five hundred miles south of the Arctic Circle. A line drawn from Seward Peninsula in Alaska southeast to Port Harrison on the eastern shore of Hudson Bay would climatically divide the Arctic of the northeast from the sub-Arctic of the southwest. The great land masses of the northwest make the summers warmer than those in the northeastern part of the Arctic, where the average mean temperature remains below fifty degrees Fahrenheit in the warmest month. Paradoxically, the winters of the Yukon have recorded temperatures of eighty-one below zero, much colder than the eastern Arctic, where thirty-five to forty degrees below zero for the coldest month of January have been recorded. The reason? Those great land masses absorb heat faster than the sea and retain the heat beneath the ice! At Igloolik, just off the tip of the Melville Peninsula, it was a hot day of forty-nine degrees.

"We have about a dozen of these days a year," Father Trebaol had explained on our arrival there. "Usually it is between thirty-five and forty on clear days during our summer, which is August. At night, even though the sun never sets for a month and a half, the temperature drops sometimes to below freezing."

Flying at five thousand over Baffin Island, I was thankful to Father Fournier for suggesting that I wear my parka and flying boots. Our wing thermometer read thirty-six degrees Fahrenheit! High over Richards Bay, I saw Fury and Hecla Strait, and they were open. This was strange, since all of Foxe Basin to the east was a solid white ice mass. I learned later from Father Lorson at Pond Inlet that it was due to the tides and winds on the ocean that changed the temperatures of the water. He said he found them open even in January and frozen in September.

Some one hundred and fifty miles north of Igloolik the snow fields of Baffin Island glistened beneath us, and the terrain became mountainous, with deep ravines and gorges. There was no sign of life on the land, but in the blue-green sea, square flipper seals and porpoise played, following a school of fish. My passenger was silent and observant. His rosary slipped slowly through the fingers of his right hand while his left lay on the map, his finger pointing to our exact position. Early in July, when we began flying together on the visitation of the Vicariate of Keewatin, I had asked him to help me with navigation by trying to follow the map. In a country so vast and with so many similar lakes and a homogeneous landscape, this is very difficult for a beginner. Usually I would fly for about fifteen minutes to gain altitude, then would point out our position on the map if Father did not have it. In a week he was at home with the map when we could get enough altitude to read check points, but often we had to fly in rain and under low fog, with visibility less than three miles. In these conditions I flew on the compass, since most of these flights were short jaunts of a hundred miles or so.

On this trip to Pond Inlet we had climbed to six thousand feet, which made map reading a pleasure. In fact, it gave him time to get "prayed up" on the trail! As we approached the northern tip of Baffin Island the mountains continued to rise over five thousand feet. First we saw the glaciers and mountains on Bylot Island. Then, as GTM was descending, Father picked out the small settlement of Pond Inlet on the south shore. Snow-covered hills gave it an ermine setting, and two huge icebergs lay grounded just off shore. It was only after a descent to a thousand feet that I noted the roll and swell of the sea. The tide was in full, and heavy seas rolled up on the beach. I circled twice, descending to three hundred feet, and was just taking note of the waves washing against the blue iceberg when Father called into my ear, "Why don't you land?"

"The swells are too long and too high in front of the settlement. I'm looking for some sheltered bay or the lee of a peninsula." He looked directly down on the water but could not detect the heavy sea swells.

"Look along the beach," I called into his ear. "Watch the rollers break there." He nodded, indicating he saw them.

People began to appear near the doors of their homes, and a group of Eskimos had come to the water's edge. After a fourth orbit I decided on a letdown deep in the throat of the inlet, where the swells seemed to diminish. My air speed was cut to sixty-five miles per hour, with twenty-five degrees of flap and very fine propeller pitch. Father made the Sign of the Cross, and smash! We hit the crest of a roller and I sensed the danger as the plane glanced off the water and sent the throttle forward. That smack had slowed us down to forty-five miles per hour. The Wasp growled like an angry bear and the propeller sprayed water over the ship as it caught the crest of a wave. We hit again and again, but with less impact than the first time, and finally broke free of the water. Those swells must have been eight or ten feet high.

"Go to the small lake," Father called frantically in my ear. He did not have to tell me. After that first smack my decision was definite. We zipped past the towering icebergs, and I orbited once over the little mission house, where the two Fathers waved at us. I pointed GTM toward a cut in the snow-capped mountains to the south.

Captain Dave Croal of Trans Air Lines had told me about a small lake in the mountains, about twenty miles southeast of the inlet, where I could find shelter in case the sea was too rough for a landing. In eight minutes we spotted it. It looked very narrow, and there was only one way in and the same way out. I judged it to be about three hundred or so yards wide and a good length of two miles, but with mountains at the far end. I flew low past the mouth to check it. This would have to be a tail-wind landing.

Father La Rochelle became quite excited and I saw his beads slide quickly through his fingers. As we passed the lake I noted it was somewhat elevated, perhaps fifty feet, from the flat land to the north. A small river with rapids drained off water from its northeastern tip. The lake water was a very dark blue, indicating good depth, and the entire lake was already in shadow, the late-afternoon sun curtained out by the towering hills.

We flew low over the rocky ledge at the north end of the lake, and with a light feathering of wavelets against the floats we settled on the quiet waters.

What a relief from those heavy seas! The rocky red walls were precipitous to at least two thousand feet. Where did Dave moor his plane? I asked myself. We came about and faced the north entrance, then I recalled seeing a little creek on my inspection orbit before landing. I taxied up to the north end of the lake, and the little creek was deep enough for the aircraft to enter, just in the lee of a small island. Using a canoe paddle, I approached the sharp-rocked shore with caution. A punctured float here would really mean trouble.

It was 5:30 P.M., with almost seven hours in the air that day. I moored the aircraft, tail to shore, with Father assisting and secured two lines to some hefty rocks, thinking all the while about that ration box and a good hot bowl of soup.

There was a hollow echo in the air, a frightening stillness that magnified the slightest noise. The high canyon walls of ice and rock began to give me the "deep-in-a-well" feeling I had experienced as a boy when I once helped my father clean a well. He had cautioned me not to look up while I was in the well, but my curiosity got the better of me and I chanced a look that shivered me with fright. The light was so far away and the whole world seemed to be slowly closing in around me. I had to come up out of that well—only twenty feet deep! Now, while my hands worked the ropes around the black, moss-crusted rocks, my wild imagination envisioned rock slides and a mad scramble to save our lives.

"Look up there on the rocks," Father La Rochelle pointed. "It looks like a white fox."

"That's an Arctic hare," I almost whispered, cautiously going to the plane for my .22. "They're usually fat this time of year, and a rabbit stew would taste good about now. Say a little prayer to St. Hubert, the hunters' patron, Father. That rabbit is too far to try a shot from here. I'll have to sneak up at least within a hundred

312

yards." I climbed with one eye on the white speck and the other picking a footing on the rocks. Just for an instant I took my eyes off the rabbit. He vanished! I sat like a stone, just moving my eyeballs, searching for the white fur against the dark red rocks.

"He's coming this way," Father called. Then I saw it hopping. I flattened out against the rocks, worked my gun in position, and found the rabbit in my sights. He stopped for an instant and I squeezed a shot at him. He went down, but I couldn't spot him from my position. Fifteen minutes of climbing and I was at the spot—a hole the size of a basketball in the rocks. It looked deep and dark inside. I could see nothing and returned to the plane.

"I see you missed the rabbit," Father teased. I told him of the hole in the rocks, but he just laughed. We decided to use the emergency rations and have a little food.

The wind was just a light breeze now and the sea would be calm enough to make another attempt to reach Pond Inlet that evening. Our appetites were satisfied with a box of sardines each, a pilot biscuit, and a healthy drink of that icy green mountain lake water.

To lighten our cabin load we pumped the three ten-gallon drums of gasoline into our wing tanks and at seven o'clock decided to make another attempt to reach the settlement. After a routine taxi down the lake we turned and took off. Eight minutes of flight brought us to the inlet, but short rollers were still running their frothy tongues along the gravel lip of the beach. A landing would not be easy.

We selected the smoothest-looking water to the lee of a huge iceberg and attempted to land. Our first contact with the water was such a surprise impact that it bounced us a good ten feet in the air. Luckily, I still had good speed. Full throttle pulled us out of those waves after two more light touches. I looked at my passenger, and he pointed toward the mountain lake. We both had the same idea. Enough of that flirting with a dip in the drink. In a flash we were past the houses, headed for our lake in the last of the day's good light. Even though Pond Inlet enjoys two and a half months without a sunset, the last days of August are shrouded in gray light, with a low sun below the rim of the mountains of Bylot Island.

Our landing was routine now, and soon we were tailed to the rocky shoreline of the little creek on the north end of the lake.

"Perhaps I could start walking to the settlement," Father said, looking toward the mountaintops north of the inlet. "It doesn't seem very far. I believe I could make it in two hours!" I assured him that he would not be able to walk there, even if it was possible, in less than eight hours! While flying he did not notice the hills and ravines, some over a hundred feet deep. And there was at least one good-sized stream to cross. Father understood, and we began to make our night camp. The tent was too small for both of us, so I elected to use it and Father La Rochelle chose the aircraft. We agreed to leave for the settlement at three in the morning.

The evening was still young, only eight-thirty, so I picked up my .22 and wandered up a ravine along the little creek to see if I could spot a rabbit or a ptarmigan. Either one would make a good breakfast. Carefully and slowly picking my way over the rocks, I thought of the advice the fellows at Churchill had dished out about this place.

"That Pond Inlet can be the devil of a place to sit down on after a storm at sea, Father," Dave Croal had cautioned the evening I spent at his home going over air maps of this country.

"Usually ice fog settles over the inlet. Remember, it's only some two hundred and sixty miles across Baffin Bay to Thule, Greenland." Father Cochard shook his official, stubby finger at me. For almost a month these cheerful hints were dropped with gentle and jesty tact, like boulders on the tender toes of my almost anemic courage.

After an hour's walk, seeing nothing but rocks, I returned to my little tent on the hillside and tried to get some sleep. Usually the motion of the plane as it rode at anchor put me to sleep. But up here on the rocks it was different. Every little while there was a rumble of some distant glacier breaking off into the sea. Then a kind of scratching at the back of the tent sent cold chills into my bones. Slowly I picked up my rifle, gently bolted a shell into the barrel, and crept out of the tent quietly. I was inching toward the back of the tent when a pure-white ermine came around the corner. It stopped, and as soon as my scent reached it the little fellow was off in a flash, bounding over the mossy rocks and into the night. It was almost a mouse and elephant story and made me chuckle a little at my timidity.

The morning sun knifed into my face through the tent flap. It was 3:30 A.M. and time to move! I slipped into my parka and outside gear, picked up my rifle, and crawled outside. It was cool there on the side of the mountain. A very thin fog had spread over the lake, but the country was quiet under the new golden glow of the morning. I had the tent down and folded before I heard "*Bonjour, mon ami,*" from the plane.

"Did you sleep a little, Father?"

"I rested but could not turn off my thinking about that rough sea and those icebergs last evening. Another thing"—Father cleared his hoarse throat—"I can assure you my idea of bush pilots has climbed into a new sublime category. Men who come so near death, so often, cannot live far away from God!"

"*Merci, mon Père,*" I said, coming down the knoll to the ship with the tent and sleeping bag. "Speaking of pilots, I think we should run off a short prayer to our patron of airmen, Father, Our Lady of Loretto, and ask her to put in a good word to the Master Pilot. We have a very cold engine to start and only one battery!" Being a thoughtful man—and one who makes others always seem tall in his presence—he nodded and handed me the ropes and shore gear silently. With everything aboard I made my usual Sign of the Cross, and hit the starter with my fingers crossed. Our Wasp turned over very slowly, took a healthy gulp of gasoline from the primer, and began to breathe and live. Father La Rochelle smiled, looked up toward the sky, and called into my ear: "We must have Friends up there."

GTM slowly left the rocky shore and we taxied down the cold, blue lake. The echoes of our exhaust must have sent every living thing in those hills scurrying for their dens. After ten minutes of turning about to get our engine oil heated we were off for the inlet.

My big concern all morning was the condition of the water at Pond Inlet. If it was too rough we would have to return to Igloolik, 290 miles south, and our gasoline supply was limited. Approaching the inlet, I was thankful that there was very little surf. As a matter of fact, a small boat high on the beach indicated low tide. We could taxi to the beach, my passenger could get off in style, and we could unload these few supplies for the mission and move out to anchor without danger of being grounded. I pointed GTM toward a huge chunk of ice some ten feet from the water line on shore. It would make a solid mooring post. About thirty feet from shore I cut the switches and climbed down on a float with a rope. We drifted in until the keelsons of the floats grounded on the gravel, and I heaved a line on shore.

A bowlegged Eskimo grinned and grabbed it. I made the line fast to the aft ballard of the float and used a paddle to push the plane free. Three Eskimos were on the line without a word. They heaved on the rope and GTM tailed up high on the gravel. Now my passenger could step off on dry land. Before I pointed to the grounded iceberg, the Eskimos had the rope anchored securely around a jetting chunk of it.

Father La Rochelle climbed down onto the pontoon while we were mooring the ship, jumped ashore, and met the Eskimos.

"Falla is coming." One of them pointed. We turned to see the two Fathers coming on the run, pulling on their parkas.

"Welcome to Pond Inlet," they both said at once. "We had a real blow off the sea all last week, which accounts for the large swells you found last evening," Father Dufour explained, his gray-flecked beard bobbing as he spoke. "When we saw you last evening, the Hudson's Bay manager was with us. He said it would be all right to tie the plane behind their boat. They have a big anchor. You will not have to worry about a little wind."

"I will come for you in the rowboat," tall, blond Father Lorson began. "Some of the Eskimos will help you with the ropes. They know what to do."

It sounded like a safe and good procedure. We unloaded the baggage and mail, and I taxied out with the aircraft. The Eskimos anticipated my instructions and moved around the boat with the agility and sure-footedness of heavy mountain cats.

"This is the first time in the history of this mission that we have four priests here on Sunday," Father Lorson commented later as we walked toward the house. "I suppose the Eskimos wonder just what's going to happen." He turned to look at them. "They're following us. Believe it or not, Father, there isn't a Catholic in the bunch! They all attend services, either ours or the Anglican, but they haven't decided what to believe yet." Then he added seriously, "We've been here a dozen years already, Father, and do you know what? Two families have entered the Church." He held up two fingers, one with a knob on its knuckle from being broken. "It takes so much patience with these people," he said, half to himself. "They look for only the material things—mostly something to eat."

The mission at Pond Inlet is built like the others in the Arctic. Everything is under one roof to conserve fuel. I liked the little chapel here. Above the altar is a large mural of igloos and Eskimos coming with their dog teams, their sleds piled high with belongings and waving children. I served Father La Rochelle's Mass and then said my Mass of thanksgiving, which he served. Only two of the Eskimos followed us into the little chapel. They were surprised that I was a full-fledged priest who said Mass like the others, I found out later. I was the first English-speaking priest they had ever met—and the fact that I was a pilot, too, made them scratch their chins in wonder.

"Our two Catholic families are hunting narwhal a hundred and seventy-five miles east at Arctic Bay," Father Dufour said, passing me a huge plate of baked sea trout. "Try some of this, Father. We usually have it cold, or raw and frozen, but this morning we baked it. We thought you and Father La Rochelle would prefer it this way."

Fish for breakfast is a little unusual even in the North, but on that special morning both of us enjoyed the Arctic char very much. And it was during this hour-long visit over morning coffee that the decision was made for Father Lorson to ride south with us. His new Obedience was taking him to Baker Lake Mission to assist Father Charles Choque. I gave him a hand packing his trunk, and after we had all his effects aboard the plane he took me on a tour of the place.

"This is our warmest time of the year. We have a full three months of daylight here, you know," Father Lorson began. "Of course that means we also have three months in winter when we don't see the sun."

"Does it actually remain pitch-dark at any time during the dark winter months?"

"No, the long night is not a continuous black night. There is usually a degree in the kind of darkness during the actual days and nights. At noon in clear weather there is a kind of eerie moonlight reflected from the snow. This is brighter, naturally, later in the day when there is a reflection of the starlight from the snow. In stormy weather," Father went on, "which at times lasts for eight or nine days without a letup, we need a flashlight to find our way to the Hudson's Bay store only four hundred feet away."

Father Lorson spoke softly, looking at a group of Eskimos standing at the corner of the Hudson's Bay store. "Our natives who live off this country really have a hard time when the weather is bad during the long night. In good weather they can at least visit their fox traps and find the seal breathing holes, but in a storm they must keep to their snowhouses sometimes for a week or even longer. As long as they have seal oil and some kind of food they can keep warm. I found a few families in my travels that had not given up hope, even with their last dog eaten."

Pond Inlet, one of the entrances to the Northwest Passage, was named after the great Peter Pond of the 1770s, an explorer and man of travel, both on land and sea. Two days after our departure I learned that the Canadian Navy's HMCS *Labrador* sailed through Pond Inlet after successfully navigating the dangerous Bellot Strait and shortening the Arctic route by over four hundred miles. Previously this strait, which is twenty miles long and cut by rocks and shoals, was considered too shallow for deep-draft ships and they sailed north around Somerset Island. The *Labrador* recorded the shallowest depth of fifty feet. This discovery will aid the United States Merchant Marine and Coast Guard ships in getting closer to land supplies to the Dew Line sites. It may even mean possibilities for commercial shipping, according to ice-breaker-manufacturing experts. As missionaries we are happy to see this hard shell of the Arctic yield to modern methods of transport. It will mean a new life for our northern people.

"By the way, Father, how do you get your supplies up in this country?" I asked.

"The Arctic Ice Patrol boat transported the lumber for the mission thirteen years ago. Each year it brings a few supplies," Father Lorson replied, taking me into the small supply warehouse.

"You must use a lot of fuel oil here during the long winter."

"See that pile of sacks? They're coal sacks. We mine our own fuel, a kind of soft coal or lignite. Speaking of the long winter," he said, rubbing his hands, "we don't heat very much. A good part of the time we are off on the trail, visiting the people. When we are home we light a fire just for cooking. It would burn too much coal and keep one of us constantly digging. That's work, I tell you." He patted the sacks. "Usually we take turns getting up early, a week at a time, to light the big kitchen range. Once the fire is started, the fireman hops back into his sleeping bag for another hour until the frost gets out of the house."

I noted that their flour and other sacked supplies were on a two-foot platform above the floor. Father explained that precaution was to keep out the mice and especially the lemmings.

In the attic of their home the Fathers stored their few freezables, including the batteries for their 32-volt wind charger. The entire upper room was lined with caribou skins to keep out the intense cold.

"Let me show you our refrigerator now that you have seen our warm storage." Father led me down the narrow stair. In the center of the large meeting room he opened a trap door insulated with three thicknesses of caribou skin on its underside. He descended the ladder first with the lantern and I followed.

"We dug the pit with picks and blasting powder before we built the house," he explained. "The terrain around here thaws out about five inches at most. All we have to do is keep a tight cover on the cellar and we are in the deep-freeze business all year round! When the walls get oily and bloody from fish and caribou, we just bring in a few gallons of fresh water and throw it on the walls and floor. It freezes immediately and our icebox is clean again."

"What about seal meat and blubber? I don't see any here."

"We have a special blubber pit for that smelly stuff." Father wrinkled his nose.

There was a pile of fish stacked like firewood in one corner, and chunks of caribou in another, all frozen like rocks. And no wonder! The thermometer on the side of the ladder read twenty-eight below zero.

We climbed out of the pit, and the warm room felt good—especially with its aroma of roasting fish. Father Dufour was sitting at the kitchen table, talking with the canonical visitor and keeping an eye on the roast.

"Look at this," Father Lorson called to me, holding a long white pole in his hands. "This is a tusk from a narwhal. Two weeks ago I was out whaling with some Eskimos and they gave me this large one and this little fellow," he said, reaching in a corner.

Here was something I had been searching for ever since I saw one at Dr. Melling's home.

"Only the male has these tusks," Father Lorson explained. "The left tooth usually erupts first in the young male narwhal. It grows into a spirally twisted horn of ivory like this from four to even eight feet long. Sometimes it weighs as much as fifteen pounds." He handed me the tusk. I examined the ivory and hefted it. What a beauty!

"Take it along for a souvenir of Pond Inlet." Father Lorson smiled. "I will have other opportunities to collect one of them."

I thanked him, took the prize out and carefully packed it in the aircraft. On my way back I took a few pictures of the settlement with the huge icebergs in the background. Seven buildings were set high on the beach, out of reach of high tide and in the lee of a two-hundred-foot graveled escarpment that kept rising to the three-thousand-foot mountains to the east and the snow fields.

A fifty-by-fifty-foot coat of arms with crest of the Royal Canadian Mounted Police is laid in multicolored rocks on the hillside as a backdrop for Pond Inlet, whose name is written in white-painted rocks in twenty-foot letters. The Eskimos had four tents perched on the eastern end of the settlement, high on the rocks, and two new white tents, like sentinels, flapped high above the Royal Canadian Police crest.

The icebergs and changing fourteen-foot tide make the beach and the inlet a continual cynosure of all eyes. Anything from large sea trout to seal or even narwhal could be grounded—after each outgoing tide—providing food, the essence of importance here. When I asked about the icebergs, Father told me that one morning they were awakened by people who were calling and climbing the hill behind the mission.

"Hurry, Falla. Ice coming on us." A huge iceberg had floated into the inlet and was heading for the settlement. It could have mashed the houses against the hill like a giant bulldozer. But Father said he noticed the tide going out rapidly and calmed the people. Actually the berg was grounded four hundred yards from shore.

After our trout lunch Father La Rochelle decided to profit by the wonderful flying weather and set 2:30 P.M. for departure time. It was a hot forty-eight degrees Fahrenheit—one of the exceptional days of their short summer. Father Dufour rowed me out to the aircraft to make a minute inspection before our long flight south. I was anxious to take a look inside the fuselage at the tail section that had taken such a pounding on those waves in the attempted landing. One look was enough. Four small wooden ribs were broken, but the fabric was still intact and the damage was not extensive enough to prevent our flight. I decided it could wait for repair at Igloolik, where I would have a good quiet harbor to work on it.

The Hudson's Bay Company could not make contact by radio with Igloolik for a late weather report, but the local weather was grand. There was even a slight northwest breeze that would sit right on our tail for a change. By two-thirty that afternoon every person in the settlement was on the beach to see us off. In no time we were looking down on the icebergs and the last good-bys from the waving people of Pond Inlet.

On the flight south Father Lorson was an interested observer of the country he traveled so often with his dog sled in winter. Occasionally he called our attention to one or more Eskimo tupiks, or skin tents, at the deltas of small rivers. Here also I saw the first flocks of blue geese with their long white necks, flying south in irregular lines a few hundred yards beneath us.

We landed at Igloolik after a very fast and enjoyable flight, and the whole population was on shore to welcome us back. I retired early that evening, relaxed now that the long, worrisome flight was over. After entering my daily flight log, and a short night prayer, I spread out my sleeping bag on the floor of GTM and flew south in dreams with the blue geese.

In the next six days, with Father Trebaol and Father Lorson as passengers, Father La Rochelle and I visited Our Lady of the Snows Mission at Repulse Bay. Here we met tides of over twenty-two feet and some sharp, unfriendly rocks and ice. But Fathers Didier and Fransen compensated for the bleak surroundings with their warm Oblate hospitality. Father Fransen even waded in the icy water to keep GTM from cutting her tender aluminum boots.

Then southeast at Coral Harbor, on Southampton Island, we were ushered into the "white house" of Father Joseph Choque.

"This is walrus country," he said, watching us gravitate to his collection of ivory carvings after the greetings were over. "The Eskimos practically live on that art work now that the bottom is out of the fur market." He uncovered his very best cribbage boards, letter openers, Eskimo figurines, polar bears, and a few dozen other items, all in ivory. Eskimos filled the room and stood beaming at our interest in their work.

At the Hudson's Bay store I was pleasantly surprised to see Bob Cruckshanks and his wife, whom I had met often at Coppermine and Cambridge Bay. Besides giving my battery a boost on his generating plant, he gave me good weather news and we flew away to Chesterfield Inlet—a flight that took a little over four hours.

When we arrived at Chesterfield, a twenty-mile-an-hour east wind churned up heavy seas on the bay, and we landed on a small lake behind the mission.

"You fellows made that northern Circle route plenty fast," Father Courtemanche called as he caught the mooring lines.

A few minutes later he introduced the new missionary for Garry Lake, Father Trinel, a young priest with a sparkle in his eye and the compact build of a hockey player.

"Father Cochard told me you would fly me and a few supplies to my new mission," he said anxiously. "If there is anything I can do to help, just say the word, Father." With all that zeal handy GTM was loaded with his cargo that evening, plus a good supply of fuel for the long trip.

Next morning he was aboard, sitting on cases of dry fruit. Father Lorson rode co-pilot, checking the maps with his knobby finger as we flew to Baker Lake, where Father Charles Choque met us at the small sandy beach near his house. This time I had letters from his brother and a new assistant. He was smiling and happy. Now he would not have to spend the winter alone.

Father Trinel helped refuel the plane, readjust the cargo, and run mooring lines out for the night. That evening I learned Father Choque was familiar with the Garry Lake area and asked him to accompany us and help us in our search for Father Buliard. We gathered all the available weather data and the following morning flew northwest two hundred miles over the rugged country to Garry Lake.

The weather was clear and we found the little tarpaper-shack mission without difficulty. When the supplies were landed I met an Eskimo by the name of Adjuk, who seemed to know a few of the answers I was after. Father Choque talked with him in his Saningayormiut language while he fed him half a dozen cigarettes and learned this story.

On October 24, 1956, Father Joseph Buliard left the mission to visit his fish nets. There was a little ground drift, but nothing to keep a man with twenty thousand miles of Arctic dog-sledding from making a little jaunt of twelve miles.

After he left, the winds intensified to blizzard force. The Eskimo waited that evening, but no sign of Father. For three days the blizzard covered the land and there was no chance to go looking for the missionary. On the fourth day, the wind died and Adjuk walked to the nets, only to discover the ice had not been chopped. Father never reached the nets. The Eskimo looked around and found no trace of broken ice anywhere in the vicinity, then went to his brother's camp a little beyond the nets. He had seen nothing of Father either. They agreed the priest did not drown but must be lost in the Barren Land. On November 14, all of Father's dogs returned except one. They were without harnesses and starving.

I fished out my flight maps of the area, and we located the exact place of the nets. With the Fathers and the two Eskimos aboard, I took off. We flew to the spot Father Buliard was aiming for with his dogs and began a series of orbits at seven hundred feet, surveying half-mile belts of country. Fortunately Father Choque knew the caretaker of an airstrip twenty miles north, used by the Spartan Air Photo planes, and we were able to get a few extra gallons of gasoline.

Our air search was spread over two days because of a little fog that grounded us awhile. After flying orbits for forty miles out of Garry Lake we returned to the lake proper. We searched thoroughly every deep bay, every ravine, river bed, and valley in the area that looked like a possible shelter from that storm.

On the fourth morning four inches of snow covered the ground, and ice laced the edges of the lakes.

"Not much use searching now," Father Choque said, looking at the snow. "It has covered everything."

Father Trinel said he would search with his canoe and on foot, when and if the weather cleared. We wished him luck, promised our prayers for his safety, and flew back to Baker Lake with four Eskimo children for the boarding school at Chesterfield. Father Lorson, meanwhile, had rounded up two more pupils.

With many regrets at not finding any trace of Father Buliard, I left the two missionaries at Baker Lake next morning and flew to Chesterfield Inlet with my six young passengers.

Archbishop Turquetil had founded this Mission of St. Therese in 1913. It was now the center of all the northern settlements.

The Grey Nuns must have sensed that I might have school children aboard that day. They delegated Sister Pelagie, the first Eskimo girl to become a nun, to meet the plane.

Father Cochard was very anxious to learn about our search. When I told about our unfruitful results, he was sad.

"He may be dead, but his work is very much alive," I consoled this man, who felt so keenly the loss of his brother missionary.

"Without his efforts you would not have Eskimo families eager to send their children to school, like those." I pointed to Sister leading the children over the rocks. He nodded, but his face became old. He must have thought about his own days of loneliness and illness at Arctic Bay, for he said:

"Thanks for risking your life in that wild country. Father Buliard will see to it from his new home that you receive the reward and protection of all faithful pilots of souls." Then he added quickly with a smile, "When Father Paul Schulte saved my life with his plane I told him I would say a Hail Mary every day to Our Lady of the Snows to keep his plane from crashing. Now I'll add another for you."

My Roman passenger completed his work the following day and we continued south to Rankin Inlet with Father Trebaol. An ocean-going vessel was in the harbor loading nickel ore from a mine in operation there when we arrived, and Father was surprised at all the activity. A few dozen houses and many tents were clustered around a high gray mine shaft.

We landed, taxied to shore, and some Eskimos came running. Father Trebaol asked them in Eskimo where the priest was, and they ran back up the hill. Father Robert Paradis soon came rushing down and took the Fathers to his mission shack.

"We're just building a little place here," he said. "Next time you come I will ask you to stop overnight. Right now we have kind of rustic accommodations."

Late that same afternoon we flew south to Eskimo Point for a visit with Father Lionel Ducharme.

"Anchor your plane well," he cautioned. "This is where Father Schulte almost lost his aircraft. A storm came up and he and Father Dunleavy spent half the night in that icy water to save the plane."

I took his advice and anchored to a large float in the bay. The local Mountie assured me that no storm would move his anchor, so I rested easy that evening.

The last leg of our eastern Arctic trip into Churchill the next afternoon made Father La Rochelle a very happy man. He was convinced of the safety and necessity of air travel in our Arctic missions. His Excellency, Bishop Marc Lacroix, also expressed sincere appreciation and the hope that I would return one day to take him on such a visit.

Flying back to my base at Fort Smith after such a full season, I had only one regret—that I was unable to find a trace of Father Joseph Buliard. After seeing the bleak country where he worked, sleeping in the shack that had been his home, saying Mass on his humble little altar, and seeing the faith of his people, I could draw only one conclusion. He was now with the sainted founder of the Oblates of Mary Immaculate, receiving a just reward for his faithfulness to our motto: "to preach the Gospel to the poor."

Chapter Nineteen

AFTER six years of hard work GTM had lost much of its air-worthiness. A secondhand plane when we purchased it, it was now thirteen years old and required too many modifications and was too costly to operate. The Bishop appealed to the Cardinal Prefect of the Society for the Propagation of the Faith in Rome for help. He knew the great need in all foreign missions, and his hopes were not very high. Then to his great surprise Archbishop Pietro Sigismondi promised help.

"You tell us how much you need and we will do our best."

The Bishop was profuse in his gratitude. Now Rome approved of his air transportation in the missions. In a special-delivery air-mail letter he sent me the good news. When he arrived in Montreal we went to the De Havilland Aircraft Company in Toronto, where the Bishop met an old friend who had given him his first airplane ride in the North, Charles "Punch" Dickins.

"What you need, Bishop, is a Beaver aircraft," Punch said. "It will fly for half the cost of your Norseman and carry practically the same load."

On June 15, 1958, I flew out of Toronto in our new Beaver with Denis Chatain of Edmonton as my co-pilot. When we met with gusty winds at Sault Ste. Marie, I was happy that my assistant was a few shades over six feet and 240 pounds! His poundage on the mooring lines saved the new plane. After an overnight stop at Fort William and refueling stops at Lac du Bonnet and Prince Albert, we arrived at the oil capital of Edmonton.

"How did you ever manage to get that personalized identification, CF-OMI?" Paul Chatain, Denis' father, asked as soon as we docked at Cooking Lake.

The Department of Air Transport in Ottawa had honored our request because of "the assistance and co-operation of the missionaries in matters of state these many years."

"And I see you have the ship painted in Our Lady's colors to match—white and Dresden-blue trim," Mrs. Chatain chimed in.

Following the suggestions of Mr. Dickins, the bush pilot who pioneered the Arctic mail route, we have equipped CF-OMI with the latest in radio aids. Long-range fuel tanks give us five hundred miles plus, and hydraulic ski wheels give the ship year-round operating facilities.

"Now you fellows are developing one step ahead of the country," Bert Bury, owner of McMurray Air Services, joshed as he took the Bishop's arm to help him out of the plane at Uranium City. It may have appeared that way to Bert, but development, all the way from Edmonton to the Arctic coast, made the Bishop ride his new plane constantly to keep abreast of it.

Throughout all of northern Canada education has suddenly become a heavy issue. Prior to 1946 there was not a government school in the North. The missions provided day schools and boarding schools from the days of their foundation in the 1850s. As is the case in primitive education around the world, teachers shouldered the cause. Devoted to a life of instructing others, they had not only to coax their pupils to attend school but also had to bring the entire education issue out of the tent and igloo stage. The desperate pleading of educators, teacher findings, and a general government survey of the whole situation finally brought results.

On January 13, 1958, a new school and hostel were officially opened at Fort Smith with eighteen classrooms and special facilities for subjects such as manual training and home economics. The greatest feature of this new center of education is its facility to accommodate two hundred children from outlying parts of the Northwest Territories. The new school is under the supervision of the Oblate Fathers, and the teaching and care of the children are in the hands of the Grey Nuns.

The Grey Nuns of Montreal are ninety-one years old down North! They were there more than sixty years, preparing generations of children for the change in their lives, when Gilbert La-Bine found pitchblende on Great Bear Lake in 1930 and rolled up the curtain on a new frontier. Along with the missionaries, the Sisters taught the people through their children the greatest lesson of all: that these little ones will not and cannot be always simple denizens of the woods. They must learn to make a living in much the same way as the rest of men.

Down through the years the patience of the Grey Nuns has been rewarded. A goodly number of young men and women have taken their place in society and adapted themselves to the new way of life. On May 3, 1959, God in His own Almighty way spoke His reward when Margaret d'Youville, foundress of the Grey Nuns of Montreal in 1753, was declared Blessed.

With such added spiritual equipment, the Sisters have more than just a new workshop to tackle the momentous task before them; they have the blessing of God's grace to strengthen and encourage them.

Besides the Fort Smith school and hostel, a hundred-student-capacity edifice of a similar nature was opened in Fort McPherson on September 1, 1958, under the supervision of the Anglican Church. Plans are now in preparation for two hostels at Fort Simpson, of one hundred pupils each, operated by the Roman Catholic and Anglican churches. And fifty miles from the Arctic coast, two large hostels of 250 pupils each, operated by the Roman Catholic and Anglican churches, were completed in July 1959 at Inuvik (New Aklavik).

Throughout his entire vicariate, the Bishop had to make readjustments in his personnel to follow the rapid changes in growth and development, but no change can compare with that of his favorite mission of Aklavik.

On December 8, 1953, the Feast of the Immaculate Conception —and the patroness of Aklavik Mission—the Cabinet in Ottawa voted to move the town of Aklavik, the largest Canadian community within the Arctic Circle.

Major General H. A. Young, who had selected the original site with Bishop Trocellier, arrived in Aklavik in 1952 to examine the site of a proposed new hospital and school. When he saw the condition of the site and the growth of the settlement, he realized the place was not only too limited for added buildings but that the foundation of delta silt was not a place to erect the proposed huge hospital and school.

A survey of the area was made and a new site east of the Mackenzie River, on high gravel-base land, was chosen. The new site, called Inuvik (the place of man), is thirty-five air miles and seventy water miles from Aklavik. Planners of the town have given it a potential of five thousand residents. Other reasons given for the move to this new site were poor sanitary facilities and threatening epidemics, no suitable location for an airstrip, and the fact that river erosion was washing out to sea the alluvial silt on which Aklavik stood.

In July and August of 1958 I made several trips to Inuvik with Bishop Trocellier. CF-OMI carried passengers and some materials for the construction of the first igloo-style church in Canada. Father Adam, who spent over twenty years with the Eskimos, and Brother Larocque were in charge of the building.

I had occasion to meet the men from Pool Construction of Edmonton who were building the school dormitories and installing the "Utilidors"—an overground four-foot-square insulated utility box that contains the water, heat, and sewage lines. It is elevated and kept off the ground on short stilts to prevent melting of the permafrost. The power plant is located near the river, and the service Utilidors run uphill to the town, which has a natural gravity flow toward the river. At Inuvik, because of the severe winters, the whole town is heated with hot water, which at the same time keeps the Utilidor from freezing.

Careful planning and discussion with experienced Northerners resulted in an isolated quiet hospital area in the north part of the settlement. The residential section for the staff is close by. Some thirty acres surrounding the hospital allow for future expansion.

The twenty-five-room school is built on the main square of the town. The two hostels are for orphan children or for those who live too far from the settlement to walk to school each day. All the large buildings sit on wooden pilings steamed into the permafrost. They were allowed to stand a year to freeze solid before carrying the weight of the buildings. An air space is arranged under each edifice to keep the ground cold, frozen. There is so much frost and ice in this permafrost soil that when it does melt it just leaves a hole and a building would sag in it.

In the residential area, where utilities are furnished for a price, the housing units are completely serviced with water, sewage, and electricity. In the area just up from the river docks, where units have been provided for the transient residents who come either to visit their children or to trade, the houses are provided with electricity, but special trucks service them with water and disposal of sewage. For heating, these units have either electric heaters that can be rented or else fuel-oil stoves are provided.

The main street begins at the waterfront and runs east to a main intersection, which is the town square, where the retail stores, Federal Administrative Offices, and the Royal Canadian Mounted Police headquarters are located. Provision also has been made for theaters and rinks.

To keep the industrial area apart from the town, twenty-five acres are walled off from the town proper by a park strip, where workshops, garages, and storage facilities, including refrigerated warehouse space, are located. Next to the warehouse area are the river wharves, where most of the freight arrives for the settlement.

The great connecting link with Outside is Inuvik's new all-weather airport. Along the eight-mile road that joins it to town are a number of new homes and more in the building stage.

In September 1959 the students of the Immaculate Conception boarding school and the Grey Nuns moved from Aklavik to Inuvik.

The vocational training center is at the federally operated hostel at Yellowknife. There students may take courses in technical and home economics as well as academic and commercial courses.

St. Patrick's Parochial School, under the supervision of the Sisters of St. Joseph in Yellowknife, has expanded with four more classrooms to accommodate over 250 pupils.

Beginning with the new school in McMurray, every settlement along the Mackenzie River system to Inuvik offers an opportunity for the North to give its children an education. Teachers have come from many parts of the Dominion and the United States to staff this drive in northern culture. In outposts, these men and women have still the problems of pioneers. Like the first Sisters who lived in a log cabin at Providence in 1867, they have come to realize that the big bottleneck is *getting there*—transportation.

Father Mansoz often said, "As the mining industry goes, so goes the North." He saw the radical change those first discoveries made in the whole motif of the country. Life and thought and progress gravitated toward the diggings.

Mining is now in high gear. A program of roads and railroads costing millions is under way. The government is pushing a sixty-million-dollar railway north to Pine Point on the southern shore of Great Slave Lake. In this area are the biggest potential mineral developments of lead, zinc, and copper deposits in the Northwest Territories. The Saskatchewan Provincial Government has begun a fifteen-million-dollar road, five hundred miles long from La Ronge to Uranium City on the north shore of Lake Athabaska. Farther north the Canadian Government is completing a twelve-million-dollar road linking Edmonton to Yellowknife. This gigantic Mackenzie Highway is a spur of the mighty Alcan Highway to Alaska. Now a tourist, hunter, or fisherman interested in fishing some virgin trout streams can climb into his car in Chicago or Toronto and drive to the Lake Athabaska or the Great Slave Lake country and have the finest hunting and fishing of a lifetime.

In the winter of 1957 and '58 convoys of diesel-driven trucks came over the Mackenzie Highway to Fort Smith with a sawmill. On September 16, 1958, the Denney Logging Company at Fitzgerald, Alberta, was officially open for business. This mill is equipped to produce a hundred thousand board feet of lumber daily from local timber, spruce and poplar. Half a dozen other sawmills, including our own at Grand Detour on the Slave River, thirty miles north of Smith, turn out lumber for consumption in northern housing and mining.

Before the Brothers cut one piece of lumber for our new hospital at Fort Smith in 1952, the Bishop made certain that the utilities of water and power would be available. In the summer of 1958 the Pool Construction Company had the work under way to enlarge the present filtration plant, pumping station, and sewage-disposal facilities.

The Power Commission operates plants at Fort Smith, at Yellowknife's Snare River Hydro, at Fort Simpson and at Inuvik. With the Pine Point mineral development in mind, the Power Commission has an eye on the 300,000-horsepower potential of the Slave River's Fort Smith rapids, sixteen miles long.

With all these developments in mind, Bishop Trocellier decided to do some immediate development in Fort Smith himself in 1958. He gave the contract to Mr. Laurent Giroux of Quebec City to build a new cathedral.

One day in late July, I was in the Bishop's room discussing a flight to Stony Rapids, Saskatchewan, where Brother Bruyère was building a new mission with Fathers Porte and Barrier, when a sharp little rap on the door brought us to attention.

It was little Mother Therese Chaloux, Provincial of the Grey Nuns.

"What can I do for you, Mother?" the Bishop asked.

"We are having a series of special conferences on the sociological problems in education here at the new school, Your Excellency. I was wondering if Father Leising would be able to fly all the Sisters here from the other missions?"

"When do these conferences begin, Mother?"

"The first week of August, Your Excellency. We arranged so they would terminate in time to allow us to participate in the

Golden Jubilee celebration at Fort Simpson," Mother added, smiling in my direction.

CF-OMI made eighteen flights as far as Aklavik to gather the Sisters. Since my co-pilot, Brother Beauchemin, was needed on the mission boat, Mother Therese profited by these trips to visit all her convents. She rode co-pilot for two weeks, but instead of juggling protractors and maps, she navigated around her rosary.

During the conferences of the Grey Nuns, Bishop Trocellier climbed aboard CF-OMI. The seat next to mine had a real co-pilot on this trip, Father John T. O'Toole from Crookston, Minnesota. I had met him while flying in God's Lake country down in Manitoba. He was flying his own small plane at the time and told me he would like to spend his vacation as my navigator sometime to see the Arctic. I consulted the Bishop and he welcomed him aboard.

"Being editor of the Catholic newspaper in his diocese, he may be able to help our missions," His Excellency said, adding: "You know how much Monsignor McDonagh of the Extension Society helps us in the Canadian *Register*."

We flew fifteen hundred miles down to Inuvik and out three hundred miles farther on the Arctic coast to Paulatuk. The Eskimo families had moved out of the vicinity of Paulatuk to the site of the Dew Line, sixty miles north at Cape Parry. They had given up trapping for a new kind of work where they could make a few dollars.

Since the Eskimos had moved, the missionary would also have to move. Out to the fog-bound Cape we flew. The polar ice sheet was just nudging the coast line when we landed in an open bay close to the Dew Line Site. I remained with the plane and said my Office while Father John and the Bishop went up with Father Leonce to inspect the place he had chosen for a new house. Ice floes came in on the rise and fall of the sea, and I did not want them to put bruises on our new ship. In an hour they were back and we flew to the old mission at Paulatuk.

"I'll take care of the cooking and you young fellows can load the plane." The Bishop smiled, taking off his cassock.

While the old chimney belched its heavy soft-coal smoke and the pots and pans rattled in the kitchen, we gathered sacks of beans, flour, and dog feed. Father O'Toole packed and carried the supplies to the water's edge, and Father Leonce and I loaded and flew them to his new home at Cape Parry.

"The people will move back to this wonderful bay in the summer," Father commented, just a little homesick for this place where he had lived alone so many years.

"We have the cemetery at Paulatuk and the grotto. The Eskimos will come. You will see when you visit next summer, Bishop," Father added hopefully when we left him at Cape Parry.

The Beaver responded like an angel anxious to get home, and climbed off those ice-infested seas on a southerly course to Fort Simpson.

"Those trees sure look good after a week on that barren Arctic coast." Father O'Toole pointed to the ground an hour and a half out of Cape Parry. "Why don't those Eskimos move south? There's nothing here!"

"It's their home," I answered.

Every time I have flown the Arctic coast route during the last nine years I have asked myself this same question. Trying to arrive at a reasonable and a truthful reply, I always remember the answer Brother William Beckschaeffer gave me: "It's their home." This was a man who knew all about a *home!* When he was a young man in his teens he said good-by to his parents in Germany and came to northern Canada. To Boulata (the Eskimos called him this for Brother) the North was his home for the rest of his life—over fifty years. He never returned to see his people, "because I miss them and love them so much, I don't think I would ever have the strength to leave home a second time."

On our return from the Arctic we were welcomed back to Fort Simpson by Ted Mercredi.

"You made it just in time for the eatin' part of the feast. We finished all the prayin' this morning." He laughed.

Ted had been one of my students in 1941 at Fort Smith. Now married and with a family, he is in charge of the Power Commission at Fort Simpson. His parents were pupils at Holy Angels School at Fort Chipewyan, and it is encouraging to see how well they put into practice what they were taught. The Grey Nuns are very proud of Ted and his family.

That evening Father Lesage and the Sisters directed the school children in a play depicting the heroism of the early missionaries, the usual battle of the elements, and the language barriers. The Bishop spoke and wished "grace and blessing that the next fifty years may be as profitable for souls as the first half century."

After the celebration at Simpson, Father O'Toole had to return to his duties at Crookston, and Father Robert Haramburu, our Provincial, took the co-pilot seat. With the Bishop and a cargo of mail we flew north again, this time to Coppermine and the various missions on Coronation Gulf, four hundred miles north of the Arctic Circle. We even included a visit with Father Henry at Gjoa Haven on King William Island. It was here that Father Provincial told me of his plans to build the Foyer Grandin Home at Fort Smith, a kind of preparatory seminary for the vicariate.

For the first time I noticed Bishop Trocellier growing tired after the slightest effort. Even a short walk of a few hundred yards left him gasping for breath. Whenever he left the plane I had to lead him by the hand. "I seem to lose my balance," he used to say.

After the 650-mile flight south to Smith from Coppermine the Bishop was so "played out," as he put it, that he had to rest in bed for three days.

"I don't know what's come over me lately," he said when I saw him just before leaving Smith for the close of the summer season. "I seem to have suddenly lost all my energy."

As usual, he expressed his gratefulness in the most appreciated manner possible, a Mass for my intention. Blessing me, he added: "Take a good rest. I'll see you in a few weeks for our trip to Ottawa."

That was one promise our Lord did not let him keep. The Chief Shepherd of us all called Bishop Trocellier to his eternal reward on November 27, 1958. Like Father Joseph Buliard and the other men and women who have given their lives in the battle of Christianity versus paganism, he will live on in the hearts of the people he loved.

When I fly our new Bishop, Paul Piché, O.M.I., on his first visit to the Indian and Eskimo people there is one question they will ask: "When is Bishop Trocellier coming?" I will reply that this time *they would be going to meet him, but only on the condition that they live by the principles he taught them.*

Bishop Trocellier's vision in promoting modern means of transportation in the missions will be recorded not only in the pages of the history of northern progress but especially in the golden ledger of apostolic work among the poor souls scattered on the Arctic wastes. He knew the great barrier of distance that kept these children of the snow fields from a knowledge of the Christian way of life. He suffered with them when sickness or injury left them in pain, helpless and alone, far away from the aid of their fellow man, in their dark cold houses of snow.

There is no force on earth that rips open the heart of a man like the rough-edged knife of human misery. And there is no greater fuel to fire the heart and mind of a man than that deep love for his fellow man, the valued life of a friend, the worthwhileness of his existence. The importance of men as creatures of God is the dynamic driving force which energizes some men's souls with a kind of high voltage of grace, making them bloodhounds of charity, or men and women who are known to us as missionaries—men and women sent to care for their fellow man and to carry a message of love. The Eskimo of the Arctic tundra, the Indians of the great Mackenzie basin, the small son of a Hudson's Bay Company manager, the wild man of Borneo, the lowest derelict on skid row, you and I—we are all important to our Creator, and He cares. And when a man or a woman is fired by this God-given grace to care for his fellow man, that man or woman is indeed a missionary.

It has been my privilege to know such men and women while flying the skyways of the Arctic. I also met the Indians and Eskimos, some of the most human and heart-warming souls in the world. I'm glad I met them and, God willing, I shall see them again for many more years. Adventure? Yes, but with a purpose and the satisfaction that will make my professor *pratique* smile from his place far above our igloo-domed earth.

The scene of disciplined dogs trotting over smooth ice pulling a sled, with fur-wrapped Eskimos running alongside, is an idyllic picture to thousands of people who have not run beside a dog sled in fifty below zero or to those who have never bucked a blinding snowstorm, eventually giving up to build a snowhouse in such a blizzard. Such is the life of the Eskimos, the Indians, and the missionaries who live among them.

They live a hard life. They know how to suffer and how to laugh. They are the happiest people I have ever known. Personally, I believe it can all be attributed to their great faith in each other and their trust in the One Who is the Master of the winds and the mighty Fireman of the sun!